THE CRIMEA QUESTION

THE CRIMEA QUESTION:

Identity, Transition, and Conflict

Gwendolyn Sasse

Distributed by Harvard University Press
for the Harvard Ukrainian Research Institute

The Harvard Ukrainian Research Institute was established in 1973 as an integral part of Harvard University. It supports research associates and visiting scholars who are engaged in projects concerned with all aspects of Ukrainian studies. The Institute also works in close cooperation with the Committee on Ukrainian Studies, which supervises and coordinates the teaching of Ukrainian history, language, and literature at Harvard University.

Publication of this book has been made possible by the Paul Sawka endowed publication fund for Ukrainian studies at Harvard University.

Library of Congress Cataloging-in-Publication Data

Sasse, Gwendolyn.
  The Crimea question : identity, transition, and conflict / Gwendolyn Sasse.
    p. cm.
  Includes bibliographical references and index.
  ISBN-13: 978-1-932650-01-3 (alk. paper)
  ISBN-10: 1-932650-01-6 (alk. paper)
  1. Crimea (Ukraine)--History. 2. Crimea (Ukraine)--Politics and government. I. Title.
  DK508.9.K78S28 2007
  947.7'1--dc22

                              2007014136

Paperback edition ISBN: 978-1-932650-12-9
Cover design: Mina Moshkeri Upton and Claire Harrison, Design Unit,
    London School of Economics

To my parents

Anna Luise Sasse
Horst Sasse (1927–1985)

Как в раковине малой — Океана
Великое дыхание гудит,
Как плоть ее мерцает и горит
Отливами и серебром тумана,
А выгибы её повторены
В движении и завитке волны, —
Так вся душа моя в твоих заливах,
О, Киммерии темная страна,
Заключена и преображена.

—Maksimilian Voloshin
from "Koktebel'" (1918)

Contents

Acknowledgments

T HIS BOOK IS BASED ON THE RESEARCH conducted for my doctoral thesis in the Department of Government at the London School of Economics and Political Science (1995–99) and subsequent research conducted in the UK and in Ukraine. For the duration of this project I have found LSE an intellectually extremely stimulating place, first as a postgraduate student and now as a member of the academic staff.

My thanks are owed to many people who have guided, discussed, questioned, challenged, and encouraged my work over many years. First and foremost, I want to express my gratitude to my academic supervisor and friend, Jim Hughes, whose constructive advice has critically shaped both my PhD and this book. Dominic Lieven has been a kind and helpful adviser during my entire time at the LSE. I am extremely grateful to Margot Light for being such a wonderful LSE mentor and to Chris Binns for his encouragement over many years.

During my time as a PhD student, Roy Allison and Andrew Wilson have made useful comments on the work in progress, for which I am grateful. I would also like to thank Gottfried Lorenz, who first provoked my interest in Eastern Europe at the Gymnasium Glinde, Klaus-Detlef Grothusen, who during my first years at Hamburg University taught me how history and theoretical thinking can be fruitfully combined, and Peter Zervakis, without whose advice I might never have gone to the LSE in the first place. Frank Golczewski and Andreas Kappeler provided much appreciated long-distance encouragement "from home" during my PhD. The Harvard Ukrainian Research Institute, where I spent the summer of 1997, deserves special mention. Roman Szporluk's scholarship, teaching, and his kind but challenging advice, were a formative experience for my work.

In Kyiv, I wish to thank Iurii Shapoval for his suggestions on archival materials and Inna Piluds'ka and Dmitrii Koublits'kyi, Vitalii Palamarchuk, Valerii Khmelko, and Ihor Shpak for their practical help and time for discussion. Thanks also to the staff of the Tsentral'nyi Derzhavnyi Arkhiv Hromads'kykh Ob'iednan' Ukraïny in Kyiv and the Rossiiskii Tsentr Khranenii Sovremennoi Dokumentatsii in Moscow for bearing with my rather work-intensive visits. In Crimea a huge thank-you is due to Liudmila Bessonova, Elena Nikolaeva, Viktor Sharapa, and Valerii Vasilev, all of whom work(ed) at the Tavrycheskyi Natsional'nyi Universytet in Simferopol, for their moral, intellectual, and practical support over many years. Without Liudmila's regular newspaper packages, the valuable information provided by Oleksandr Formanchuk, Andrei Mal'gin, Andrei Nikiforov, and Volodymyr Prytula, and all the Crimean politicians, businessmen, activists, and academics who agreed to my interviews, the research on which the book is based would have been impossible. A special *spasibo* to Liudmila, Anya and Katya; Antonina, Evgenii and Natasha; Galya and Lyosha, Valya, my uncle Friedrich, whom I first and unexpectedly met in Crimea, and his wife Natalia—all have helped me with their friendship, humor, and initiative. Thanks also to Norbert Ruetsche, a fellow Crimean traveler, who found original postal routes to pass on some of the final missing pieces of the jigsaw.

I want to express my gratitude to the Studienstiftung des deutschen Volkes for providing continuous financial and intellectual support throughout my studies (1991–99). The Economic and Social Research Council covered the fees of my PhD program (1996–99); the LSE Graduate School, the London University Central Research Fund, and the Travel Fund of the British Association for Slavonic and East European Studies provided me with additional maintenance and travel grants without which my doctoral research, fieldwork, and attendance at many conferences would have been impossible. My neighbors and friends of over thirty years, Joachim and Edeltraud von Rantzau, deserve special mention, not least due to their generous financial support towards my stay at Harvard University in 1997.

I want to thank my friends Linda, Tony, Elisa, Razmik, Gloria, and Albert for their companionship and help during the crucial phase of my PhD—without you I would not have reached the finish on time! Thanks also to my former colleagues at the Central European University, whose collegiality helped me through the final months of my PhD. Since my return to the LSE, I have benefited enormously from the discussions with my colleagues and friends in the European Institute. Sabbaticals spent at the Freie Universität Berlin (2002–3) and the European University Institute in Florence (2003–4) gave me the space and time to complete this book amidst other ongoing research projects. I am grateful to Klaus Segbers for arranging my affiliation with the Osteuropa-Institut at the FU Berlin and to Christoph, Jan, Fritz, Björn, and Simon for making me feel welcome in their midst. At the EUI the list of individuals I have to thank for making that year so unforgettable is too long—you all know who you are! The helpful comments on draft book chapters by Jim Hughes, Jennifer Jackson-Preece, Brendan O'Leary, and Christoph Zürcher and the moral support from Waltraud, Juliana, Rachael and Sean, Linda and Tony, Neil, Tinki, Judith, and Jan during the final stretch (which felt like a marathon) are most gratefully acknowledged.

Earlier versions of the research presented in some chapters of this book were published in *Österreichische Osthefte* 42, nos. 3–4 (2000), *Regional and Federal Studies* 11, no. 3 (2001), and *Nationalism and Ethnic Politics* 8, no. 2 (2002). At the end of a long odyssey the Harvard Ukrainian Research Institute saw this manuscript through to publication; here my thanks go to Pat Wright, Michael Flier, Marika Whaley, Louise Smith, and Mary Ann Szporluk. My thanks also go to the anonymous referees, who gave most helpful comments and advice, and to Mina Moshkeri Upton and Claire Harrison from the LSE Design Unit, who prepared the maps and the cover design. All translations of quotations are my own unless otherwise indicated.

Finally and most importantly, I thank my parents, Anna Luise and Horst Sasse. This book is dedicated to them. They have encouraged and guided me over many years and enabled me to pursue my scholarly interests. My father did not live to see me study and take up an academic job, but the love and determination of both my parents have been a constant source of inspiration.

London, March 2007

Maps

Map 1. Crimea.

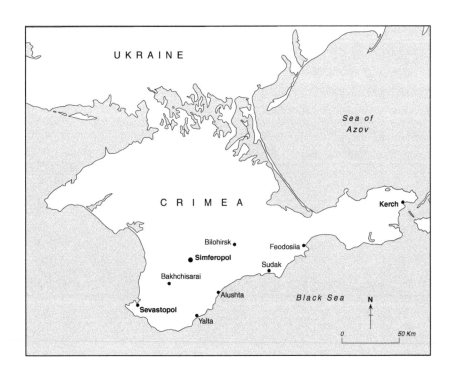

Map 2. Ukraine and its international neighbors.

Map 3. Ukraine's regional borders.

Introduction

UKRAINE OCCUPIES THE STRATEGICALLY IMPORTANT SPACE between the newly enlarged European Union, the Russian Federation, and the Black Sea region. In modern times this region was the interface of the Russian, Habsburg, and Ottoman empires. The history of states is shaped by location, and the modern history of the state of Ukraine is no exception.

Ukraine's experiences of statehood between the seventeenth and early twentieth centuries were short-lived. Within its contemporary boundaries Ukraine now exists for the first time in its history as an independent state. As part of a fourth empire, the Soviet Union, Ukraine enjoyed some of the trappings of statehood, but remained closely subordinated to Moscow's power and control structures. Ukraine's territorial map was completed only during the Soviet period: its western border is by and large a result of World War II, and the transfer of Crimea from the RSFSR to the Ukrainian SSR in 1954 shifted Ukraine's southern border. The collapse of the USSR left behind a complex territorial, political, and socioeconomic legacy that continues to shape Ukraine's development. The various ethnic, linguistic, religious, and socioeconomic identities and cleavages, and its different historical memories and political orientations, make regional diversity Ukraine's single most important characteristic.

By defining Ukraine as a "state of regions"[1] we neither call Ukraine's territorial integrity into question nor preclude the prospect of a successful post-Soviet transition. It simply highlights the fact that the management of historically determined regional differences was bound to shape every aspect of Ukraine's post-Soviet political and economic transition. Regional diversity often embodies potential for friction and conflict, in particular when it involves territorialized ethnicity and divergent historical experiences. Political elites interested in stability and conflict prevention must find ways either to accommodate or to control this diversity. Postcommunist transition has opened up the political system to the redefinition of center-periphery relations and the rebalancing of the interests of different ethnic groups.

Crimea was Ukraine's most immediate and most serious center-periphery challenge. The multiethnic composition of Crimea, especially the tense interaction between Russians, Ukrainians, and Crimean Tatars, created a widespread image of Crimea as "a fateful peninsula"[2] that was prone to conflict, an idea that permeated the Western media and the discussions of policymakers and academics in the early to mid-1990s. In July 1993, the *Economist* dramatically warned of a "long-running, acrimonious, possibly bloody and conceivably nuclear, dispute over Crimea."[3] Alarmist comparisons were also drawn with the wars in the former Yugoslavia and Kashmir so as to highlight the potential worst-case scenario.[4] Commentators pointed to a range of factors in the politics of post-Soviet Crimea that are generally closely associated with the risk of conflict:[5] the difficulty of reconciling competing historical and cultural claims in a multiethnic society, the demand for an institutionalization of regional autonomy, the peripherality of the region and its capacity for secession, the depressed socioeconomic conditions, and the destabilizing influence of external actors, in particular Russia. These factors, moreover, were operating during a transition period when institutions, power relations, and access to resources were undergoing a fundamental reordering. The dense buildup of events in the early 1990s caused a spiral of mounting tension: Crimea's referendum on autonomy in 1991, the establishment of a regional autonomy at a time when other Soviet-era autonomies were being dismantled in the context of the disintegration of the USSR, the influx and settlement of over 200,000 Crimean Tatars returning to the region from which they had been deported under Stalin in 1944, and the rise of a Russian separatist movement in Crimea fueled by Russia's rhetoric and influence.

However, the expected conflict in Crimea did not materialize. With the exception of a small number of clashes between Crimean Tatar returnees and the local authorities, a descent into large-scale conflict and political violence in the region has been averted. Contrary to the earlier predictions, Kyiv has managed to integrate Crimea into the new Ukrainian polity.[6] How did this happen, given the presence of so many regional characteristics typically associated with conflict and a complex postcommunist transition process?

This is the "Crimea question" this book seeks to answer. Taking as one's subject of analysis a widely expected conflict that did *not* occur is neither the usual approach in the study of conflict regulation nor the main focus in studies of postcommunist state and nation building. However, understanding why conflicts do *not* occur is as important as analyzing those that do, especially if the conflict potential includes the principal structural conditions that are typically regarded as the main causes of conflict.

Studies of postcommunist conflict have tended to focus on the role of historical legacies in their causation, viewing the conflicts as a resurgence of "unfinished business" from the past and as the result of irreconcilable identities or so-called "ancient hatreds."[7] This explanation draws on the experience of key hot conflict areas in the postcommunist region, such as former Yugoslavia, Chechnya, Georgia, Nagorno-Karabakh, Transdnistria, the Ferghana valley, and Tajikistan. This narrow focus on violent conflicts does not take due account of those areas with similar conflict-prone legacies that have so far remained peaceful. It is this variation against the backdrop of similar conditions and legacies that needs to be explained rather than only the outbreak of violent conflict. Mark Beissinger concluded from his study of the role of nationalism in the collapse of the Soviet Union that "the typical Pandora's box metaphor often used to describe the collapse of the USSR does not hold true, since in quite a number of cases the demons refused to leave the box or did so under the influence of the actions of others."[8] This observation is equally valid, in my view, for the aftermath of the collapse of the Soviet empire.

The Crimea Question: Identity, Transition, and Conflict is a study of the ethnoregional challenge Crimea posed to the "new" Ukraine. It explores how regional and ethnic identities became embedded, by uncovering firstly the cultural raw materials from which these identities have been formed, and secondly the key historical and institutional legacies that have shaped Crimea's political landscape. While Crimea is a critical case in which conflict has not erupted despite a structural predisposition to ethnic, regional, and even international conflict, a single case study cannot explain variation across the whole of the former Soviet Union (FSU). But it can demonstrate that the study of post-Soviet conflicts has to take the dynamics of nonviolent conflicts into account. This is particularly important given the recent trend for large-scale statistical analyses of conflicts that can produce skewed analyses and generate misunderstanding of the causes of conflict by a focusing too narrowly on those cases that become violent.[9] The sources of instability in Crimea, brought to a head by the experience of transition, are generally considered to involve several factors: geography; a history of fractious multiethnicity; institutional legacies, including various experiments with autonomy and specific regional socioeconomic and political structures; political, economic, and social conditions; as well as the interference of external forces. To what extent can the analysis of such factors help us to evaluate the conflict potential in Crimea?

Geography

Geography is generally seen as a determining feature of conflict potential, because it is an important factor in the capacity for autonomy or secession. As the southernmost region of Ukraine, and as a peninsula jutting into the Black Sea that is connected by a narrow ribbon of land to Ukraine *propre*, Crimea is a place apart from Ukraine. Indeed, Crimea has been described as "a world unto itself."[10] This difference should not be exaggerated, however, since the Black Sea littoral has been a historical crossroads of different cultures, and Crimea in particular has been pivotal to the historical development of the whole area. Neal Ascherson aptly described Crimea "as a sort of theatre, an apron-stage, for events important to the whole Black Sea region and its peoples."[11] Historically, then, Crimea was Ukraine's main interface with the Black Sea region, which in turn provided an important connector to Europe and the Ottoman empire. The main episodes of Crimean history, from the era of Crimean Tatar rule beginning in the fourteenth century through to the incorporation of Crimea into the Russian Empire in 1783, the brief interlude of changing governments after the 1917 revolution followed by over seventy years of Soviet rule, place the region at the heart of any understanding of the interaction of Russian, Ottoman, and Ukrainian history.

Multiethnicity

Crimea's political geography facilitated numerous settlement waves throughout history, making multiethnicity one of the region's key characteristics. Ethnic demography is a structural determinant of conflict potential, in particular if it undergoes radical changes. Crimea's multiethnic map was redrawn repeatedly in the context of colonial settlement and targeted state policies. In recent memory it was radically transformed by the Soviet policy of violent forced mass deportation and resettlement affecting, above all, the Crimean Tatars, as well as the Armenians, Bulgarians, Germans, and Greeks based in the region (see appendix 1). Stalin ordered the deportation of the entire Crimean Tatar population from Crimea in 1944 to Central Asia and Siberia based on the false claim that the Crimean Tatars as a group had cooperated with the Germans during World War II.[12] In view of Soviet repression, parts of the Tatar population greeted the new German occupation of Crimea from October 1941 as a relief. The hope that the Nazi regime would grant the Crimean Tatars national territorial autonomy proved unrealistic. The German army, the SS, and the administration disagreed about how to deal with the Crimean Tatars. Hitler himself was most intrigued with the "Gotland project," the fantastical idea of settling Germans from South Tyrol in Crimea, though nothing came of it. Archival material demonstrates that some Crimean Tatar organizations did indeed cooperate with the German authorities during World War II.[13] Evidently, the German army hoped to exploit Crimean Tatar nationalism for military and strategic purposes. The establishment of local Crimean Tatar committees was permitted, and six Crimean Tatar battalions numbering about twenty thousand troops were set up in rural Crimea under German military control as combined forces with local police "self-defense contingents." Many Crimean Tatars, however, supported the Soviet war effort; at least 20,000 fought in the Soviet army. Nevertheless, the victory of Soviet troops in Crimea in April 1944, coupled with Soviet allegations of large-scale Crimean Tatar collaboration with the Germans, culminated in the deportation of the entire Crimean Tatar population in May 1944.

The multiethnicity of Crimea is reinforced by deeply rooted symbolic, literary, and historical memories that provide ample material for ethnopolitical mobilization and exclusive claims to the territory. Crimea is the only region within Ukraine with an ethnic Russian majority. The post-1991 return of the Crimean Tatars to Crimea, especially from Uzbekistan, has marked the most significant recent change in the ethnopolitical profile of the region.[14] In the 1990s the Crimean Tatar segment of the regional population grew from near zero to over ten percent, making them the third biggest ethnic group in Crimea. According to the 2001 Ukrainian census, Russians account for 58.3 percent of the Crimean population, Ukrainians for 24.3 percent, the Crimean Tatars for 12 percent, followed by about eighty other small national minorities.[15]

Institutional Legacies

The deportations masterminded by Stalin were accompanied by a further punishment: the downgrading of the status of the region from an autonomous republic (ASSR) to a region (oblast). Thus, Crimea first experienced a series of different types of autonomy after 1917, and then the deinstitutionalization of Soviet autonomy status in 1945. Another pivotal event with ramifications beyond the Soviet Union's existence was the transfer of the Crimean oblast from the jurisdiction of the RSFSR to the Ukrainian SSR in 1954, an event commonly and rather superficially referred to as Khrushchev's "present" to Ukraine. The redrawing of borders was common practice in the Soviet era, but this change proved to be a time bomb with a long fuse. It became one of the foci of the post-Soviet disputes both between the Russian and Ukrainian governments and between the Ukrainian government and the Crimean authorities.

Crimea's post-Soviet transition has involved grappling with severe problems arising from a distinctly Soviet socioeconomic legacy. The regional economic slump placed it among the worst affected parts of Ukraine, given its bankrupt military-industrial complex, a once well-developed Soviet tourism industry that collapsed together with the Soviet Union, appliance-based industries dependent on disrupted supplies from outside the region, and its lack of energy and water resources. The specific characteristics of the regional economy, together with the high proportion of retirees from the former Soviet administrative and military hierarchies reinforced the region's "Soviet" political culture. Persisting Soviet values made for high levels of resistance to the reforms of the transition.[16]

External Actors

The emergence of Crimea as a salient post-Soviet political issue made the region a key interface between the two distinct, but interrelated, processes of state and nation building in Ukraine and Russia. To a somewhat lesser degree the region has also shaped the geopolitical triangle Russia-Ukraine-Turkey, which has made it important for regional stability in the Black Sea region.

The study of how this complex regional challenge has been managed offers a prism for the analysis of three interlocking dimensions of Ukraine's transition: regional, national, and international. Crimea represents a critical case not only for Ukraine's own identity and transition, but also within the wider context of postimperialism, post-Soviet transition and democratization, and for conflict prevention in general. In essence, this book is a study of the state, the nation, and the region in transition. These interrelated processes make for an empirically rich setting for the study of the highly contested concepts of nationalism, regionalism, and ethnic conflict. Moreover, Crimea is a good case for the comparative study of conflict management and the role of institutions, such as autonomy arrangements. Ukraine's dual state-building model of centralization and selective autonomization may offer elements to be drawn on in the search for peaceful solutions to other more violent or "frozen" regional challenges in the FSU or elsewhere.

Crimea is the only region in Ukraine with the status of a territorial autonomy, anchored as the "Autonomous Republic of Crimea" in the 1996 Constitution of Ukraine. This book suggests that this constitutionalized asymmetric institutional arrangement played a vital role in conflict prevention. An examination of Crimea's autonomy status, however, reveals it to be constitutionally ambiguous and weakly implemented. The apparent legal and political fragility of Crimean autonomy, on paper and in practice, raises the question of how important a role autonomy really played in resolving the complex territorial challenge posed in 1991–98. The argument developed in this book is that the political *process* of negotiation, of central and regional elite bargaining, rather than the institutional *outcome* per se was the critically important factor for conflict prevention.[17] The analysis presented here emphasizes the importance of the process of institution making rather than the institutional outcome itself. Thus, the dynamics of conflict prevention in Crimea speak to the eternal social science debate about the relative importance of structure and agency in politics. The making of a Crimean autonomy aptly demonstrates the interaction between the two. For what appears to be a feeble and symbolic institutionalized solution—Crimean autonomy—cloaks the deeper causality of conflict prevention arising from a process of compromise and consensus building.[18]

The tracing of events and processes in this study reveals four key background conditions that provided a favorable environment for resolving constitutional issues at the national and regional level in Ukraine. First, Crimea's multiethnicity has prevented clear-cut ethnopolitical mobilization and polarization. Second, Russian nationalist mobilization in Crimea proved unsustainable because of a blurred Soviet-Russian identity, the movement's inability to address the bread-and-butter issues of regional socioeconomic problems, and a lack of unity and leadership. Third, the central elites chose a pragmatic approach and opted to bargain over cultural and linguistic concerns in Crimea rather than pursue an uncompromisingly nationalizing strategy in state building. Fourth, neither of the main external governmental actors, Russia and Turkey, actively supported regional political mobilization in Crimea, but rather prioritized inter-state relations with Ukraine.

*

The book is divided into two parts. Part 1 frames the analysis both conceptually and historically in order to establish the type of challenge Crimea posed to post-Soviet Ukraine. Three constants running through Crimea's history are emphasized: the role of multiethnicity, the political aspirations for a special status or autonomy, and the impact of location in a triangle of competing geopolitical interests framed by Ukraine, Russia, and Turkey. These three elements provide the basic parameters for contemporary identity construction, transition politics, and post-Soviet conflict dynamics. Chapter 1 locates the analysis of developments in Crimea within the conceptual debates about national and regional identities, transition, and postcommunist conflict. Based on literature, travelogues of the eighteenth and nineteenth centuries, and historiography, Chapters 2 and 3 chart Crimea's cultural and historical legacies, which provide the material available for ethnopolitical mobilization. Chapter 4 traces the historical institutional experience of self-government, which resonates in contemporary politics, by surveying the different and often short-lived autonomy experiments in Crimea, in particular in the aftermath of the 1917 revolution and in the early Soviet period. The USSR tried to manage territory and ethnicity by linking the two institutionally within the socialist monist system.[19] Chapter 5 reassesses another institutional landmark: the 1954 transfer of Crimea from the RSFSR to the Ukrainian SSR, a frequent point of contention in post-1991 Russian-Ukrainian relations. The legality of the transfer procedure itself has been disputed, largely due to ambiguities in the Soviet constitutions and the minimum of documented procedure employed in the process. The picture that emerges from the analysis of the archival evidence presented in this chapter diverges somewhat from the clichéd image of Khrushchev "giving" Crimea to Ukraine as a symbol of Russian-Ukrainian friendship to mark the 300th anniversary of the Pereiaslav Treaty between Cossack Hetman Bohdan Khmel'nyts'kyi and the Russian tsar in 1654. In sum, part 1 maps those elements of Crimea's cultural and political history that have been instrumental in framing the political claims of the post-Soviet period by being incorporated into platforms of mobilization, thus underpinning the potential for conflict.

Part 2 concentrates on the post-Soviet cycle of political mobilization in Crimea and the dynamics of conflict and conflict prevention. Crimean and Ukrainian politics are examined from the first demands for autonomy in 1990 to the constitutionalization of the Autonomous Republic of Crimea in 1996 and 1998, followed by the implementation of the autonomy arrangement up to the present. Chapters 6 and 7 concentrate on the first phase of this cycle, the rising tide of political mobilization from 1990 to 1994. Chapter 8 deals with the second phase of the cycle, during which the mobilization was rechanneled from the unstable populist politics of the street into more stable institutional forms. The analysis focuses on the domestic aspects of the Crimean issue, namely the roles and interactions of elites and institutions at the regional and central state level. The argument concentrates on the stop-go institutionalization of Crimean autonomy, which structured the politics of the period 1990–98 (and beyond) and has played an important role in the prevention of conflict. The international dimensions of the Crimea question are addressed in chapter 9. Chapter 10 discusses the final constitutional settlement between Kyiv and Simferopol in 1998, and charts how the agreement has performed in the national and regional political context after 1998.

The book deals with the Crimea question as a complex territorial challenge. It presents an answer to the question of why conflict has so far been avoided in Crimea by highlighting the "constructive" rather than the "subversive" dimension of autonomy. The key to conflict prevention in Crimea was the process of formulating the region's autonomy status. Thus, this study emphasizes the institutional *process* over the final institutional *outcome*. To date, different types of conflict have been prevented in Crimea: a clash between Ukraine and Russia, an intraregional political conflict among different ethnopolitical groups, internecine conflict among the Crimean Russian elites, and a center-periphery conflict between Kyiv and Simferopol. A fourth potential for conflict involving the Crimean Tatar minority has only temporarily and intermittently been stabilized. The political and social integration of the Crimean Tatars is far from complete and remains one of the key factors—if not the key factor—for the future stability of Crimea.

PART ONE

1 Identity and Conflict in Transition

THE CORRELATION BETWEEN THE END OF COMMUNISM and the rise of conflict potential is undisputed. It fits a broader trend identified by authors like Daniel Horowitz and Jack Snyder—namely, the correlation or causal link between ethnic conflict and the processes of transition or democratization.[1] Scholarly agreement ends, however, with this general premise. Assessments of the importance of the opportunity structures created during the transition process, or the cultural, political and institutional legacy, or indeed the scope for accommodation, vary significantly in the scholarly literature.[2] This book draws on a number of literatures, on nationalism and regionalism, transition and ethnic conflict, to explore these issues in the Crimean context. The Russian nationalist political mobilization in Crimea in the early 1990s was a continuation of the tide of nationalism that had washed away the Soviet state. This nationalist challenge posed a serious test for Ukraine's attempts to build and consolidate new democratic institutions, and to define a new "Ukrainian" political identity. Why did the Crimea question not derail the process of state and nation building in post-Soviet Ukraine?

Identity and Conflict: Redefining Center-Regional Relations in Ukraine

The Crimea question goes to the heart of Ukraine's state and nation building process—the choice between an inclusive and an exclusive definition of the national identity, as well as the choice between a centralized and a decentralized democratic state. Political identity, after all, is a composite. It is made up of multiple identities, including national and regional identities, some of which coexist, while others are in conflict. The emotional appeal and political relevance of these identities vary from context to context. Experience shows that identities are malleable despite attempts to anchor them in the seemingly fixed attributes of culture, territory, gender, or social origin, to name but a few. At times of crisis or societal change a sense of identity, whether newly created or revived, takes on a particularly potent function as a mobilizing force, whether to promote internal cohesion, or to denote differentiation from the "other." Identity politics is invariably based on competing claims as to who can be legitimately included or excluded. Postcommunist transition is a moment when political legitimacy of this kind is being redefined. It brings to the fore an identity crisis at different levels: individual, group, regional, national, and international. The simultaneous redefinition of national and regional identity is a crucial dimension of postcommunist identity politics, and together they form an integral part of the reconfiguration of the institutional relationship between the center and the regions.

There is a tendency to conflate nationalism and regionalism, or to treat them in isolation. Nationalism and regionalism involve similar processes of identity construction and political legitimacy but are separated by different levels of governance. Either can exist without the other, but they can also feed off each other in a conflictual or constructive manner. As a result, nationalism and regionalism are not always clearly distinguishable. In Crimea, regionalism was overtaken by nationalism as the driving force of political mobilization. The prevailing orientation towards Russian language and culture on the part of the majority of Crimea's population, the region's short-lived but influential Russian nationalist movement advocating separatism, and the Crimean Tatar's "homeland" politics, have generated rival claims to autonomy or statehood for Crimea. Ukraine, consequently, embarked on its transition with unresolved issues as to its territorial integrity and the relationship between the state and the nation.

The terms "nation" and "nationalism" are among the most ambiguous concepts in political thought.[3] The distinction between *Kulturnation* and *Staatsnation*—or between ethnic and civic nations, respectively—is widely employed in the study of nationalism. Whereas the former denotes an "exclusive club" based on ethnocultural criteria,[4] the latter is a liberal political construct that defines a citizen's loyalty and affiliation in terms of state institutions. This latter idea of contractual loyalty and identity was encapsulated in Ernest Renan's famous formula that the concept of the "nation" was the result of a "daily plebiscite" by citizens.[5] There is, moreover, a common distinction made between Eastern and Western nationalism, following Hans Kohn. This associates ethnocultural definitions to the states of Eastern Europe, whereas the civic political notion is linked to the Western European states.[6] The notion that "Eastern" nationalism is substantially more prone to violent interethnic clashes than its "Western" counterpart is reflected in the hyperbolic observations cited in the introduction about the potential for conflict in Crimea that were prevalent in the media, academic discourse, and among policymakers in the 1990s. There is a tendency for conflicts in Eastern Europe to be quickly labelled "ethnic" and located within ethnically defined historical patterns. The categorization of "Eastern" and "Western" nationalism, consequently, substitutes essentialism for analysis of the historical developments that structure the different temporalities in nation and state building.

Nationalism as a modern political phenomenon is at the heart of the study of ethnic conflict. The distinctions both between ethnic and civic nations, and their respective geographical zones, however, are misleading simplifications because "every nationalism contains civic and ethnic elements in varying degrees and different forms."[7] The respective significance of ethnic and civic criteria depends on the specific political context. As John Breuilly puts it, "the identity of the nation will be related to 'tradition' and to existing cultural practices, but the decisions as to what is relevant and how it should be used in establishing the national identity will rest with the state."[8] Post-Soviet state and nation building provides an opportunity to investigate the mechanisms through which the balance between ethnic and civic criteria is being institutionalized. In the case of post-Soviet Ukraine, the management of the Crimean issue was a defining episode for the newly democratizing state in achieving this balance.

How then may a clash of identities, especially if they are rooted in ethnicity or culture and are attached to claims to statehood or autonomy such as in Crimea, be channelled into nonviolent politics, and rendered amenable to political bargaining? How may a newly democratizing state, such as Ukraine, reconcile state and nation building with the presence of territorialized multiethnicity and demands for autonomy or secession? An instrumentalist view assumes basic rational choice and emphasizes the use of the concept of the nation and its potential for political purposes. It takes seriously the analysis of the raw material out of which national and regional identities are formed and the ways in which identity is channeled into mobilization.

The idea of the nation-state, famously defined by Ernest Gellner as "a political principle that holds that the political and the national should be congruent" or as "culturally homogenous, internally undifferentiated, cultural polities,"[9] remains an unrealized ideal. Only very few states around the globe fit the narrow definition of a nation-state. Most states must continuously accommodate diversity within their boundaries. Nevertheless, the ideal type of the nation-state retains its political appeal and surfaces during periods when the state is being redefined.[10] In many postcommunist countries, the process of nation and state building fulfils at least a dual function: it helps to distance the current regime from the communist past, and it legitimizes the new regime. The key question is how a context of multiethnicity shapes these processes.

Despite highlighting the significance of the political mobilization of the idea of the nation, many "modernist" analyses of nationalism that see the nation-state as a function of modernization remain strangely apolitical, often neglecting concrete political actors, case studies, and, in particular, the role of institutions below and above the level of the nation-state. Thus, they understand the nation simply as "the necessary consequence or correlate of certain social conditions,"[11] a necessity and reality during state building. Brendan O'Leary has rightly criticized Gellner, arguably the most prominent "modernist" scholar of nationalism, for his narrow functionalist approach that makes nationalism unintentional in nature, for his lack of interest in political institutions, and for his failure to address the interdependency between nationalism and democratization.[12] Rather than studying nationalism as a set of ideas or as a functional necessity, Breuilly stresses the need to analyze the particular political context in which some of these ideas become politically significant. Accordingly, he places nationalism in the context of modern state power and politics: "Nationalism redefines the nature of legitimate authority. Nationalism is frequently associated with political change which favors new elites. Nationalist politics are typically crisis politics, and crises threaten the *status quo*."[13] A post-Soviet territorial conflict such as Ukraine's with Crimea fits well within this approach, as it elaborates the crisis elements, opportunity structures, and forms of mobilization during post-Soviet state and nation building. Arguably, the redefinition of the center-regional relationship forms the cornerstone of identity politics in post-Soviet Ukraine. Moreover, as Gellner observed, "the clue to understanding nationalism is its weakness at least as much as its strength."[14] Crimea is a case that furthers our understanding of the strengths and weaknesses of nationalism and regionalism and widens the horizon of the study of conflict beyond its narrow focus on forms of violence.

Regional identities and regionalism are even more disparate outlets for identity politics than nationalism. In the imperial Russian and Soviet tradition, regions primarily performed administrative functions and had little political salience. The communist system, based on Leninist democratic centralism, denied any substantial regional self-government. Like many *guberniias* in the tsarist period, Soviet-era regions often lacked historical roots and had arbitrary or deliberately redrawn boundaries. Thus, the regional legacy in post-communist states consists of different overlapping regional concepts tied to historically formed regional identities, Soviet administrative regions, and communist economic planning regions. Over a decade of postcommunist and postimperial state building has highlighted the significance of subnational or substate actors and institutions. Political and economic transitions have underscored regional legacies, demands, and discrepancies. "Bringing the regions back in" to the study of transition seems to be a timely variation on an earlier theme. Crimea is a special case in this respect, as its distinctiveness was recognized, debated, and manipulated in the Russian imperial period and the Soviet era in ways that continued to resonate in the politics of post-Soviet Ukraine.

Gradually, scholars of post-Soviet politics have paid more attention to regional political dynamics. Publications on Russian federalism or specific regions within the Russian Federation and on individual ethnoregional conflicts in the FSU have increased.[15] Russia has remained the dominant subject for the study of regional issues because it has remained a federal state after the collapse of the USSR. The absence of an explicit federal system in other post-Soviet states, however, does not preclude the existence of distinct regional identities, regional political demands, and the need for accommodative strategies.

Ukraine's considerable regional and ethnic diversity makes it an obvious choice for the study of conflict and conflict prevention. Apart from the Russian Federation, which revitalized an asymmetric federal structure inherited from the Soviet period, Ukraine has been a pathfinder among the post-Soviet states for a peaceful equilibrium between the central state and the regions. Within Ukraine, the Crimean case puts other regional challenges in perspective: if ethnoregional conflict did not erupt in the region where it was most expected, pessimistic predictions regarding a possible East-West fracturing of Ukraine[16] as well as the emphasis on Russian nationalism in the study of post-Soviet state and nation building may not be well founded. Thus the regional prism can provide a useful corrective to some of the general assumptions about states in transition.

Generally, the comparative politics literature on regions resembles the literature on nationalism and ethnic conflict. It is preoccupied with classifying regions as, for example, political, economic, administrative, or cultural, or with the "freezing" of cleavage structures into voter alignments and party systems.[17] Regionalism, understood as peripheral mobilization, results from the incongruity among political, economic, and cultural roles. The concept does not explain, however, who the actors are and how the cleavage structures offer the incentives and resources for actors to mobilize for distinct purposes. Given that the cleavages themselves are still in flux across the postimperial space in the FSU, and that party systems are weak or nonexistent, this starting point for the study of regional diversity is rather problematic.

However, even those authors who emphasize that regionalism is concerned with types of cleavages, and territorialized roles and identities, have tended to concentrate on the regions where the ethnic cleavage is predominant, thereby further blurring the distinction between regionalism and nationalism.[18] "Distance, difference and dependence"[19] as the key characteristics of a periphery offer a more flexible framework for understanding regional identity and the scope for regional political mobilization. As the two parts of this book will show, they capture the dynamics of Crimea's relationship with the imperial center of the tsarist and Soviet empires and its interaction with Kyiv in the post-Soviet period.

Transition and Conflict: Challenging Ukraine's Stateness

The "triple transition,"[20] understood as the simultaneous process of political change, economic reform, and state and nation building, is the common denominator in the comparative study of postcommunist transition. Whether the postcommunist transitions are part of the tail end of the so-called third wave of democratization or are a new fourth wave, or something qualitatively different, is much debated.[21] The third wave began in Southern Europe in the 1970s, swept across Latin America, and reached Eastern Europe and the FSU in the late 1980s.[22] The theory of transition to democracy shares with classic definitions of liberal democracy a basic premise: the utility of homogeneity for democratic consolidation.[23] Thus, Dankwart Rustow singled out "national unity" based on the "overwhelming majority" of the population as the precondition for transition.[24] Conversely, multiethnicity is presented as a serious obstacle to democratization, and the "ethnification" of transition politics appears as an almost insoluble problem.[25] The "stateness" question, raised by Juan Linz and Alfred Stepan, is thus a variation on an old theme.[26] It underscores the need to settle issues resulting from the incongruence of ethnic and political boundaries prior to or alongside the establishment of democratic institutions. In conditions where multiethnicity contests the state, state building per se becomes the prerequisite for the establishment of democracy, posing a formidable obstacle. Although calling something a prerequisite unduly limits the available paths or choices, the problem of state building is widely seen as a distinct marker of postcommunist transition. Unlike most of Southern Europe, Latin America, and East Asia, Eastern Europe—especially the FSU—is not only engaged in a transition "from authoritarian capitalism to liberal democracy" but also simultaneously involved in "a virtual reinvention of the state and a comprehensive reordering of the economy."[27] Consequently, theory of transition suggests that successful democratization in conditions of multiethnicity such as those prevailing in Ukraine, or in conditions of territorial challenges to the state as was the case with Crimea, would be virtually impossible to achieve.

The second key condition for regime change, suggested by transition theory, is the significance of pacts among the divided elites at the central state level. Despite the undisputed role of elites and elite bargaining during transition,[28] interethnic or regional cleavages do not figure in these conceptual discussions. What is generally missing is a detailed analysis of when ethnic or regional differences become politically relevant, who mobilizes them, and what mobilizational strategies are being pursued to what effect. Crimea illustrates the relevance of elite pacts not only at the center, but also at the regional level, and between the center and the region.

The third element stressed in the study of transition is the role of institutions or, more precisely, the significance of institutional design as embodied in the process of constitutional engineering. One of the most prominent debates in this field has been the argument about the perils or benefits of presidentialism and the choice of particular electoral systems. In more recent work, Stepan has acknowledged that the early transition literature failed to draw on the immense literature on the role of a range of state institutions in managing multiethnicity (e.g., consociationalism, federalism, autonomy).[29] The case of Crimea, where parallel constitution-making processes were pursued at the regional and national levels, allows us to test arguments as to the scope and efficacy of institutional methods of managing multiethnicity and separatism in transition states.

The fourth characteristic of the studies of transition that emerged in the 1980s and 1990s was the assumption that transition and democratization are primarily endogenous processes. Laurence Whitehead and Philippe Schmitter were among the first to provide some basic analytical tools to classify and study the international dimension of transition. Their emphasis remained on Western influences on countries in transition rather than the equally important interdependency of transition states or the specific role of Russia as the former colonial power and aspiring regional hegemon.[30] In

Crimea, both of these neglected dimensions are present through Russia's stake in the region and its structural interdependencies with Ukraine and with Crimea itself.

The focus on Crimea also helps to integrate domestic and international dimensions of state building and transition, as the region is of interest to not one, but two post-Soviet transitions. The Crimean issue in post-Soviet Ukraine goes to the heart of the "making" of one nation (and state): Ukraine; it goes to the "unmaking" of another: Russia.[31] Crimea is, in effect, a periphery within a periphery, located at the margins of the former tsarist and Soviet empires and the "new" Ukraine. Thus, it finds itself at the borderlines between two distinct but interrelated processes shaped by postimperial legacies. Former imperial peripheries are faced by intricate difficulties of state and nation building, in particular if they find themselves in close proximity to and economic dependence on the former metropolis. Moreover, imperial perceptions take much longer to change than state borders.[32] For the former imperial center—Russia—previously domestic or regional issues suddenly became foreign policy. Russia had to come to terms with Ukrainian independence, and Russian elites have found it particularly hard to accept as permanent the loss of Crimea resulting from its transfer to the jurisdiction of the Ukrainian SSR in 1954. For post-Soviet Ukraine, the political integration of this overwhelmingly ethnic Russian region became a litmus test for its new foreign policy vis-à-vis Russia. Thus, Crimea illustrates the complexities of postimperialism, a process involving both the establishment of new states at the core and at the periphery of the old empire, and the political and economic interaction or interdependence among these new polities.[33] Among the unresolved issues emerging from the Soviet empire's rubble are unclear and contested borders,[34] resource dependencies, the loss of status of the former imperial center, and ample scope for ethnic and regional conflict. It is important, however, to emphasize that competing national and regional identities are only one of many sources of instability in the aftermath of empire and tend to disguise other destabilizing factors, such as political or socioeconomic interests.

Although there is considerable variation along all three dimensions of postcommunist transition—political change, economic reforms, and state and nation building—the latter has been on bal-

ance more protracted in the successor states to the USSR than in
Central and Eastern Europe. While all postimperial states share a
certain "deflation in state capacity" due to institutional changes and
adjustments, pre-independence experiences with statehood matter greatly for the post-independence period.[35] Many post-Soviet
countries such as Ukraine are building independent states within
their current boundaries for the first time in their history. As a result
of this ongoing "process of competitive and contested polity building,"[36] institutions and identities are both malleable and contestable.
While constitutional crafting and choices are generally considered to
be vitally important for newly democratizing states, it is important
to add that they are even more important in conditions of multiethnicity. The majority of postcommunist states have opted for a
type of nation-state building that is based on the centralization of
power. Much depends, however, on the mode of state organization,
"institutional engineers," and leadership.

Conflict and Postcommunism: Equating State Capacity with Centralization

The study of ethnic conflict has generated a number of taxonomies for conflicts and means of conflict regulation.[37] A taxonomy,
however, explains neither the causes and dynamics of conflicts nor
the rationale for choosing a particular strategy to deal with a real
or potential conflict. The study of the causes of conflict revolves
around a relatively small set of structural preconditions (such as ethnic composition, demography, geography, historical legacies, and
socioeconomic factors). Depending on the range of cases and the
time period studied, the prioritization of individual factors may vary,
and vague correlations have been drawn up, such as "the greater the
discrimination the more likely is organized action" or "the more
strongly a person identifies with a group the more likely is action."[38]
David Carment and Patrick James sum up the dilemma: "Agreement
exists that some combination of economic, political and psychological
factors can explain ethnic conflict. Consensus, however, ends at that
point."[39] Beissinger convincingly cuts through the circular study of
structural preconditions by demonstrating statistically that the same

structural factors are present both in cases where conflict becomes violent and where it does not.[40] The works of Arend Lijphart, Donald Horowitz, Joseph Rothschild, and Eric Nordlinger also offer ways to break out of this deadlock by considering the significance of elite motivations to play the ethnic card, the potentially stabilizing role of crosscutting cleavages, and the structural-institutional and distributional mechanisms of conflict management.[41]

A key argument running throughout the debates on conflict regulation is the impact of power sharing based on ethnically defined groups: do these institutions ease tension and effectively deal with conflict potential in the long run, or do they simply entrench divisions and postpone the conflict? A territorial autonomy status acknowledges the political significance or distinct nature of a particular region. Often the ethnic composition of a territorial unit leads to demands for a special administrative or political status and cultural rights. Thus, autonomy can reinforce the link between ethnicity and territory. Multiethnicity can become a stimulus for a special regional status, although an autonomy status in a multiethnic setting does not guarantee the accommodation of all relevant groups. Crimea, as the historical and political analysis provided in this book will demonstrate, exemplifies both trends.

Since the late 1980s, eight violent conflicts have occurred in the territory of the FSU (Nagorno-Karabakh, Abkhazia, Ferghana Valley, South Ossetia, North Ossetia/Ingushetia, Transdnistria, Tajikistan, Chechnya) and at least eight significant potential conflicts have not erupted into violence (Crimea, Tatarstan, Bashkortostan, Gagauzia, Ajaria, Northern Kazakhstan, Estonia, Latvia).[42] Ethnopolitical mobilization in the aftermath of the USSR has underlined the internationally observed shift from interstate to intrastate conflicts.[43] Several commentators see the year 1992 as the cutoff point for the initiation of ethnopolitical protest and rebellion in the FSU and, perhaps prematurely, refer to the "stabilization of the post-Soviet space" as a result of state building, Russian influence, and processes of internationalization.[44] Others see conflict potential as being high primarily because most of the governments lack the commitment and resources to make power sharing a real priority.[45] In any event, a certain degree of stability should not distract from a detailed analysis of the dynamics of postcommunist conflicts and the mechanisms of conflict prevention or conflict management.

The academic study of post-Soviet conflicts has focused on the role of ethnicity, in particular the presence of the Russian (or Russian-speaking) diaspora across the FSU, as the key to postimperialism and potential conflict.[46] These studies explicitly or implicitly map a potential for conflict. By comparison, less emphasis has been on the systematic analysis of the dynamics of conflict prevention and conflict management, especially in multiethnic settings. Quantitative studies of postcommunist conflicts have concluded that power-sharing institutions are less important for conflict management than demographic and cultural factors, in particular cultural proximity between the core group and the minority.[47] This argument appears to be shaped by the notion of building institutions "from scratch" and neglects the fact that divided societies and a complex institutional architecture for managing multiethnicity were already in place when the Soviet Union collapsed. How these institutional legacies were managed was critical for the stability of interethnic relations in the aftermath of the collapse.[48]

Centralization, despite the wishes of its proponents, does not necessarily stabilize or strengthen a divided society or a state in transition. The general centralist preference across the postcommunist region was fostered by insecurities and tensions over inherited Soviet administrative boundaries, now fixed as state borders, and perceived threats to state integrity. Moreover, the governing elites at the level of the former Union Republics, who had just seceded from the political center in Moscow, were often at the vanguard of the nationalist mobilization that brought the Soviet Union to collapse, and thus they were not politically sensitive to the need for carefully managing complex ethnoterritorial and regional demands. The Soviet legacy of institutionalized multiethnicity in the federal state was almost universally associated with a tendency to separatism, and thus its disassembly was an urgent priority for many new nationalist governments. The dilution of the central state by federalism or autonomy was generally equated with an automatic weakening of state power, thus limiting the space for accommodative strategies. These sentiments were also prominent among Ukraine's ruling elite vis-à-vis Crimea.

The concept of federalism remains deeply tainted by the Soviet experience and has been a taboo topic in post-Soviet Ukraine. According to Ukraine's first president, Leonid Kravchuk, federalization was never discussed as a real option.[49] Since the late Soviet period, federalism has been an idea of the political opposition in Ukraine.[50] In the run-up to the collapse of the Soviet Union, the idea of federalism figured prominently in the political debates in the west of Ukraine as a vehicle for the national movement with Viacheslav Chornovil, leader of the Narodnyi Rukh Ukraïny party (Rukh) and chairman of the Lviv regional council as its main proponent.[51] Once Ukrainian independence had been proclaimed, however, Ukraine's national-democratic forces reversed their positions and turned into the most staunch supporters of a unitary Ukrainian state. State consolidation became inextricably linked with centralization, while the "federal idea" translated into a vague concept of regional autonomy that traveled to the east and south of Ukraine. In the 1994 presidential elections, Leonid Kuchma's campaign, orchestrated by the Inter-regional Bloc of Reforms, successfully tapped into these regional sentiments.[52] Once elected president, however, Kuchma followed his predecessor Kravchuk in concentrating on issues of central state capacity. Ideas about Crimea as a first step towards regionalization or even federalism in Ukraine were kept alive in academic and political circles in the east of Ukraine, for example in Donetsk and Kharkiv.[53] During the protracted constitution-making process from 1991 to 1996, the predominant argument for the preservation of a unitary state was the need to preserve Ukraine's territorial integrity and to ensure central state capacity during transition, whereas the necessity to address regional specificities and regional economic rights as a precondition for economic transformation was among the arguments put forward by a marginalized group of supporters of decentralization and federalism.[54] Ukraine's most outspoken proponent of federalism at the time was Volodymyr Hryn'ov, leader of the Interregional Bloc of Reforms. As soon as Kuchma had taken office, however, Hryn'ov was politically sidelined. *Nova Ukraïna*, the book in which he developed his idea of federalism, earned harsh public criticism, illustrating the extent to which federalism has been considered a taboo topic by the central Ukrainian political establishment.[55] In the 2006 parliamentary elections federalism resurfaced as a vague goal on the agenda of Viktor Yanukovych's Party of Regions, which has its stronghold in Donetsk. As soon as Yanukovych became prime minister—after a four-month long political struggle—he dropped his federalist rhetoric, thereby once again demonstrating that federalism remains a tool of the political opposition.

The focus on central state capacity in the postcommunist countries is mirrored by an emphasis in the transition and democratization literature on the elites and institutions at the state or "national" level. This emphasis is in line with a trend in the social sciences since the 1980s that was best captured in the evocative title of a book edited by Peter Evans, Dietrich Rueschemeyer, and Theda Skocpol: *Bringing the State Back In.*[56] This book made a strong case for taking the state seriously both as an organizational structure and a potentially autonomous actor. This emphasis on state capacity came as a reaction against society-centered pluralist, functionalist, and neo-Marxist approaches that had reduced the state to "a mere arena in which social groups make demands and engage in political struggles or compromises."[57] The study called for an analysis of the state's role in revolutions and reforms, its social and economic policies, and their effects on political conflicts.[58] Published well before the onset of transition in Eastern Europe, it is illuminating for the analysis of postcommunist state building. As Stephen Hanson has observed, "statehood itself—that is, the very identity of the country as a distinct, sovereign national unit—has been far more problematic in the postcommunist world than in most other regions."[59]

The state—whether defined as a nation-state, the bearer of domestic or international sovereignty and identity, a regulatory mechanism, or the sum of effective monopoly functions within a territorially bounded entity—remains central to comparative politics. In the post-Soviet setting, many of the questions about state capacity (or incapacity), or the "unevenness" of capacity across policy areas, are relevant, but the starting point is different: we are dealing with new states, most of which have never experienced sovereignty. This book on Crimea applies some of the ideas about state capacity and goes beyond national-level analysis. It calls for "bringing the region back in" by focusing on its role in the ongoing process of postcommunist state building. Accordingly, the conceptual emphasis switches from the analysis of "old" and relatively stable states to the construction of "new" states and to the immediate and active role of regions and regional actors in this process. Insofar as sovereignty is classically understood to be effective control over territory and people, the status of regions and their interaction with the central government are fundamental to the understanding of state building (and state disintegration). In many stable Western democracies, the accommodation of the "regional factor" has remained a contentious and ongoing process, even in federal and consociational states. In conditions of weak statehood and of political and economic volatility, as exhibited during transition, the regional challenge can be expected to be even more serious.

"Subversive" versus "Constructive" Institutions

The Soviet legacy of federal ethnoterritorial institutions is an important influence on how post-Soviet elites are seeking to manage these two challenges. The management of this legacy in the FSU has occasioned political responses ranging from negotiation and bargaining to violent conflict. By controlling and manipulating ethnic identities, the socialist system fulfilled a dual function: on the one hand, as Gellner noted, it acted as a "deep freeze" for nationalism and nation-state building,[60] and on the other hand, by institutionalizing and territorializing ethnicity in the organization of the federal state, it provided an incubator for embryonic nation-states. This mixed legacy of "institutionalized multinationality"[61] provided the backdrop for the rise of old and new conflict potential. The resurgence of ancient ethnic hatreds has become the shorthand explanation of the wars in the FSU and former Yugoslavia. Much less attention is focused on how the quasi-federalism of the communist period created "subversive institutions" by providing ready-made platforms for nationalist mobilization in the event of a disintegration of the central state.[62]

The Soviet federal system consisted of ethnoterritorial political units at four territorial levels: the union republic (*sovetskaia sotsialisticheskaia respublika*), the autonomous republic (*avtonomnaia respublika*), the autonomous region (*avtonomnaia oblast'*), and the autonomous district (*avtonomnyi okrug*). A passport entry formally identified every individual by nationality in addition to the ethnoterritorial units. Under Soviet rule, the hierarchical federal system had little overall political significance. The "leading" role of the Communist Party and the lack of meaningful procedures for shared power and jurisdictional autonomy made Soviet federalism a sham. For example, the constitutional right of the union republics to secede was merely a paper guarantee; no legal mechanism for realizing this right existed. Nevertheless, the different ethnically-defined autonomy constructs within union republics may have constrained ethnopolitical mobilization, because they helped to embed a set of formal and informal cultural and recruitment practices benefiting the titular ethnic groups of the autonomies. Thus, the ethnofederal units formed part of the counterbalancing mechanisms and protections within the Soviet system against nationalist mobilization, including against Russian national chauvinism.

As soon as the center's overarching control began to unravel, however, this kind of state organization no longer acted as a constraint on nationalism; rather, the ethnically denominated federal units became a platform for nationalist mobilization and provided resources to project ethnic power. The collapse of the Soviet Union, and the subsequent transition, led to a reorganization of the inherited ethnoterritorial framework. By and large the successor states were "nationalizing states" whose titular ethnic groups engaged in a redefinition of political, economic, and cultural power to their advantage over other ethnic groups. The incentives and opportunity structures that transition provided in the political and economic spheres made for a speedy disassembly of institutional constraints on ethnic power.

The legacy of "institutionalized multinationality" was further complicated by the either arbitrary or deliberate manner by which the Soviet Union had drawn federal boundaries over time, often without sensitivity to ethnic demography, and by the patterns of communist-era population settlements, in particular the "settler colonialism" of Russians and Russian-speakers, and the consequences of the rehabilitation of deported peoples who had been dispossessed of their homes and homelands.[63] Demonstration effects among ethnofederal units within or across union republics, often crosscutting the hierarchy of formal or imagined autonomy, added to the buildup of what Beissinger aptly describes as the "tide of nationalism" leading to the collapse of the Soviet Union and a phase of "noisy politics" characterized by nationalism, separatism, and violent conflicts.[64]

Institutions fulfil a number of important functions by defining the boundaries of inclusion and exclusion, formalizing incentive structures and constraints, aggregating the action of individuals, and stabilizing expectations and patterns of interactions."[65] Douglass North's analysis of institutions as including formal structures and rules as well as informal norms and codes of behavior is particularly appropriate for the transition state, in which institution making is an ongoing process and the distinction between formal and informal is even more blurred.[66] Institutionalized patterns of behavior, social interaction, and recruitment, conditioned by different historical experiences, can either bolster the state or, in the wake of a loosening of control at the center, reinforce and accelerate the subversion of multilevel state institutions and state-society linkages.

The subversive power of Soviet-type federal structures is confirmed by the fact that almost all the socialist-era federations broke up (with the exception of the Russian Federation). The legacy of Soviet federalism, however, continues to play an important role in the aftermath of systemic collapse. The ways in which socialist-era institutional legacies were addressed, managed, readjusted, disassembled, or ignored have affected the causation and duration of conflicts and the management of conflict potential.[67] The Soviet institutional legacy has also acted as a constraint on some post-Soviet "nationalizing states."[68] By examining how this Soviet institutional legacy impinged upon the management of the Crimean issue during post-Soviet state building in Ukraine, this book will argue that the institutional legacy of the Soviet era has explanatory power not only for the collapse of the USSR, as Rogers Brubaker and Valerie Bunce have argued, but also for the patterns of state and nation building in the postcommunist period. The ways in which institutional legacies were undone, picked over and reassembled, were of crucial importance not only for the causation of conflicts, but also for the dynamics of conflict prevention. This study of Crimea puts forward the argument that one institution—an autonomy status—can be both "subversive" and "constructive." It can be subversive in one place in one period of time, and constructive in another place and time, or it can take on these different roles over time in the same place.

Ukraine's "State of Regions"

The significance of regional diversity in Ukrainian history and politics has been acknowledged without, however, attempting to write a history of Ukraine through a regional prism.[69] Ukraine's post-Soviet state and nation building process has been studied from different conceptual angles, such as nationalism, constitution making, party politics, civil society, rent seeking, corporatism, and foreign-policy making.[70] Andrew Wilson stresses the role of regional divisions, but he is primarily interested in ethnolinguistic differences as an explanation for the weakness of Ukrainian ethnic nationalism.[71] Ukraine's sizable Russian minority (eleven million according to the Soviet census of 1989, and 8.3 million—17.3 percent—according to Ukraine's 2001 census),[72] plus the significant segment of Russian-speaking Ukrainians in the southwest of the country, figure prominently in the discussion about the weakness of state identity. In fact, the study of Ukraine's Russian-speaking minority was part of a wider concern about the impact of the twenty-five million ethnic Russian and Russian-speaker minority scattered across the FSU, which proved a fashionable research topic in the 1990s.[73] A key assumption in these studies was that where this minority was present, Russian nationalist mobilization would follow and turn into a major destabilizing factor for the successor states.

Studies of Ukraine tended to reinforce the perception of clear-cut ethnolinguistic cleavages in the country and assume that they made for an inherent conflict potential.[74] Several authors, however, have questioned this thesis. Taras Kuzio has strongly disagreed with the emphasis on ethnolinguistic divisions.[75] His own assessment remains somewhat ambivalent: while describing regional identities as a sign of an incomplete national identity and thereby as a transitional phenomenon, he also recognizes the continuous existence of multiple identities, ethnic and territorial, in regions such as Crimea or the Donbas.[76] Similarly, George Liber observes a "common desire for peace and stability" that tends to overshadow regional divisions and acts as a guarantee against the disintegration of the state.[77] Stephen Shulman puts forward an argument about the complementarities of Ukrainian and Russian identities in the formation of a common civic

Ukrainian identity.[78] In contrast, Roman Solchanyk concedes that Ukraine may not be in danger of fragmentation, but he singles out the overlapping regional, ethnic, and linguistic cleavages as "one of the most serious obstacles to state building and nation building and, by extension, to the country's stability and security."[79]

This intriguing relationship between state and regional identities and the stability and legitimacy of state institutions is the main theme of this book. It follows other works on regional identity in Ukraine which have mainly focused on the predominantly Russophone eastern regions such as the Donbas and Zaporizhzhia.[80] These studies have revealed the fluid nature of regional and national identities, both as ethnic and territorial categories, and provide new evidence to refute the ubiquitous overemphasis on the politics of the Russian language issue in eastern Ukraine.

Public opinion research has continually revealed a link between place of residence within Ukraine and issue polarization, but the sheer existence of territorial characteristics says little about their political significance or how they may be mobilized.[81] Survey and focus group data tend to confirm a generally positive attitude of ethnic Ukrainians and ethnic Russians in Ukraine toward each other, an attitude previously identified by Ian Bremmer in the early 1990s.[82] There is also much evidence of the blurring of the ethnic boundary through language, intermarriage, and the strength of regional identities.[83] In fact, the data suggest that regional territorial identification can weaken ethnic identity.

Most attention has been paid to regional differences in national elections. Ukraine's electoral geography in 1994, the year of the first post-Soviet parliamentary and presidential elections, suggested that ethnolinguistic divisions along an east-west divide translated into anti- or pro-reform voting behavior and support for leftist or national-democratic parties respectively.[84] Over time, the regional distribution of votes became more complex, as did the analyses of the regional factor in the elections.[85] Birch has argued that region and ethnicity have distinctive effects on separate segments of the electorate.[86] The parliamentary elections of 1998 underscored the importance of regional socioeconomic concerns and the fact that the regional effect on voting behavior varies across regions and parties: in the western regions cultural-historical experience is strongly correlated with the national-democratic vote, whereas socioeconomic factors make for a more salient explanation of the leftist vote in the east of Ukraine.[87]

The idea that an ethnolinguistic regional east-west divide dominates Ukrainian politics over all other dimensions is also extrapolated from the debates over Ukraine's foreign policy orientation since the early 1990s. It is widely accepted that Ukraine operates a so-called multivector foreign policy—the official description of the balancing act between East (Russia) and West (the European Union and U.S.). This balancing act between Western and Russian interests is reflected in the opinion polls over time.[88] The foreign policy rhetoric of the various political forces in Ukraine sometimes reinforces the simplistic view of an East-West divide. In fact, Ukraine's regional divisions cover a range of ethnic, linguistic, political, ideological, and socioeconomic issues which often crosscut and blur the political fault lines.

Most recent publications on Crimea emphasize the Russian-Ukrainian disputes over Crimea, Sevastopol, and the Black Sea Fleet, or focus on the ethnic issue, whether Crimea's ethnic Russians, or the Crimean Tatars.[89] The common assumption shared by different studies of Crimea is that it had one of the greatest potentials for ethnic conflict among the successor states to the Soviet Union, comparable to Transdnistria, Abkhazia, or Chechnya.[90] Crimea's multiethnicity has often been described—implicitly and explicitly—as the potential motor of conflict.[91] In Crimea or elsewhere in the postcommunist space, little attention has been paid to multiethnicity as a complex political phenomenon—defined by a dynamic interaction among a whole range of identities, interests, and institutions—the boundaries and political relevance of which are neither rigid nor unchangeable. Moreover, ethnicity may only be one, though possibly the most visible, marker of difference; it may also fuse with or cloak other salient interests or demands.

Studies of the political events and developments in Crimea have primarily concentrated on the high point of separatist sentiment in 1994.[92] Russian media and academic publications have tended to stress the "illegitimate" transfer of Crimea in 1954, as well as to express concerns about the strategic security implications of the loss of Crimea.[93] Much of the original focus among analysts was on the significance of Crimea as a foreign policy issue between Russia and Ukraine.[94] Few authors, particularly at the time of the 1994 high-water mark of separatist sentiment, emphasized the distinctive domestic dynamics of the Crimean issue in Ukrainian politics.[95]

A study of Crimea's autonomy status is by and large absent from the field of conflict studies. One exception is Philip Chase's essay on Crimea as an example of the limits of international law in dealing with ethnic enclaves and claims to autonomy.[96] Susan Stewart also analyzes the tensions between the Crimean Tatars and the Russophone population irrespective of Crimea's autonomy status. She argues that Crimea's multiethnicity fuels ethnopolitical competition, and thus severely limits the chances for autonomy to work.[97]

This book, in contrast, demonstrates that the potential for conflict and instability arising from multiethnicity and the mobilization of regional political identities can be managed by center-regional and intraregional bargaining. Crimea has to date been one of the biggest tests of Ukraine's post-Soviet transition, but it has been successfully managed so far by developing an institutionalized autonomy. This autonomy has been both "subversive" and "constructive," for it was a product of a destabilizing nationalist mobilization, but also the result of political compromise and constitutional consensus. Measured on the commonly used institutional criteria of a federal state, Ukraine does not qualify. Unitary and federal states, however, mark only the theoretical endpoints on a scale. Between them lies an array of institutional arrangements, including many different types of autonomy. Democratic theory assumes that state stability requires homogeneity and, in the case of a federation, institutional symmetry.[98] Comparative experience has shown, however, that asymmetric autonomy arrangements can be flexible and effective mechanisms for stabilizing and accommodating diversity within a state. Ultimately, Crimea's autonomy inscribes the federal principle de facto in Ukraine's constitutional framework.[99] As we shall discuss in the latter part of this book, it is not the inherent power of the Crimean autonomy per se that has been stabilizing, but the process of deliberation by which the autonomy was created. Ukraine's state and nation building defies the widespread theoretical assumptions that the "ethnic East" is more conflict-prone than the "civic West" and that unresolved stateness issues can derail democratization. It has achieved this through an institutional compromise that is a significant achievement in a newly established democracy.

2   Imagining Crimea: The Symbols and Myths of a Politicized Landscape

EXPLORING THE CULTURAL MATRIX OF A REGION is an important complement to the analysis of conflict and conflict potential. In order for conflict to erupt over a combination of structural conditions (such as the ethnic composition of an area, socioeconomic discrepancies, or interested external actors), these risk factors have to be channeled through collective memories inscribed in symbols and myths. This process is an essential part of the mobilizational cycle accompanying conflict, but in itself it should not be mistaken for the key cause of conflict.

The cultural and political context shaping the symbolic use of landscape has proven difficult to trace systematically. Similarly, the effects of symbols and myths defy the assumptions of causality-driven social science research. Omitting these aspects from the study of conflict, however, would situate our analysis in an artificial vacuum of the present. Conflicts tend to be framed by rival claims to historically evolved identities rooted in territory, ethnicity, and experience. Competing claims to history can translate into rival claims to territory. These political claims often cloak more tangible interests pursued by particular groups of actors, but they fulfill a range of important functions: they link elites with wider parts of the population through collective recognition, they reinforce the bonds of common interests vis-à-vis "otherness," they instill a sense of security by emphasizing the continuity of group identification, and thus they provide a basis for political action.

Memory, Symbol, and Myth

Memories, symbols, and myths are the raw material for the construction and political mobilization of identity. Markers of identity will endure and be fit for mobilization only if they resonate. Thus, they are best understood as social constructs which effectively weld and interpret historical and cultural memories of a place and its people. Accordingly, Benedict Anderson's famous phrase "imagined communities" does not describe a fictitious or false sense of community, but rather the active process of making sense of the world by imagining a community larger than one's personal environment.[1] He grasps the idea that geographical distances in the modern world are shrinking while the horizons of abstraction are expanding. Even though this book takes a political perspective, Crimea's rich cultural landscape must be analyzed in order to understand its resonance in contemporary politics and public discourse. The extent to which there is both a regular use of shared historical and cultural memories and a sense of the depth of this attachment to the territory provides us with a yardstick to measure and understand the scope of political mobilization. Memories, translating into symbols and myths, are only one element in the context of transition politics and conflict potential, but an important one.

Symbols combine suggestive, emotional, and political power. They function as a conscious and subconscious form of communication, and they organize speech patterns, daily routines, and personal and political interaction. Symbols foster collective identities by reinforcing shared historical or cultural memories, and they are often the triggers by which these memories become politically activated. Language as the reservoir of memory and information is the broadest tapestry for symbolic expression, one in which everyday codes can act as abstract *pars pro toto* affirmations of vague notions of identity.[2] Anthony Smith identifies a long list of elements that mark the identity of nations and nation-states:

> flags, anthems, parades, coinage, capital cities, oaths, folk costumes, museums of folklore, war memorials, ceremonies of remembrance for the national dead, passports, frontiers—as well as more hidden aspects, such as national recreation, the countryside, popular heroes

and heroines, fairy tales, forms of etiquette, styles of architecture, arts and crafts, modes of town planning, legal procedures, educational practices and military codes.[3]

Some of these symbols of national identity also resonate at the regional level; others find their complementary or rival outlets.

Symbols can be the "building blocks of myth,"[4] story lines that link and interpret a selected set of memories, some of which might be transmitted through symbols. The word "myth" implies a coherent narrative following certain patterns, but myths can vary in their scope and time span, their themes and density. The process of mythmaking and the dissemination of myths help to forge, maintain, and mobilize identities. There is no clear-cut boundary between fact, memory, symbol and myth, because they all revolve around perceptions and interpretation. Nevertheless, the term "myth" contains an a priori judgment and suggests resemblance with fiction rather than with reality. However, the actual construction, transmission, and function of myths are more relevant to the study of identity politics than the disentangling of fact from fiction. Myths represent traditions of storytelling about the past, parts of rituals, and constructs of reality which assist to maintain a social order.[5] Myths politicize space, historical experience, and cultural heritage. Symbols and myths are points of reference that locate individual actors and groups in ongoing political and social processes. Some myths, particularly myths of origin and place, tend to conflict with the myths of neighbors, whereas other myths are mutually compatible. The most powerful myths are explicitly linked to nationhood, to the nation's origins, evolution and glorious struggles that can be called upon in the quest for self-determination.[6] Myths can also focus on other units of society, such as families, extended kin groups, regions and other localities.

A distinct geographical location and landscape, the presence of diverse cultures, and a turbulent history—this is the stuff of which potent memories, symbols, and myths are constructed. Crimea's natural beauty and distinctive history readily inspire national and regional mythmaking. Imperial Russian, Soviet and Soviet-Russian, Crimean Tatar, and Ukrainian mythmaking are the predominant perspectives in contemporary Crimean politics. The collapse of the

Soviet Union in 1991 tore apart the cultural and historical map—in
Serhii Plokhy's words, the "sacred space"[7]—created by Russian imperialism and Soviet ideology. An intricate web of memories, symbols,
and myths, woven into the fabric of the Russian and Soviet empires,
began to unravel. Crimea occupied a prime position in Russian and
Soviet symbolism and mythmaking, yet in 1991 it found itself outside
Russian sovereign territory after the disintegration of the USSR. The
shock of this dislocation led to an urgent recovery of the old symbols
and myths.

Landscape as Identity

Historical memories and literary images are closely interwoven with
landscape. Landscapes, writes Simon Schama,

> are culture before they are nature; constructs of the imagination
> projected onto wood and water and rock.… Once a certain idea of
> landscape, a myth, a vision, establishes itself in an actual place, it has
> a peculiar way of muddling categories, of making metaphors more
> real than their referents; of becoming, in fact, part of the scenery.[8]

Similarly, Smith describes the "territorialization of memory" as "a
process by which certain kinds of shared memories are attached
to particular territories so that the former ethnic landscape (or
ethnoscape) and the latter become historic homelands."[9] In the
term "homeland," the territorialization of memory culminates and
acquires political potency.

Despite the centrality of territory in national and regional identity construction, social science analysis does not focus on the role
of culture in the interaction between geographical boundaries and
membership boundaries. In fact, the perception of shared historical
and cultural experiences is usually tied to a particular territorial setting, as is the modern notion of political sovereignty. The generalized
conception of "nature" was gradually transformed into the definition
of "landscape." The word "landscape" entered the English language
as a technical term used by painters. Landscape painting became an
integral part of the representation and imagination of territory. In
the context of growing national consciousness in Europe, the concept
of "landscape" was applied to an ever wider range of cultural and

social dimensions.[10] By the eighteenth and nineteenth centuries, "landscapes" and supposedly unique national myths were inextricably bound.[11]

The name "Ukraina" itself denotes a landscape: the borderland of the Russian Empire towards the rest of Europe and the Ottoman Empire. Folk songs and legends, rituals, literature, and art reflect this idealized landscape. Ukraine's striped blue-and-yellow national flag is composed of two timeless abstract images of its landscape: a blue sky over a ripened wheat field. Alternatively, the Ukrainian landscape is a mythologized steppe. By comparison, the symbolic English landscape is a tamed and cultivated rural paradise, while the sublime Alps dominate the Swiss landscape, the boundless frontier is embedded in the American psyche, and the awe-inspiring vastness of space between Europe and Asia weighs on the Russian mentality. The focus in these imaginations by insiders and outsiders has remained on the nation as the point of reference. Regional or local identifications with the surrounding environment can be equally strong, and often national landscape imagery draws on specific regional or local landmarks.

Eric Kaufmann and Oliver Zimmer date the explicit linkage between landscape and national characteristics to nineteenth-century Romanticism,[12] but the institutional foundations of these links were developed much earlier, for example in the geographic societies of the seventeenth century. Representations of landscape increased with modernization, especially with new opportunities for traveling and encounters of people and places. Travelers from "inside" and "outside"—mappers, scientists, artists, writers, estate owners, government officials, and diplomats—increasingly shaped and disseminated landscape mythologies. Kaufmann and Zimmer refer to the projection of memories, myths, and national virtues onto a landscape as the "nationalisation of nature."[13] Their comparative study of Canada and Switzerland suggests that in addition to the mere presence of dramatic landscape, countries with a high degree of ethnic pluralism make landscape a preeminent marker of a shared identity. This finding might apply regionally in Crimea, where the landscape has been part of the shared mythology of different ethnic groups for centuries, if not millenia.

The building blocks of the symbols and myths surrounding

Crimea's landscape include images created both by indigenous artists, writers, and storytellers of different nationalities and by various
outsiders, in particular official Russian accounts from the time of
the annexation of Crimea onwards, descriptions by foreign travelers
from the eighteenth through the twentieth centuries, and by Soviet,
Crimean Tatar, and Ukrainian literary accounts and historiography.
These different narratives tend to draw on similar images. Their
common thread is that Crimea combines natural beauty with ethnic
diversity. Into a shared landscape full of distinctive features—the
Black Sea coast, the peninsula's mountain ridges and steppe—different groups have embedded their communal symbols and myths.
Successive tides of settlers have appropriated parts of the already
culturally mapped landscape and imbued it with their own symbolic
meaning. There is a sense of both authenticity and continuity in
the mythologization of the Crimean landscape. Some of Crimea's
most vivid myths and legends, based on the region's natural features,
originate in the Crimean Tatar era (from the thirteenth century to
the incorporation of Crimea in the Russian Empire in 1783) and,
thus, considerably predate the Romantic era in Western Europe.
The Crimean Tatar memory is crucially shaped by the landscape of
Crimea and its distinct steppe, mountain, and coastal areas, each of
which is closely associated with specific subgroups of the Tatars.

Ascherson divided Crimea's history into three zones: the zone
of the mind—the coast and its towns and ports; the zone of the
body—the inland steppe behind the coastal mountain range; and
the zone of the spirit—the mountain area dividing the other two
zones.[14] Cultural and political developments continually reinforced
the region's geographical distinctiveness. The myth of Crimea
in the Russian imagination began as an imperial exotica with the
journey of Empress Catherine II in March 1787 through the newly
conquered southern provinces of the Russian Empire, including the
Tavricheskaia guberniia.[15] Catherine II and her companions—Joseph
II of Austria along with French, English, and German counts and
envoys—were spared any evidence of disorder and unrest thanks
to Grigorii Potemkin's adept stage-managing of the tour.[16] They
encountered seemingly happy, well-fed peasants en route (hence
the term "Potemkin villages"), and in Crimea they met peaceful
Tatars who swore eternal allegiance to the Russian state.[17] Catherine

was taken with the climate and beauty of the peninsula, and she recognized both its commercial potential and its geopolitical role in further confrontations with the Ottoman Empire. Contemporaries interpreted the journey as a political demonstration of the grandeur of Russian imperial power, but it was also the beginning of the Russian romance with the peninsula. Crimea's beauty, its pendantlike shape, and borderland location inspired Russians to call it "the jewel in the crown" of the empire.[18]

In the nineteenth century, Crimea became the summer retreat and "luxurious playground"[19] for the wealthy and the literati of tsarist imperial society. The Crimean Riviera was the Russian equivalent to the Côte d'Azur. This period gave rise to some of the most vivid and enduring images of Crimea. In the Soviet era the Crimean landscape became embedded in Soviet ideology. In official rhetoric and popular imagination, the peninsula was successfully proletarianized as a zone of working-class tourism, and the sanatorium became "the real *genius loci* of Crimea."[20] Today the memory of Crimea as the Soviet Union's number-one holiday resort still reverberates throughout the FSU. Interestingly, many of Crimea's natural features retained their Tatar names even during the tsarist and Soviet periods.[21] Parallel Russian names and translations of Crimean Tatar names were introduced, but in public and literary imaginations they never fully replaced the older names.

The collapse of the Soviet empire has resulted in the return, rather than "the end of history," coupled with "the return of geography."[22] During the years of glasnost and perestroika, environmental concerns were an important part of the "econational" movements, intensified by the Chornobyl disaster in 1986. National sovereignty and environmental sovereignty were fused in the imagination and in political mobilization. Even in Crimea, a late riser in comparison to the rest of the country, political mobilization crystallized around concerns over a nuclear power station in the north of the peninsula.[23] In the early phases, these environmental movements were civic in nature and embraced the territory of the whole state or region, but political or ethnic cleavages subsequently undermined these movements. In Crimea, references and claims to the territory soon became ethnicized. With the large-scale return of the Crimean Tatars, the exclusivist notion of "homeland"—the most powerful fusion of geography, historical memory, and political claim—became a key theme in debates over Crimea's political status, its institutions, and the rights of its different ethnic groups.

Mapping Crimea: The Politics of Toponymy

The map is one of the essential tools for the imagining of communities.[24] It can be used flexibly for classificatory purposes, for example to define and categorize people, regions, religions, languages, products, and monuments. The map is also a logo deeply ingrained in popular imagination as an objective representation of space and landscape. Maps and mapping exercises are deeply political. The parameters chosen to define a place and integrate it with a broader regional or global view of space are not free of prejudice. Pierre Bourdieu's analogy between maps and culture underlines the relevance of different mapping exercises for the construction of identity.[25]

Toponymy, the naming of places, is by definition part of this mapping exercise. The origin of the name "Crimea" itself is unclear. In the nineteenth century, European historians originally traced it back to the Cimmerians, a people living in Crimea in the eighth century BC. Later etymological studies located its origin in the Crimean Tatar word "Qırım" (Russian: Krym), meaning "stronghold" or "fortress," and the name of the administrative center of the Crimean Tatars (from the thirteenth to the fifteenth century), the town of Eski Qırım (Russian: Starii Krym).[26] Wherever the name originated, the repeated renaming of the region throughout its history highlights its close association—real or imagined—with the Tatars. After the Russian annexation in 1783 the region was divided into three districts; most of Crimea became Tauride Province (*Tavricheskaia guberniia*). This choice reflected the contemporary fashion for neoclassicism and for Hellenistic names. Moreover, a return to the Hellenistic toponym known since the Greek colonization of Crimea, which began in the seventh century BC, was regarded as being more "European." The Byzantine Greek influence, however, although stronger than the impact of early Slav settlers, had ended with the rise of the Genoese and Venetians in the medieval period.[27] When the Golden Horde lost its internal cohesion in the 1420s, an independent Crimean Khanate emerged; it, in turn, came under the protectorate of the Ottoman

Empire in 1475. The Khanate eventually succumbed to the Russian Empire when the Nogai Tatars in the north of Crimea acknowledged Russian suzerainty during the 1768–74 Russo-Turkish war.[28] Khan Şahin Giray cooperated with Catherine II but lacked the support of the different regional, ethnic, and political groups. There was still no unified sense of Crimean Tatar identity when Russia finally annexed Crimea.

At the time of its annexation in 1783, Crimea was largely an unknown entity to the Russian elites. Only its geopolitical significance in the Black Sea region was widely acknowledged.[29] The subsequent surge in studies about Crimea's nature, climate, and population, often encouraged and sponsored by the government, reflects the recognition of the need to master, physically and mentally, the newly conquered region.[30] Archaeological expeditions focused on Crimea's ancient history, looking for traces of Hellenistic civilizations that were deemed compatible with, or seen as acceptable antecedents to Russia.[31] Some changes were made to Crimea's toponymy, replacing Tatar names by Greek- or Russian-sounding ones.[32] The philhellenism that characterized this period is reflected in the Greek-sounding names chosen for existing or newly created cities and towns, for example Evpatoriia (replacing the Tatar name Gözleve) or Feodosiia (instead of Kefe). Simferopol, the new Orthodox capital, first enveloped and later replaced the Tatar village Akmescit. Sevastopol became the new naval base and port replacing the Tatar village Akyar. Simferopol means "the city of gatherers," a name widely seen as referring to its mixed ethnic composition. Sevastopol connotes "city of victors." Some foreign travelers wondered why the Russians did not simply translate the Tatar place names.[33] Greek names affirmed Russia's claim to be the successor of the Byzantine Empire, and Crimea was the geographically closest part of the new Russian Empire to the old Byzantine Empire. Similarly, the coat of arms of the Tavricheskaia guberniia showed the double-headed eagle and the Orthodox cross.

From the reign of Peter I onwards, Russia was divided into *gouvernements* (*guberniias*), each overseen by an appointed governor. Each governor was responsible to the senate and had the right of personal report to the tsar. Loyalty to the tsar afforded a governor powerful status in his area. Tavricheskaia guberniia became one of the new administrative units on the new southern fringe of the Russian Empire. A guberniia included 200,000–300,000 people.[34] In its asymmetry and hierarchical order, the tsarist administrative system prefigured the Soviet one, although during the tsarist regime ethnicity was not a regular institutionalized marker at the regional level. Nevertheless, the privileges granted to some areas, for example the Baltic provinces, had ethnoterritorial overtones. Until the second half of the nineteenth century, local administration in the Russian Empire was firmly controlled by the central power.

Under Tsar Paul in 1796, Tavricheskaia guberniia was incorporated into the much bigger Novorossiiskaia guberniia (Novorossiia). Some Tatar place names were revived, however without any "re-turkification" of the peninsula or its administration.[35] Alexander I redivided Novorossiiskaia guberniia into three smaller guberniias, one of them being Tavrida. This administrative structure remained largely intact until 1917 except for the establishment of separate administrations for the garrison cities of Kerch, Balaklava, and Sevastopol. The special administrative status of these cities emphasized the strategic role of Crimea as a Russian military stronghold.[36] In the case of Sevastopol, this special status contributed to the ensuing mythmaking about the city. Debates about the city's separate administrative status resurfaced even in the post-Soviet era, and today Sevastopol is—apart from Kyiv—the only Ukrainian city with a special administrative status comparable to that of an oblast.

After the October Revolution, the Crimean Tatar National Assembly (Kurultay) revived the name "Crimea" (Qırım). Under the slogan "Crimea for the Crimeans," the Kurultay and the National Party (Milli Firqa) proposed a multiethnic Crimea as an autonomous unit within the Russian Federation.[37] In 1921, the official Soviet label for this new unit became the Autonomous Crimean Soviet Socialist Republic (*Avtonomnaia Krymskaia Sovetskaia Sotsialisticheskaia Respublika*). Despite this territorial definition, the ASSR resembled a de facto Crimean Tatar national autonomy, a status that fostered the Crimean Tatars' modern conception of Crimea as their national homeland.

Stalin's deportation of the Crimean Tatars in 1944 brought about the next change in the region's political and ethnic outlook, as reflected in its toponymy, which changed even more radically than after 1783. An orchestrated attempt was made to write the Crimean Tatars out of history. Over 1,400 historical names of towns and villages were forcibly and speedily erased from the Crimean map; the names of over 1,000 landscape features and buildings linked to the Crimean Tatar (or imperial Russian) past were changed so as to be more politically acceptable to the Stalinist regime.[38] After the deportation of the Crimean Tatars, all references associating them with the Crimea were banned. Subsumed under the general category "Tatars," they were dissolved as a distinct ethnic group. Until the collapse of the USSR in 1991, the Crimean Tatars were excluded from Soviet statistics and were not listed as a separate census category. The state-sanctioned definition referred to them as "Tatars who previously lived in Crimea and are now based in Uzbekistan," albeit without giving a reason for their "resettlement."[39] It was only in 1994 that the Supreme Soviet of Crimea under Mykola Bahrov [Nikolai Bagrov] restored the name of the Crimean Tatars and asked the Ministry of Internal Affairs to make the appropriate changes in passports and other documents.[40] The revival of historic place-names abolished in the period from 1944 to 1948 has remained a controversy among Crimean and Ukrainian politicians and academics. Crimean Tatar representatives have been recommending a revival of the old place-names. In practice, however, this revival not only incurs administrative costs but also occasions a highly emotional and politicized debate. Many old Tatar names have been lost to the shared imagination of the Crimean population.[41]

It is, however, important to note that a considerable number of Crimean Tatar toponyms relating to landscape have survived largely intact. This defiance of tsarist and Soviet imperial policies of repression demonstrates continuity in collective memories and regional identities. That Crimean Tatar names, in particular for mountains and rock formations that feature in popular legends, have remained an integral part of the collective memory in the region illustrates the depth of the Crimean Tatar affiliation with this territory and the readiness of other groups to appropriate parts of this culture into their own regional history.

Landscape as "the Other": Crimea in Travelogues

In the imperial discourse on Crimea, travelers' impressions have helped to shape perceptions. The categories and images travel literature employs can influence colonizers and colonized, outsiders and insiders alike. Travelogues were also key to intelligence gathering in the pre-satellite era. The increasing number of journeys undertaken by eighteenth- and nineteenth-century West Europeans to and within Russia, particularly in southern regions, reflects their interest in an area perceived as exotic and new, if not their concern about the expansion of the Russian Empire on the fringes of Europe and the Ottoman Empire. Edward Clarke expresses this feeling: "The capture of the Crimea excited the attention of all Europe."[42] One of the earliest and best-known travelers to the southern province was the scientist P. S. Pallas, who brought back from his journey in 1783–84 a detailed description of Crimea's geology and nature, its inhabitants and politics. His relatively detached observations have been historically important for the recording and preserving of many Tatar names for villages, mountains, and other features.[43] By contrast, other official Russian expeditions, such as the 1837 expedition of artists and scientists led by M. Anatole de Demidoff, resulted in superficial and uncritical accounts.[44]

Around the same time that Pallas published his research on the new southern provinces, a different tradition of travel writing reached Crimea, as English, French, and German travelers, mostly officials or their wives, wrote down their personal impressions of the region. Without having any profound knowledge of the culture or people they encountered, these travelers were intrigued by the area's history and natural beauty. Their impressions and memories, disseminated through the travelogues published in their home countries, helped to construct a lasting image of Crimea well beyond the boundaries of the Russian Empire. Their authors' individual and cultural biases notwithstanding, all of the travel reports share vivid images of Crimea and, in the absence of systematic Crimean Tatar records for this period, constitute a valuable contemporary source of information on Crimean Tatar life. For instance, they record differences among the Tatar groups settled in various parts of Crimea; they describe houses, gardens, and complex irrigation systems; they explain the role of Islam as the Tatars' primary communal bond; and at times they even point out the Russian repression of the Tatars. These accounts thus offer a counterweight to later Russian and Soviet imperialist portraits of an unsettled and undeveloped society which became "civilized" only through Russian rule. The distinctions noted among groups of Crimean Tatars similarly question contemporary Crimean Tatar myths of ethnic homogeneity and territory as the primary marker of identity.

For instance, Lady Elizabeth Craven praised "Tauride" for its "climate and situation." She was fascinated by the remnants of Greek history in Crimea and by the links between Greek and Russian civilization.[45] Another traveler, inspired to explore the "celebrated peninsula" by Herodotus's writing about the Cimmerians and Greek settlements, saw Tatar settlements merely as accretions on the sites of superior ancient civilizations.[46] On the whole, the Tatars exist only on the margins of these narratives. To the European aristocrats setting foot in Crimea, they belong to an "exotic" alien and intimidating "Oriental" culture.[47] Many travelers were heavily influenced by the official Russian views on Crimea, since conversations with local "society" were perforce held with the governor, other officials, and their wives. Due to the lack of direct contact, the Tatars are inevitably presented as a successfully subdued people.[48] Russian policies towards the Tatars, such as land confiscations, are noted by a few more skeptical observers.[49] Even apolitical reports like Lady Elizabeth's, however, note the military significance of Sevastopol.[50] Mary Holderness conjures up the poetic image of "the rendezvous of the Russian fleet in the Black Sea."[51] In other reports Sevastopol is described as "the present mistress of the Black Sea," as a city with "no traces of the past," as a city of "war-like animation and bustle,"[52] with an "immense fortification,"[53] and as "the southern stronghold of Russia."[54]

Descriptions of Crimea as the "Tauric Arcadia" became firmly embedded,[55] and comparisons with Italy and Greece abounded.[56] All foreign travelers were keenly aware of the contrast between Crimea and the rest of Russia. H. D. Seymour sums up this feeling best:

> We cannot be astonished at the Russians themselves being much struck with it, for after a weary journey over the flat steppe from Petersburg or Moscow, the total change which it presents to the gloomy and monotonous aspect of their own country must make it seem to them like a land of enchantment. The temperament of the

Russians also, like that of all Slavonic races, is highly poetical, and it is no wonder that they should be strongly affected by their first glimpse of a southern land—that they flock to the only spot in their empire (except the Caucasus) where they can feel the genial warmth and admire the beauties of the Mediterranean region, or that they covet a larger share of those countries where such charms can always be enjoyed.[57]

In this description lies a kernel of the century-long Russian—and Soviet—infatuation with the peninsula. Unlike the Caucasus, it was experienced as a safe though exotic destination, a place where Russia could get close to Europe's ancient civilizations.

The reports by foreign travelers were usually circulated among Russian officialdom and high society. Thus, the reports were generally aimed to please the Russian hosts and were often even dedicated to the tsar.[58] In the imagining of Crimea, the link between outsider and insider views is of crucial importance. From the very outset, foreign travelers played an active part in the making of Russia's enduring images of Crimea and the symbolic reverence for the region. Consequently, when the age of tourism began, certain features of the peninsula had already become stereotypical throughout the Russian Empire, as J. G. Kohl observes:

> The southern shore of the Crimea is always spoken of, even now, as a distinct country, and in the interior of Russia and in Moscow it is common enough to hear it spoken of simply as the "south-coast." "Those wines from the south-coast," people will say, without mentioning that they allude to the south coast of the Crimea.[59]

Throughout the nineteenth century, Yalta was experienced and portrayed as "the great rendezvous of tourists."[60] For Russians and foreign visitors alike, Yalta became *the* symbol of the Russian Crimea.

Crimea remained the great interface between Europe and the Orient. Travelogues routinely contrasted the wealth of the Russian nobility and Russian architecture with the poverty of local Tatar villages, thereby defining and reinforcing the clash of the two cultures.[61] Despite the condescending attitude towards the Crimean Tatars that prevails in the travel literature, most writers used and explained the Tatar names of mountains and villages and thereby inadvertently helped to spread and familiarize them. Paradoxically, the image of the barbarous Turks and Tatars was often paired with an equally exaggerated romantic and exotic image of Crimean Tatar life, usually observed from a "safe" distance.[62] Crude stereotypes are commonplace: Tatars are seen as "indolent,"[63] "honest and hospitable,"[64] "a primitive race,"[65] uneducated and "unsophisticated,"[66] but "sober and chaste,"[67] "extremely sincere and faithful," and with "the highest character for integrity,"[68] as "gracefully made, quick and courageous."[69] Their agricultural methods are "rude and simple"[70] and their villages and houses abound in "neglect and filth."[71] The widely held image of the Tatars is summed up by one rather sympathetic traveler: "They are an inoffensive, indolent set of people, fond of smoking their chibonks, talking gossip, and telling or listening to wonderful tales; but when roused, they are exceedingly passionate and revengeful."[72] In contrast, some travelogues describe the Tatars' well-cultivated orchards and vineyards maintained with the help of complex irrigation systems, their well-built terraced houses, and their reverence for the surrounding nature.[73]

Many travel reports single out Crimea's multiethnicity and multilingualism as distinct regional features, particularly when describing the new capital Simferopol (the old Akmescit).[74] An English lady captured the ethnic and social diversity:

> Were the reader to be transported blindfold into the middle of Simpheropol, it would be a puzzle difficult for him to solve to what nation or empire this half-European, half-Asiatic town belongs. At every turn, Russians, Germans, Jews, Greeks, Armenians, and Tartars, with their peculiar costumes and physiognomic characteristics, mingle with ladies and gentlemen whose style, dress and general appearance might pass unobserved in Hyde Park or the Tuileries.[75]

Another traveler conveys an equally multiethnic image, albeit of an ethnically segregated society including "Armenians, Greeks, Jews and others": "although naturalised in this peninsula for ages...they still preserve their national religion, customs and so on and do not seem to have mixed their blood in any considerable degree with the Tartars."[76]

The more experienced travelers, or those who spent some years in the region, note that the Crimean Tatars were in general unable to maintain their customs under Russian law.[77] These observers also note that the Russian authorities granted the Tatars exclusive residency rights in Bakhchisarai and Karasubazar and funded the restoration of the Khan's Palace, an indirect admission of their otherwise secondary role.[78] In the various travelogues, Bakhchisarai often appears as a last residue of a dying Tatar civilization.[79] The great exodus of Tatars to the Ottoman Empire did not go unnoticed, and some writers appear conscious of recording customs for posterity, but the causes of emigration remain largely unexplored.[80] There are, however, some explicit references to repressive policies towards Tatar peasants, the destruction of Tatar architecture, and the prospect of the group's extinction.[81] The disruptive effect of the imposition of the Russian system of land ownership on the Tatars' own traditional organizational patterns is mentioned, as is its indirect effects upon the Tatars' connection with the land. The expropriation of communal land increased the dependence of the Tatar peasantry, destroyed their support structures, and triggered famine and illness.[82] These travelers' comments hint at the effects of the imposition of Russian imperial rule without spelling out their dimensions. While the immediate out-migration of Crimean Tatars after the Russian annexation of Crimea was limited to about 8,000, the Ottoman defeat in the Russo-Turkish war of 1787–92 that asserted Russian control over Crimea unleashed a wave of mass emigration. The estimates vary, but about 100,000 Crimean Muslims fled to the Ottoman Empire.[83]

A remarkable insider account, neither travel report nor fiction, was written by Evgenii Markov (1835–1903), a teacher who was appointed director of the schools and colleges in Tavricheskaia guberniia in 1865. He established Tatar and Russian-Tatar schools and founded the newspaper *Tavrida*. His collection *Ocherki Kryma* (Essays on Crimea), published in several illustrated editions, resembles a diary of personal impressions, reminiscences, and facts about the nature, life, and history of Crimea.[84] That Markov diverged from the official view and proved difficult to incorporate into Soviet ideology largely explains why the *Ocherki* were republished only in 1995. Markov saw Crimea as part of "Malorossiia" (Little Russia) and its inhabitants as closest to the *khokhli*, defined as the "inhabitants of the Black Sea steppe and south" and the "historical late-comers" to the region.[85] This view sits comfortably with post-Soviet Ukrainian arguments about the historical links between Crimea and Ukraine. Interestingly, Markov's Crimea is one where the Crimean Tatars have a special role, and their capital Bakhchisarai is "the East in its purest form."[86] He takes an unusually strong critical view of the repression of the Crimean Tatars: "He who has spent in Crimea barely a month, will realise immediately that the Crimea died after the removal of the Tatars.... In a word, the leaving of the Tatars, makes Crimea like a house after a fire." Anti-Tatar policies are strongly attacked, and the Tatars are praised, for example, for assisting the local population to survive the hunger of the Crimean War.[87] Markov's account pictures a much more harmonious interethnic relationship than that generally portrayed in Russian historiography. His harshest criticism is reserved for the stereotype of the "indolent" pipe-smoking Tatar, an image created and routinely reinforced by Russian and foreign travelers.[88] On the whole, Markov's account offers a much more nuanced insight into Crimean Tatar culture and life. Most importantly, it captures the religious-spiritual attachment to the predominantly Tatar names of Crimea's natural features.[89]

Markov's description of Sevastopol still slumbering after the destruction of the Crimean War explains why Russian and Soviet historiography must have found it difficult to endorse his views.[90] Markov explicitly attacks the Sevastopol myth: "In Russia we do not have anything similar to Sevastopol, and there is nothing Russian in it except the flag. It is a child of the nineteenth century, dressed completely in European style." He sees Sevastopol as "currently a dead man," a strange and frightening city in which buildings and people hold out in "a grave-like silence and seem to wait for something." Expressing his surprise at the extent of destruction visible in Sevastopol, Markov notes that Russians were told little about the reality in the city. His account of conversations with soldiers and local inhabitants illustrates "the side of the great war hidden behind the scenes" and supports his conclusion that Sevastopol was, in fact, less significant than the official Russian mythology held.[91] Markov's account is ahead of its times, in particular with regard to three key points: the emphasis on tolerance in a multiethnic setting, the definition of Crimea as part of Ukranian territory, and the dynamics of potent Russian mythmaking based on Crimea.

Landscape as Literary Memory

Literature can turn landscape, history, and personal experience into cultural and mental reserves. Russian writer Andrei Bitov eloquently referred to the poet as "the last farmer."[92] Crimea has been a literary topos since the ancient Greek myth of Iphigenia of Tauris. In Russia, the literary imagination of Crimea was rivaled only by that of the landscape of the Caucasus. Literature can be highly political, even when it deals with the ostensibly nonpolitical. Even where there is no conscious link between the reference to literary images and political claims, the continuous use and transfer of these points of reference from generation to generation make them an integral part of people's identity. The extent to which literature becomes absorbed into one's identity depends on a country's cultural and political tradition and, more specifically, on the school curriculum. In Soviet society literature had great significance. Between the extremes of official propaganda (in the guise of literature) and dissident outlets lay a vast area of literary awareness: songs, stories, slogans, quotations, and wordplay that permeated people's daily lives. In the Soviet era, the Russian literary canon of the eighteenth and nineteenth centuries was part of the school curriculum and was published on a massive scale. This canon shaped popular imagination and identity. Although literary images are not explicitly linked to political turbulence and conflict, they nevertheless belong to the cultural fabric of perceptions and, by extension, of conflict potential. The omnipresent Russian-Soviet literature imprinted a Russophile image of Crimea on the minds of generations of Soviet citizens and fostered an ownership mentality in Russia.

There were alternative literary traditions in the work of Crimean writers of different national backgrounds, especially Crimean Tatar writers in exile and the bearers of oral storytelling traditions among the deported Tatars, but the residues of Soviet linguistic and literary Russification dominated popular imagination when the Soviet Union collapsed and mobilization around the Crimean issue began. Post-Soviet developments prompted a revival of Crimean Tatar literature: old texts have been rediscovered and republished, and contemporary writers often link collective memory with a running commentary on current events so that literary work, historical records, and political activism can be difficult to distinguish.

The boundaries of this cultural space may, however, be difficult to draw. Russian, Soviet, Soviet-Russian, Ukrainian, and Crimean Tatar literary images overlap and complement each other, creating complex ethnocultural, imperial, ideological, and regional associations.[93] The literary symbols and myths about Crimea share an emphasis on the geography of the peninsula, the beauty of its landscape, its diversity, its special atmosphere, its distance from the mainland, and its distinct path of development. Tracing the resonance of literary images from three centuries in contemporary discourse reveals their continuity across different social structures and political regimes. This continuity of powerful images underscores both their role in identity construction and their scope for manipulation. The exact degree to which literary images of Crimea are present in today's public or private discourse is hard to measure, but some fragments are easy to spot, and those point the way. Among the most favorite literary topoi—summoned in the national and regional media, in political discourse, and even everyday conversation—are references to old legends about Crimea, Pushkin's poems, the work of the twentieth-century Crimean poet and artist Maksimilian Voloshin (1877–1932), and the Soviet-era novel *Ostrov Krym* (The Island of Crimea) by Vasilii Aksenov.

Mythmaking through Legends

The legend of Iphigenia of Tauris, immortalized by Greek mythology, is probably the most widely known literary reference to the shores of Crimea and its early inhabitants, the Taurians. The extent to which this myth has taken on a cultural life of its own has almost disconnected it from its original place. Today's Crimean population is widely familiar with a stunning variety of regional, orally transmitted legends, many of them published only in the twentieth century. In the early 1990s, a peculiar blend of Russian and Soviet-Russian tales about Crimea were published for children that continued the Russian-Soviet tradition of literary images of Crimea.[94] From the mid-1990s onwards, there has been a surge in more authentic collections of legends, combining Russian, Ukrainian, Crimean Tatar, Greek, and other legends, sometimes without identifying the national origin of a particular story.[95] A collection designed for preschool and primary school children and sponsored by the International Renaissance Foundation combines regional legends of Bulgarian, Crimean Tatar, German, Greek, Russian, and Ukrainian extraction. One legend per nationality is written up in all six languages (plus an English translation).[96] Thus, the rich and diverse heritage of legends inspired by the region is consciously being turned into an entertaining source of mutual understanding, regional identification, and collective identity.

A few prominent examples of storytelling suffice to add some flavor to the notion of Crimea as a multiethnic literary landscape. Among the most widely known legends are those connected with distinctive rock formations along the southern shore of Crimea. The most famous are the legends about the Ayu-Dag (Bear Mountain) near Gurzuf, a bear turned into stone. Tatar legend tells that the bear was sent by Allah to punish and destroy the unruly inhabitants of these shores. When he takes too long to rest and to drink the water of the Black Sea, defying Allah's orders to continue, he is turned into stone as he kneels to drink. A more romantic version describes a girl stranded on the shore, which is only inhabited by wild animals. The bears rear and treasure her. When she falls in love with a young man washed ashore and decides to flee in a boat the couple have made, the bears start drinking the sea water in order to pull them back to land. The beautiful voice of the singing girl makes them stop, except for one bear who is turned into stone (depending on the version) by the sound of the girl's voice, as a result of Allah's punishment, or because he simply remains in the same position watching his beloved girl disappear.

Another legend shared by all Crimean inhabitants is about the Skaly Bliznetsy (Twin Rocks) or Adalary near Gurzuf. These rocks form an image of twin sisters who refuse to be forced into loving the twin princes of this land. Similarly, the town of Miskhor is tied to the legend of Rusalka, the beautiful daughter of a Tatar farmer, who is kidnapped at the Miskhor fountain during her wedding night and brought to the Sultan's harem. She gives birth to a son and in her desperation jumps into the sea. Since then, once a year, a woman with a child in her arms appears close to the fountain of Miskhor. Other more political legends recall Tatar raids on the Cossacks of the steppes, Tatar power resting on the gold deposits of the Crimean mountains, and the Tatar struggle for independence from the Otto- man Empire. A Soviet edition of Crimean Tatar legends, published in 1936, claimed to be the first systematic collection of these legends. This edition "sovietized" and distorted many of the legends. Surpris- ingly, not even the original preface, with its references to Stalin's views on national culture, was changed for the new edition of 1992.[97] By now a range of Crimean Tatar–language editions of the legends has been published and disseminated.

Russian and Soviet Literary and Visual Images of Crimea

Pushkin spent but a few weeks in Crimea on his way to the Cau- casus, yet the inspiration was such that he produced some of his best-known work based on this experience. The claim to have spent the "happiest minutes of his life" (*shchastliveishie minuty zhizni*) in Crimea echoes through his poetry and beyond. His poems evoke the image of a distant and magic region (*volshebnyi krai, shchastlivyi krai, krai prelestnyi*). Pushkin's poetic cycle *Tavrida* expresses strong emotions, sad and hopeful at the same time; it is about Crimea's lush vegetation, the beautiful scenery and, above all, the surrounding sea. For Pushkin, the Crimea is Russian land; the Crimean Tatars, their lives, and their gardens form the picturesque background.[98] It is exactly this largely apolitical, yet overtly romanticized, view that has come to dominate the Russian literary image of Crimea. One of Pushkin's best known poems commemorates the legendary Fountain of Bakhchisarai (*"Bakhchisaraiskii Fontan"*).[99] Rumor has it that the Khan's Palace survived Stalinist campaigns of destruc- tion intact thanks only to Stalin's regard for this poem. The poem and its shorter version *"Fontanu Bakhchisaraiskogo dvortsa"* retell the story of Khan Giray and his love for a Polish Christian woman he brought to his palace. After one of the khan's jealous wives murders her, he erects a memorial: an ever-weeping fountain of white stone decorated with roses. This old legend was transformed into a Russian (and Polish) literary topos that blends a supposedly "Turkic" image of romance and violence.[100] Undoubtedly, these poems helped to preserve a number of Crimean Tatar symbols in Russian, Soviet, and Western literary awareness.

Pushkin's poems demonstrate that, only about forty years after the conquest of Crimea, the region still represented a new and exotic place. In contrast, by the time that another great Russian literary figure, Anton Chekhov, settled there in the late nineteenth century, images of Crimea were already deeply ingrained on the Russian mind. By then Crimea had become *the* most fashionable holiday resort for the fin de siècle upper-class society of St. Petersburg and Moscow, including all its seediness. Chekhov's short story *"Dama s sobachkoi"* (Lady with a Lapdog) epitomizes this image.[101]

In the immediate postrevolutionary era, the poet and artist Maksimilian Voloshin had an immense influence on the development of Crimea's regional cultural memory.[102] Voloshin became a mythical figure during his own lifetime.[103] Born in Kyiv, he spent part of his childhood in Crimea. After having spent time in Russia and engaged in extensive traveling across Europe, he settled on Crimea's southeastern shore in Koktebel in 1916. In the 1920s, the house in Koktebel, which Voloshin had designed to resemble a combination of church and boat, became a meeting place of Silver Age poets, writers, and artists including Tsvetaeva, Gumilev, Mandel'shtam, Belyi, Bulgakov, Erenburg, and many others. After his political disgrace in the late 1920s, Voloshin's work was suppressed until the 1960s. Since then his contribution to Crimea's literary image has been gradually revived.

Marina Tsvetaeva, a frequent guest in Voloshin's house, drew inspiration from her visits to Crimea; her poems portray its archaeology, its cities and their history, and above all its landscape of mountains and the sea. The mood of melancholic reflection that she creates out of these Crimean fragments recalls that of Pushkin's work.[104] Without making explicit political statements about Crimea's status, one of Tsvetaeva's poems (*"Dneval'nyi"*) addresses Crimea as the "khan's land" (*zemlia khanska*), and links "holy Rus'" with Tavrida. The poem's speaker turns right and left while looking around, a gesture that has been interpreted as observation of the still-undecided struggle between Russia and the Crimean Khanate, the Ottoman Empire or Turkey, respectively.[105] Tsvetaeva's poems for Voloshin, written shortly after his death, tie his name forever to a memorial:

his house and grave in Koktebel, as well as a nearby mountain that resembles Voloshin's profile and that the Tatars called the "Mountain of the Big Man."[106] Another Crimean writer, who is known more locally, is Aleksandr Grin, the Armenian-born and Feodosiia-based inventor of a literary and visual fairy tale image loosely based on Crimean motifs.[107]

Crimea's literary images, especially in their Russian tradition, have a self-replicating element. Poets and writers bridge centuries through allusions and indirect references to each other. They have deliberately evoked symbols and myths, recycled them, and embedded their works firmly in a common cultural tradition. Most references center on Pushkin's work and his deep, albeit brief, impression of Crimea.[108] The Tatar's place in Crimea, evoked by Pushkin and echoed by others, is a distorted and romanticized image.[109] That the works and lives of so many major Russian writers, poets, and artists are linked with Crimea reinforces the region's place in Russian cultural heritage.

Visual art has had a similarly profound impact on the imagining of Crimea. The fusion of literary and visual imagery of Crimea has been most potent in the region itself. The numerous seascapes of the Crimean Armenian Ivan K. Aivasovskii (1817–1900) have undoubtedly left a vivid imprint on popular imagination. Equally well-known and cherished by local residents are Maksimilian Voloshin's watercolors depicting the sparsely populated, rocky southeast of Crimea near Koktebel and capturing the haziness which lends this area its peaceful and slightly mystical atmosphere. The paintings illustrate Voloshin's poetry, particularly his cycles of poems *Kimmeriiskie sumerki* (1907) and *Kimmeriiskaia vesna* (1910). Here the combination of different art forms enhances the lasting effect of the images of the Crimean landscape.

A very different, and widely quoted, image is coined by the anti-Soviet science fiction novel *Ostrov Krym* (1981) by Aksenov.[110] Banned in the Soviet Union, it plays on the old travelogues' notion of Crimea as a real island, an image borrowed from the Crimean Tatar reference to Crimea as their "green island." Aksenov's preface to the English-language version of the novel places the image in a political context:

Every peninsula fancies itself an island.... What if Crimea really were an island? What if, as a result, the White Army had been able to defend Crimea from the Reds in 1920? What if Crimea had developed as a Russian, yet Western democracy alongside the totalitarian mainland?

The novel describes a delicately balanced relationship between Soviet Moscow and a booming capitalist Simferopol bearing a fancied resemblance to Hong Kong. The Soviet Union regards Crimean independence as a temporary phenomenon; in contrast, some regional groups advocate the emergence of a new multiethnic nation rooted in Crimea, and others propound the "common fate" that ties the region to the rest of Russia and the Soviet Union. The novel is interspersed with playful references to historical events in Crimea. The enduring image is of Crimea as a place set apart from Russia, a place that is different, that needs to take a distinct path, and that demands special treatment. The theme of regional distinctiveness fits within a larger trend in Russian and Soviet-Russian culture, but taken to its political extreme as in Aksenov's novel, it represented a threat to the Soviet state and ideology.

Official Soviet propaganda went only so far as to embrace Gorkii's poems about Crimea and elicited work of little literary value but significant ideological importance, especially after the 1954 transfer of Crimea to the Ukrainian SSR. Examples include the Ukrainian-language stories about the "successful" resettlement of Ukrainian peasants in Crimean kolkhoz farms.[111] On the whole, Russian and Soviet authors share an imperial, romanticized, and functional perspective on Crimea: they focus on Crimea's beauty, its geopolitical location, or its function as a resort without, however, attempting to engage with the region's history, in particular its Crimean Tatar history.[112] Russian and Soviet cultural ownership affirmed political power over Crimea.

Ukrainian Literary Images of Crimea

Ukrainian cultural organizations have tried recently to increase public awareness of their own Crimean heritage. This attempt cannot disguise the fact that today Crimea's literary memory is by and large

Russian or Soviet-Russian, extended by a separate Crimean Tatar tradition of storytelling and legends, a tradition that is still only partially accessible for non-Tatars.[113] A recent collection of Crimean writers and poets writing in Ukrainian is indicative of a move to integrate the Ukrainian heritage into the regional school curriculum.[114] The collection samples the works of twelve Ukrainian writers, most of whom were born in some other part of the Ukrainian SSR and moved to Crimea in the 1950s for study or work purposes. Both the difficulty in finding pieces of an appropriately literary standard and the distinction between official Soviet authors and original Ukrainian national or regional literature are all too apparent. The themes are typically Russian and Soviet: Crimea's landscape, particularly the Black Sea and the mountains, a description of Bakhchisarai as an exotic place, the heroic struggle of Crimea against fascism in World War II, Crimea as a resort, or the military profile of Sevastopol.[115] In addition to such collections, the Crimean publishing house *Tavriia* has printed a number of Ukrainian-language publications on a range of political, historical, and literary topics.[116] On the whole, the perspectives are Russian and Soviet, but the language is Ukrainian.

Crimean Tatar Poetry and Song

Politics, poetry, and song are linked throughout Crimean Tatar history and are critical for the formation of Crimean Tatar identity.[117] Both the belief in the Koran as the only holy book and the late spread of literacy explain the dearth of written Crimean Tatar literary work before the twentieth century.[118] Instead, literature was constantly on the move, a characteristic that fits the repeated experience of migration, exile, and deportation. Under the Crimean Khanate, traveling poets (*keday* or *akey*) enjoyed great prestige and popularity as the conveyors of cultural heritage. The importance of poetry to the Crimean Tatars is signified in numerous inscriptions that survived, most notably above the entrance gate of the Khan's Palace in Bakhchisarai, the inscription above the Bakhchisarai Fountain, or on the gravestones on its grounds.[119] The cultural heritage of song, music, dance, and story has been crucial in maintaining and fostering group identity among the Crimean Tatars during centuries of Russian (and Soviet) rule and oppression.[120] Religious ballads, sung by

traveling bards, formed an integral part of Crimean Muslim culture
in the nineteenth century. By celebrating the sacred "white soil" (*ak
toprak*), a symbolic reference to the Ottoman Empire, these ballads
emphasize the role of religious identification as the strongest bond
among the Crimean Muslims in this period. In addition to presenting religious reasons for emigrating to the Ottoman Empire, the
emigrant ballads also dramatize the pressures exerted by the Russian
authorities and landowners, and resonate with the sorrows of exile
and the memories of the beloved villages left behind in Crimea.[121]
The emphasis is on the overarching religious bond, but some of the
songs reflect a territorial memory of Crimea which contributed to
the gradual building of the homeland image.

Folklore, songs, traditional dances, and poems kept the Crimean
heritage alive in exile. The songs of the Crimean Tatar composer
Yahya Sherfedinov (born in 1894) and performances by the ensemble
Qaytarma, reestablished in 1957 in Central Asia, played key roles.
Songs in the diaspora projected an enduring image of the "Green
Isle" (*Yeşil Ada*). A prominent example are the two poems titled "The
Green Island" and "The Green Homeland" written by the Crimean
Tatar poet and educator Mehmet Niyazi, an important figure in the
establishment of the national movement in Dobruca (the Ottoman
region in today's Bulgaria and Romania) between 1900 and 1930. The
poems praise the beauty of Crimea, liken it to "a finely organized
bouquet," and express the longing to return to the region.[122] The novels by the popular Crimean Tatar writer Cengiz Dağci, for example,
who made his way from Crimea to London at the end of World War
II, kept the memory of Crimea alive in the Western diaspora.[123] The
Soviet deportation and repression diminished the role of religion in
the Crimean Tatars' identity construction in the twentieth century.
Only the end of the Soviet empire and the return to Crimea marked
the beginning of a gradual revival of religious practices.

In exile a small but active circle of Crimean Tatar writers, poets,
and composers created forceful images of an oppressed community
and a lost homeland. Such homeland images, tied to the hope of
return and restoration, are evoked in the poem "What Is the Homeland's Scent?" (1989) by Lilia Bujurova, who since the 1990s has been
a prominent political figure in Crimea:

Of what does the homeland smell?
Of a dry blade of grass,
Caught in a child's hair,
Of a pine branch, of bitter wormwood,
Or, of separation, buried in the heart?
Or, of lamb's wool, of aromatic coffee,
Tinkling as it pours into thin little cups,
Of mountain tea, of almonds, fragrant with mint,
Of today's reality, of yesterday's dream?
Or, of the searing cry of a lone seagull?
Or, of the snowy peak of Chatir-Dagh?
Of distant music from an ancient song?
Oh no, my homeland smells of hope.[124]

Bujurova's poetic "homeland" links historical memory, dream, and present-day reality, thereby capturing the different elements inherent in the construction of symbols and identities. Bujurova dedicated her poem "We Returned Today" (1991) to the delegates of the newly established Kurultay. This poem weaves literary images into the contemporary political struggle and aptly demonstrates the confluence of history, culture and politics:

Our happiness comes from being together,
In spite of the awful calamity,
We gathered in the old place, in order
Once more to make our history.[125]

These poems underpin a strong communal spirit by merging the experience of the individual with that of the group as a whole.

Individual memoirs, a genre that like the travelogue sits between literature and historiography, have been another important element shaping Crimean Tatar national identity. Personal stories have been handed down from one generation to the next; they are integrated with a tradition of similar stories through symbols related to the homeland (vatan), and further personal experiences are added in the process. The discourse itself creates, maintains, and spreads memories, customs, and identity.[126] The younger generation, brought up in Central Asia, knew its homeland only through these oral histories. This grassroots tradition provides an important corrective to the assumption that cultural and political elites construct symbols and myths "from above." The personal stories that center on the self-immolation of Crimean Tatars in the Soviet period make for a particularly powerful communal bond that is actively being renewed through collective imagining every time the story is told.[127] Omnipresent Soviet and Russian idealizations of Crimea and its beauty must have been an additional source for the imagining of the homeland among the younger generations of Crimean Tatars in the Soviet Union.

Conclusion

Crimea is a good example of the construction of identities based on a wide range of parallel and overlapping memories and images inspired by the landscape, often condensed in recurring symbols and myths, that have been transmitted through maps, toponymy, travelogues, legends, literature, and art. Over centuries Crimea's multitude of images has been shaped by both insiders and outsiders. The images vary in their resonance and outreach. Symbols and myths from the imperial Russian period, kept alive during the Soviet era, dominate Russian public imagination and were readily available for the separatist Russian nationalist movement of the early 1990s to tap into. With the return of the Crimean Tatars to Crimea, their symbols and myths have rapidly reclaimed their position since the early 1990s, underpinning a strong political claim to the peninsula as the Crimean Tatar homeland.

Crimea's rich cultural history imbues identity construction and political claims with a sense of authenticity. In the public discourse the cultural references may appear as a shorthand or as a tool at the disposal of elites and the media. The Russian and Crimean Tatar images of Crimea have mass support and, more generally, act as the sounding board against which identity and transition politics unfold. Not all of the memories and images attached to Crimea are mutually exclusive and conflict-prone. Captured in a whole range of different genres, they are shaped by a general recognition of Crimea's multiethnicity and a collective identification of all main ethnic groups with Crimea's landscape, location, and natural beauty. A shared imagining of the region can provide ample raw material for rival claims during political mobilization, especially in times of uncertainty, but it can also underpin the attempts to accommodate diversity.[128]

3 The Making of History: Writing and Rewriting "Crimea"

THE FUNCTION OF A NATION'S HISTORIOGRAPHY is to establish what Edward Shils called the "consensus through time": streamlining the past and relating it to the present.[1] Memory of the past is meant to help people locate themselves and others on a "historical map." By anchoring a sense of identification with the past and present, it underscores feelings of commonality and otherness as well as the legitimacy of new states and institutions. The past is reconfigured in close relation to the present, and history becomes a malleable resource in the process of identity construction. Thus, national historiography is essentially a "dialectic of collective remembering and forgetting, and of imagination and unimaginative repetition."[2]

Making history by writing and rewriting it is central to the reclaiming of the past for political use, especially when historiography is considered to be incomplete, biased, or distorted. Refashioning history creates continuity and national unity out of the relics of historical memory and thus can bolster the authority and legitimacy of newly created states and institutions. As such it is an integral part of state and nation building. By definition, the rewriting of history challenges and "unmakes" the history written by others.[3] Dramatic political changes, for example in a postimperial era, make it essential for successor states "to think the nation" and tackle national historiography anew.[4] The new perspective is potentially as selective as the accounts it replaces, but in the longer run, at least in a pluralist society, the more plausible narratives will stand up to questioning.

A typical "biography of nations" rests upon continuity—real or invented—through time and space.[5] Post-Soviet Ukrainian historiography, however, cannot easily gloss over obvious discontinuities in Ukraine's state and nation building process, especially the lack of real progeny as an independent state and the constant flux in the idea of what the Ukrainian nation is—territorially, politically, and culturally. Discontinuity and a circuitous path to nation- and statehood are the key themes in contemporary Ukrainian historiography.[6] Another challenge is how to integrate some aspects of the Soviet past: oppression and famine are easy to incorporate into national history, but (in contrast to the Baltic states) Ukraine cannot distance itself clearly from World War II, which shaped most of its western borders.

Finding a place for Crimea in Ukraine's new historiography is a delicate task. From the outset Ukraine had to counter Russian claims and perceptions. Crimean Tatar claims have been easier to integrate, as they are explicitly formulated in a way that recognizes the post-Soviet Ukrainian state. The post-Soviet fact of a "Ukrainian" Crimea directly challenges Russian and Soviet-Russian conceptions of history and politics. In particular, the Soviet transfer of the region in 1954 has to be integrated into Ukrainian historiography. This has been managed by reiterating its constitutionality and the pragmatic Soviet reasons for the decision (minus the rhetoric about Russian-Ukrainian friendship). Historical links between Crimea and the territory of today's Ukraine have existed, but presenting them as a continually harmonious relationship would overstretch the historical imagination of even Ukrainian nationalists.

As with history, public symbols play a key role in constructing national identity and legitimizing the state. In every country, the flags on public buildings, the home news, weather reports, and sports events all showcase national identity on a daily basis. In a new and as yet weakly established state, the imagining and projecting of the nation are initially less "banal" and more deliberately staged than in established nations.[7] Official symbols have occupied a prominent position in post-Soviet state and nation building. The choice of flags, insignia, and anthems triggered debate in many post-Soviet countries. In Ukraine, a similar debate occurred at the regional level. Regional political mobilization in Crimea employed regional "state" symbols, such as a tricolor flag that is conspicuously similar to the pan-Slavic flag adopted at the Pan-Slavic Convention in Prague in 1848.[8] Despite the presence of Crimean symbols around the peninsula, the Ukrainian parliament tried to prevent their use in public administration. Eventually, their use was regulated by Crimea's 1998 Constitution, albeit without their recognition as "state" symbols. Well before the status of the Crimean symbols was decided, history books used in local schools had already introduced them as the official regional symbols.[9] Official buildings in Crimea now raise the Ukrainian and the Crimean flags, whereas during the heyday of the Russian movement in 1994, the Ukrainian state symbols were virtually absent.

In addition to historiography and official symbols, history is commemorated by monuments and rituals, often in conjunction. A totalitarian regime like the Soviet Union was acutely aware of the instrumental function of monuments and ritual. As early as April 1918, a decree by Lenin ordered all tsarist monuments to be destroyed. An ideologically correct list of people and events worthy of commemoration was drawn up, initiating the era of "Leninist monumental propaganda" (Leninskaia monumental'naia propaganda).[10] In Crimea, particularly in Simferopol and Sevastopol, historical and literary monuments abound, subconsciously shaping people's historical perceptions. In Simferopol, various Russian imperial and Soviet monuments commemorate Crimea's most prolific Russian and Soviet poets, writers, and scientists. Recently, Crimean Tatar monuments have been erected, most notably commemorating the deportation of 1944. Sevastopol, on the other hand, resembles an open-air war museum where monuments to the great sieges of the nineteenth and twentieth centuries stand side by side. The monuments of Sevastopol reinforce a Russian-Soviet identity in possibly the most potent blend to be found in the FSU.

Trends in Russian, Soviet, and Post-Soviet Historiography

Prerevolutionary Russian historiography was shaped by tsarist imperial ideology. Nikolai Karamzin, Sergei Solov'ev and Vasilii Kliuchevskii are among its best known historians. They were key disseminators of the official ideology of autocracy, orthodoxy, and nationality. They present territorial expansion of the Russian Empire as a natural process—the "gathering of the Russian lands"—and the annexation of Crimea forms part of this process. By contrast, the

Crimean Tatar Khanate symbolizes a dangerous rival and hostile out-post of the Ottoman Empire that Russian colonization subdued and pacified.[11] These tsarist historiographical themes also framed Soviet historians' perceptions and interpretations. After all, the ideologies of empire in tsarist Russia and in the Soviet Union had much in common, especially since the 1940s, when Soviet historians deliberately revived and built on tsarist-era myths, promoting an undertone of Russian nationalism. By the time of Stalin's death, official Soviet historiography had turned "into a near replica of the official Tsarist interpretation."[12]

This tsarist and Soviet historiography never presented Crimea as the territory of one national group. Prewar Stalinist Soviet historiography attached great importance to Russian colonial expansion into Crimea turning the region into a model of interethnic relations.[13] Nevertheless, "an army of trained archaeologists, anthropologists, historians, and linguists who sought to provide all Soviet nations with a secular Marxist 'national' history"[14] actively fostered the Crimean Tatars' awareness of themselves, their origins, and their communal identity. This historiography "rooted" the Tatars in the Crimean territory. In contrast, P. N. Nadinskii's post–World War II multivolume history of Crimea adapts earlier Russian historiography to the Soviet ideology, but retains the stress on the inherently "Russian" or "Slavic" character of Crimea. Crimea is defined as primordial Slav or Russian territory, and even the Scythians appear in the guise of proto-Slavs.[15] Only a short section of Nadinskii's account is dedicated to the Crimean Khanate, which is portrayed as a parasitical state living off the trade in slaves of Slav origin. This era is presented as an historical aberration and a temporary break in the traditional link between Slavs, in particular Russians, and Crimea. The Crimean Tatars appear as the foreign occupiers raiding the region and are presented as an underdeveloped society in flux, a society that failed to properly settle in the region. The Tatars are wrongly portrayed as puppets at the hands of the Turkish sultans, although the khanate retained considerable autonomy after becoming a vassal of the Ottoman Empire in the fifteenth century. Such Soviet claims deliberately underestimate the organization and power of the Crimean Khanate and deny the historical attachment of the Crimean Tatars to the territory. Soviet propaganda also kept alive the image of war, raiding, and plunder as the Tatars' key occupations.[16]

This simplistic approach to the region's history was part of Stalinist policy to eradicate Crimean Tatar traces in the aftermath of the deportation in 1944. Only in the late Soviet period, as part of a general rethinking of history, is the alleged "Russian" character of Crimea toned down, the ritualistic denigration of the Crimean Tatars abandoned, and Crimea's historical multiethnicity taken seriously.[17] In line with this change in approach, earlier Soviet accounts, portraying the Scythians as proto-Slavs in order to demarcate Crimea as primordial Slav territory, are criticized. Historical sources are now revealed to show that Slav settlements can be traced back only to the late tenth century.[18]

Although some of the most blatant historical bias and error of Soviet-era historiography has been abandoned, the predominant post-Soviet perspective on Crimea remains Russocentric. Crimea's history is seen as a sequence of settlements and wars, culminating with the Russian "unification" with Crimea in the late eighteenth century.[19] Popular history is void of references to the imperial policies towards the Crimean Tatars. Instead, Crimea is still presented as a symbol of Russian imperial power. Even the late imperial era is glorified; for example, the widely available book *Romanovy i Krym* (The Romanovs and Crimea; 1993) combines historical vignettes, illustrations, and Crimean holiday snapshots taken by the tsar.[20]

A series of books under the title *Krymskii al'bom* (Crimean Album), published in Crimea since 1996 and financed in part by the Fond Moskva-Krym, provides one of the best examples of how the Russian identification with Crimea is kept alive.[21] Each year the publication brings together a wide range of literary texts, essays, historical fragments, and illustrations on topics as diverse as the two-hundredth anniversary of Pushkin's birth, Sevastopol, the link between Moscow and Crimea, early Christianity in the region, excerpts from the works of Crimean writers and essays about their lives, and cultural portraits of important regional towns. The preface by Moscow Mayor Iurii Luzhkov to the first edition, co-financed by the Russian government, sums up the main elements of Russia's Crimea myth discussed in the previous chapter: the landscape motif, the ethnic "coloring" and diverse history of the region, the belief by Russians that Crimea is "a dream island," and numerous associations with Pushkin, Voloshin, Aivasovskii, and Grin. The Soviet-era slogan *Da zdravstvuet, Krym!* ("Long live Crimea!") completes this list of elements of the Russian myth.[22] These Russocentric views are incompatible with the vocal Crimean Tatar claims to their homeland. Accordingly, the *Krymskii al'bom* series is almost completely devoid of references to or documents about the Crimean Tatars.[23]

The Sevastopol Myth

While Crimea's landscape and diversity have coined lasting images and symbols in the arts, Sevastopol is a symbol of a different kind, signifying Russian national resistance of a "glory unto death" kind. This mythic Sevastopol is the "holy-of-holies of Russian (and Soviet) imperialism."[24] The Sevastopol myth, one of the most powerful "mental shrines of Russia,"[25] results from what Anderson calls "museumizing imagination."[26] It is a fusion of literary and historical myths. As early as Catherine II's spectacular tour through the recently conquered southern provinces in 1787, the newly built port at Sevastopol and the young fleet—all masterminded by Potemkin—made a strong impression on the empress and her European travel companions.[27] The Sevastopol myth in the Russian image of Crimea was established as a result of the Great Siege during the Crimean War (October 1854–September 1855). This first siege of Sevastopol, the imperial base for the Black Sea Fleet, lasted 349 days before the imperial army had to abandon the city.

The Sevastopol myth was reinforced a century later by a second siege during World War II (30 October 1941–3 July 1942). Thus, Sevastopol became a "double" myth, a tsarist and a Soviet one that was unified in the Russian consciousness. In Russian and Russian-Soviet historiography, Sevastopol had even more salience than Crimea as a whole. The myth is emblematic of the close link between Russian nationalism on the one hand and Russian or Soviet imperialism on the other. The emphatic Soviet title *gorod geroi* (heroic city) was awarded by a decree of the Supreme Soviet of the USSR on 1 May 1945 in commemoration of the defense against the Germans.[28] This prestigious title and the variant *gorod slavy* (city of glory) are deeply ingrained in Russian historiography, political rhetoric and popular imagination alike. The extended title *gorod russkoi slavy* (city of Russian glory) is used interchangeably. The collapse of the Soviet Union has not diminished the usage or power of these labels, a testimony to the endurance of the myth.

Plokhy calls the Sevastopol myth "the cornerstone of all Russian claims to the Crimea and Sevastopol."[29] The post-Soviet political struggle between Russia and Ukraine over the status of Sevastopol and the division of the Black Sea Fleet have not only demonstrated the significance of the historical memories, but have, in fact, reinforced the Sevastopol myth in Russian nationalisms of all shades, both in the region and in Russia itself. The myth permeates the political and public discourse. Prominent Russian politicians managed to integrate the Sevastopol myth into their new political careers, one of the best examples being Moscow mayor Iurii Luzhkov, who turned it into his *cause célèbre* in the mid- to late 1990s.

Sevastopol, like Borodino, was a Pyrrhic victory for the outside invaders. The blood sacrifice tied to such places turns them into inviolable holy ground in the national psyche. Both sieges involved huge losses of human life, the destruction of the city, and significant, though temporary, strategic setbacks to Russian power. Mythmaking integrated these losses into a "scorched-earth mentality": destroying Russia denied it to the enemy and hence ultimately saved it. The Sevastopol myth is not simply a product of state-sponsored propaganda. The Pyrrhic victory is as much, if not more, a triumph of the people. Accordingly, the first monument to Russia's Crimean War commanders was erected in 1856, thanks to the donations of Black Sea Fleet sailors. The official mythmaking also began with celebrating the *people* of Tavricheskaia guberniia, a gesture sealed with the highest honor (*gramota*) for the heroic defense of the city and fatherland, awarded on 26 August 1856 (the coronation day of Tsar Alexander II).[30] This document represents one of the earliest expressions of the region's and, in particular, Sevastopol's heroic image. The text of the *gramota* itself already provides many of the referents for the myth propagated in later tsarist and Soviet historiography. In 1869, a committee for the establishment of a Sevastopol military museum was founded in St. Petersburg, again by private initiative.[31] Official mythmaking intensified only during the Russo-Turkish War of 1877–78.

The rather hesitant participation of the state in the mythmaking process meant that the official myth had to incorporate figures that were revered by the public but played only a secondary role in the defense of Sevastopol, such as Admiral Pavel Nakhimov.[32] In the late 1860s, an official initiative asked veterans to write up their war experiences. These personal stories were published in three volumes between 1872 and 1877.[33] Similarly, Tolstoi's *Sevastopol'skie rasskazy* (Sevastopol Stories) on the siege, another Russian and Soviet literary classic, mythologized not the achievements of great commanders, but the sacrifices and heroism of ordinary soldiers and the civilian population.[34]

By the beginning of the twentieth century, Sevastopol, along with Borodino, had been established as one of the most symbolic and revered places in Russian history. This image was also projected into the outside world.[35] In the 1890s monuments to the admirals Vladimir Kornilov and Pavel Nakhimov were erected in Sevastopol, and the new building of the Sevastopol military museum was opened.[36] The fiftieth anniversary of the siege of 1854–55, which coincided with the Russo-Japanese war of 1904–5, was marked with the opening of the Sevastopol "Panorama." Half painting, half installation, this in-the-round display of human dimensions vividly brings to life the heroic defense of the city. The Panorama's popularity as a modern icon and tourist sight has remained unchanged. The Panorama was later complemented by a Soviet version, the so-called Diorama commemorating the siege during World War II. When Sevastopol was again besieged in 1941–42, the already existing myth needed little help to renew itself. Admiral Nakhimov resurfaced as an heroic figure in Stalinist war propaganda, taking his place beside other Russian heroes such as Aleksandr Nevskii, Mikhail Kutuzov, and Aleksandr Suvorov. Later a military order and medal were named in Nakhimov's honor.

A large number of pseudoscholarly and popular accounts of both sieges shaped Soviet-Russian identity. In the Cold War era, the memory of Russia's fighting against Britain, France, and Turkey during the Crimean War acquired yet another political meaning. The Soviet historian Evgenii Tarle anchored the honorary title of Sevastopol in his bestselling blend of Soviet ideology and Great Russian nationalism, *Gorod russkoi slavy: Sevastopol' v 1854–1855 gg.* (City of Russian Glory: Sevastopol in 1854–1855).[37] After the transfer of Crimea to the Ukrainian SSR in 1954, Russian nationalist rhetoric was modified to underscore the heroism of the Soviet people in general and the Slavic peoples in particular, above all the Ukrainians. Thus, the siege of Sevastopol originated as an imperial myth of the Russian people, was appropriated by the tsarist state, was revived in its Soviet-Russian variant during World War II, and was gradually transformed by the Soviet state back into a myth of the whole "people." The steady development of the myth over time allowed its powerful grip on the Russian imagination to tighten.

The Sevastopol myth became a shorthand for the memory of both the Crimean War and World War II. As such, it was closely intertwined with a negative perception of the Crimean Tatars. Regardless of their real role during both wars, the image of the Tatar as traitor and the ally of the enemy—first of the Ottoman Empire, then of Nazi Germany—was continually recreated by the official myth. In fact, during the Crimean War the Crimean Tatar peasants were little more than "spectators to the massive battles between modern armies."[38] They did not exploit the volatility of the situation, and there is some evidence that the Tatars supported the local Slav population during the siege.[39] In the aftermath of the Crimean War, rumors about the Russian government's plans to deport the Tatars to Siberia as punishment for war treachery further accelerated the Tatars' emigration to the Ottoman Empire.[40] The experience of the Crimean War and subsequent mythmaking thus prepared the way for the Crimean Tatars' fate during World War II.[41]

The breakup of the USSR set the stage for a new adaptation of the Sevastopol myth to a new set of political realities. Sevastopol and the Black Sea Fleet have occupied prominent places in the Russian and Ukrainian national discourse, respectively. While Ukrainian nationalism has difficulties integrating Crimea into its national historiography, post-Soviet Russian nationalism has been quick to endorse a blend of the imperial Russian and the Soviet-Russian myths of Sevastopol in order to assert the "Russianness" of Crimea. The myth taps into and fosters Russian national identity in a period of uncertainty, and some politicians have used it to boost their electoral appeal.

The myth, however, also acquired a new foreign policy dimension. It was manipulated by both Russian politicians and intellectuals as a way to directly challenge Ukrainian sovereignty and independence.[42] Aleksandr Solzhenitsyn's claim that Crimea is Russia's "natural southern border" is but one prominent example of this rhetoric, readily taken up by populist Russian politicians like Iurii Luzhkov or Vladimir Zhirinovskii. The Communist Party under Gennadii Zyuganov also has kept alive the Soviet-era myth. The Russian movement in Crimea has used the Sevastopol myth to lend itself historical credibility and to connect with the claims of certain Russian politicians. The Sevastopol myth dominated the rhetoric of the early post-Soviet polarization in Crimea. Admiral Igor' Kasatonov, for example, claimed that the loss of the Black Sea Fleet, which he commanded, would throw Russia back to the time before Peter I.[43] In 1996, in what can only be described as a coup of the regional media, the alleged descendants of three famous Crimean War commanders—Pavel Nakhimov, Vladimir Kornilov, and Vladimir Istomin—appealed to the Russian authorities not to loosen their control over Sevastopol.[44] The local fears of linguistic and political "Ukrainization" of Crimea, real or imagined, led to talk of a "third Sevastopol siege."[45]

Crimean Tatar Historiography

The ethnogenesis of the Crimean Tatars is presented differently depending on who wrote its history.[46] The Crimean Tatars resent the predominant Soviet portrait of their relatively late arrival in Crimea during the Mongol era, which projects their origin into the depths of Asia or presents them as a subgroup of the Volga Tatars. This view effectively undermines the Crimean Tatars' claims to be an indigenous group with a special right to the territory. Crimean Tatar historians take issue with this interpretation and emphasize the Crimean Tatars' pre-Mongol links to Crimea. Williams describes the Crimean Tatars as "an eclectic Turkic-Muslim ethnic group that claims direct descent from the Goths, Pontic Greeks, Armenians, the Tatars of the Golden Horde, and other East European ethnic groups." For most of their history, the Crimean Tatars were not a homogeneous group; their differences resulted from the diverse geography of Crimea itself. Against the background of these diverse ethnic and geographic loyalties, Islam increasingly became the primary marker of a collective cultural identity which linked the inhabitants of Crimea to the wider international Muslim community (*umma*) rather than the territory of Crimea. By the fifteenth century, the process of Islamization had created the foundation for a wider Crimean Tatar group identification.

The historically most contested period is that of Russian colonial rule over Crimea. Crimean Tatar and Turkish historiography provide the mirror image of the Russian and Soviet-Russian views. For Crimean Tatar and Turkish historians, the year 1783 represents a national disaster. The subsequent waves of emigration to the Ottoman Empire are linked to Russian repression. An estimated 400,000 Tatars emigrated from Crimea to the Ottoman Empire in the eighteenth and nineteenth centuries, and about forty percent of the Crimean population emigrated after the Crimean war, reducing the number of Crimean Tatars to about 100,000 by 1865. However, Crimean Tatar historiography tends to downplay both the religious incentives to emigrate, which still superseded territorial attachments, and the mass response to the explicit invitation by the Ottoman sultan.[47]

The identification with Crimea as an ethnically defined Crimean Tatar homeland is by and large a twentieth-century creation. Paradoxically, "it was the Soviet state that completed the development of a secular Crimean Tatar national identity…and the construction of the Crimea as a homeland."[48] The Soviet regime first fostered this ethnoterritorial identity in the 1920s. After the deportation of 1944, this fused territorial and cultural identity served as a common bond and means of survival in exile. The urge to find out more about Crimean Tatar history, a taboo subject under the Soviet regime, was one of the starting points for the Crimean Tatar national movement from the 1950s and 1960s and the Soviet dissident movement in general.[49] As elsewhere in the FSU, the "history debate" of the perestroika period from 1986–87 marked a key turning-point for nationalist mobilization. In the case of the Crimean Tatars, this momentum grew into a mass return to Crimea in the early 1990s.

Oral history plays an important part in the historical consciousness of the Crimean Tatars. The written historical record prior to the early twentieth century is sparse.[50] Moreover, the Tatars "have generally had their enemies as their historians."[51] A modernization of educational policies for the Muslims in the Russian Empire got under way only at the end of the nineteenth century.[52] The key formative stage in the development of Crimean Tatar national consciousness was the period from 1905 to 1917. By the time of the Russo-Japanese war, the notion of the homeland had begun to shift from a political one (the Ottoman Empire) to a territorial one (the Crimean peninsula), and increasingly became the focus of political mobilization. Ismail Gaspıralı (in Russian: Gasprinskii), born in Crimea to an ennobled Tatar and trained at a traditional Muslim school, a Russian gymnasium, and the Russian Military Academy, became a key figure in the struggle for the reform of Muslim education. He also established the first bilingual Russian-Tatar newspaper (*Tercümen*), which critically shaped Tatar national consciousness and had an impact beyond the Russian Empire. The newspaper was a vehicle for promoting Gaspıralı's idea of a Turkic nation within the Russian Empire and based upon ethnicity rather than religion. Despite his opposition to a narrow definition of the nation, he is today commemorated as a founding father of the Crimean Tatar nation.

Around this time, numerous nationalist organizations were established among the Crimean Tatar diasporas. These organizations consisted mainly of students based in Istanbul, St. Petersburg, Moscow, and, to a lesser extent, in Crimea itself. Secular education for Crimean Tatars, in particular higher education, was severely restricted by the Russian imperial authorities in Crimea. The national movement drew its recruits from abroad, mainly from the Ottoman Empire. The so-called Fatherland Society (Vatan Cemiyeti), set up among Crimean Tatar students in Istanbul in 1909, was one of the secret radical associations demanding the liberation of the Crimean Tatar nation and independent statehood.

The nationalists sparked a renewed interest in Crimean Tatar history. Initially, nationalist organizations such as the Fatherland Society had distanced themselves from the Khanate past, because they disapproved of autocracy and despotism. With Halim Giray Sultan's 1911 publication of a fourteenth-century history of the Crimean Khanate, the whole Crimean Tatar past was recovered as part of the national historical memory.[53]

The Fatherland Society created national symbols that are still the focus of Crimean Tatar national identity today. A flag was designed in 1917 as the national flag of the Crimean Tatars and the independent Crimean state. Its turquoise color refers to a pan-Turkic identity and originated in the pan-Turkist movement in Istanbul, and the golden trident seal of the Crimean khans (Tarak Tamgha), which had been discovered on some material relics from the khanate, is imprinted on the upper left corner of the flag. It symbolizes the independence of the Crimean khans and their successors. Historical authenticity was less important than symbolic expressiveness. In these early twentieth-century nationalist circles, the long-forgotten Crimean term Kurultay (assembly) was revived. These fundamental symbols remain important today.

The first new Kurultay in 1917, for instance, took place in the Khan's Palace in Bakhchisarai, a setting that dramatically symbolized historical continuity and political claims. At the opening ceremony in November 1917 for three new cultural institutions—the National Museum, the Ismail Gasprinskii Pedagogical Institute, and the National Art School—Çelebi Cihan, then president of the Crimean Tatar government, gave a key speech. It exemplifies the poetic imagery of nationalist discourse:

> In Crimea many flowers, different colors and scents flourish. These flowers represent the peoples living in Crimea—Muslims, Russians, Jews, Greeks, Germans, and others. The aim of the Kurultay is to combine them all, to make out of all of them a wonderful bouquet and out of Crimea a truly cultural Switzerland. The National Kurultay will not only look after the Muslims, but also after the other peoples; it calls upon them for their cooperation.[54]

Cihan's speech also expresses his strong political claim to represent Crimea in all its national diversity. After his death in 1918, Cihan's poem *"Ant enkennen"* ("I Have Sworn"), which depicts oppression against the Crimean Tatars, became the Crimean Tatar national anthem.

Other culturally symbolic steps were taken in the early Soviet period to make the language and history distinctively Crimean. In 1924, Shevki Bektore (1881–1961) created the first Arabic-script alphabet specifically modified for the Crimean Tatar language. He also wrote one of the most popular patriotic songs in Crimean Tatar music, "My Tatarness," which was later revised and further popularized by another cultural leader, Bekir Sitki Chobanzade (1893–1938). The cultural and political leaders of the national movement attempted to modernize the educational system while preserving and embedding the literary language and historical memory.

Crimean Tatars are naturally very critical of the Russian and Soviet imperial historiography of the khanate. One of the histories endorsed by the current Crimean Tatar movement is the account by Valerii E. Vozgrin.[55] Though the author is Russian, he often reflects a pro–Crimean Tatar perspective. In his view, only the Crimean Tatars have a historical right to Crimea as their homeland. Like some of the post-Soviet Ukrainian rewriting of history discussed above, Vozgrin's history traces the Crimean Tatar ethnos back to Crimea's prehistoric settlers, in this case to the legendary Tavry. In addition to making factual errors about Crimea's ancient history, Vozgrin deflects attention from the impact of Crimean Tatar raids into Slav-populated lands by arguing that the Russian and Cossack raids were of a similar, or even larger, scale. Vozgrin also contributed to a collection of essays, combining Voloshin's general pieces about the special culture of Crimea with various political documents and forgotten pieces on Crimean Tatar history.[56] This collection emphasizes the distinct nature of the Crimean Tatar ethnopolitical claim to Crimea. In 1992, the official documentation regarding the preparation and execution of the deportation of the Crimean Tatars, including the exchange of instructions and reports between Stalin and Lavrentii Beria, was published and thereby finally took its place in the public domain.[57] Current Crimean Tatar historiography is closely tied up with pressing the political struggle for recognition as the region's indigenous people.[58] The Soviet denial of the Tatars' pre-Mongol roots in Crimea is consistently refuted.[59] In general, the Tatars' connection with the Golden Horde and the influence of the Ottoman Empire tend to be downplayed. Despite inherent contradictions, Crimean Tatar nationalist historiography has also portrayed the khanate as a national dynasty with the attributes of a modern nation-state.[60]

The museum and library of the Khan's Palace in Bakhchisarai represent an important resource for the study and dissemination of Crimean Tatar history. Moreover, in 1990, the Crimean Tatar library in Simferopol, named after Gaspıralı (Gasprinskii), was restored. The library's archive and the collection of the Crimean Tatar museum in Simferopol gradually are establishing themselves as centers for the preservation and display of Crimean Tatar historical memory. Moreover, the rewriting of history from a Crimean Tatar perspective includes the revival of both the Crimean Tatar language and cultural traditions, in particular among schoolchildren, and an increased awareness among the population in Crimea, and Ukraine at large, about Crimean Tatar history and legacy.[61] The three volumes of historical and contemporary documents on the national movement compiled by Guboglo and Chervonnaia, were crucial for raising the profile and consciousness of the Tatar national movement in the post-Soviet space as well as among Western scholars.[62] The strong twentieth-century notion of Crimea as the Crimean Tatar homeland has remained unbroken, but the identification has seamlessly moved from the "return to the homeland" to the modern legal notion of an "indigenous people" entitled to special rights over its territory.

Ukrainian Historiography of Crimea

Compared to Russian and Crimean Tatar historical and literary images, Crimea does not figure in nineteenth-century thinking about the Ukrainian nation. Mykhailo Drahomanov's ethnographical map of Ukraine (1880) unites the lands of the Right and Left Bank, Galicia, and Bukovyna as a territorial space sharing a common culture exemplified by the historical-political content of songs. This marker of identity explains Drahomanov's approach of entirely excluding Crimea from the map of Ukraine.[63] However, the very first census in the Russian Empire, conducted in 1897, indicates a considerable number of Ukrainian speakers (611,121 or 42.2 percent of the population) in Tauride, which was classified as "Ukrainian borderland."[64] Stepan Rudnyts'kyi, geography lecturer at Lviv University in the early twentieth century, takes this census data as a starting point for his own ethnographical map of Ukraine, in which he includes Crimea. Rudnyts'kyi in particular points to the northern part of Crimea, with its denser Ukrainian settlements.[65] The historian and politician Mykhailo Hrushevs'kyi, in turn, treats Crimea's status ambiguously. In his fundamental work *Istoriia Ukraïny-Rusy*, he argues that Crimea lies outside the national territory.[66] He presents the Crimean Khanate as having a twofold impact on the Ukrainian people: Crimean Tatar raids devastated Ukrainian lands, but strengthened communal bonds among the Ukrainian Cossacks.[67] More generally, national thinking on the position of Crimea shifted in the early twentieth century. Rudnyts′kyi and the historian Vasyl′ Dubrovs′kyi, for example, tied Crimea historically and geopolitically to Ukraine.[68]

Post-Soviet Ukrainian historiography primarily focuses on the formation of the Ukrainian people and its state structures, often following the Hrushevs′kyi tradition. Crimea occupies only a marginal position in the majority of these accounts. Some historians and politicians, however, assert a dubious ethnogenesis, trying to prove a direct ancestral line between the earliest inhabitants of Crimea and the Ukrainian ethnos.[69] Others concentrate on the links between the Zaporozhian Sich and Crimea, which Catherine II had supposedly destroyed. These analysts emphasize the common bonds of repression in Ukrainian-Crimean relations within the Russian Empire and in the Soviet period, including the deportations of Ukrainians and Crimean Tatars. This approach is the basis for interpreting the 1954 transfer of Crimea as the lawful and historically justified "normalization" in relations between Ukraine and Crimea.[70] These pseudo-historical accounts, shaped by political interests, aim to underscore Crimea's "rightful" place in Ukraine while playing down its demand or need for a special status. Some of these studies do concede the possibility of cultural autonomy for the Crimean Tatars.[71] The argument that Crimea was primordially Ukrainian[72] requires such implausible historical revisionism, however, that it has yet to be taken seriously by the majority of Ukrainians themselves. The Ukrainian media are trying to raise the historical awareness of Ukraine's impact on Crimea through serialized popular history accounts.[73] Professional historical research by Ukrainian academics points more promisingly towards the demystification of the historical links between Ukraine and Crimea.[74]

Conclusion

Similar to the cultural images transmitted through literature, storytelling, travelogues, and art—and often linked to them—making history is crucial for nation building. History, just like literature, has to be taught in order to play a part in identity construction. The writing and rewriting of Crimean history is not simply a revision process of "rectifying historical grievances," but also translates into special claims to territory or rights and can thus serve as a catalyst for political mobilization. So far the symbols, myths, and politicized historical discourse on Crimea have been dominated by official Russian and Soviet-Russian interpretations, but these views are increasingly being challenged by the Crimean Tatars' perspective. Historiography acts as an interpretive frame and a legitimating device. It can create powerful links between the past and the present that resonate with political elites and the population at large. In a context of political change the potency of history increases sharply, especially if supported by tangible institutional points of reference. In the following two chapters we will explore how a sense of history was tied to specific institutional arrangements for the administration of Crimea. These institutional legacies, implicitly or explicitly creating links between territory and ethnicity, have shaped Crimea's political mobilization in the post-Soviet period.

.

4 The Institutional Legacies of Territory and Ethnicity

IN PERIODS OF STATE BUILDING, the political memory of previously existing ethnoterritorial institutions helps to legitimize nationalist mobilization and imbues it with a sense of historical rootedness. The existence of particular institutions at some point in history, however, does not make for current identity clashes, ethnic competition, or conflict. Like the literary or historical memories discussed in the previous chapters, this institutional legacy has to be politically activated. Political mobilization in Crimea in the late Soviet and early post-Soviet period was shaped by a range of Soviet-era institutional legacies, in particular the special autonomy status that the region had been granted at various times in the past, and the 1954 transfer of Crimea from the jurisdiction of the RSFSR to that of the Ukrainian SSR.

Crimea as a Contested Territory

The debates about Crimea's status in the twentieth century occurred following two key historical moments of imperial collapse: the collapse of the tsarist empire in the revolutions of 1917 and the collapse of the USSR in 1991. Despite the long interval between these periods, the political discourse in Crimea in both periods stresses the same options: Crimean independence, Crimean autonomy within a Ukrainian state, and incorporation into Russia.[1] The geostrategic importance of Crimea and the sensitive question of how to divide up the tsarist Black Sea Fleet are also discussed in both periods.

There were four competing views of what Crimea's status should be after the 1917 Revolution: the Crimean Tatars aspired to national Crimean autonomy, the Ukrainian nationalists wanted to incorporate Crimea into independent Ukraine, the Bolsheviks aimed to establish control over as much of the former tsarist empire as possible, and the White Russians wanted to defend Crimea as a bastion of anti-Bolshevism. A highly complicated interplay of these different forces unfolded in Crimea in 1917–21, with the then large population of Crimean Tatars playing an even more pronounced role than today.[2]

The Crimean Tatar national movement had begun to crystallize into a significant political force at the turn of the twentieth century. In the aftermath of the February Revolution of 1917, numerous nationalist Crimean Tatar cells surfaced across Crimea. Two thousand popularly elected delegates, mostly with links to the Fatherland Society, convened the All-Crimean Muslim Congress in Simferopol in April 1917, paving the way for the new Tatar national intelligentsia to enter leading political positions.[3] The Congress set up the Crimean Muslim Central Executive Committee, which declared that it was taking control of all Crimean Tatar affairs. The next step in institutionalizing Crimean Tatar influence was the establishment of a permanent ruling organization under the historic name Kurultay, originally denoting an assembly of tribal leaders to choose a new khan. The memory of this traditional institution was now revived as a secular nationalist platform.[4]

However, the Provisional Government, which had formed in Petrograd after the February Revolution of 1917, did not release the control over land and kept conservative mullahs in charge as state representatives. In response, Crimean Tatars began spontaneously to seize land.[5] After the first direct, secret elections, which afforded universal suffrage (including the vote for women) for the first time ever in the Muslim world, the Crimean Tatar National Parliament, the Kurultay, was opened in the Khan's Palace in Bakhchisarai on 9 December 1917. The initial demands of the Kurultay were for Crimean Tatar autonomy and the transfer of state property to its control. The seventy-plus members of the Kurultay, many of whom were close to the new nationalist party Milli Firqa, stressed the equality of the different ethnic groups in Crimea in order to dispel fears of an imminent "Tatarization," while at the same time demanding full territorial autonomy.[6] The political right (conservative clergy and landowners) and left (socialists) were represented with only about ten deputies each.[7] The Kurultay elected the first Crimean Tatar government, the National Directorate, with Çelebi Cihan as its president. When the Crimean Tatar cavalry, about three thousand strong, returned from the front, the power of the Kurultay was greatly enhanced.[8] On 26 December 1917, the Kurultay passed a progressive constitution setting forth the principles of an independent Crimean Democratic Republic.[9] This step followed the declaration on 20 November 1917 of an independent Ukrainian People's Republic, including three northern districts of the Tauride province but excluding Crimea, which was officially still recognized by Ukraine as a part of the Russian Empire.[10] Thus, the tsarist Tauride province was de facto partitioned. In Crimea proper, with the exception of the districts of Sevastopol and Kerch, the Crimean Tatar population was now a relative majority. In this period, Crimea had two rival power centers: the Tatar Kurultay and the Bolsheviks' base in Sevastopol.

The relations between Kyiv and Petrograd deteriorated increasingly until the end of 1917, ending in a division of the Black Sea Fleet along national lines. The "Ukrainization" of parts of the armed forces had little practical impact, given the widespread demoralization of the soldiers.[11] The Crimean Tatars' bid for independence was short-lived, as it was crushed by the Bolsheviks in January 1918. The delay in the Bolshevik takeover of Crimea was due in part to their weakness vis-à-vis the Crimean Tatar institutions and the strength of Mensheviks and Social Revolutionaries in the region. When conflicts occurred among the different political organizations, the Bolsheviks seized the moment for their invasion. The Bolshevik Central Executive Council proclaimed the "independent" Republic of Tauride, claiming Crimea and the Black Sea Fleet for the RSFSR.[12] Cihan was arrested and shot by the Bolsheviks in February, thus becoming the Crimean Tatar movement's first national martyr. His memory was kept alive underground in the Soviet period through his poem *"Ant Etkenmen"* (I Pledge), which is the Crimean Tatar anthem today.

Only three months after the takeover of Crimea, the Bolsheviks were forced out of Kyiv by Ukrainian forces and the German army. This happened shortly after Ukraine had signed the Treaty of Brest-

Litovsk and was given military support from the Germans. During the Brest-Litovsk negotiations, Crimea had neither been discussed nor awarded to Ukraine, although the peninsula was effectively cut off from the rest of the Russian Empire.[13] The Kurultay was briefly revived in May 1918, following the German occupation of Crimea. Tatar forces assisted the German army in defeating the Bolsheviks in the hope of achieving not only Crimean Tatar autonomy but also in the expectation of an ambitious repatriation of the Crimean Tatar diaspora under the German regime.[14]

The German administration of Crimea was headed by General Suleiman Sulkiewicz, a Lithuanian Tatar. At the end of June 1918, he formed a coalition government of different nationalities represented in Crimea (Crimean Tatars, Russians, Germans, and Armenians).[15] Russian remained the official language, but Crimean Tatar and German were also used. Sulkiewicz's government introduced Crimean citizenship and state symbols.[16] The turquoise flag of the Crimean Tatars was made the official Crimean flag, and the old tsarist coat of arms of the Tauride government, the eagle, became the coat of arms of the Crimean government. New elections were scheduled as a kind of plebiscite on Crimean independence. Sulkiewicz's attempt to build up a Crimean military force, consisting of either local forces or parts of the Russian Black Sea Fleet, failed due to German resistance. During this period, as in the post-Soviet situation in Crimea, two sets of institutions coexisted: on the one hand, the coalition government of Crimea, and on the other, the Kurultay and the Crimean Tatar National Directorate. However, the Crimean population recognized neither the Kurultay nor the Directorate as being representative of the whole of Crimea.[17] The failure to both build an armed force capable of defending an independent Crimea, and to widen interethnic support for independence, accelerated the fall of the government.

Although Crimean-Ukrainian relations were initially friendly, and the Crimean Tatar Executive Committee expressed its support for the recognition of the Ukrainian People's Republic,[18] these relations worsened considerably when Ukrainian forces reached Crimea in the spring of 1918.[19] A Ukrainian newspaper listed the Crimean ports of Evpatoriia, Feodosiia, and Kerch as Ukrainian, provoking angry reactions in Crimea and Turkey. On 13 March 1918, the Provisional

Law on the Naval Forces of the Ukrainian People's Republic declared the Black Sea Fleet to be a Ukrainian naval force, and at the end of April the Ukrainian flag was hoisted on most of the ships.[20] Given that the Black Sea Fleet was commanded by the Bolsheviks and that the German occupiers did not support the moves of the Ukrainian Central Rada, the Ukrainian actions were essentially declaratory.

There are many examples of the increasingly possessive claims on Crimea of Ukrainian nationalist rhetoric. Mykhailo Hrushevs'kyi published an article entitled "The Black Sea Orientation," stressing Ukraine's gravitation towards the Black Sea, which he called the "Ukrainian Sea."[21] The strongest assertion of a Ukrainian Crimea can be attributed to Pavlo Skoropads'kyi, the tsarist general and head of the short-lived Ukrainian Hetmanate (Cossack state) in 1918. His authoritarian regime envisaged a greater Ukrainian state, possibly as a part of a federation with Russia. Crimea and the Black Sea Fleet became important components of this idea. First, Skoropads'kyi tried to achieve his goal via diplomatic means, through the German ambassador to Kyiv and the German authorities in Berlin. In a memorandum to the German ambassador in May 1918, he presented the integration of Crimea with the Ukrainian state as both an economic necessity (to secure Ukraine's economic independence with the help of Crimean salt, tobacco, wine, and fruit) and a geopolitical necessity (to overcome Ukraine's isolation from the Black Sea and its ports). In his memoirs, Skoropads'kyi coined a rather crude image: "Ukraine cannot live without Crimea; without Crimea it would be a body without legs. It does not matter whether this will be a full merger or far-reaching autonomy. This will depend on the wish of the Crimeans themselves."[22] It seems that Skoropads'kyi deliberately underestimated the Crimean Tatar population at only fourteen percent in order to refute any rival Tatar claims to a state.[23] Skoropads'kyi also emphasized the significance of the Black Sea Fleet for "Ukrainian national pride" and military security, and he asked for German support in this matter.

Ukrainian Foreign Minister Dmytro Doroshenko followed up on these suggestions with a similar memorandum to the German ambassador at the end of May 1918. In Berlin these suggestions found little support, and in Turkey they evoked immediate protest. In September 1918 Skoropads'kyi traveled to Berlin to begin direct negotiations with Germany and even with Kaiser William II personally. According to Doroshenko, Germany subsequently withdrew its objections to the formation of a regular Ukrainian army and passed the Black Sea Fleet on to the Ukrainian government.[24] Germany remained hesitant about Skoropads'kyi's proposal regarding the unification of all lands populated by Ukrainians (including Crimea, the Kuban, and Bessarabia).[25] On the whole, the German government lacked a coherent strategy while the war on the western front continued, and proved ill-prepared to deal with the Crimean issue.[26] Generally, Bolshevik occupation of Crimea was perceived as the worst possible option, while cooperation with the Crimean Tatars was perceived as an important means of preventing communist control over Crimea. Eventually, Germany seemed to favor the construction of a new regional Crimean entity that would be associated with Ukraine and open for German colonists. Independent Crimean statehood was not on Germany's agenda, but prolonged German influence over Ukraine could have created the precedent of Crimean autonomy within an "independent" Ukraine, albeit under a German protectorate. Germany's increasing support for a Ukrainian-Crimean agreement forced the Crimean government to resume talks with Ukraine. Sulkiewicz insisted on full Crimean independence as a possible basis for a federal union with Ukraine.[27] This struggle for Crimean independence offers some parallels with the post-Soviet period.

Rival delegations from Kyiv and Crimea tried to gain German support at meetings in Berlin between August and October 1918. Germany's position wavered, but eventually it pressed the Crimean government to resolve its conflict with Kyiv through an international treaty. Direct negotiations between the two parties were held in early October 1918, after Kyiv had temporarily interrupted its blockade of Crimea. The two positions proved irreconcilable: while the Ukrainian delegation insisted upon the integration of Crimea into the Ukrainian state, the Crimean delegation advocated a federal union between Ukraine and Crimea on equal grounds, a union that would be open to other member states. When negotiations broke down in Kyiv in October 1918, the Ukrainian government held talks with representatives of Crimea's main ethnic groups who, unlike the Crimean government, were able to find a consensus. In autumn 1918, a preliminary treaty made Crimea an autonomous region within Ukraine, with its own regional parliament, territorial army, and administration, as well as a permanent state secretary in the Ukrainian Council of Ministers. This status would have gone far beyond any autonomy rights Crimea has been granted in the post-Soviet era, but the treaty was never implemented. Instead, with the collapse of the German army on the western front in November 1918, German forces in the East began to withdraw to German territory. The Sulkiewicz government quickly fell after the German withdrawal from Crimea. It had already been severely weakened by the loss of the support of the Crimean Tatar organizations, and it ultimately failed to build a broad base of support. When Skoropads'kyi published a manifesto on 14 November 1918 announcing the unification of Ukraine and Russia, he had already lost in influence.

The sudden end of German dominance led to a series of unstable governments in Kyiv. Skoropads'kyi was replaced by a pro-Ukrainian Directorate under Symon Petliura and Volodymyr Vynnychenko. Torbakov sums up the situation: "The collapse of the Hetmanate, the new stage of the civil war in Ukraine, the Bolshevik victory in this war, and the subsequent formation of the USSR officially closed discussions over the status of Crimea and the Black Sea fleet."[28] Both issues were kept in a deep freeze, ready to be thawed and mobilized under a new political tide. In November 1918, the Sulkiewicz government was replaced by an interim government which lasted until April 1919. It was dominated by the Kadets, who opposed both Crimean and Ukrainian independence. Crimea fell under the de facto rule of General Anton Denikin's Volunteer Army, which was strongly opposed by the Crimean Tatars. In April 1919, the Bolsheviks took control of Crimea and proclaimed the Soviet Socialist Republic of Crimea, ruled by a provisional government. But by June, this republic too ceased to exist, falling after an attack by Denikin, whom the Entente (the alliance between France, Russia, and the United Kingdom) supported. Denikin reinstated a Tauride government that did not recognize the national autonomy of the Crimean Tatars. Under Denikin and his successor, Baron Piotr Wrangel, a considerable number of Crimean Tatars retreated into the mountainous areas of the peninsula to avoid the repressions of the Whites and to fight a partisan war. In November 1920, Wrangel's government was finally defeated and expelled from Crimea by the Red Army. The Bolshevik regime then swiftly integrated Crimea politically and institutionally with Soviet Russia.

The Legacies of Soviet Autonomy

The Soviet Union institutionalized ethnoterritorial federalism in the 1920s and from the 1930s onwards complemented this with a system of individualized national identification fixed in every Soviet citizen's passport. Soviet pseudofederalism was subordinated to the control of the Communist Party apparatus and was staffed by the nomenklatura system of party-approved appointments.[29] From 1977 the fifteen constituent republics of the USSR theoretically had the freedom to secede from the Union. The absence of an actual procedural mechanism, however, meant secession was impossible in constitutional terms. The 1977 USSR Constitution established the federal hierarchy as fifteen union republics, twenty autonomous republics (ASSR; sixteen in the RSFSR, one in Azerbaijan, two in Georgia, one in Uzbekistan), eight autonomous regions (*avtonomnaia oblast'*; five in the RSFSR, one each in Azerbaijan, Georgia, and Tajikistan), and ten autonomous districts (*avtonomnyi okrug*; all in the RSFSR). This complex hierarchy of autonomous units was characterized by different levels of formal self-government, each with its own specific cultural rights for the main "titular" ethnic group. Almost all of the territorial units of the federation were named after a particular ethnic group or nation (thus the "titular" nationality), and next to Russians they tended to be the most privileged in enjoying political, economic, and cultural rights. The ASSR was an instrument in the nationality policy of the new Soviet state to win the support of the most politically important national groups. Most autonomous entities belonged to the RSFSR, the only republic formally structured as a federation. Despite the existence of ethnically defined territorial units, titular groups were often outnumbered by the Russian population. Moreover, most of the autonomous units were highly heterogeneous in their ethnic, cultural, and socioeconomic composition.

The smallest autonomous units, the ten autonomous districts, were first set up in 1925 for smaller national groups in the northern territories of the RSFSR. Under the 1936 Constitution they were represented in the USSR Council of Nationalities by one deputy each.[30]

The eight autonomous regions sent five deputies each to the Council of Nationalities, the second chamber of the Supreme Soviet of the USSR, whereas other regions had no direct representation at the central level. Autonomous regions enjoyed administrative autonomy within a union republic, namely the right to propose to the Supreme Soviet of the union republics a law governing the region and the right of the region's organs to conduct their affairs in the language of the titular national group. Ultimate control was concentrated at the union republic level, thus limiting rights at the oblast level to administrative functions. A symbolically higher status was assigned to the twenty ASSRs, each of which sent eleven deputies to the Council of Nationalities. The ASSRs were entitled to their own constitutions, which did not need to be approved by the union republics, although these constitutions obviously had to accord with the constitutions of the Soviet Union and the relevant union republic. The autonomous republics could initiate legislation in the Supreme Soviet of the union republics, and they had their own executive, legislature, and judiciary, as well as their own flags, anthems, and emblems. Under the "nativization" (*korenizatsiia*) policy implemented by the Bolsheviks in the 1920s, titular national groups were supposed to staff the majority of important posts within their jurisdiction, but this practice weakened as a result of the steady pursuit of control by the appointment of Slavs, and policies of Russification and assimilation by the Soviet leadership. Despite this complex hierarchical structure of autonomous units, the Constitution of the USSR strictly defined the overarching framework. In reality, little real power over administration and cultural policy was left to the autonomous units, and in the Council of Nationalities the autonomous units' representatives usually rubber-stamped the suggestions coming from the central party bodies.

Formally, autonomous republics were established within union republics with the approval of the USSR institutions, and the territory of autonomous republics was not to be changed without their consent. Like the union republics' right to secede, however, this limit on territorial changes was in essence a declaratory one, as there was no specific procedure for either laid down in the Soviet constitutions. Throughout the Soviet era, several federal units changed their status as a result of Stalin's whims or other decisions at the highest level of the state. The Karelian ASSR, for example, was elevated into the Karelo-Finnish SSR in 1940, before being demoted to an ASSR again in 1956. In other instances, autonomous regions were elevated to autonomous republics (for example, Udmurtiia and Yakutiia). Under Soviet rule, these changes amounted to little more than administrative corrections, justified either as a means of improving an area's development or as punitive measures. Soviet boundary changes are often described as "arbitrary." In fact, many changes were driven by an inherent logic of technocratic pragmatism and cynical calculations wrapped up in Soviet ideology. Crimea's status changed repeatedly during the Soviet era: from an ASSR within the RSFSR to an oblast in 1945, then to an oblast within the Ukrainian SSR in 1954, and a poorly defined ASSR in early 1991.

The Crimean ASSR

The All-Russian Central Executive Committee and the Soviet of People's Commissars (*Sovnarkom*) of the Russian Socialist Federal Soviet Republic passed a resolution "On the Autonomy of Crimea" on 18 October 1921, establishing Crimea's status within the RSFSR.[31] The Constitution adopted on 10 November 1921 by the First All-Crimean Congress of Soviets established a Crimean Socialist Soviet Republic (*Krymskaia Sotsialisticheskaia Sovetskaia Respublika*). Reflecting the constitutional flux of the period, Crimea was not explicitly defined as a part of the RSFSR. However, it was set up in line with the 1918 RSFSR Constitution that referred to constitutent "autonomous regional unions" (*avtonomnye oblastnye soiuzy*) without spelling out the details of this status.[32] Despite its confusing name, suggesting union republic status, the 1921 Crimean Constitution stipulated that the Crimean SSR was meant to adopt the laws and legal acts of the RSFSR.[33] The new Crimean SSR was proclaimed as a workers' republic that would end colonization and the oppression of classes and nationalities. In addition to defining a territorial autonomy status, the Constitution also embodied provisions for a hierarchy of nations within Crimea. While the Bolshevik mantra of "equality of all nationalities" was repeated throughout the Constitution, Russian and Tatar were defined as the two state languages (*gosudarstvennye iazyki*).[34] Moreover, the Crimean Tatars were singled out as the most important national group.[35] Reflecting early Bolshevik practice, both the Constitution and Crimea's new coat of arms combined socialist and national symbols. The official name of the Crimean SSR appeared in Russian and Tatar on both the red flag and the coat of arms; the latter added the slogan "Proletarians of all lands, unite!" in both languages.[36]

The status of Crimea as an ASSR within the RSFSR was gradually spelled out in more detail in the Soviet and regional constitutions of the 1920s and 1930s.[37] In contrast to other ASSRs the Crimean ASSR was named after a territory rather than its "titular" nationality. Although the Crimean Tatars did not enjoy the official status of a titular group, in practice Crimean autonomy in the early 1920s resembled that of other ASSRs. Williams observes of this institutional arrangement that it "completed the development of a mass-based, modern Crimean Tatar national identity."[38] During a phase of relatively liberal Soviet nationality policies in the 1920s, the key positions in Crimea's political structures were dominated by Crimean Tatars, yet as an ethnic group they accounted for only about twenty-five percent of the Crimean population (about 150,000 people) in 1921. The local communist Crimean Tatar Veli Ibrahim chaired the Central Executive Committee, and Crimean Tatars headed the Sovnarkom and several People's Commissariats, and held a significant proportion of administrative and legal posts. There were many Crimean Tatars among the directors of enterprises and farms, and Crimean Tatar language and culture saw a revival throughout the 1920s. The Soviet policy of *korenizatsiia* via ethnic quotas for leading positions led to the Tatarization of government, the judiciary, trade unions, newly established educational institutions, and industry. Accordingly, the Crimean ASSR can be accurately described as an exercise in "state-sponsored identity construction."[39] When Crimean Tatar politicians refer to this period and demand the reestablishment of a similar type of autonomy today, they indirectly acknowledge the Soviet contribution to their cultural and political identity. Today, the Crimean Tatars claim that the Soviet ASSR—like other ASSRs—recognized the Tatars' status as the indigenous people. Post-Soviet Russocentric historiography, in contrast, has emphasized the multiethnic, "international" nature of the territorial status of the ASSR.[40]

In 1926–28, a struggle arose with the Communist Party in Crimea over the question of official languages and the transliteration of Turkic languages from Arabic to Roman characters. From the late 1920s onwards, with the rise of Stalin, a new wave of "Sovietiza-tion" brought the policy of *korenizatsiia* to an abrupt halt. In the 1930s a period of repression of "bourgeois nationalism" and forced collectivization resulted in thirty-five to forty thousand Crimean Tatars being deported to Siberia. The Tatars were seriously affected by the famines, political repressions, and the Russification during this period.[41] A large Slavic population influx occurred in the 1930s as a result of the Soviet policy of regional development, mainly by forced industrialization (shipbuilding, machine building, and chemi-cal industries) and the establishment of Crimea as the USSR's prime tourist resort. These demographic changes permanently altered the ethnic balance in the region (see appendix 1). According to official Soviet data for 1936, 43.5 percent of the Crimean population were Rus-sians, 23.1 percent Crimean Tatars, 10 percent Ukrainians, 7.4 percent Jews, and 5.7 percent Germans; the remaining 10.3 percent comprised other small nationalities.

In his speech "On the Draft Constitution of the USSR," deliv-ered at the Extraordinary Eighth Congress of Soviets of the USSR on 25 November 1936, Stalin admitted, maybe inadvertently, that the name and status of the Crimean ASSR were linked to the Crimean Tatars. He used the Crimean ASSR as a model of how to demar-cate the characteristics of a union republic from those of an ASSR. According to Stalin, a union republic had to be located on an external border, the overall population had to exceed one million, and the titular nationality had to be the majority within that territory.[42] The Crimean ASSR in 1936 fulfilled the first and second criteria; Stalin had clearly added the third criterion so as to preempt potential claims (in this region and elsewhere) as early as possible: the Crimean Tatars accounted for 19.4 percent of the Crimean population in 1939.[43] Soviet rhetoric and political practice clearly diverged, as the example of the Karelian ASSR demonstrates: although it did not fit Stalin's second and third criteria—having less than half the required total population (469,000 in 1939), of whom only 23.2 percent identified themselves as Karelian—it was elevated in 1940 to the status of a union republic, the Karelo-Finnish SSR.[44]

According to the Crimean ASSR Constitution of 4 June 1937, the Crimean ASSR remained an integral part of the RSFSR, and all laws adopted at the all-union or republic level applied automatically in Crimea.[45] Despite new centralizing nuances, the Constitution restated the provision of the previous Constitution as regards the need for the consent of an ASSR before any change could be made to its territory, though as previously, no procedure was laid down for such matters.[46] While Soviet realities made this clause a mere formality, its existence in the Constitution left an institutional point of leverage in later discussions about the legitimacy of changes in status and territorial boundaries.

According to the 1937 Constitution, the coat of arms and flag of the Crimean ASSR retained their writing in Russian and Tatar.[47] Even though repressions against the Crimean Tatars were long underway by 1937—and although the Constitution's wording hardly guaranteed its implementation—the new Constitution of the Crimean ASSR prescribed that all laws passed by the Crimean Supreme Soviet were to be published in Russian and Tatar.[48] Legal proceedings in rural areas and parts of towns and villages with a Tatar, Russian, German, or Jewish majority could be conducted in that majority's language or, if necessary, translation would be provided.[49] In the wake of an immense influx of Slav settlers into Crimea and ongoing Stalinist repression, this seemingly liberal language provision applied to ever fewer settlements.

The deportation of the Crimean Tatars in May 1944 paved the way for the downgrading of Crimea's ASSR status to that of an ordinary oblast within the RSFSR on 30 June 1945. This change in status can be seen as a belated recognition of the link between the Crimean Tatars and the region's special status. By physically removing the Tatars, the Soviets also eliminated the need for a special territorial status.[50]

The "Gift" of 1954: The Beginning of a "Ukrainian" Crimea

The transfer of Crimea from the RSFSR to the Ukrainian SSR in 1954 completed the territorial definition of modern Ukraine. The transfer is often described as a "present" or "gift" by Soviet writers. The "gift" solidified the institutional, territorial, and political links between Crimea and Ukraine while leaving the region's status in the overall Soviet federal hierarchy untouched. Seemingly innocuous at the time, the "gift" assumed great political significance after the collapse of the Soviet Union in 1991.[51] Crimea is one of the best examples of how some Soviet-era decisions, especially those involving boundary changes or shifts in competences, assumed a radically different dynamic in the post-Soviet era. Post-Soviet state and nation building in both Ukraine and Russia invested the institutional legacy of the border change with a politically salient link between ethnicity and territory. In the aftermath of empire, the 1954 transfer became a source of serious contention in the relations between independent Ukraine and Russia. Although post-Soviet debates over the status and ownership of Crimea are deeply grounded in history, the actual transfer of Crimea in 1954 has not elicited a systematic investigation of how the transfer came about. Recently released archival materials in Moscow and Kyiv allow us to revisit the 1954 transfer and assess its rationale and implications.

References to Khrushchev's "gift" to Ukraine are ubiquitous in Soviet writing on the subject. They have created a Soviet-era myth that has remained unchallenged.[52] Moscow Mayor Luzhkov referred to the "tsarist present to the Ukrainian communists" in a book published in 1999, illustrating the continuing resonance of the 1954 transfer in recent politics.[53] Existing scholarship tells us very little about the motivations, the politics, and the actors or procedures surrounding the decision to transfer Crimea to the Ukrainian SSR. These questions had repercussions for the post-Soviet Russian and Ukrainian debate about which state had legitimate sovereignty over Crimea. The legality, rationale, and context of the transfer are, consequently, crucial issues.

In Western historical accounts, references to the 1954 transfer tend to be extremely brief, despite the knowledge provided by hindsight as to its post-1991 importance. Taubman's comprehensive biography of Khrushchev (2003) devotes only a few lines to the event. Taubman repeats the standard interpretation that there was no ulterior motive: "Khrushchev extracted the Crimea from Russia and benevolently presented it to Ukraine," but also mentions that Khrushchev "tried to pull off the same trick in 1944," in the context of the resettlement of Ukrainians in Crimea after the deportation of the Crimean Tatars (see chapter 5). Orest Subtelny is one of few authors to pass a judgement on the transfer. Like most others, he sees it as a "friendship token" of Moscow's new approach to Ukraine as the junior partner within the USSR, but he also points out that the "gift" was in reality far less altruistic than it seemed. Crimea was, after all, the historical homeland of the Crimean Tatars. Thus, Subtelny concludes, the Russians did not have the "moral right to give it away nor did the Ukrainians have the right to accept it."[54] Furthermore, he points to a functional logic behind the transfer based on Crimea's geographical closeness to and economic dependence on Ukraine. What he terms the "annexation" of Crimea saddled Ukraine with the region's economic and political problems arising from the deportation of the Crimean Tatars.[55] The transfer occurred during a time when destalinization was under way. According to Paul R. Magocsi, the transfer was, in fact, part of destalinization. Instead of focusing on Khrushchev's involvement in the transfer of Crimea, he focuses on the evolution of Soviet interpretations and perceptions of that event. For Magocsi, the events of 1954 epitomize the dual approach: closely integrating Ukraine into the Soviet system, while loosening the center's political control as part of destalinization.[56]

Other scholars see Khrushchev's "gift" to the Ukrainian SSR in 1954 as an act to mark the three-hundredth anniversary of the Pereiaslav Treaty between the Cossack hetman Bohdan Khmel'nyts'kyi and Muscovy. In Andrew Wilson's words, it illustrates Soviet Ukrainian state building as "ersatz statehood through external agency."[57] Brian G. Williams calls the transfer "a (at the time!) purely symbolic gesture celebrating the 300th anniversary of the Cossack Ukraine's unification with Russia in 1654"[58] and agrees with Edward Ozhiganov, who speculates that Khrushchev may have tried to use Crimea as an enticement to gain the support of the Communist Party of Ukraine in the struggle for power after Stalin's death.[59] Alexander J. Motyl explicitly recognizes the limited knowledge about the transfer: "Then, in 1954, for reasons that are still not fully clear, Nikita Khrushchev granted Ukraine the Crimea as a 'gift' from Russia on the occasion of the 300th anniversary of the Pereiaslav Treaty."[60] The notion of the "gift" also informs Alan Fisher's study of the Crimean Tatars. Like Wilson and Motyl, he sees the territorial transfer as an "award" to the Ukrainian SSR on the occasion of the three-hundredth anniversary

of the Pereiaslav union with Moscow. He quotes Kliment Voroshilov,
then chairman of the Presidium of the Supreme Soviet of the USSR,
who stressed that the transfer recognized the strategic importance of
Crimea and was a symbol of Russia's trust in its Ukrainian partner.
Fisher adds that through the transfer of Crimea, Moscow delegated
responsibility for the Crimean Tatar problem, the complex contours
of which were slowly beginning to take shape around this time. By
involving Kyiv in this issue, Moscow diluted its responsibility.[61] In the
end, the transfer of Crimea had serious long-term implications for
Ukraine, making it the only post-Soviet government directly responsible for the financial support and accommodation of the Crimean
Tatars.

    Yaroslav Bilinsky is one of few authors to mention the Soviet
attempts to permanently alter the demographic balance by resettling
a significant number of families from Western Ukraine to Crimea
so as to help rebuild the regional economy, in particular agriculture,
after the deportation of the Crimean Tatars.[62] Solchanyk chides the
"conventional wisdom" about the transfer, but his criticism refers to
the commemoration of the allegedly historical "reunion" of Russia
and Ukraine rather than to the "transfer of title" itself.[63] Solchanyk's
publication briefly summarizes the official archival documents about
the transfer (see below) and concludes that the highly politicized
debate in Russia and Ukraine about the "Soviet legality" of Crimea's
transfer misses the point. Soviet laws and procedures were often
applied erratically, flexibly, and secretly.[64] Thus, the important issues
for post-Soviet politics are the political dynamics of the transfer and
their effect on political mobilization after the Soviet collapse, rather
than the legal niceties of the actual procedure used in 1954.

    The transfer received little attention in the Western press,[65]
which (like the Soviet media) allowed the three-hundredth anniversary celebrations of the Pereiaslav agreement to overshadow the
border change.[66] And just like their colleagues in the Soviet Union,
Western scholars took the three-hundredth anniversary as an occasion for historical discussions about the events in 1654 but avoided
any thorough engagement with the "gift" as such. They either underestimated the significance of the border change, the disintegration
of the USSR being hard to envisage in 1954, or they deemed it safer

to discuss the distant past without addressing the current or future implications.[67]

The Western media were obviously not well informed about what was going on in the USSR and, more specifically, in Crimea. The *New York Times* at least saw the increasing importance of Ukraine in Soviet politics reflected in the celebrations and the transfer.[68] Reporting on the Soviet Union was strongly shaped by Cold War perceptions. Accordingly, the *New York Times* interpreted the border change as just another sign of the arbitrariness of Soviet rule without popular consent, a caution to Western audiences that any Soviet decision, not only in foreign policy, was to be treated with suspicion.[69] In a reply to that view, Ivan Rudnytsky drew attention to the conflict potential inherent in the territorial change, a potential that manifested itself several decades later. Today his words seem prescient: "This concession by Moscow to the old Ukrainian demand is of considerable psychological significance, and in the future the question may become even more important."[70] Rudnytsky called the transfer a "natural solution" to the historical anomaly whereby the Ukrainians had always objected to "Russian encirclement." Rudnytsky wrote in the spirit of the Ukrainian diaspora in the West, and his observations provided a counterweight to the predominant Soviet-inspired view of Russian-Ukrainian friendship. The Ukrainian diaspora became the main source of criticism of the celebrated union with Russia, but equally it promoted the idea of a "Greater" Ukraine that included Crimea.[71] The *Ukrainian Bulletin* published a series of articles condemning Moscow's "struggle for the Ukrainian soul" and arguing for Ukrainian ownership of Crimea:

> They [the Ukrainians] know that the Crimea is not a Russian territory but Russian loot. They cannot forget that the Russians by heinous genocide actually eradicated the Crimean Tatars, original inhabitants of the region. It is true that there are now many Ukrainians in Crimea. Some have settled there recently, others have come since the turn of the century. It is also known that for economic and strategic reasons the Crimea has always been an integral part of the Ukrainian mainland.[72]

Ukrainian exiles in West Germany at the Third Congressional Session of the Ukrainian National Assembly in May 1954 called for the right of self-determination of all native Crimean peoples and, thus, reflected on the transfer by pointing to the still unresolved Crimean Tatar question. Ukrainian nationalists feared that given the ethnic Russian majority in the new Crimean oblast of Ukraine, the transfer was an attempt by the Soviet leadership to dilute the notion of "Ukrainianness" in the Soviet Union.[73]

The Soviet Silence about the Transfer

The absence of any references to the transfer of Crimea in contemporary Soviet accounts is rather puzzling. The fact that major political actors, including Khrushchev, who was not averse to describing the minutiae of meetings and events, did not discuss the transfer of Crimea in their memoirs is equally odd. It is possible that Khrushchev wanted to distance himself from his involvement in the transfer. One could argue that perhaps by the time Khrushchev began to write his memoirs the Crimean Tatar question had become so acute that any discussion of Crimea was deemed too sensitive and he was reluctant to admit his role in this question. In 1967 the Soviet leadership finally rehabilitated the Crimean Tatars, albeit without granting them the right to return to Crimea.[74] The silence on Crimea's transfer is analogous to Khrushchev's Secret Speech of 1956, in which he denounced the repressions against the party and the deportation of certain peoples under Stalin, but did not mention the Crimean Tatars, Volga Germans, or Meshketian Turks in his list of deported peoples.

Apart from Khrushchev's own memoirs, which only briefly mention the transfer, the accounts of his key adviser Fedor Burlatsky and other more critically-minded contemporaries, such as Roy Medvedev, are devoid of any mention of the transfer.[75] Khrushchev's son, Sergei Khrushchev, is extremely vague on his father's role in the early post-Stalin years.[76] In a whole range of studies from the 1960s onwards, including both standard items and less-known publications, Crimea does not figure in the descriptions of Khrushchev's rise to power during 1953–57.[77]

Pravda, the central press organ of the Communist Party, and the government newspaper *Izvestiia* also were eerily silent on the transfer. *Izvestiia* reported the ratification of the transfer at the final meeting of the Presidium of the Supreme Soviet of the USSR on 19 February 1954, and included some excerpts from the official speeches. *Pravda*, however, simply published the final decision without reporting any prior discussion.[78] The sole focus of the press was on the 300th anniversary of the Pereiaslav Treaty at the end of May 1954. If the transfer was to commemorate Pereiaslav then it is odd indeed that aside from Voroshilov's statement cited earlier, Crimea played no other visible role in the celebratory events. Either the Crimean "gift" was deliberately played down by the Soviet authorities for its political sensitivity, or it was simply not deemed sufficiently important at the time, given the official Soviet view of Ukraine as being little more than an extension of Russia. The collapse of the Soviet Union was obviously an inconceivable scenario for the political actors, both at the time of the transfer and for another three decades. Thus, the practical relevance of the border change was limited and may simply not have been deemed worthy of much attention. In the absence of a more complete release of archival documents, if they exist, a definitive explanation of the motivations for the 1954 transfer remains elusive. As we will discuss in chapter 5, however, the idea of the transfer was not new in 1954; it was part of a package of resettlement and development policies, and Khrushchev could not have administered the change singlehandedly.

The 300th Anniversary of Pereiaslav and the Symbolism of the Transfer

The Soviet press and other publications from Moscow and Kyiv in 1954 paid great attention to the pomp and circumstance of the celebrations of the Pereiaslav Treaty. Every detail of the extended celebration was obviously carefully staged, including the ideological manipulation of history. Crimea and the territorial transfer, however, are nowhere mentioned in the minutiae of the preparations, which lasted for about a year. The absence of Crimea from the official script suggests that the decision on the transfer was taken hastily in early 1954, or that it was contested within the party.[79] While the Pereiaslav agreement cannot be described as a bilateral agreement between equals, it served as a useful starting-point for the historical myth of Russian-Ukrainian friendship fostered during the Soviet era. Official Soviet history presented the historical "union" as a Ukrainian initiative to voluntarily join the Russian state.[80] Official publications stressed the many ways in which the Ukrainian people benefited from the treaty, for example: "The unification of Ukraine and Russia accelerated the transformation of the Ukrainian people into a nation."[81] The celebrations of 1954 reaffirmed the notion that Ukraine was an adjunct of Russia. Only very occasionally were references made to the transfer of Crimea as a "friendship token."[82]

Crimea's role in the anniversary celebrations was minimal. The photographs of the official celebrations, published in *Pravda*, did not show any Crimean officials. There were none of the usual speeches and statements of support by lower-level officials and "ordinary citizens"—a standard Soviet device to fabricate consultation and input to decision making "from below"—perhaps because none could be found in Crimea. This neglect could also be interpreted as evidence of the relative unimportance of regional officials in the decision. It could also, however, be evidence for the thesis that there was regional party opposition to the transfer of Crimea.[83]

Writings on "Soviet Ukraine" published around 1954 emphasized the significance of the Ukrainian economy as an integral part of the Soviet economy and combined this with rebuttals of any assertion of national Ukrainian aspirations.[84] The choice of words leaves no doubt as to who was considered the predominant group in the Soviet Union: "the older Russian brother" (*starshchii russkii brat*) and "the Great Russian people" (*velikii russkii narod*) are the phrases recurring in the Soviet publications of this period. In Crimea, no serious attempts were made at Ukrainization (*ukrainizatsiia*). While there were moves to establish Ukrainian language classes at school and university level, and a Ukrainian language edition of the newspaper *Krymskaia pravda* was introduced, the overwhelmingly Russophone Crimean population remained the hegemonic ethnic group in the region.[85]

Some scholars view the emphasis on Ukrainian-Russian solidarity as an attempt to elevate Ukraine's image, while at the same time denying its distinct features: "the Ukrainians are not to be concerned with the status of their nation, but rather to glorify Russia's achievements as their own."[86] The envisaged result was subordination: "a

Ukrainian nation, whose entire destiny is to play forever the role of a younger brother and accomplice of Russia, differs little from pre-revolutionary Little Russia—a tribal branch of a single Russian nation."[87] Though not directly linked to the Pereiaslav celebrations in 1954, the later construct of the "Crimean borderland [*ukraina*] of the Russian state" (*Krymskaia ukraina russkogo gosudarstva*) fits this rhetoric of 1954 very well.[88] A large number of contemporary pseudo-scholarly brochures followed a rigid formula of terms to applaud Russian-Ukrainian "brotherhood" (*bratstvo*), "friendship" (*druzhba*), and to glorify the "reunification of Ukraine with Russia" (*vossoedine-niia Ukrainy s Rossiei*). Equally, a whole body of literature devoted to Crimea was published in 1954 and thereafter. It ranged from programmatic brochures titled "Crimea—the Oblast in Which We Live" (*Krym—oblast' v kotoroi my zhivem*) to popular history books and travel guides. This was also a time of massive expansion in Soviet tourism. Crimea was a key destination for Soviet tourism, and information booklets on the region were in great demand. In these publications, the references to the overarching Soviet identity overshadow every other aspect. Soviet identity is used to smother any sense of Crimea's "Ukrainianness."[89]

Three layers of Soviet identity were promoted simultaneously: the Soviet bond throughout the USSR, the common Slavic roots of Russians, Ukrainians, and Belarusians, and the Russian nation and its achievements.[90] Nowhere else did these elements fuse so tangibly as in the official representations of Crimea as the preeminent Soviet holiday resort. In imagining Crimea, the Soviet idea crystallized. The burgeoning popular press and literature on Russian-Ukrainian culture appeared in both languages. Each culture's distinct features were dissolved and the point about unity was illustrated with carefully selected "safe" bits of Ukrainian literature, such as the Soviet promotion of Ukrainian writer Nikolai Gogol's works. Despite the fact that Gogol had chosen to write in Russian, his works were published in Ukrainian to mark the political occasion of 1954.[91]

A repetition of the Pereiaslav celebrations in 1979 (the 325th anniversary) shifted the focus slightly, putting less emphasis on Ukraine's special role but reverting back to the equality of all republics.[92] This shift is an indicator of the development of political dissent and growing national consciousness across the USSR in the 1960s. In the 1970s the Soviet authorities still believed that the 1954 myth had some currency; it just had to be readjusted to fit the political agenda of the day.

Having been deported and written out of history, the Crimean Tatars were excluded from the 1954 celebrations and the transfer of Crimea. They were not specifically mentioned in the official proceedings, documents, the contemporary coverage, as well as the publications on Russian-Ukrainian friendship and Crimea issued around this time. The official interpretation of the 1654 treaty stressed the negative role of the Tatars, claiming that the union of the hetmanate with Muscovy was directed against Polish and Tatar "enemies."[93] The celebration of this "union" three hundred years later automatically reinforced the images of the hostile Tatar "other."[94] Polish-Ukrainian historical links were also simply edited out of official Soviet historiography in line with the Soviet agenda after World War II. According to Stephen Velychenko, the peak of the Kremlin's intervention in Polish affairs was reached between 1948 and 1956, and the 1954 commemorations were accompanied by a wave of state-sponsored anti-Polish historiography:

> Until 1956, under the guise of struggle against Polish nationalism, outlines demanded more references to Russian events, more emphatic positive assessments of anti-Polish revolts in Ukraine, and less mention of Polish events east of the Bug. In general, historians were not to treat events in the area as if they were an integral part of Poland's past.[95]

Despite the anti-Polish overtones of the Pereiaslav myth, Poland sent an official delegation to the Moscow celebrations of the three-hundredth anniversary in 1954, officially endorsing the Soviet policy of a "friendship of peoples."[96]

In the post-Soviet era, the 1954 transfer has been one of the major controversies between Russia and Ukraine. The focus of Ukrainian and Russian historians has remained primarily on the events of 1654, thereby not diverging much from the Soviet pattern of history.[97] The fear of igniting Russian-Ukrainian tensions over the issue may well have blocked an open debate and seems to account for the fact that the official documents of the transfer were published without any further analysis or discussion. Moreover, the historical irony behind the celebratory events of 1954 has been explored neither in the FSU nor in the West. At the time of the Pereiaslav Treaty in 1654 most of the Ukrainian lands were occupied by the Poles, an important fact that had to be ignored to make history fit Soviet purposes.[98] Moreover, in 1654 Crimea was still a stronghold of "anti-Russianness," personified by the Crimean Tatar Khanate.

In the Ukrainian diaspora, and in post-Soviet Ukraine, Hetman Khmel'nyts'kyi has been widely acclaimed as a fighter for Ukrainian independence and a national symbol of heroism.[99] Today this view predominates in Kyiv's official rhetoric, which glosses over the historical ambiguities of Khmel'nyts'kyi's role. After all, Khmel'nyts'kyi's Ukraine was driven into the Pereiaslav "union" with Russia as a defense against the Polish threat because the alternative—cooperation with the Crimean Khanate—had failed to materialize. This historical fact is difficult to reconcile with the common post-Soviet references to Ukrainian–Crimean Tatar friendship commonly employed to counter Russian claims. The dilemma of 1654 illustrates some of the difficulties and contradictions inherent in the current politically motivated rewriting of history.[100]

In the post-Soviet era, Pereiaslav has been seen as both a marker of Ukrainian assertiveness and a sign of Slavic friendship. In his study on the historiography surrounding the Pereiaslav Agreement, John Basarab has demonstrated how the accord has continuously been reinterpreted and captured by different ideologies.[101] On the occasion of the four-hundredth anniversary of Khmel'nyts'kyi's birth in December 1995, for instance, President Leonid Kuchma praised the hetman for unifying the Ukrainian lands and introducing a new concept of the Ukrainian state and nation. Kuchma explicitly marked the Pereiaslav Treaty as the birth of the Ukrainian state and the symbolic entry of Ukraine into international affairs.[102] This attempt to fit 1654 into present-day Ukrainian national historiography jars with the official praise of the poet Taras Shevchenko, who harshly criticized Khmel'nyts'kyi for making the union with Russia. The parallel use of selective and contradictory historical myths is part of everyday reality in post-Soviet Ukraine. It is not unique to postcommunist societies, or modern states generally, but the context of transition gives these contradictory dynamics a particular salience. In the case of post-Soviet Ukraine, the events of 1654 and 1954 are of immediate relevance to the politics of the present.[103]

Conclusion

Two different types of institutional legacies from the Soviet period reinforce the link between territory and ethnicity in Crimea's case. First, Crimea's position within Ukraine's short-lived independent state in the aftermath of the revolution and the precedent of a Crimean autonomy in the Soviet period until 1944, were a de facto recognition of Crimea's ethnoterritorial distinctiveness, including its multiethnicity and the presence of a sizable Tatar minority. This institutional legacy was the backdrop against which the discussions from 1990 onwards about a new autonomy status unfolded. As we will see later, Crimea's post-Soviet autonomy is defined in territorial rather than ethnic terms, but the region's distinctive ethnic makeup arguably provided the rationale for this autonomy status.

Second, the institutional legacy of the 1954 transfer of Crimea to the Ukrainian SSR marks the real beginning of Crimea's link to the Ukrainian state. Whatever the original motivations for this territorial administrative change, and however much it is legally disputed in the relations between Russia and Ukraine, the transfer of Crimea in 1954 has assumed an ethnic dimension in the context of post-Soviet Ukrainian nation building. After 1991 the management of Russian and Crimean Tatar nationalism in Crimea became a major challenge for any attempt at an exclusive ethnic definition of the Ukrainian state or nation.

5   Reassessing the 1954 Transfer of Crimea

A COLLECTION OF OFFICIAL DOCUMENTS about the transfer of Crimea was published in the Russian historical journal *Istoricheskii arkhiv* in 1992, at a politically sensitive time when the mobilization of Russian nationalism was underway.[1] This collection appears to provide the only written documentation of the actual decision to transfer Crimea, since neither the protocols, nor the stenographic records of the three Presidia of the Central Committee of the Communist Party of the Soviet Union (KPSS)—in September 1953, February and March 1954, and June 1954—nor the records of the party conferences of this period mention the transfer.[2] Discussions in the higher party arenas in this period are devoted to one of Khrushchev's great obsessions: the development of agriculture. The official documents published in *Istoricheskii arkhiv* reveal interesting details and raise some questions about the legality of the decision-making process.

It was not a common practice for the Russian and Ukrainian Supreme Soviets to adopt the same decree on different occasions.[3] The Presidium of the Russian Supreme Soviet made its decision on 5 February 1954 by adopting a resolution following the recommendations of the RSFSR Council of Ministers; the Presidium of the Ukrainian Supreme Soviet followed suit on 13 February 1954. The archive contains no record of the speeches given at the Presidium of the Supreme Soviet of the RSFSR on 5 February.[4] Usually, only the names of the participants and the nature of the decision or resolution are recorded, though often brief summaries of the speeches are appended.

The newly released official documents present the decision about the transfer as an administrative act preceded by a well-staged "decision-making process." The formality of the transfer is underscored by a lack of details on the motives. There are slight inconsistencies between the resolution of the Presidium of the Supreme Soviet of the Ukrainian SSR of 13 February and the resolution of 19 February, signed by Dem'ian Korotchenko, chairman of the Presidium of the Supreme Soviet of the Ukrainian SSR. On the whole, the evidence presented in *Istoricheskii arkhiv* confirms that the norm of Soviet decision making of this period was in operation: to plan the decision "from above" and then make it seem to have come "from below." The transfer had all the hallmarks of a typical Soviet decision: no detail seems random, every contribution at the different sessions was planned, and the outcome was evident from the beginning. The procedure, however, was rushed. The number of people involved at each stage of the process and the balance among officials from Moscow, Kyiv, and Crimea suggest that a very limited circle of people around Khrushchev, then general secretary (*Gensek*) of the Central Committee (party leader), Georgii Malenkov, the chairman of the Council of Ministers, and Kliment Voroshilov, chairman of the Presidium of the Supreme Soviet of the USSR, were involved. The planning behind the scenes seems to have been supported by a small group around Leonid Kyrychenko, then a candidate member of the Central Committee, and first secretary of the Central Committee of the Communist Party of Ukraine. The formal procedure for the transfer was complex and repetitive. As was the norm with Soviet decisions, the draft decree of the Presidium of the Central Committee, as the Politburo was then known, remained unchanged in the subsequent resolution and decree of the Presidium of the Supreme Soviet of the USSR. The Presidium of the Central Committee approved its first resolution on the transfer on 25 January 1954. A draft decree was prepared by the Presidium of the Supreme Soviet of the USSR to be signed by Voroshilov and Nikolai Pegov, chairman and secretary respectively.

The Presidium of the Central Committee of the KPSS at the time consisted of nine members and three candidates.[5] It was dominated by Russian nationals, but they did not play the "Russian" nationalist card. They were preoccupied with bureaucratic and technocratic "scientific" programs aimed at streamlining the Soviet economy and agriculture. The official reasons put forward for the incorporation of Crimea into the Ukrainian SSR stressed economic reasons and planning functionalism.

On 1 February 1954, Mikhail Suslov, then a member of the Presidium of the Supreme Soviet of the USSR, and Pegov wrote a memorandum to Khrushchev asking him to confirm the agenda for the session of the Presidium of the Supreme Soviet of the USSR scheduled for 19 February.[6] A list of speakers and their messages was prepared, which Khrushchev affirmed in handwriting on the document. The Presidium of the Supreme Soviet of the RSFSR was then asked by the Council of Ministers of the RSFSR on 5 February to consider the transfer, referred to by the ministers as "expedient." The draft resolution of the Presidium of the Supreme Soviet of the RSFSR, addressed to Voroshilov, was transmitted for approval to the Presidium of the Supreme Soviet of the USSR. It was also issued no later than 5 February. Almost half the members—eleven of the twenty-six—were absent from the meeting of the Presidium of the Supreme Soviet of the RSFSR on 5 February. Since decisions were always adopted unanimously, absence was one of the few ways in the crypto-politics of the early post-Stalin era to express disapproval.

At all the sessions and in all the resolutions, territorial proximity and the close economic and cultural-historical ties between Crimea and Ukraine were given as the main reasons for the transfer. Despite the poor economic situation in Crimea, the transfer was said to be a generous "present" rooted in Soviet Ukrainian-Russian friendship which, it was hoped, would "assist the further development of Ukraine."[7] The Presidium of the Supreme Soviet of the Ukrainian SSR accepted the decision by its Russian counterpart on 13 February. Representatives of the Ukrainian SSR, namely Dem'ian Korotchenko, the chairman of the Presidium of the Supreme Soviet of the Ukrainian SSR, formally asked that the Crimean oblast be included in the Ukrainian SSR, expressed Ukraine's gratitude, and promised that it would seek to foster the future economic and cultural development of Crimea.

One of the most detailed documents available, including extracts from various speeches, is the protocol of the final session of the Presidium of the Supreme Soviet of the USSR on 19 February

1954. Though in attendance, representatives of both the Crimean oblast and its city councils (including the head of the Sevastopol city council) did not speak to the motion. Even if they had spoken, it is unlikely that they would have diverged from the official line. Their presence may be seen as part of the stage managing of a demand "from below" for the transfer. It is odd that there were no speeches from the Crimeans, even if only to approve the transfer. Silence cannot automatically be interpreted as opposition, but the participation of Crimean officials in the transfer was evidently minimal and local activism around the decision was limited, if not altogether absent.

The ultimate decision to transfer Crimea was made in Moscow and formally approved in Kyiv. Confining the decision to the Presidia of the Supreme Soviets (RSFSR, Ukrainian SSR, USSR) limited the discussion and made for a quick passage of the decree.[8] In the end, a total of just over thirty people, including "guests," attended the final Presidium session.

The official documents present the transfer as a decision made within the highest ranks of the party, a decision then filtered through the highest-level state procedures and institutions before being activated by a decree of the Presidium of the Supreme Soviet of the USSR on 19 February 1954 and sealed by a law approved by the Supreme Soviet of the USSR on 26 April 1954.[9] Subsequently, the RSFSR Constitution was amended accordingly. Two questions—whether there were legal irregularities in the procedure, and whether the Constitution of the RSFSR authorized the Presidium of the Supreme Soviet of the RSFSR to initiate the border change—are difficult to answer, but the law of the Supreme Soviet of the USSR in April 1954 was certainly in line with Soviet constitutional practice regarding border changes.

Anecdotal evidence reinforces the impression that the decision about the transfer was made by a clique around Khrushchev in Moscow and Kyiv without the Crimean officials being informed. L. G. Mezentsev, second secretary of the Crimean *obkom* at the time, remembered Pavel Titov, the first secretary of the Crimean party, being summoned to Moscow in January 1954, where he was informed of the decision on the transfer. Apparently, Titov protested and was immediately replaced by the Ukrainian Dmytro Polians'kyi.[10] The transfer might simply have been an opportune moment to remove

Titov, but the temporal coincidence supports the interpretation that there was opposition to the transfer in Crimean party circles. At the Crimean party conference in March 1954, Polians'kyi simply introduced Crimea as "the youngest oblast of the Ukrainian republic." In line with the rhetoric at the center, the transfer was referred to as an act of friendship. Mentioning geographic, economic, and cultural links, Polians'kyi emphasized the historical ties between Crimea and Ukraine and the joint effort of the Russian and Ukrainian people to protect Crimea from common enemies. He likewise expressed hope that the transfer would help to spur the necessary development in Crimea, which, in turn, could have a positive effect on the Ukrainian SSR as a whole. Given that Polians'kyi had only just been appointed first secretary, he could easily criticize the regional party organs under his predecessor and hold them responsible for the lagging development.

Claims about the illegality of the transfer have recently found support from documents in the newly opened archives. In 1992 Evgenii Ambartsumov, deputy head of the Russian Supreme Soviet Committee on International Affairs, said that the archives had substantiated the claim that Khrushchev had already announced the decision to transfer Crimea on a visit to Kyiv in January 1954; that is, after the Politburo decision but before the Soviet procedures had run their course. Ambartsumov also noted Khrushchev's comment to *Pravda* Editor Dmitrii Shepilov about the pressure Kyrychenko and other Ukrainian officials had exerted with regard to a quick transfer of Crimea. Khrushchev apparently admitted to the Ukrainian leaders that he could not deny them Crimea, and that he needed their support in the intensifying power struggle in Moscow. Ambartsumov argues that the decision to transfer Crimea was illegal, since the RSFSR Constitution at the time required that any decision on a territorial change had to be taken by the highest organ—the entire RSFSR Supreme Soviet, not just its Presidium. He also quotes article 18 of the 1936 Constitution of the USSR, according to which the territory of a union republic could not be changed without its own consent.[11] Similar provisions in article 16 of the RSFSR Constitution and article 19 of the Constitution of the Ukrainian SSR have been cited in order to show that the transfer contravened Soviet law.[12] Ambartsumov claims that his committee, which sought to defend the rights of Russians in Crimea,[13] intended neither to provoke Ukraine nor to seek border revisions, since neither the Russian nor Ukrainian people had any real impact on the top-level decision of 1954. This claim, however, had to ring hollow in the ears of Ukrainian politicians. In particular, his analogy between the transfer of Crimea and the infamous Molotov-Ribbentrop Pact reinforces the perception of illegality, historical injustice, and the loss of national territory.

The USSR Constitution of 1936 indeed stipulates that alterations of boundaries between union republics fall under the jurisdiction of the highest organs of the USSR, namely the Supreme Soviet, unless specified otherwise, and that the territory of the union republics may not be changed without their consent.[14] The RSFSR Constitution, in its variants of 1948 and 1952, declares that the establishment of new ASSRs, oblasts, and *krais* within the RSFSR must be confirmed not only by the highest state organs of the RSFSR, but also by the Supreme Soviet of the USSR.[15] It also includes a general article stating that the territory of the RSFSR cannot be changed without "the consent of the RSFSR" without, however, specifying exactly the procedure by which consent is to be expressed and what is meant by "RSFSR."[16] Since the Supreme Soviet of the RSFSR is defined as the highest state organ of the RSFSR, it is reasonable to assume that its decision would have qualified as "the consent of the RSFSR." The Constitution also stipulates that the Presidium of the Supreme Soviet of the RSFSR is responsible to the Supreme Soviet of the RSFSR. Consequently, the fact that the 1954 transfer decision was not approved by the RSFSR Supreme Soviet as a whole means that it contravened Soviet constitutional law. Although many Soviet constitutional provisions existed only on paper and could easily be overruled by party decisions, the nonadherence to procedural norms suggests extreme haste, if not a subterfuge conducted for some underlying political motive. With hindsight, post-Soviet political actors have tended to imbue Soviet constitutional provisions with more significance and legitimacy than they had enjoyed during the Soviet period. Given the political elasticity in the application of Soviet law, it seems more important to understand the context in which decisions about the territorial makeup of the USSR were made, how these institutional changes were interpreted and operationalized, and what momentum they developed over time.

The territorial setup of the Ukrainian SSR underwent further adjustments in 1954, but these did not involve interrepublican transfers. The small Ismailovskii oblast, for example, was incorporated into Odesa oblast, while some *raions* (districts) of the old Odesa oblast were reassigned to the bordering Kirovohrad oblast.[17] The goal was simply to correct an extreme variation in oblast size. The procedure for such territorial swaps was more straightforward: the Central Committee of the Communist Party of Ukraine forwarded a draft resolution in the name of the Presidium of the Supreme Soviet of the Ukrainian SSR, along with some supporting documentation about the administrative changes, to Khrushchev at the Central Committee of the KPSS, where the decision was approved. Another administrative creation of that time was Cherkasy oblast, made up of parts of the neighboring oblasts of Kyiv, Kirovohrad, and Poltava. The official explanation for these territorial changes was that they would strengthen Kyiv oblast, improve the administration of far-flung *raions*, and administratively integrate economically linked areas.[18]

A more apposite comparison could be drawn with the redrawing of boundaries in the Caucasus. The Chechen and Ingush peoples had been deported to Central Asia in February 1944 on grounds of alleged collaboration with the Nazi regime,[19] the same grounds that had been used for deporting the Crimean Tatars. As with Crimea, the Chechen-Ingush ASSR was abolished in 1944, losing parts of its territory to Georgia, North Ossetia, and Dagestan; the remainder was turned into a territorially defined oblast. New settlers—Russians, Ukrainians, Ossetians, Dagestani, and others—were brought into Chechnya to replace the deported workforce.[20] Khrushchev's Secret Speech of 1956 rehabilitated the Chechens and Ingush, and in response to the growing number of Chechen and Ingush returnees, the Soviet regime conceded the restoration of a Chechen-Ingush ASSR in 1957 on the basis of the Grozny oblast, which had replaced the old ASSR. Districts belonging to Stavropol *krai*, the Dagestani ASSR, and the North Ossetian ASSR—most of which did not originally form part of the Chechen and Ingush homeland—were added to the territory and thereby partially diluted the ethnic Chechen majority in the ASSR. The procedure through which the regional map was redrawn in the North Caucasus resembled the interrepublican transfer of Crimea. The changes were specified in a decree of the Presidium of the Supreme Soviet of the RSFSR rather than the full Supreme Soviet of the RSFSR.[21] Again, as with Crimea, the reason for this unconstitutional mode of transfer could hinge on the political sensitivity of the territorial changes or merely be a result of undue haste.

The Role of Khrushchev

Khrushchev's Ukrainian descent is often thought to account for his interest in Ukrainian affairs.[22] Whatever Khrushchev's personal thoughts were, he adhered closely to the ideology of the day, according to which Ukraine was in everlasting union with Russia. His own background seemed to confirm this union: he was born in an area that later fell within the Soviet Kursk oblast in Russia, but was brought up in what became the Soviet Donetsk oblast in eastern Ukraine. His career spanned positions in Ukraine and Russia. Khrushchev had risen to the ranks of the party leadership through the patronage of Lazar Kaganovich, one of Stalin's most loyal associates, who was known for his unquestioning obedience. Khrushchev's career trajectory in the party apparatus was closely intertwined with Stalin's rise to power. Working in the propaganda department of the Ukrainian Communist Party, Khrushchev came to the attention of Kaganovich when the latter was first secretary of the Communist Party of the Ukrainian SSR from 1925 to 1928. When Kaganovich was moved by Stalin to leading positions in the party apparatus in Moscow in the late 1920s and early 1930s, Khrushchev followed in his wake. In 1930 Khrushchev worked in the Moscow *obkom* apparatus and became first secretary in 1935. In 1938, Stalin appointed him general secretary of the Communist Party of Ukraine. Stalin viewed and presented Khrushchev as an "authentic" Ukrainian who could be called upon to perform his native folksongs and dances at Stalin's dacha parties and was the butt of Stalin's jokes. Khrushchev skillfully played the court jester role. It was no coincidence that, as a Ukrainian, Khrushchev was put in charge of the 1930s purges targeting Ukrainian "bourgeois nationalism" and "national communism." These purges he implemented rigorously. Khrushchev's leadership role in Ukraine from 1938 to 1949 allowed him to build up patronage networks that proved crucial to his rise to power in the post-Stalin leadership struggles of the mid-1950s.

Khrushchev's son-in-law and unofficial foreign policy adviser, Aleksei Adzhubei, published one of the few insider accounts of the events preceding the transfer of Crimea.[23] Accompanying Khrushchev on a trip to Crimea in October 1953, he observed Khrushchev's impressions and increasing impatience with the poor economic conditions in Crimea, the widespread dissatisfaction of its population (particularly among the Russians who had been resettled in the region after World War II), and the still visible traces of wartime destruction. According to Adzhubei, Khrushchev's discontent with what he saw in Crimea provoked one of the spontaneous reactions for which he became famous.[24] On the spot, he decided to fly to Kyiv on a military plane that he saw sitting in an airfield by the roadside. At the subsequent dinner with party officials in Kyiv, most of whom he knew from his time as head of the Communist Party of Ukraine, he voiced the idea of the border change as part of the plan to rebuild and develop Crimea. Adzhubei's account reduces the motivation behind the transfer to a spontaneous decision based on an efficiency argument. Furthermore, it attributes the idea and initiative behind the transfer squarely to Khrushchev. Adzhubei stresses that the details of the transfer of Crimea were not discussed on this occasion. As far as it is possible to judge, the Crimean Tatar issue remained absent from these informal discussions.[25]

Khrushchev had first voiced the idea of the transfer some years before, in 1944, according to Lavrentii Pogrebnoi, an apparatchik close to Nikolai Shvernik, the first secretary of the All-Union Central Council of Trade Unions (VTsSPS) and head of the Presidium of the Supreme Soviet of the RSFSR in the 1940s.[26] At the time, Stalin had ordered Khrushchev, then first secretary of the Communist Party of Ukraine and head of the Ukrainian Sovnarkom, to relocate one hundred thousand Ukrainians to Russia to help with the postwar reconstruction. Pogrebnoi had to obtain Khrushchev's written consent for this order. Many years later, he vividly recalls Khrushchev's angry reaction, how he swore, cursed, and complained about Russia pulling people away from Ukraine when Ukraine itself was in as much, if not greater, disarray. Khrushchev confided that, on his most recent visit to Moscow, he had proposed the transfer of Crimea to Ukraine in exchange for the resettlement of Ukrainians to Russia. From memory, Pogrebnoi quotes Khrushchev's recollection of his meeting in Moscow: "Ukraine is in collapse and everything is pulled out of her. What about giving her Crimea? How they cursed me and what a hard time they gave me after that." Khrushchev had to concede the resettlement of the Ukrainians to Russia, but is said to have added: "The people I will provide, but Crimea I will have, no matter what."[27] Pogrebnoi interprets the decision to transfer Crimea soon after Khrushchev became first secretary of the Central Committee as part of his personal crusade to avenge the unsatisfactory meeting of 1944. There is, however, no other proof for Pogrebnoi's claim that Khrushchev's decision was rooted in his national loyalty to Ukraine, hurt pride, and sense of injustice.

The various fragments of evidence suggest that the idea of the transfer of Crimea can, in fact, be traced back to the 1940s. As early as September 1943, a comprehensive study on Crimea, commissioned by the Central Committee of the Communist Party of Ukraine under Khrushchev, had been prepared by I. N. Romanenko, a senior research associate of the Institute of Economics at the Ukrainian Academy of Sciences.[28] It presents Crimea's geographical, socioeconomic, and multinational profile, and it sums up the region's history over the last fifty years, in particular its changing ethnic composition. Khrushchev must have found a stimulus for, or confirmation of, his plan in this study, which stresses Crimea's historical links with the rest of Ukraine and especially emphasizes that the population of Ukrainian descent had begun to consider itself part of the Russian nation. A further summary of Crimea's administrative structure and economic potential was prepared in 1943, probably in conjunction with the report mentioned above. In the changed political, economic, and ideological climate in the 1950s, Khrushchev revived the idea and helped to rush it through Soviet legal procedures.

Resettlement of Ukrainians in Crimea

Although most studies stress the large influx of Ukrainians into Crimea following the incorporation into the Ukrainian SSR,[29] substantial numbers of Ukrainians were settled in Crimea well before the 1954 transfer. The history of these early Ukrainian settlers has not been sufficiently researched. In August 1944, a resolution by the USSR State Committee of Defense ordered the resettlement of nine thousand Ukrainian collective farm peasants to Crimea. The resolution was followed up by a decree by the Sovnarkom of the Ukrainian SSR and the Central Committee of the Communist Party of Ukraine on 18 August 1944 on the resettlement of nine thousand kolkhozniks, mainly from northern and central Ukraine.[30] The main resettlement areas in 1945–47 were the *raions* of Alushta, Balaklava, Bakhchisarai, Bilohirsk, Kuibyshev (Simferopol), Staryi Krym, Sudak, and Yalta.[31] The resettlement program was to compensate for the labor shortage caused by the deportation of Crimean Tatars.[32] Each farm reportedly received a one-off payment of 2,500 rubles as compensation for the move.[33] The logistics of the resettlement seem more like that of a deportation than a voluntary move.[34] The flood of documented complaints by the new Crimean settlers shows that their living conditions were worse than on the kolkhoz farms from which they had come.[35]

There are slight discrepancies in the documentation regarding the number of resettled people, but the party report—according to which 10,017 people had arrived in Crimea by 3 October 1944—seems to be a fair estimate.[36] The resettlement programs continued up to and beyond the transfer of Crimea.[37] By the end of 1953, the plan for the resettlement in Crimea had been exceeded by 11 percent according to the official reports.[38] The USSR plan for 1954 envisaged the resettlement of a total of 22,075 families from western regions of Ukraine—14,075 of them outside the Ukrainian Republic, and 1,750 of them in the Crimean oblast.[39] At the beginning of March 1954, an internal party report addressed to Kyrychenko indicates that significantly fewer families from western Ukraine were resettled than had been planned.[40] The slowing pace hints at the pressure that had to be exerted to move people. The continuation of the resettlement program was linked to the expansion of agriculture in the region, but the targeting of western Ukrainian farmers for resettlement suggests that this also had a political motive, as an attempt to undermine the recorded anti-party sentiment, underground activity, and resulting low productivity levels in western Ukrainian collective farms.[41] The resettlement program faced an additional challenge: in response to bad living conditions and unfulfilled promises, many newly settled farmers returned to their old homes.[42] By 1949 alone, 10,210 families (56.5 percent of the new settlers) had already left Crimea.[43]

The Political Background of the Transfer

The transfer of Crimea occurred during a period defined by collective leadership and destalinization when a power struggle was looming. The cursory claim that Khrushchev "gave away" Crimea implies that he had already established a firm position of power by February 1954, only a year after Stalin's death. This assumption is easy to disprove.[44] As a means of protection against possible rivals, Stalin himself had deliberately avoided naming a successor or institutionalizing a smooth procedure for succession. His death created a political vacuum, in which "none of his heirs could claim the empty throne and, if necessary, support such a claim by force."[45] Instead, the power vacuum was filled by so-called "collective leadership," with primary positions changing hands among a number of individuals, all wishing to limit each other's power. In a complex struggle, an oligarchic elite with delicately balanced interests formed.[46] The term "collective leadership" inadequately conveys the undercurrent of competition and insecurity framing decision making in the early post-Stalin period.

The elite consensus was firm on certain issues: for example, the need to reassert the party's role. Khrushchev became first party secretary in September 1953. His post differed from that held by Stalin, since the position of the general secretary had been abolished. Initially there were no significant anti-Khrushchev alliances in the leadership, because he was not considered to be much of a threat. The official listings by rank of the party hierarchy placed Khrushchev fifth—after Malenkov, Molotov, Beria, and Kaganovich.[47] The putsch against Beria and his subsequent execution in December 1953 elevated Khrushchev to number two—after Malenkov—in terms of real power. The rebuilding of the party's power by extension enhanced Khrushchev's authority as party leader. The "Malenkov era" lasted from August 1953 until April 1954, when the struggle between Malenkov and Khrushchev came to a head. The decision to transfer Crimea came just as Khrushchev was launching his first attacks against Malenkov's agricultural and reform policies. Khrushchev's virgin lands campaign, initiated in March 1954, made him the undisputed leader and resulted in the ouster of Malenkov, who was replaced as chairman of the Council of Ministers "at his own request" in February 1955. Nevertheless, it was not until the Central Committee was elected at the 20th Congress of the Communist Party in 1956 that the real shift occurred in favor of Khrushchev and his supporters, paving the way for his defeat of the "anti-party group" in 1957.[48]

Khrushchev's destalinization had a clear political rationale: it was a means of political struggle against his opponents, the most dangerous of whom had been closer to Stalin than Khrushchev himself. In such a tense and conspiratorial environment, it seems unlikely that any decision, including the transfer of Crimea, was made regardless of the cutthroat power struggle within the political elite. That Khrushchev started criticizing the Presidium of the Central Committee of the Communist Party as early as February 1954—at the time when the decision about Crimea was being made—illustrates that his political ambitions were beginning to take shape. At that time, however, he was not yet in a position to impose his personal will on the Presidium. Thus, whether the initiative behind the transfer lay with Khrushchev or not, high-level opposition to the transfer was evidently absent.

Given that Khrushchev himself later apparently hinted at demands voiced by Ukrainian party secretaries to make Crimea part of the Ukrainian SSR,[49] the transfer could be seen in connection with his proposal to allow Ukraine its own armed forces, a proposal that Malenkov rejected but that was obviously an attempt to attract the support of the Ukrainian Communist Party in the ongoing power struggle.[50] Given Khrushchev's involvement in the 1938 purges in Ukraine, a genuine pro-Ukrainian nationalist disposition on his part is questionable, although he may have softened somewhat Stalin's anti-Ukrainian policies in the 1940s and 1950s. Rather, Khrushchev played on his Ukrainian image for pragmatic political purposes. While Crimea was in the process of being "gifted" to Ukraine, the Soviet armed forces and NKVD were in the final stages of their campaigns to eradicate the nationalist Ukrainian Insurgent Army (UPA). Significantly, in May 1954, in the midst of the Pereiaslav celebrations, the Soviet media announced the execution by military firing squad of a prominent émigré leader of the Organization of Ukrainian Nationalists (OUN), Vasyl' Okhrymovych, who had been captured by the NKVD in early 1953. There was a disproportionately large share of Ukrainians in Soviet prison camps and the regime was clearly concerned about a Ukrainian nationalist resurgence as the dismantling of the gulag system got under way.[51]

Ever the tactician, Khrushchev fostered and used the support of the Ukrainian party apparatus, especially through his close ally Kyrychenko. Further support came from Dem'ian Korotchenko and Aleksandr Korneichuk, both of whom were members of the Central Committee of the KPSS.[52] The timing of the power struggle with Malenkov lends plausibility to the thesis that Crimea was a "gift in return" for support from the leaders of the Communist Party of Ukraine. The stenograms of the Ukrainian party conferences in 1949, 1952, and 1954, however, disclose no clues about the party's interest in the transfer. A detailed study of the administrative setup of the Crimean oblast—its demographic structure and economic conditions, including the number of enterprises in different ministerial branches and their plan for fulfillment—was prepared for the Ukrainian Central Committee in January 1954.[53] This document appears to be one of the few indications that the Ukrainian leadership was preparing for the possibility of a border change.

The transfer of Crimea fits a number of post-Stalinist trends and policies. This good fit does not ex post facto inject necessity into the decision or the procedure behind the transfer, but it goes some way towards explaining the speed of the process and the effectiveness of the myth of Khrushchev's single-handedly making a "gift" to Ukraine in 1954. As he rose to power, Khrushchev skillfully molded his personal image, creating a cult closely tied to Lenin and, initially, even Stalin. His leadership cult was first exposed on a large scale during the Pereiaslav celebrations of Russian-Ukrainian unity in May 1954. In his speeches in Kyiv and Moscow, Kyrychenko, the Ukrainian first secretary, paid tribute to Khrushchev's outstanding achievements: Khrushchev personally came to symbolize the celebrated unity of Ukraine and Russia.[54] The transfer of Crimea as a symbol and proof of this unity became an integral part of the myth.

During the Khrushchev era, Ukraine's position as *secunda inter pares* within the USSR became more pronounced. In return for loyalty, it was assigned the role of Moscow's "little brother" and the Ukrainian party elite was fully co-opted into the Soviet leadership. The overt state-sponsored Russian nationalism of World War II was replaced by "Soviet patriotism." Ukraine's size, location, and resources, its devastating experiences during the war, and its cultural proximity to Russia were important factors that made it the most obvious choice for consolidating a Slav-dominated KPSS and USSR. The events and speeches during the Pereiaslav celebrations must be seen within this context.[55] The transfer of Crimea drew Ukraine closer to Moscow. Soviet-Russian interests in Crimea, particularly in Sevastopol, were never called into question. Furthermore, the economic rationale behind Crimea's transfer fits Khrushchev's drive for economic and administrative efficiency from 1954 onwards, something he sought to achieve through economic decentralization.[56]

Integrating Crimea into Soviet Ukraine

In connection with the development of Crimea's agriculture the number of new settlers was continuously increased: altogether 31,392 families reportedly moved to Crimea between 1954 and 1960; but 5,345 families returned to their previous homes between 1955 and 1958 due to low pay and lack of housing and provisions.[57] That the repopulation of Crimea was no easy task in postwar conditions is clear: by 1959, the population of Crimea totaled 1,201,500 people, just seventy-four thousand more than at the outbreak of World War II.[58] The 1959 and 1970 census data show that various efforts were made to settle Ukrainians in the region, but the increase in Russian settlers was proportionally the same. Thus, the overall ethnic balance remained approximately the same.[59] The increase in Ukrainian language high school teachers from two in 1950–51 to 345 in 1955–56 reflects the introduction of obligatory Ukrainian-language classes at school, possibly to cope with the needs of the new settlers in Crimea.[60] The Ukrainian authorities attempted to partially "ukrainize," for example, by increasing the use of Ukrainian-language signs on administrative buildings and shops, and by renaming some streets in Crimean cities and towns to commemorate famous Ukrainians. A Moscow-sponsored official drive to Russify Ukrainian educational policy, however, overshadowed these largely symbolic moves.

Following the transfer, efforts to improve the economic and social conditions in Crimea increased. On 7 April 1954, a group of officials from different levels of the Soviet hierarchy, including Mykola Pidhirnyi, then deputy secretary of the Ukrainian Communist Party, and Dmytro Polians'kyi, first secretary of the Crimean Communist Party, handed over a collection of materials to Kyrychenko in conjunction with a draft resolution about the economic development of Crimea.[61] The Central Committee of the Communist Party of Ukraine addressed the all-union authorities on 10 April 1954 with suggestions about the future development of agriculture, towns, and sanatoria in the Crimean oblast.[62] To intensify construction work, expand the collective farm system, and increase agricultural production, 17,800 new settler families were deemed necessary in the period from 1954 to 1958. These plans—as well as the collection of materials mentioned above—included Sevastopol as part of the Crimean planned economic development. Although it had enjoyed special status as a city of "federal jurisdiction" (viz. under the direct control of the USSR authorities) since 1948, economic plans and other decisions affecting Sevastopol often followed the same administrative channels as the rest of Crimea. This practice contradicts post-1991 Russian claims that Sevastopol had always been administered separately by Moscow irrespective of the transfer.[63] There is sufficient archival evidence to suggest that the legal status of Sevastopol within the USSR after 1954 did not always match the practice whereby in administrative matters it was governed by Ukraine.[64]

Soviet statistical data is problematic and can, at best, indicate trends. Tracing economic developments in Crimea over time helps to measure the extent to which the transfer had an impact on the peninsula. Kyiv's expenditures on Crimea over a period of almost forty years adds weight to post-Soviet Ukraine's claim to legitimate sovereignty over the territory. Of course, Kyiv did not enjoy economic or political independence when dealing with Crimea. Any decision initiated at the republic level had to be approved by Moscow. Nevertheless, as part of Khrushchev's decentralization drive in the mid-1950s, the primary responsibility for enterprises shifted downwards to the republic, oblast, and *raion* level and, thus, affected the majority of Crimean enterprises.[65] A detailed five-year plan (1954–58) aimed to reach and even exceed prewar levels in all spheres of agricultural and industrial production.[66] From the required investment listed, it is not evident where the money would come from: the all-union budget or the budget of the Ukrainian SSR. Labor was still a scarce resource despite the resettlement programs. These detailed plans described a bleak state of affairs in Crimea at the time of the transfer. Crimea had fallen behind other regions of the RSFSR and Ukrainian SSR due to a lack of investment, labor shortages, and poor planning. The post-1954 effort to channel resources and rebuild Crimea reads like a retrospective confirmation of the arguments for efficiency that had been offered as the official rationale for the transfer. Ten years after the war, that effort seems to have been the first serious attempt at reconstruction and modernization.[67] In September 1954, the Central Committee of the Communist Party of Ukraine received a report about persisting deficiencies in the work of the party organs and soviets in the Crimean oblast.[68] The report gives a good insight into the attempts by the Ukrainian authorities to secure more direct administrative control and more effective planning in Crimea. The report refers to several fact-finding visits to Crimea by Ukrainian party and state officials.[69] These visits are another hint that the decision to transfer Crimea in early 1954 was sudden. Had it been long-deliberated, these fact-finding missions would have taken place before the actual border change occurred. The report paints a particularly pessimistic picture of the state of industry, agriculture, party activities, and the development of the region. For example, it criticized weak implementation of plans and the lack of control by the party organs. The party committees at the *obkom* and *raikom* levels were singled out for criticism, no doubt in anticipation of personnel changes.[70]

Annual industrial growth rates developed evenly, without a noticeable effect after the transfer.[71] There is no indication of a sudden increase, or an improvement of the general economic situation, despite the official declarations to this effect at the time of the transfer. After a serious drop in 1954, agricultural production started to pick up again but then decreased considerably by 1956. This fluctuation seems to be the outcome of overall agricultural policies rather than a reflection of Ukrainian or Crimean policies. Overall, most of the envisaged capital investment in Crimea in 1955–57 was earmarked for industries and for social and cultural infrastructure

projects that fell within the orbit of Moscow-based USSR ministries, and only about one-seventh came under the jurisdiction of
the Ukrainian ministries.[72] An increase in capital investment in the
oblast from 809.1 million rubles to 951.3 million rubles in 1956 suggests
that the state paid more attention to Crimea.[73] The construction
of the Dnipro Canal, supplying Crimea with much-needed water,
accounts for this increase. The canal was seen as the key to Crimea's
further development, a compensation for the lack of water resources
for agriculture, local industry, and private households.[74] Although
the centrally controlled construction of the canal was not dependent on the transfer of Crimea to the Ukrainian SSR, the canal itself
increased Crimea's economic dependence on Ukraine.[75] It constituted a material and psychological "Soviet-Ukrainian investment" in
Crimea. The canal exemplified the new administrative relationship
between Ukrainian and Crimean institutions in decisions affecting
Crimea. The Central Committee of Ukraine had to submit measures
to the Central Committee of the Communist Party in Moscow.[76]
While, on the one hand, an additional step was thus inserted into
an already complicated bureaucracy, on the other, a new level of
administration—one in closer contact with the region—now bore at
least some responsibility and proposed issues for Moscow's agenda.
Gosplan USSR and the Soviet Ministry of Finance had to allocate
funds from the USSR budget to the Ukrainian Council of Ministers
before the funds could reach their final destination.[77] Moreover, the
Council of Ministers of the RSFSR was to continue its work on the
canal through 1954–55 with the financial means earmarked by the
Gosplan USSR. The total sums assigned to RSFSR organs involved
in the construction are clearly below those of the Ukrainian SSR
and primarily confined to the completion of the excavation work.
While the relevant resolutions single out the Council of Ministers
of the Ukrainian SSR as the primary institution to receive money
and coordinate the project, only the USSR ministries, for example
the Ministries of Defense, Internal Affairs, Construction, and various sectors of production, are assigned concrete tasks. Within the
hierarchy of decision making, the line of vertical power now ran
from Moscow to Kyiv, and then to Crimea. Thus, secretary of the
Crimean *obkom*, Polians′kyi, proposed suggestions—mainly about
additional funds needed to complete the construction of the canal

and housing—to the Central Committee of the Communist Party of Ukraine, asking Kyrychenko to refer the suggestions to the Soviet Council of Ministers.[78]

Shortly after the decreed transfer of Crimea, Polians'kyi wrote to Kyrychenko on 15 March 1954 to ask the Central Committee of the Communist Party to impose a general ban on the return of the deported peoples to Crimea.[79] He copied his draft letter to Khrushchev. This letter reveals that, from the very outset of the new administrative order, the Ukrainian and new Crimean political leadership were anxious to put an early stop to any return of the Tatars. It also illustrates that although Ukraine had gained administrative responsibility, Moscow retained final authority. The Central Committee of the Ukrainian party, acted as the intermediary authority. In April 1954, for example, Kyrychenko passed on a toned-down version of Polians'kyi's letter to Khrushchev, informing him about the problems arising from the return of deported Armenians, Greeks, and Bulgarians, who by reclaiming their confiscated property caused a standoff with the new settlers in Crimea.[80] Kyrychenko suggested treating the deportees like other settlers, provided they agreed to settle not in Crimea but in other designated parts of the USSR.

Conclusion

The newly available archival material suffices at least to challenge the conventional wisdom about the transfer of Crimea to the jurisdiction of the Ukrainian SSR in 1954, namely the widely held Soviet (and Western) myth that it was Khrushchev's sole decision to make the transfer as a "gift" in commemoration of Pereiaslav. Khrushchev played the central role, particularly in conceiving the idea and timing its implementation, but he as yet lacked the political strength to impose such a radical change unilaterally. Constitutional and procedural ambiguities attached to the transfer have fed into the post-Soviet Russian-Ukrainian debate about the legality of the transfer of Crimea. Moreover, the transfer began a process whereby Crimea was Ukrainized in some key aspects: Crimea was henceforth part of Ukraine within the Soviet command-administrative structure; there was a substantial resettlement of Ukrainians from other parts of Ukraine in Crimea; the region was integrated into the central planning mechanism of the Ukrainian SSR; and the first major infra-structural linkages (such as the construction of the Dnipro Canal) were developed.

Part 1 of this book has examined the historical-cultural and institutional particularities of Crimea. Part 2 will explore how these legacies shaped the potential for conflict when they became part of a nationalist and regionalist agenda during the late Soviet and post-Soviet periods.

PART TWO

6   The Last Soviet ASSR: The Mobilization of Crimean Separatism

WHEN A TERRITORY HAS A COMPLEX HISTORICAL and institutional legacy it offers elements that may both ignite and defuse conflict. The cultural, historical, and institutional aspects of Crimean politics—its multiethnicity, the competing claims to Crimea as a homeland or national symbol, and the history of a territorial autonomy status with ethnic overtones—were associated primarily with a high potential for conflict during the period of transition from the Soviet Union to an independent Ukraine. An uneasy mixture of old and new structures and actors defines the arena of postimperial and postcommunist politics. This setting provides ideal conditions for political mobilization around nationalist and separatist regional demands. The legacies are only one part of the fabric of sentiments and mobilizational strategies. It is not the legacies per se or the transition environment that fully accounts for the occurrence of conflict or conflict prevention. Rather it is the interaction of the two elements, resulting from the opportunities opening up for new actors to come to the fore and for new kinds of mobilization to emerge, that drives political action. The postcommunist transition saw an aggressive competition between old and new structures, elites, and ideas.

The issue of autonomy for Crimea became politically salient during Mikhail Gorbachev's liberalization, well before Ukraine had declared itself an independent state. After the Belovezha Accord of December 1991, which sealed the breakup of the USSR, Crimea, as a territory ethnically dominated by Russians and strongly adhering to Soviet values, suddenly found itself within the newly democratizing independent state of Ukraine. The issues of Crimea's jurisdiction and status quickly and forcefully emerged as the focal points of political mobilization and became a major challenge for Ukraine. In Crimea there were two cycles of mobilization. First, the period from 1990 to 1994 straddles the collapse of the Soviet Union and the early course of state and nation building in Ukraine. This period saw the rapid rise of a regional Russian nationalist political mobilization that culminated in a push for Crimean separatism. Second, the period from late 1994 to 1998 saw the tide of separatist mobilization recede as speedily as it had emerged, and following protracted negotiations the Ukrainian parliament adopted a special constitutional autonomy status for Crimea in December 1998.

What is striking about the relations between Ukraine and Crimea is that the elite interaction primarily centered on constitution making and a muddling-through for a new stable consensus on how the status of Crimea would be managed within the new democratic Ukraine. The deliberations between political forces over Crimea were a textbook version of a negotiated elite pact during transition, albeit a very protracted one that involved different national and regional elites over almost a decade-long process. Part 2 of this book traces the processes of separatist mobilization and negotiation over Crimea not only as a dimension of Ukrainian domestic politics, but also as a dimension of Ukrainian-Russian relations in the post-Soviet period.

Gorbachev's Liberalization and the Periphery

Crimea was an administrative unit on the periphery of the Ukrainian SSR and the Soviet Union as a whole, and it was at the fringe of the political struggles of perestroika. In the ferment of perestroika Crimea's slow political awakening can be attributed to its party organization, which had a long-standing reputation for conservatism and unquestioning conformity—characteristics embedded by decades of close interaction between Crimea's political elites and the highest echelons of the Soviet nomenklatura, which regularly vacationed and often retired in the region. The "upward mobility" of many party officials in Crimea who moved to positions in Moscow without a detour via Kyiv further testifies to Crimea's close integration into the Moscow-based party and soviet structures.[1] Thus, even when the region found itself at the epicenter of the putsch of August 1991, when Gorbachev was held prisoner at the presidential retreat in Foros, the Crimean leadership and the population at large remained passive and "slept" through the whole episode, no doubt hoping that the putsch would succeed.[2]

Crimean politics was only slowly shaken out of its Soviet inertia. The strands of a Russian nationalist regional political mobilization began to crystallize in the perestroika period. The opening up of the past accelerated an intelligentsia-led nationalist resurgence across the USSR, which after the Chornobyl catastrophe in April 1986 proliferated in the form of "econational" movements. This was the form in which Crimean identity as a political issue first surfaced in the mid-1980s. The Crimean Green movement promoted an ecology debate that questioned both Kyiv's and Moscow's right to impose their policies on the region. Environmental concerns and the protest against Moscow's reckless economic policies were inextricably linked with the growing political claims to nationally defined territories and self-rule decision-making powers. Indeed, "self-rule" (*samoupravlenie*) was one of Gorbachev's slogans, but this was empowered by Green nationalists. The Crimean Greens formed in opposition to the construction of a nuclear power station in the northeast of the peninsula. Its leadership was initially composed of scientists and the literary elite of Simferopol. Protests got under way in 1987, and by early 1988 the idea of protecting the Crimean environment was high on the regional political agenda. The regional Communist Party organization, after an initially ambiguous stance, hijacked the environmental movement to strengthen its control over the region. Some party members and others infiltrated the environmental movement, triggering the exit of many of its founding scientists and writers. As a result, the movement changed "from an independent intellectual organization that was willing to challenge the region's political elite to a relatively docile and apolitical organization."[3]

In the spring of 1989, the Crimean *obkom* and the Crimean Supreme Soviet imposed a moratorium on the construction of the nuclear power station, even though the authority in energy questions lay with the USSR ministries and the central party organs in Moscow. It was thus one of the first occasions when central power structures were overruled by a local decision in response to popular protest. Eventually, in October 1989, the USSR Council of Ministers acceded to Crimean demands, and the Crimean nuclear project was stopped.[4] The Crimean environmental movement turned out to be a classic example of a successful but short-lived, single-issue mobilization. Once the construction of the nuclear power station had been halted, the movement dwindled.

In Crimea, unlike other parts of the USSR, the antinuclear movement did not directly become a surrogate outlet for nationalist sentiment. The movement was not defined as a "Russian" one, but rather it established links with both Russian and Ukrainian environmental organizations.[5] The importance of the Crimean Green movement lies in how it raised the political awareness of a Crimean identity, though it was a predominantly "Slav" one. The Crimean Tatars, however, who were just beginning to embark on their mass return to Crimea, declined invitations to participate in the environmental protests and chose to concentrate on their own specific ethnoterritorial demands and grievances instead.[6]

Crimea entered the post-Soviet period as a stronghold of Soviet perceptions and power structures. An island in a sea of change, Crimea turned Aksenov's idea of the capitalist *Ostrov Krym* on its head. Crimea had an unusual concentration of Soviet structures, ranging from a strong Soviet military presence and military-industrial complex to the numerous resort facilities of the USSR ministries, trade unions, and other Soviet social and cultural organizations. There were many retired Soviet personnel residing in the region. These were ideal conditions for making Crimea a bastion of Soviet-minded conservatism. Soviet demographic policies had further reinforced the Soviet identity of the region: a substantial part of the regional population comprised recent, mostly post–World War II settlers.[7] The conservatism of the Crimean Party organization manifested itself in the desire to bolster the crumbling USSR.[8] Only a few prominent Communist leaders—notably Mykola Bahrov, former first secretary of the *obkom* and head of the Crimean Supreme Soviet in the early 1990s—adjusted to the transition. As Bahrov polemically put it in 1996, the Crimean Communist Party remained an unreformed "party of general secretaries" that missed the opportunity to transform itself.[9] Resistance to Gorbachev's liberalization was also driven by local interests. Gorbachev's antialcohol campaign in 1985–86, in particular, led to the deliberate destruction of many of Crimea's prized vineyards, thus alienating the regional party elite and public opinion from Gorbachev, and reinforcing the conviction that regional decision making had to be strengthened.

The democratization and independence movements that swept across large parts of the USSR in the late 1980s largely bypassed Crimea. A regional umbrella movement, Democratic Crimea (*Demokraticheskii Krym*), had emerged in the late 1980s, but the group soon splintered due to divisions over policies on Crimea's status and the Crimean Tatars. Democratic Crimea formed a small faction of only about twenty deputies in the Crimean Supreme Soviet.[10] One breakaway faction joined the Soviet apparatchiks, who then supported the idea of a Crimea within a sovereign Ukraine. A different faction that advocated "Crimea first" formed the Russian Movement of Crimea (*Russkoe dvizhenie Kryma*), the foundation for separatism and ethnopolitical polarization from 1991 onwards.[11] Under perestroika the question of Crimean autonomy came to dominate regional politics, followed closely by the serious concern at the prospect of the large-scale return of the Crimean Tatars from exile. As the USSR disintegrated the communist elite in Crimea resorted to a typically Soviet political instrument as a lifeline for securing its position of power: the creation of a Crimean ASSR.

The Rise of the Crimean Autonomy "Movement"

The establishment of a Crimean ASSR within the Ukrainian SSR in June 1991, when the USSR still existed, was unusual. It occurred when the status of existing ASSRs and autonomous regions in other republics was increasingly being challenged—both from above, by the demands from republic-level elites for their abolition, and from below, by local elite pressures that they be upgraded. The issue was directly related to the high-level power struggle between Gorbachev and Boris Yeltsin. Gorbachev saw in the autonomous units of the USSR a useful tool to control the "parade of sovereignties" led by Yeltsin. Gorbachev's strategy to counter Yeltsin's rise was to raise the status of lower-ranking administrative units, especially the ASSRs (most of which were located in the RSFSR), in order to increase the chances for the approval of a new Union Treaty to refederalize the USSR and to make secession from the USSR all but impossible constitutionally. Yeltsin, concurrently, was urging the ASSRs of the RSFSR to seize as much "sovereignty" as they could "swallow," and his challenge was designed to undermine Gorbachev's authority as Soviet leader.

The "Law on the Division of Powers between the USSR and the Subjects of the Federation," passed by the Congress of People's Deputies on 26 April 1990, officially eradicated some of the key constitutional distinctions between union republics and autonomous republics. A union republic exercising its constitutional right to secede from the union could now be faced with similar secessionist demands from an autonomous republic within its boundaries. Instead of providing the leverage Gorbachev had hoped to gain over the "unruly" union republics, this law strengthened the claims to sovereignty at the level of ASSRs from Nagorno-Karabakh and Abkhazia to Tatarstan and Bashkortostan.

By giving itself the status of an ASSR, the Crimean political elite attempted to acquire a mechanism that would provide an exit from Ukraine, should it secede from the USSR. Thus in Crimea, a Soviet-era federal institutional form was created precisely at the moment when the federal institutional bonds of the USSR were unraveling. From the viewpoint of the Crimean Communists, an ASSR status promised not only to contain the uncertainty over the region's future within an independent Ukrainian state, but would also preempt the Crimean Tatars' exclusivist ethnoterritorial demands. The Crimean Communist Party leadership saw autonomy as a means of physically controlling the return of the Crimean Tatars.[12] The 14 November 1989 decree by the Supreme Soviet of the USSR paved the way for the return of the Crimean Tatars to Crimea.[13] The issues of their return and of Crimea's status were closely linked despite the regional elite's attempts to keep them separate. The surge of Crimean Tatar returnees galvanized the Communists' reasoning about regional autonomy, and it strengthened popular support for it.[14] The timing of the declaration of ASSR status, however, raised the political stakes over the issue, for it came to the fore as Ukraine and other republics were pushing to secede from the USSR, while the Soviet government under Gorbachev was in disarray and seeking to impose more centralized control.

While a Crimean ASSR was seen by the regional elites as a bulwark against the political changes taking place in Kyiv, Moscow, and elsewhere in the USSR, the political discourse in Crimea at this time presented autonomy as an inherent part of the democratization process.[15] One could argue that the autonomy movement became a regional substitute for a democratic movement. The first senior Soviet leader to raise the question of a Crimean ASSR was the head of the Ukrainian Communist Party, Volodymyr Ivashko, at the Twenty-Eighth Ukrainian Party Congress in June 1989. Ivashko envisioned a "multinational autonomy," though he gave no more details.[16] The question began to be addressed seriously in Crimea itself from August 1989, when the Sevastopol city party organization issued a recommendation on the need for a referendum to restore the Crimean ASSR, to regulate the status of the Ukrainian language, and to control the resettlement of the Crimean Tatars. From January 1990, these issues topped the agenda of the Crimean *obkom*, which First Secretary Bahrov had led since late 1989.[17] The local elections in March 1990 confirmed the Communist Party's grip on regional government, and the debate about autonomy intensified thereafter. In July 1990, the Crimean Supreme Soviet set up a committee to study Crimea's future status. Deputies from the soviets at the all-union level, the Ukrainian SSR, and the Crimean oblast, as well as representatives of cultural organizations and the media, were invited to take part in the committee's meetings.[18] The demand for autonomy was also articulated by the Crimean deputies in the Ukrainian Supreme Soviet.[19]

The discussions enlivened a debate about Crimea's previous experiences with autonomy.[20] The committee deemed unconstitutional both the downgrading of Crimea's status in 1945 and the transfer of Crimea from the RSFSR to Ukraine in 1954, and it discussed the possibility of a Crimean referendum on whether the region should join Russia or Ukraine. Opinions were divided: some saw Crimea as an internal matter for the Ukrainian state; others supported Crimea's right to exercise sovereignty and act independently.[21] In 1990, Yurii Meshkov, a deputy in the Crimean Supreme Soviet who was to become the leader of the Russian movement (formally registered as the Republican Movement of Crimea in November 1991) was one of the first and most vocal advocates of a far-reaching autonomy status.[22]

In September 1990, the Crimean Supreme Soviet reviewed the special committee's report but postponed a decision on the referendum. Instead, the Crimean Supreme Soviet acted on the recommendation in the report regarding the downgrading of the Crimean ASSR to an oblast in 1945 by issuing a statement addressed to the Supreme Soviets of the USSR and the RSFSR, declaring that act unconstitutional and demanding its annulment. It asked for any decision about the region's status to be based on "popular will" (implicitly a call for a referendum). The Crimean Party organization adopted a resolution at its conference in October 1990, calling for the restoration of the ASSR status and for a regional referendum. The Secretariat of the Central Committee of the Ukrainian Communist Party instructed the Supreme Soviet to consider the question of Crimea's status and came out in support of the referendum.

On 12 November 1990, an extraordinary session of the Crimean Supreme Soviet convened to consider Crimea's status. It issued a new statement on the Crimean population's right to determine the region's ASSR status. In effect, the Crimean leadership sought to enhance the region's status and make it a signatory to Gorbachev's Union Treaty. At the session, Leonid Kravchuk, then chairman of the Ukrainian Supreme Soviet, supported the notion of a Crimean ASSR but urged the deputies to make the decision, rather than putting the issue to a referendum.[23] Nevertheless, the Crimean deputies committed themselves to a referendum and adopted a new referendum law.[24]

The regional media, still closely tied to the official power structures, strongly supported the notion of a Soviet territorial autonomy status. Throughout the second half of 1990, the main regional newspaper, *Krymskaia pravda*, published a series of articles, "What Should Crimea Be?" (*Kakim byt' Krymu?*), engaging regional and national politicians and other readers in the discussion. The media criticized the Crimean Tatars, the newly established ethnic Ukrainian organizations in Crimea, and the extremist pro-Russian politicians as obstacles to a more powerful and more civic Crimean autonomy.[25] The media campaign was aimed at strengthening a Soviet definition of Crimean identity among the population.[26] The campaign in the run-up to the referendum, masterminded by the Crimean Communists, emphasized an overarching and multiethnic Crimean regional identity. Exclusive ethnic claims were avoided, as is illustrated by newspaper headings such as "Crimea—our common home" and "Crimea is not Ukraine and not Russia. Crimea is a unique region."[27] The Soviet regional elite emphasized economic arguments, above all the benefits and financial resources to be derived from regional self-control over real estate and infrastructure, especially in the tourism sector. Autonomy was also held up as a shield against what was perceived as growing Ukrainian nationalism.[28] The Ukrainian language law of October 1989 was seen as a threat to Russian culture in Ukraine by decreeing a complete shift to Ukrainian as the sole state language within a decade, and it thereby acted as a catalyst for regional separatist sentiments.

Elite struggles over political power and positioning are often waged in emotive historical or cultural terms. Language makes for a particularly effective symbol of identity in times of regime change and uncertainty, and it can easily be politically mobilized in multiethnic and regionalized societies.[29] According to the 1989 census, as many as 47.4 percent of Crimean Ukrainians considered Russian to be their native language, and over ninety percent had Russian-language fluency:[30] only about four percent of Crimea's population considered themselves to be Ukrainian speakers.[31] Despite their high degree of identification with the Crimean Tatar language, the returning Crimean Tatars have in practice spoken Russian as their the primary language. The language factor in post-Soviet Crimea, thus, is not a useful indicator of political cleavages based on ethnicity.

The regional discussions about autonomy led to a Crimea-wide referendum on 21 January 1991 on the establishment of a Crimean ASSR within the USSR, demanding more democratic and regionalized decision making than was prevalent across the USSR. The aspiration to a Crimean ASSR status within the USSR, rather than the Ukrainian SSR, followed Gorbachev's equalization of union and autonomous republics, which created incentives to participate in the new Union Treaty. Through this referendum, Crimea claimed a direct say in the negotiations of a new Union Treaty. The phrasing of the referendum question deliberately employed a misnomer: according to Bahrov, the question asking for the "reestablishment of the ASSR status" suggested historical continuity and justice even though a Crimean ASSR had existed only within the RSFSR.[32]

Paradoxically, the establishment of the Crimean ASSR in 1991 made it the last Soviet ASSR, but also the first and only one to have been established by a popular vote. It was an attempt to channel the emotions and political interests of the time in both an old "Soviet" way (that is, into an ASSR status) and a new "democratic" way (that is, through a referendum). The referendum resulted in a massive "yes" vote: the turnout was heavy (81.4 percent of the eligible electorate), and 93.3 percent voted for a Crimean ASSR within the USSR and for its inclusion in the Union Treaty.[33] This outcome strengthened the regional political leaders' claim to be acting on a popular mandate in their pursuit of an autonomy status. Those Crimean Tatars who had already returned to the peninsula but lacked official representation in regional politics had boycotted the referendum. They remained the group most notably alienated from this early regional consensus on autonomy.

Kyiv acted quickly after the referendum to contain the issue, fearing that an escalation was looming. The Ukrainian government was also keen to resolve the issue without interference from the USSR level. The referendum result, however, was not fully implemented in Crimea. The Ukrainian Supreme Soviet passed by a clear majority a special law on 12 February 1991, which affirmed Crimea's ASSR status but within the Ukrainian SSR rather than within the USSR, as the referendum question had suggested by the use of the term "reestablishment."[34] The debate over the law marked the beginning of a lengthy post-Soviet constitution-making process at the national and regional level. Deputies from western Ukraine, for example, questioned the justification of the autonomy status, regarding it as a de facto Russian national autonomy. They also pointed out that the Crimean Tatars not only had boycotted the referendum but also had not even returned fully to the peninsula. The Crimean deputies stressed the need for the ASSR given the common regional identity based on multiethnicity. They pointed to the unjustified downgrading of Crimea's status from an ASSR to an oblast in 1945, but preferred to recognize the Soviet Crimean ASSR as a territorial rather than a national autonomy.

In his concluding remarks at the Supreme Soviet session, Leonid Kravchuk strongly supported Crimea's autonomy status within Ukraine, declaring it a test of democracy for the newly independent state. He compared the Crimean referendum to the vote on Ukrainian sovereignty and highlighted the need to accept the will of the people in order to prevent political instability. On this occasion, Kravchuk optimistically spoke about Crimean autonomy as an arrangement that would guarantee equality and harmony among all the peoples of Crimea. The new status of Crimea was constitutionally embedded in article 75 of the Ukrainian SSR Constitution in June 1991. It defined the Crimean ASSR as a constituent part of the Ukrainian SSR and referred vaguely to the ASSR's right to decide questions independently within its competence. Furthermore, the detailed relations between Crimea and Ukraine were envisaged to be regulated in a bilateral treaty between the Republic of Crimea and the Supreme Soviet of the Ukrainian SSR.[35]

The first session of the renamed Supreme Soviet of the Crimean ASSR opened on 22 March 1991.[36] In April, Bahrov separated the posts of first party secretary and head of the Crimean Supreme Soviet, thereby following a trend throughout the USSR whereby the party nomenklatura shifted their power bases from the party apparatus to the soviet structures. He chose to stay in the Supreme Soviet, and with his support Leonid Hrach [Grach] was elected first party secretary. Unlike Bahrov, Hrach was unwilling to embark upon reforms.[37] The price Hrach had to pay for his principles was to find the party outlawed after the putsch and to see his support in the regional parliament dwindle to just two deputies in 1994–98 (he later made a powerful political comeback). Before the new autonomy status was fully elaborated in a Crimean constitution, Gorbachev's Union Treaty initiative took center stage. As it had supported the regional referendum in January 1991, the regional press now supported the new Union Treaty. The draft Union Treaty was widely supported in Crimea. Even the Crimean Tatars supported the idea, because they feared they would lose the "guarantees" of return that the USSR had only just granted them.[38] The negotiations about the Union Treaty were eventually cut short by the August coup in 1991. Had Gorbachev succeeded in implementing a new Union Treaty, Crimean autonomy would almost certainly have been defined differently.

Following the failed August putsch and Ukraine's declaration of independence on 24 August, the Crimean Supreme Soviet joined in the scramble for power by issuing a "Declaration of Crimean State Sovereignty" in September 1991.[39] This document confirmed that Crimea would remain an integral part of Ukraine, but the language used and the claims made by this self-proclaimed "Crimean Republic" went beyond a mere autonomy status. Both Soviet state- and KPSS-owned property located on the peninsula's territory was defined as belonging exclusively to the people of Crimea. This declaration was followed up by a resolution of the Crimean Supreme Soviet, calling into question the legitimacy of the 1954 transfer of Crimea by pointing out that the transfer had been made without the consent of the people. Once the USSR had disintegrated, the growing Republican Movement reinterpreted the January 1991 referendum result as the legal starting-point for a push for Crimean sovereignty and independence.[40]

The Popular Mandate for Separatism

A range of Ukrainian cultural and political organizations (Narodnyi Rukh, Prosvita, Ukrains'ka Respublikans'ka Partiya, Ukrains'kyi Kongres Natsionalistiv, Ukrains'kyi Hromadians'kyi Kongres) had opened regional offices in Crimea from 1989 onwards, but their scope for political mobilization remained very limited. In the spring of 1992 "Crimea with Ukraine" was founded as an umbrella movement for the Ukrainian groups in the region. The August putsch of 1991 acted as a catalyst for the formation of new political organizations, and the divisions over Crimea's status became an important political cleavage. The Republican Movement of Crimea (*Respublikanskoe dvizhenie Kryma*), headed by Yurii Meshkov, increasingly set the regional political agenda.[41] Other groups were the Movement of December Twentieth, Democratic Tavrida, and the Russian Society of Crimea (*Russkoe obshchestvo Kryma*). These movements demanded a regional referendum on Crimea's status to coincide with the nationwide referendum on Ukraine's future on 1 December 1991.

Business structures, in particular the association Impeks-55-Krym, supported a high degree of regional independence, as did the most popular regional newspaper, *Krymskaia pravda*. This newspaper became one of the main instruments in the post–August 1991 pro-Russian and separatist movements, propagating even extreme "solutions" such as Crimea's return to Russia or an independent Crimean state. The magnitude of the popular mandate for separatism in Crimea is disputed. Opinion poll data from late 1991 are inconclusive. The results varied significantly depending on the choice and phrasing of the questions, the geographic spread of the poll, and the contexts in which all or parts of the results were published. While *Krymskaia pravda* published figures demonstrating widespread support for Crimea's integration with Russia and significant (though less than majority) support for Crimean independence, other polls showed a more even balance between supporters of a Crimean future within Ukraine and supporters of Crimean independence within a new union, and they showed less support for Crimea's integration with Russia.[42]

The uncertainties of this period of transition were reflected in the overarching public and political ambivalence about autonomy, sovereignty, statehood, and independence. A question about Crimean independence, for example, produced different results when a reference to the "new union" was added. In late 1991, when the Soviet ASSR status had lost its potency, the terms "sovereignty," "independence," and "statehood" seemed promising, whereas "autonomy" now seemed to be one of the weaker political visions.

When Ukraine's independent statehood was initiated by a national referendum and presidential elections on 1 December 1991, in both cases the regional results in Crimea diverged significantly from those elsewhere. They can, however, be read as a continuum of the voting trends in other eastern and southern regions. The referendum on Ukrainian independence reflected the Crimean population's ambivalent allegiances. Altogether 67.5 percent of the Crimean electorate took part in the referendum; 54.2 percent expressed their support for Ukraine's declaration of independence (42 percent voted against); and a 90.3 percent turnout compared to 84.2 percent in Ukraine as a whole.[43] In Simferopol and Bakhchisarai, only 36.4 percent and 38.7 percent, respectively, favored Ukrainian independence, whereas in Yalta and northern Crimea the results were above the

Crimean average.[44] The close result was subsequently instrumental-ized by Crimean Tatar organizations, claiming that their support for Ukrainian independence had been crucial in the voting.

The Crimean result was the closest any Ukrainian region came to a "no" vote, but the majority's preference for Ukrainian indepen-dence should not be underestimated. It proves that ethnic cleavages were not completely polarized in 1991–92. Pragmatic choices, rather than deeply rooted ethnic cleavages, appear to have determined the voting behavior. The widespread image of Ukraine's economic potential, fostered by Kyiv and Western analysts alike, undoubtedly fed into this result. Crimea's support for Ukrainian independence eased the country's path into the post-Soviet period and may have distracted the political elite at the center from the urgency of the regional issues. The Crimean margin of confidence in Ukrainian politics was small to begin with. It was only a matter of time before confidence had to turn into disappointment, once regional socio-economic problems became more pressing and Ukraine's overall economic performance worsened in comparison with Russia's.

The first Ukrainian presidential elections coincided with the national referendum on 1 December. Leonid Kravchuk won the sup-port of 56.7 percent of the Crimean voters, a result in line with the close independence vote. Throughout Ukraine, Kravchuk was elected on a platform of Ukrainian independence and state building. He was the best known candidate, both a prominent Communist-era figure and a reformer and national democrat. During the presidential campaign, Kravchuk had supported Crimean autonomy and a clear division of powers between Kyiv and Simferopol, a position going some way towards addressing the Crimeans' concerns. This message boosted his electoral appeal.

Crimean Autonomy in Ukraine's Transition

By the time the USSR collapsed in late 1991, Crimea's new autonomy status had been only vaguely defined and was barely operational. Consequently, the loss of the autonomy's Soviet institutional and legal bases undercut its legitimacy and placed it constitutionally in a legal vacuum. The incomplete and redundant ASSR status had to be adjusted to post-Soviet realities in the midst of a constant battle between Kyiv and Simferopol over status and the division of power. A regional analyst aptly described the formidable challenge: Crimea "needs to find a model of territorial self-government which, on the one hand, suits all the ethnic groups and peoples represented and, on the other hand, the states which have an interest in this region."[45] In the first years of independence, Kyiv seriously underestimated the Crimean issue and failed to develop a clear regional policy quickly. In its absence, regional political forces took the initiative to expand Crimean autonomy. The early post-Soviet period saw an intense political mobilization that produced two Crimean constitutions and a claim of Crimean separatism that centered on Russian nationalist sentiments.[46]

Ukraine's "zero option," anchored in the citizenship law of October 1991, automatically granted Ukrainian citizenship to every person then living in Ukraine, regardless of nationality. Thus, the Crimean voters were guaranteed a say in regional and national political processes. The issue of dual citizenship—either Ukrainian-Russian or Ukrainian-Crimean—became important in the regional rhetoric of mobilization. The most protracted debate regarding citizenship, however, concerned the Crimean Tatars. Despite their loyalty to the Ukrainian state, they faced the most serious practical difficulties in obtaining Ukrainian citizenship. The vast majority of Crimean Tatars arrived in the peninsula only after 1991. Amendments to the citizenship law throughout the 1990s gradually eased the process for the Crimean Tatars. Ukrainian legislation alone, however, did not remove all the obstacles: while Ukrainian legislation does not allow for dual citizenship, the process of giving up Uzbek citizenship proved to be protracted and costly, preventing the majority of Crimean Tatars from pursuing this path. Only a Ukrainian-Uzbek agreement at the presidential level finally broke this deadlock in 1998.

These different strands of political mobilization in Crimea never followed strict ethnic fault lines. Many of the prominent political leaders in Crimea were ethnic Ukrainians—among them Bahrov and Hrach, as well as some of the activists of the Republican Movement. Thus, the claims for autonomy, sovereignty, independence, and closer links with Russia were rooted in a regional political identity that was not exclusively defined in ethnic terms. This identity rests upon a sense of Crimea's distinctiveness from the rest of Ukraine and a recognition of the profound Russian cultural orientation, embodied in the predominant use of the Russian language. The Russian language is a key marker of regional difference in Crimea, as it is shared by the majority of the regional population irrespective of their ethnic background. This regional identity provided a foundation for a minimum popular consensus on the claim for a special status for Crimea. There was, however, no agreement on how this regional difference should be institutionalized or empowered. Without agreement on the nature and scale of the autonomy, the rhetoric of mobilization became radicalized, and was hijacked by nationalist extremists who tapped into ethnoterritorial, cultural, and historical memories.

The regional media played a crucial role in this kind of radical mobilization and helped to deepen the ethnification of Crimean politics. In the run-up to Ukrainian independence in 1991, the communist and pro-Russian regional press propagated and popularized the slogans that came to frame the conflict between Crimea and Kyiv by nurturing unfounded fears of Ukrainian nationalism.[47] In Crimea's predominantly Russian-language media market, the importance of the regional media as a source of information and political influence increased as a result of the collapse of the distribution of the central media, both Russian and Ukrainian.

The campaign for a second regional referendum got under way as soon as the Soviet Union had disintegrated in December 1991. The signatures required to initiate a referendum were quickly collected. The political threat of a vote for secession forced Kyiv to engage more systematically with Simferopol. Incidents like the visit of members of the Ukrainian extremist organization UNA-UNSO to Sevastopol in early March 1992 further caused concern about local or regional clashes.[48] The Ukrainian parliament set up a Working Group, consisting of deputies of the Verkhovna Rada and the Crimean Supreme Soviet. Negotiations generated a draft law as the basis of a power-sharing arrangement between Kyiv and Simferopol. This agreement demonstrated that a considerable section of Crimea's political elite aimed to avoid the confrontational course of the Republican Movement. Nevertheless, Bahrov, who led the Crimean delegation in these negotiations, found himself under increasing regional pressure from the Republican Movement with regard to the referendum. This issue was due to be discussed in the Crimean parliament on 5 May 1992—the same day that the Working Group was to announce its agreement.

Under Bahrov's leadership, two tentative center-periphery agreements were reached but neither was implemented: a draft law on the delineation of powers, and a presidential decree approving a regional economic reform program. The Ukrainian Rada adopted the draft law "On the Delimitation of Power between Ukraine and the Republic of Crimea" in the first reading on 22 April 1992. The law conferred a symbolic status by defining Crimea as an autonomous part of Ukraine, but the law also neutered Crimea's power by declaring vaguely that Crimea only had the right to decide independently matters "within its competence," and the latter was vaguely defined.[49] This chance of an amicable bilateral agreement between Kyiv and Crimea passed unrealized, because the final version of the law, approved by the Ukrainian parliament on 29 April, unilaterally further reduced Crimea's constitutional position by limiting the scope of the regional authorities' property ownership, and the right for independent relations with CIS states, and even removed the clause about Crimean conscripts serving primarily in Crimea.[50]

The Crimean response was swift. In the absence of a new Ukrainian Constitution, regional politicians decided to raise the stakes by formulating Crimea's status more ambitiously. The Act on the State Independence of the Crimean Republic, which treated Crimea as a subject of international law, was adopted by a clear majority at the Crimean parliamentary session on 5 May 1992, and it was envisaged to enter into force through a regional referendum. The Russian wording of the Act on State Independence is difficult to convey in English, but the declaration referred to Crimea's *samostoiatel'nost'* (an undefined degree of independence, closer to self-rule) rather than *nezavisimost'* (full legal and political independence). The latter was used in the Ukraine-wide referendum on independence on 1 December 1991. Thus, the wording did signal a different kind of independence from that being claimed by the country as a whole. A bilateral treaty between Kyiv and Simferopol was proposed as the basis for future relations between the two centers of power. The developments accelerated with the Crimean Supreme Soviet setting the date of the referendum for the beginning of August 1992. The wording of the referendum questions remained cautiously ambiguous, however, in particular the question, "Are you in favor of an independent Republic of Crimea in union with other states?"

The moderate Crimean Supreme Soviet, under Bahrov, had boarded the bandwagon of more radical autonomy demands in hopes of controlling them: "We did not equate Crimean autonomy with Crimean separatism. We strived for Crimea's economic independence, which is something very different from political separatism."[51] Gradually though, the issue slipped from Bahrov's control, and the regional intra-elite balance began to tip towards the as yet amorphous Russian movement. When Crimea's independence was declared in 1992, the radical faction around Meshkov that had initiated this move still lacked a clear vision of how to realize Crimean independence.[52]

The first Constitution of 6 May 1992, passed in the name of "the multiethnic people of Crimea" (*mnogonatsional'nyi narod Kryma*), took an overtly separatist stance, defining the "Republic of Crimea" as a "state" (*gosudarstvo*) with sovereign powers over its territory (including all resources) and independent foreign relations.[53] Western media and academia alike have often characterized this Constitution as the embodiment of Crimean separatism. The Constitution of 1992 was later revived as a provocative instrument in the power struggle with Kyiv and was reinstated in 1994.[54] In fact, its text was highly ambiguous. Article 9 affirmed that the "Republic of Crimea" was part of the state of Ukraine and would regulate its relations with the Ukrainian state on the basis of a bilateral treaty.[55] The regional institutions were defined as "state organs" (*gosudarstvennye organy*); the Crimean Constitution and Crimean laws were declared the sole bases of its sovereignty, and the Supreme Soviet was referred to as the parliament.[56]

By adopting the Constitution and threatening a referendum on independence, Bahrov apparently wanted to force Kyiv to make concessions and negotiate a better deal based on the mutually agreed draft law of April 1992. The Constitution, which both Bahrov and the more radical representatives of the emerging Republican Movement had endorsed, was rejected by the Ukrainian parliament as soon as it was enacted.[57] On 13 May, the Ukrainian parliament declared the Act on State Independence illegal, and the Crimean Supreme Soviet was asked to amend its Constitution by 20 May. A Ukrainian parliamentary committee was instructed to review the constitutionality of Crimea's legislation, and the possibility of the Ukrainian president using emergency powers to restore law and order in Crimea was discussed. However, the Ukrainian parliament also signaled that the dialogue with Crimea would continue on the basis of the Ukrainian Constitution and the new law on Crimea's status adopted in April. Bahrov's gamble, therefore, had partly paid off. The May 1992 Crimean Constitution had created a precedent. That Bahrov first backed this Constitution but then was willing to compromise with Kyiv eroded his personal authority in the eyes of more radical Crimean politicians, and he also lost much popular support.

A special session of the Ukrainian parliament on 12 May addressed the Crimean question. In his memoirs, Bahrov conveys the atmosphere of this session in which he participated.[58] Some deputies accused him of "anti-state actions," described his leadership of Crimea by adding the pejorative Russian ending *-shchina* to his surname, as in *"Bagrovshchina"* ("Bahrov's time"), and demanded that his parliamentary immunity be withdrawn. In his speech, Bahrov tried to explain the decisions of the Crimean Supreme Soviet, referring to the wish to take decisions independently, to the historical links between Ukraine and Russia, to the opposition to the Ukrainian language law, to the fear of the "Ukrainian national idea," and to Crimea's economic links having been damaged by the disintegration of the USSR.[59] Most important, by describing the Act on State Independence as a merely "political document" which would require a referendum in Crimea to become legitimized, Bahrov indicated his willingness to compromise. Moreover, he claimed that the Act did not call Ukraine's territorial integrity into question, since Crimea would remain part of Ukraine. He referred to Kravchuk, who had previously spoken out for economic and political *samostaiatel'nost'* for Crimea.

The Ukrainian parliament passed a resolution on 13 May declaring Crimea's Act on State Independence and the planned referendum "unconstitutional" and the Crimean Constitution invalid. Nevertheless, it was obvious that both sides were interested in a continued dialogue, and Kravchuk promised to resume the dialogue if the Crimean Supreme Soviet renounced its most radical statements. Bahrov managed to forge a regional compromise, once again demonstrating that Meskhov's Republican Movement was contained. On 23 May, the Crimean Supreme Soviet annulled the declaration of independence and suspended the regional referendum.[60] Furthermore, it was suggested that Kyiv suspend both the law on Crimea's status and a draft law on the presidential representative in Crimea, in order to make room for new proposals regarding the delineation of powers between Kyiv and Simferopol.

On 1 June, the negotiations were resumed when the whole Presidium of the Ukrainian parliament came to Crimea to meet its regional counterpart in Yalta. Under the leadership of Ivan Pliushch and Bahrov, it was agreed that the Ukrainian parliament would reconsider the draft law On the Delimitation of Power between the Organs of State Power of Ukraine and the Republic of Crimea, which defined a far-reaching autonomy including land ownership, property rights, and joint Crimean-Ukrainian citizenship.[61] In return, the Crimean Supreme Soviet was to amend its Constitution and enforce a moratorium on the regional referendum.[62]

The escalation of the Transdnistria conflict into violence in June 1992, including the involvement of the Russian military on the "Slav" or Russian-speaking side, provided an additional warning for the regional and national elites of how events could go terribly wrong when nationalist radicalization becomes dominant. The draft law on "delimitation" was adopted by the Ukrainian parliament on 30 June 1992, but Kyiv made its ratification contingent on the Crimean Supreme Soviet's suspending the referendum and bringing the Crimean Constitution and regional legislation into line with national law. Thus, the much-discussed law never entered into force (and was explicitly declared invalid by the Ukrainian parliament in June 1994).

In early July 1992, the Crimean parliament eventually managed to agree on a moratorium on its referendum resolution. Amendments were inserted into the Constitution of May 1992 and approved by the Crimean Supreme Soviet on 25 September 1992.[63] The first article now frontloaded the ambiguous formulation about the "Republic of Crimea" being a "state" within Ukraine.[64] Further references to Ukraine as the "sovereign power" were added throughout the text, which left intact the main responsibilities of the Crimean institutions, defined as "state organs" (*gosudarstvennye organy*) as in the May variant of the text. Both 1992 constitutions had defined Crimea's status and powers in territorial terms, referring to the "multinational people of Crimea" and "the people of Crimea" (*mnogonatsional'nyi narod Kryma* and *narod Kryma* respectively).

While this Constitution stipulated that every citizen of the Republic of Crimea was a Ukrainian citizen (article 21), the term "citizen of the Republic of Crimea" used throughout the constitutional text was at least open to misunderstandings. The Constitution left room for regional lawmaking (article 108) but the legal system had to conform to Ukrainian law. The organization of elections, use of land and resources, the regulation of property issues through Ukrainian and Crimean legislation, regional economic policy and budget formation, and independent foreign relations remained within the regional competences. According to this Constitution, the Crimean Supreme Soviet would have had to agree to the location and movement of military units based in Crimea (article 10). National Guard units stationed in Crimea were to consist primarily of citizens living in Crimea (article 11). The heads of the National Guard and the SBU (the successor organization to the KGB) in Crimea, the Crimean Procurator, the chairs and the members of the Crimean Constitutional Court, Supreme Court, and Arbitrage Court were to be appointed and removed with the approval of the Crimean Supreme Soviet (article 115). The deputies of the Crimean Supreme Soviet were guaranteed immunity from prosecution while in office (article 113), and the position of the Crimean president as the head of the regional executive was inscribed in the institutional structure as the guarantor of Crimea's "state sovereignty" (article 129). Russian, Ukrainian, and Crimean Tatar all enjoyed the status of "state languages" in Crimea (article 6).

Whose Autonomy? The Mobilization of the Crimean Tatars

The early phase of the movement for autonomy had excluded the participation of the Crimean Tatars, despite their ongoing mass return and increasingly effective political organization. The Crimean Tatars were one of the best organized and politically mobilized ethnic groups in the FSU, with structures that originated in the 1950s and 1960s during de-stalinization and their campaign to return from exile. The Soviet authorities carefully prohibited a formal right of return for decades. In 1956, a decree by the Presidium of the Supreme Soviet of the USSR released the Tatars from the direct administrative control of their "special settlements" without allowing them a right of return to Crimea. Similarly, a decree in 1967 restored the Crimean Tatars' "full rights" under the Soviet Constitution; however, the Soviet system of residence permits (the so-called *propiska* system) was powerfully employed to prevent Crimean Tatars from resettling in Crimea. This policy of control and discrimination fueled the Crimean Tatar movement. In the 1960s–1980s, it emerged as one of the most active elements in the Soviet dissident movement generally, and as one of the most vocal of the national movements.[65]

By the time of Gorbachev's liberalization in the mid-1980s, the Crimean Tatars were challenging the Soviet system's political constraints by taking their protests to Moscow and forcing their demands onto the agenda of the Soviet leadership. The Soviet authorities' surreal response was to form a new ersatz homeland for the Tatars in two sparsely inhabited *raions* in Uzbekistan, in the steppe land south of Samarkand and Bukhara.[66] The most prominent Crimean Tatar activist of the Soviet era was Mustafa Jemilev, widely regarded as a "living legend" of the Crimean Tatar people, a leader who linked the Soviet and post-Soviet experience of Tatar activism.[67] His release from jail in 1988 and return to Crimea in 1989 were landmarks in the campaign for a Tatar right of return to Crimea. In the summer of 1987, as the liberalization under Gorbachev accelerated, the Central Committee and the Supreme Soviet of the USSR had tried to contain the Tatar movement by ruling out the Tatars' return to Crimea. However, the USSR Supreme Soviet on 14 November 1987 declared the deportation of the Crimean Tatars a criminal act of repression. Then, on 28 November, the Supreme Soviet of the USSR endorsed the proposals of its special commission on the Crimean Tatars: to review the Soviet policy vis-à-vis the Crimean Tatars, to recognize their right to return to Crimea, and to consider options for organizing this return. A Crimean ASSR within the Ukrainian SSR, defined on a multinational basis, was also recommended.[68]

Finally, in August 1991, the Soviet Council of Ministers approved a resettlement program that envisaged a controlled and phased return of the Crimean Tatars up to the year 2000.[69] A state commission set out to implement the program, financed by the RSFSR and the Ukrainian, Uzbek, and Tajik SSRs. A Committee on the Affairs of the Deported Peoples, headed by Yurii Osmanov, was set up under the Crimean oblast *ispolkom* (regional executive committee). But the slow, bureaucratic process of planning the return was simply overwhelmed by the growing wave of returnees. By 1991 an estimated 142,200 Crimean Tatars were already living in Crimea.[70] They had not waited for Soviet programs to be implemented but had decided to take matters into their own hands and took advantage of the liberalization under Gorbachev to move to Crimea. The increasingly hostile environment in Uzbekistan gave the Tatars an additional incentive to leave their homes and move to Crimea. Although the violent clashes in the Ferghana Valley in 1989 had affected the Meshketian Turks rather than the Crimean Tatars, the increasing disorder and disintegration of the late Gorbachev era nurtured fears about physical and socioeconomic insecurity in Uzbekistan. In such conditions, the Tatars preferred to live in their historical homeland. Upon their arrival in Crimea, they seized and occupied land illegally, lived in caravans, and started to build their own homes without planning permissions. Shantytowns mushroomed around Crimea's towns. The living conditions were harsh; the new settlements were without water and electricity supplies, and big families crowded into small, ramshackle houses.

The return to Crimea and the obstacles the returnees faced when trying to rebuild their lives from scratch intensified their political activism. More radical factions broke away from the original umbrella organization, the National Movement of the Crimean Tatars (*Natsional'noe dvizhenie krymskykh tatar*; NDKT), and set up the Organization of the Crimean Tatar National Movement (*Organizatsiia krymskotatarskogo natsional'nogo dvizheniia*; OKND) in 1989. The NDKT had proposed a draft Constitution for a restored national autonomy in a Crimean ASSR in 1990, which was based on the Sovnarkom resolution of 1921 to establish the Crimean ASSR. The draft declared the transfer of 1954, which had excluded the Crimean Tatars from any say in the process, an illegal act, along with the genocide of 1944 and the downgrading of Crimea's status in 1945.[71] Subsequently, however, the transfer of 1954 did not play a prominent role in Crimean

Tatar rhetoric about autonomy, because the Tatars endorsed the independent Ukrainian state rather than Russia as the only guarantor of their rights in the aftermath of the Soviet collapse.

While elements of the NDKT cooperated with the old nomenklatura in Crimea, the Crimean Tatars had no official political representation. After the regional referendum on the establishment of the Crimean ASSR in January 1991, which the Tatars had boycotted, the OKND organized the first Crimean Tatar Kurultay in Simferopol at the end of June 1991. The Declaration of National Sovereignty claimed Crimea as the Crimean Tatars' national homeland and demanded a return to the national-territorial Crimean ASSR of the 1920s. The Kurultay elected the Mejlis, a new core body combining executive and legislative functions. In effect, the Crimean Tatars set up their own protogovernmental institutional framework in parallel to the official regional institutions. In response to this challenge, the Crimean Supreme Soviet declared the Kurultay decisions illegal.

By December 1991 the Mejlis, headed by Jemilev, had drawn up its own draft constitution for a Crimean Republic, recognizing the special role of the three "indigenous" or "rooted" peoples (*korennye narody*): the Crimean Tatars, the Krymchaks, and the Karaim. It also guaranteed the Crimean Tatars' right to self-determination. The returnees' vast numbers, combined with their organization's commitment and discipline, constituted the strength of the Crimean Tatars' ethnoterritorial identity. The institutional ideas and demands advanced by the Crimean Tatar movement in the early 1990s, however, remained by and large peripheral to the dominant regional political discourse. Nevertheless, Crimean Tatar activism and their parallel institutions increasingly worried the Crimean regional elite and the Russophone population.

In 1992, the leaders of the Mejlis repeatedly met representatives of the Crimean Supreme Soviet, Bahrov in particular, but these meetings failed to produce tangible results. The Mejlis tried to present itself as Kyiv's natural ally in the struggle against the new Crimean ASSR. In turn, the Ukrainian national democratic forces and nationalist splinter groups, rather than the Ukrainian authorities, supported the Crimean Tatar institutions and demands. In the absence of effective state institutions dealing with the Crimean Tatars' self-empowerment through land seizure, the increasing local tension between the new settlers and the Slav population led to Crimea's first interethnic violent clashes. The Ukrainian authorities refrained from getting involved, and the Crimean institutions could do little more than limit the damage. On 2 October 1992, Crimean Tatars clashed with the local security forces on a sovkhoz farm near Alushta (*Krasnyi rai*), where Tatars had occupied land. When over twenty Tatars were arrested, the protest among the Crimean Tatars grew quickly. From 5 October onwards, they blocked several key roads to Simferopol, and on 6 October several thousand Tatars tried to storm the Crimean Supreme Soviet building, demanding that their compatriots be released. A tense standoff with the local OMON (*Otriad militsii osobogo naznachenia*) troops left over one hundred people injured. The arrested Crimean Tatars were subsequently released. The Supreme Soviet session on 8 October declared the Mejlis an illegal organization, thereby paving the way for a confrontation between the "official" regional institutions and the parallel Crimean Tatar institutions.[72] The Crimean Tatars had no say yet in the negotiations over Crimea's autonomy status.

Conclusion

The drama of the first years of Ukrainian independence left the Crimea question as a secondary issue in Ukrainian politics. Consequently, politicians in Kyiv lacked a coherent regional policy once separatism was on the rise. The first crisis in the center-periphery struggle over Crimea's status in 1991–92 had been defused by ongoing negotiations between Kyiv and Simferopol. The very existence of an as yet unspecified autonomy status and a reluctance to take extreme measures locked regional and national elites into a process of continuous negotiation supposedly to define and elaborate the form and extent of the autonomy, though the details of power-sharing were consistently postponed by Kyiv. However, the result of the first stage of negotiations, the amended regional Constitution of September 1992, turned out to be no more than a prelude to a more serious crisis. In the early phase of mobilization there were popular expectations in Crimea that economic prosperity would follow autonomy. Such views informed both the regional referendum in January 1991 and the national referendum on Ukrainian independence in December 1991. When these expectations were not realized in the first years after the collapse of the USSR, and it seemed that Kyiv was stalling on the autonomy issue, a more radical and separatist ethnic Russian regional mobilization began to gather pace. Simultaneously, Crimean Tatar political mobilization was growing into a powerful regional force claiming a stake in the political process.

7   Crimea's Post-Soviet Russian Movement: The Rise and Fall of Separatism

THE DISCUSSIONS ABOUT HOW TO AMEND the controversial Crimean Constitution of May 1992 widened a nascent split in the Russian movement of Crimea. In October Meshkov's movement joined with a number of smaller groups and parties to form the separatist Republican Party of Crimea–Party of the Republican Movement of Crimea (*Respublikanskaia partiia Kryma–Respublikanskoe dvizhenie Kryma*; RPK-RDK). The old Republican Movement of Crimea continued to exist in parallel and served as a recruitment base for the new party. Party development in Crimea accelerated in 1993 with numerous parties forming around national-cultural or economic interests.[1] The Democratic Party of Crimea (*Demokraticheskaia partiia Kryma*), for example, envisaged a special status for Crimea within Ukraine and offered a basis for cooperation with the Crimean Tatars.[2] The centrist Party of Economic Revival in Crimea (*Partiia ekonomicheskogo vozrozhdeniia Kryma*; PEVK) was established by influential businessmen with links to the regional and national authorities.[3] As part of its so-called social-democratic agenda of economic reforms, it advocated the political stabilization of Crimea within Ukraine. The Union in Support of the Republic of Crimea (*Soiuz v podderzhku Respubliki Krym*), another centrist party founded in 1993, was formed by economic interest groups from the heavy industry sector located in the north and east of Crimea. This party sought good relations with Kyiv as a basis for securing governmental subsidies. On the whole, however, the center of the political spectrum in Crimea remained weak.[4]

In the absence of strong democratic or centrist parties, the polarization along ethnically defined cleavages accelerated. The idea of a

Russian movement, not confined to the original Republican Movement of Crimea, was increasingly seen by the ethnic Russian majority in Crimea as a defense against Kyiv's officially proclaimed attempts at Ukrainization, and its support surged rapidly. A whole range of other pro-Russian organizations were established in 1993–94 in addition to the RPK-RDK, such as the Russian Party of Crimea (*Russkaia partiia Kryma*), the Russian Community of Crimea (*Russkaia obshchina Kryma*), the Russian Society of Crimea (*Russkoe obshchestvo Kryma*), and the Russian-language Movement of Crimea (*Russkoiazychnoe dvizhenie Kryma*). None of these groups were stable party political organizations, though the core organization of the Russian movement was the RPK under Meshkov's leadership. The Russian movement in Crimea in its various party guises was a highly amorphous conglomerate of politicians and activists, who were only united by the general ideas of Crimean separatism, Russian nationalism, and reintegration with Russia. The movement was so diverse that it is difficult to characterize it with just one label such as "separatism," "nationalism," or "irredentism," but rather it encompassed different levels of support for all of these concepts, and moreover this support ebbed and flowed over time.

According to Wilson's estimate, by the end of 1993 the political balance in the Crimean Supreme Soviet was as follows: of the 196 deputies, 23 to 25 were close to the Crimean Communists, 28 belonged to a conglomerate of pro-Russian groups, 10 were affiliated with the RPK-RDK; 10 with the Russian-language Movement of Crimea, and 3 to 8 with the Russian Party of Crimea; in contrast, 36 to 40 deputies supported PEVK, and 10 to 15 the Union in Support of the Republic of Crimea.[5] Thus, while the Communists' hold on power was in decline, and the Russian movement was ascendant, the centrist forces concentrating on economic issues and integration with Ukraine were still about equally strong.

The Crimean Presidency

A conflict over the powers of the Crimean presidency marked the next round of confrontation. In September 1993, the Crimean Supreme Soviet adopted a law defining the president of the Republic of Crimea as its highest-ranking official and the head of the executive. This law came in the wake of a new collection of signatures to initiate a referendum, this time including a question about fresh elections of the Supreme Soviet.[6] The Ukrainian parliament consented to the enhanced role of the Crimean presidency, assuming that Bahrov would be elected to the post and use it to cultivate cooperation and compromise with Kyiv. Bahrov's own calculation must have been that the Crimean presidency would provide him with new powers to contain separatist sentiments. Bahrov must have planned on exchanging his position as parliamentary speaker for the presidency. It was a high-risk strategy at a time when separatist sentiment was being whipped up by the Russian movement—and it backfired.

On 17 October 1993, the Crimean Supreme Soviet adopted a new regional electoral law. It amended an earlier law of April 1993 by introducing national quotas in the Supreme Soviet for one legislative period. The amendments were made in response to strong lobbying from the Mejlis, the executive representative organ of the Crimean Tatars, and Crimean Tatar street protests about their lack of representation. The regional electoral system diverged from the majoritarian system practiced at the national level in Ukraine in the 1994 elections. In Crimea sixty-six of the now ninety-eight deputies were to be elected in single-member constituencies, fourteen deputies were elected on party lists based on proportional representation; fourteen seats were reserved for the Crimean Tatars in one national multi-member constituency; and four seats were filled in single-member national constituencies for the four other deported peoples (Armenians, Bulgarians, Germans, and Greeks).[7] Bahrov strongly supported the national quotas, a factor that might have damaged his popularity with ethnic Russian voters in the Crimean presidential elections the following year. The presidential elections were scheduled for January 1994, and the regional and national parliamentary elections for March 1994. These elections defined the next phase of political mobilization in Crimea.

The Elections of 1994

The year 1994 saw an electoral marathon: along with the Ukrainian presidential and parliamentary elections, there were parallel elections to the Crimean presidency and the Crimean Supreme Soviet. Elections are a time of heightened political mobilization, and the bunching of these elections in 1994 at a time when the Russian movement was on the rise meant that electoral politics would play a crucial role in shaping Ukrainian-Crimean relations.

Six candidates competed for the newly created Crimean presidency. The frontrunners were Bahrov, the incumbent speaker of the Crimean Supreme Soviet; Hrach, the head of the Crimean Communist Party; and Meshkov, the leading figure of the Russian movement. Bahrov campaigned on the concept of Crimea's economic autonomy, and his role as a leader who could deliver interethnic peace and regional stability. I Ie advocated the need for dual citizenship for Crimea's population—a concession to the separatist sentiment—but also firmly held that Sevastopol was an integral part of Crimea, thus defending the territorial integrity of Ukraine.[8] Hrach campaigned on a revanchist communist platform for the establishment of a new state with Russia at its center. Meshkov ran on the ticket of the newly established Russia Bloc (*Blok Rossiia*), made up of the RPK-RDK and other pro-Russian organizations. He promised to lift the moratorium on a referendum about Crimea's status and employed the slogan "Crimea's Unity with Russia" without advocating a complete separation from Ukraine. He proposed that Crimeans would serve only in the Crimea-based military units of Ukraine's armed forces, and advocated that Crimea return to the Russian ruble zone.

Bahrov symbolized the rejuvenated old Soviet elite, and Meshkov represented a new dynamic Russian nationalist style in regional politics.[9] Meshkov's campaign appealed more to the amorphous pro-Russian sentiment of the ethnic Russian majority of Crimea (and many Russian-speaking Ukrainians), whereas Bahrov was seen as being in the pocket of economic oligarchs (he was supported by PEVK), too conciliatory to the Crimean Tatar Mejlis and, more generally, too close to Kyiv. Bahrov's support base was slightly larger in the constituencies with a higher concentration of Crimean Tatar settlements (for example, Bakhchisarai and Bilohirsk), and in northern Crimea, where a higher proportion of ethnic Ukrainians live. However, given the large majority of ethnic Russians, neither of the two main minorities in the region could influence the electoral outcome. Moreover, Crimea's ethnic Ukrainians were politically undermobilized or too Russified, while the Crimean Tatars were still numerically too weak though well organized politically. The majority of the Tatar returnees had not yet acquired Ukrainian citizenship and, thus, were disenfranchised. The first round of the elections on 16 January, in which just under seventy-seven percent of the eligible electorate took part, narrowed the field to the two front-runners: Bahrov and Meshkov (see table 7.1). That Shuvainikov, the head of the Russian Party of Crimea, came third in the first round indicates that Russian nationalist and irredentist sympathies dominated the voting. The voters decisively rejected both Bahrov's compromises with Kyiv and Hrach's outdated communist ideology. Voters chose Meshkov not because of his program (for this was largely nonexistent) but because he stood for the vague nationalist and separatist ideas of the Russian movement.

Table 7.1. Crimean presidential election results, 1994.

	Percent of vote	
	First round 16 Jan 1994	Second round 30 Jan 1994
M. V. Bahrov (independent)	17.55	23.35
V. A.Verkoshanskii (independent)	0.98	
L. I. Hrach (Communist Party of Crimea)	12.20	
I. F. Iermakov (independent)	6.22	
Yu. A. Meshkov (Russia Bloc)	38.50	72.92
S. I. Shuvainikov (Russian Party of Crimea)	13.56	

Source: Official results of the first round published in *Krymskaia pravda*, 19 January 1994, 1; for the second round of voting see *Krymskaia pravda*, 1 February 1994, 1.

The election campaign was fought ruthlessly and amidst sporadic violence. Most prominently, Yurii Osmanov, the leader of the NDKT, was assassinated. In the second round, Meshkov trounced Bahrov by an overwhelming majority of just under 73 percent against just over 23 percent.[10]

While the Crimean presidential elections can be interpreted as a vote in favor of a vaguely defined "Russian idea" in Crimea, neither the electorate nor the politicians representing the Russian movement had a clear vision of how to develop, implement, or institutionalize this idea.[11] Meshkov's pre-election rhetoric had toned down the separatism issue and had remained deliberately noncommittal. Shrewdly, he portrayed the prospect of a "union" with Russia as a solution to the region's economic problems. The campaign of the Russia Bloc was based on simple populist slogans emphasizing the need for the further development of Crimea's statehood, stabilization of the economic crisis, the improvement of living standards, protection of Crimean citizens' political and economic interests, and the establishment of an independent foreign policy.[12] The need for a regional referendum on Crimea's status, however, occupied a prominent place in Meshkov's election campaign. The political discourse during the campaign and, in particular, the omnipresent references to "Crimean independence within Ukraine" made for a confused political scene, but it also obscured the underlying differences within the Russian movement.

Meshkov's victory handed the political initiative in the center-periphery struggle between Kyiv and Simferopol to the Russian movement. Kyiv responded by tightening its constitutional capacity to stem the rising tide of separatism in Crimea. Between the two rounds of the presidential election, the Ukrainian parliament amended the state Constitution on Kravchuk's initiative, allowing the president to annul any acts of the Crimean authorities that violated the Ukrainian Constitution. The second round of voting was followed by a resolution of the Ukrainian parliament detailing the limitations of Crimean autonomy and ordering the Crimean authorities to bring the regional Constitution and laws into line with those of Ukraine.[13]

During the first half of 1994 Kyiv increasingly found itself in a reactive role to developments in Crimea and rapidly lost influence over the region. Decisions made by the authorities in Kyiv had little or no impact in Crimea. Despite the lack of a clear program, Meshkov's first moves after his electoral victory put him on a collision course with Kyiv: he proceeded with plans to hold a regional referendum, though he claimed that it would be non-binding; he appointed Evgenii Saburov, a Russian citizen and Moscow economist, to the post of Crimean deputy prime minister in charge of economic affairs in March 1994;[14] and he called for a regional boycott of the elections to the Ukrainian parliament. Regional politics emphasized the Crimean parliamentary elections. Meshkov literally put Crimea into a new time zone by switching the clocks to Moscow time.

The coincidence of Ukrainian and Crimean parliamentary elections in March–April 1994 further polarized politics in Crimea. In the election campaign the Russia Bloc and the Crimean Tatar organizations marked the two ends of a spectrum of regional political mobilization along ethnic lines. At this stage, Ukrainian organizations were completely overshadowed and the Crimean Communist Party was swept aside by the "Russian" wave. In late February 1994, the Ukrainian parliament passed a resolution on Crimea's autonomy status, ruling out a Crimean citizenship, special military formations, and an independent foreign and financial policy. The scene was set for a major confrontation.

The first round of elections took place on 27 March 1994 and decided the seats distributed according to party lists and national quotas (14 seats for the Crimean Tatars, and one seat each for four further deported peoples: Armenians, Bulgarians, Germans, and Greeks). Most of the deputies in the single-member constituencies were elected only in the second round of voting. Party lists had been drawn up by the Russia Bloc, the Communist Party of Crimea (KPK), PEVK, the Union in Support of the Republic of Crimea, and the Crimean Party of Social Guarantees. The latter two parties clearly failed to pass the five-percent threshold. The Crimean Tatar list of the Kurultay-Mejlis took all fourteen reserved seats. Many of the independents entering parliament after the second round of voting were businessmen considered to be close to PEVK.

In the run-up to the 1994 regional elections the differences among the Tatars (the umbrella movement NDKT under Osmanov, the OKND, and the Mejlis) had become more and more apparent.

Table 7.2. Crimean election results, 1994.

	Party lists		Round 1		Round 2	
Party	percent	seats	percent	seats	percent	seats
Russia Bloc	66.8	11		12		31
KPK	11.6	2		0		0
PEVK	12.2	1		0		0
Kurultay (on separate Crimean Tatar list)	89.3	14	8	0	6.3	0
Other deported groups		4*				
Independents				1		19

* one seat for each nationality

Source: *Krymskaia pravda*, 6 April 1994, 1; 8 April 1994, 1; 12 April 1994, 1; *Krymskie izvestiia*, 12 April 1994, 1. On the four ethnic minority lists, three independents, and one PEVK member were elected. Four seats were filled only in July 1994.

The moderate NDKT, intent on cooperating with the authorities, was increasingly sidelined. Osmanov was killed in November 1993, an attack interpreted by some as an "outside" attempt to divide the Crimean Tatars, though he also had Tatar enemies. The regional elections of 1994 reaffirmed the Mejlis as the key Crimean Tatar voice and a powerful actor in Crimean politics despite having been declared "illegal" by the Crimean Supreme Soviet in 1992.

The political role of the Crimean Tatars had been transformed by Gorbachev's reforms and the collapse of the USSR. As a well-organized ethnic group, they were in a position to retain a strong sense of political identity and cohesiveness on their mass return to Crimea in the early 1990s. The resistance of the Crimean Russians and Russian-speakers to the integration of the Tatars, whether politically, economically, or socially, both intensified the marginalization of the Tatars and fueled their mobilization. Like the other regional political actors the Crimean Tatar political leaders had to adapt to the new politics of democratization. Their organizations began to fracture and readjust, as some favored participation in the political structures in Crimea, and recognized the need for compromise, while others held to more radical positions and were prepared to use violence to realize their goals irrespective of the negotiations between Simferopol and Kyiv over the future status of the region. These different orientations have coexisted, albeit under the umbrella of a moderate leadership represented by the Mejlis and Jemilev.

The sweeping overall electoral victory of the Russia Bloc with almost 67 percent of the popular vote consolidated the gains that the Russian movement had made with Meshkov's presidential win (see table 7.2). In the mixed regional electoral system, the Russia Bloc proved strong on the party lists as well as in the single-member constituencies.[15] Other regional parties, most notably the KPK and PEVK, gained representation thanks to the party lists. Among the independents, a roughly equal number was inclined to the Russia Bloc and PEVK. The new Supreme Soviet was divided by two big segments, with the Russia Bloc holding the large majority at 54 seats, and the Crimean Tatars loosely allied with PEVK holding 35 seats. There was now clear and overwhelming popular support for the Russian movement, but what exactly did this mean for policy and the future of Crimea?

The regional "consultative opinion poll" attached to the regional parliamentary elections in March 1994 further complicated the relationship between Meshkov and Kyiv. It had been initially announced as a "referendum," but was downgraded to a "poll" due to pressure from Kravchuk. Nevertheless, the poll gauged the support for the restoration of the controversial Constitution of 6 May 1992 and for a treaty-based relationship between Crimea and Ukraine, the right to dual citizenship, and granting the force of law to the Crimean president's decrees on issues not yet covered by Crimean legislation. The poll further bolstered the popular mandate for the Russian movement and steered Crimea towards a direct confrontation with Kyiv: 78.4 percent supported the idea of a treaty-based relationship with Kyiv as suggested by the May 1992 Constitution, 82.8 percent were in favor of dual citizenship, and 77.9 percent agreed that decrees issued by the Crimean president should acquire the force of laws.[16]

Kravchuk's decision in late March 1994 to appoint Valerii Horbatov as his representative in Crimea, between the first and second round of voting in the parliamentary elections, actually served to reinforce the support for the pro-Russian forces. The office of the presidential representative had remained vacant up to this point, and Kravchuk's move seemed like a provocation to the Russian nationalists. Meshkov called for a boycott of the Ukrainian parliamentary elections. The turnout was much lower in Crimea than elsewhere in Ukraine though not disastrously so: 60.8 percent in Crimea and 50.5 percent in Sevastopol in the first round, and 61.5 percent and 53.5 percent, respectively, in the second round, as compared to 74.8 percent and 66.9 percent in Ukraine as a whole.[17] The relatively low turnout left thirteen out of twenty-three seats vacant, given that the majoritarian electoral system required obstructively high benchmarks for voter turnout (over fifty percent). It took until 1996 to fill the remaining seats.

The low regional turnout mirrored the close results in the referendum on Ukrainian independence and the first Ukrainian presidential elections in December 1991. It clearly revealed the Crimean population's weak identification with the Ukrainian state. Russia Bloc's boycott of the Ukrainian elections left the Russian movement without representatives in the national parliament and no lobbying power. Parties supportive of Crimea's links with Kyiv, particularly the Communist Party and PEVK, benefited from the "abstention" of the Russia Bloc. Moreover, the elections suggested that the electorate was less radical in its voting in national elections than in the regional elections. The elections also exposed the difficulty faced by the Crimean Tatars to win representation in Ukrainian state bodies under a majoritarian electoral system.

The Institutional War of Laws and Decrees

A conflict between Kyiv and Meshkov was unavoidable after the elections. Meshkov had visited Moscow immediately after his win in the presidential elections, but he did not receive the guarantees of Russian support that he must have hoped for. The details about his meetings with high-ranking Russian officials are sparse, but the issue of economic cooperation between Russia and Crimea seems to have dominated the agenda. Subsequently, Meshkov moderated his stance by no longer insisting on holding the regional referendum. The most serious moment in the confrontation between Kyiv and Simferopol was over a struggle for control of the security and military forces based in Crimea. When Kyiv reinforced its military presence in the region with loyal units, Meshkov backed down.[18]

Kravchuk stepped up the pressure and on 2 April 1994 he reversed as a breach of Ukrainian law Meshkov's decision that Crimean conscripts would serve exclusively in Crimea.[19] Despite this reversal Meshkov continued to expand his power by unilaterally replacing in mid-April the head of the Crimean Ministry for Internal Affairs, the head of the regional SBU, the Ukrainian successor to the Soviet KGB, and the head of Crimean state television and radio. Kravchuk responded with a further set of decrees, dissolving the Crimean Ministry of Internal Affairs, replacing it with the Main Directorate of the Ukrainian Ministry of Internal Affairs (MVS) in Crimea, and reorganizing the regional SBU and judicial organs.[20] This tit-for-tat series of decrees created de facto parallel security structures in Crimea and it seemed as if violent conflict was a distinct possibility. A delegation of high-ranking Ukrainian officials to Crimea, including the Ukrainian defense minister and the chief of the Ukrainian National Guard, demonstrated just how tense the relations were.[21] The actual control over the local MVS forces was unclear at this point but during the night of 18–19 May 1994, staff of the Ukrainian Ministry of Internal Affairs tried to take control of the Crimean MVS headquarters to begin implementing Kravchuk's decree. Rumors spread about the movement of Ukrainian troops within Crimea, and that Ukraine's National Guard in Kyiv and other regions was put on standby.[22] On 20 May the Crimean Supreme Soviet added to the tension by reinstating the May 1992 Constitution and by formally strengthening regional control over military and security organs based in the peninsula. The Crimean Tatar faction boycotted these bold moves.

The Ukrainian parliament gave Crimea ten days to revise its legislation and Constitution. The deadline passed without Crimea following Kyiv's orders. The Ukrainian parliament began to prepare legislation that would allow it to nullify the Crimean laws it deemed unconstitutional. Meshkov, presumably after consultation with Moscow, backed down and advised the Crimean Supreme Soviet not to implement its decision on reinstating the May 1992 Constitution.

He thereby averted an open and possibly violent clash. On 24 May 1994, Kuchma gave a speech in which he recalled "the lessons" of Nagorno-Karabakh, Transdnistria, South Ossetia, and Abkhazia.[23] He feared the demonstration effects of the other post-Soviet conflicts on the crisis in Crimea.

The Political Economy of Separatism

In 1989 and 1990, Crimea was still among the seven financially strongest Ukrainian regions (excluding Kyiv city), according to official budgetary figures.[24] By 1993, Ukraine's economic situation had deteriorated considerably. Following price liberalization, prices shot up and hyperinflation wrecked the Ukrainian economy. In Crimea and, even more so, in Sevastopol, social discontent and alienation surged, increasing the pro-Russian sentiment. People took to the streets, and mobilization both by the Russian movement and the Crimean Communists gained in strength, since both stood for closer links with Russia. Support for Crimea's unification with Russia grew,[25] since the disruption of economic links with Russia was blamed for Ukraine's economic collapse.

The long and inconclusive struggle between Russia and Ukraine over the Black Sea Fleet and the status of Sevastopol contributed to the city's socioeconomic problems. Most of the military industrial complex was bankrupt, but new investment was hard to attract to a conflict-ridden city. Tourism also declined. By 1990 over six hundred sanatoria and childrens' camps in Crimea had attracted between six and eight million people from all over the Soviet Union each summer, about one-fourth of organized recreational tours (*putevki*). After the collapse of the USSR, however, the numbers decreased drastically: by 1994 only four million vacationers were reported, and numbers have fallen since then.[26] Only twenty to twenty-five percent of the sector's capacities were being used.[27] Unresolved ownership questions—most of the sanatoria belong to ministries, other authorities, and trade unions—and a repeated stop on privatization from 1992 onwards minimized investment in this sector. A considerable number of sanatoria enjoyed tax privileges or paid tax to the central authorities in Kyiv, thus limiting Crimea's regional tax base.

As for mineral resources, Crimea has iron ore deposits in the

Kerch area, chalk, and mineral salts. In the early to mid-1990s, oil and gas resources covered only about a third of Crimea's needs, the rest being delivered from Russia via Ukraine.[28] Explorations in the Black and Azov Sea shelves raised hopes that additional oil and gas reserves could be exploited to reduce regional energy dependence, but massive investment in extractive capacity required funds that were not available. Crimea is highly dependent on Ukraine for water, both in terms of its agricultural output and the needs of its population: about eighty percent of the water supply of its large cities such as Simferopol and Sevastopol comes from the Dnipro Canal.[29] By cutting supplies to Crimea, Kyiv has repeatedly used Crimea's dependence for water and energy to exert pressure for political compliance much as Russia has in its relations with Ukraine. It is estimated that in 1989 the military-industrial sector accounted for about sixty percent of Crimea's gross production. In addition to military personnel and civilians supporting military infrastructure, thirty-five to forty percent of the workforce was involved in the production of military goods.[30] Russian orders decreased dramatically, while new markets have not been explored and most factories closed down or struggled with conversion programs. Crimea's military-industrial complex and its light manufacturing, machine, shipbuilding, and chemical industries were all assembly operations, highly dependent upon component manufactures and design in Russia and Ukraine.[31] The disruption of economic links, the breakdown of communications infrastructure, and the changing patterns of demand and supply after the collapse of the USSR led to a rapid economic decline in the Crimean economy. An unclear legal basis for investment and ownership and the political instability of the early 1990s did not make for a beneficial investment climate.[32] Crimean agricultural production is unable to meet regional needs. Wine and fruit cultivation, which could become the most lucrative agricultural export sector, remains underdeveloped.

The Crimean elite saw the movement for regional autonomy not only as a demand for special political recognition but also—and equally important—as a way to secure their special economic benefits.[33] The Crimean Supreme Soviet under its chairman Bahrov had prepared in 1992 for the establishment of a free economic zone embracing the whole of the Crimean peninsula, thus introducing this economic concept (then widely discussed in Russia) into Ukrainian politics.[34] The idea of smaller economic zones, for example a special offshore zone along the southern coastline, was also raised around this time. Between late 1992 and early 1993, a group of regional experts developed what they called an "open economic regime" for Crimea. It was conceived as a way out of Crimea's economic crisis through economic autonomy. The project proposed the establishment of a regional Crimean bank with far-reaching rights, a regional tax administration and independent tax policy, the right to register and open foreign enterprises in Crimea, and the right to issue licenses and quotas. Moreover, the program included an ambitious privatization plan. The ideal envisaged was Crimea as an offshore zone: a Crimean Cyprus for the CIS.[35] These plans met with general approval in Kyiv. Regional economic rights had to appear less threatening than political demands. In an attempt to appease the Crimean leadership Kravchuk signed a decree in June 1993, "On the Regime of an Open Economy on the Territory of the Republic of Crimea," followed by a resolution of the Crimean Supreme Soviet about the division of property between Ukraine and Crimea. These plans, pushed primarily by representatives of PEVK, were never realized because the communists and different sections of the Russian movement opposed them.

On coming to power, Meshkov's economic plans initially sounded more radical than those of Bahrov. On 11 April several decrees by Meshkov initiated an ambitious economic reform plan resembling earlier plans for Crimea's "open economic regime," a plan that the Ukrainian National Association of Businessmen approved.[36] The new Crimean government under Saburov, installed on 12 April 1994, consisted of a mixture of Moscow and Crimean politicians who regarded the plan as too ambitious to implement. The government's decision to raise the price of bread and its inability to cope with the epidemic of infectious diseases (especially cholera) caused by drought in the summer of 1994 made the Saburov government's regional support base crumble. Moreover, Meshkov and the Saburov government faced increasing opposition from the Crimean Supreme Soviet. Representatives of PEVK opposed the economic course of the new government: some of its supporters were associated with structures of the shadow economy which disagreed with the economic reform course, while parts of the Russia Bloc felt bypassed by

Meshkov's personnel decisions, most importantly his appointment of outsider Moscow-based politicians. Thus in the second half of 1994, the conflict between the Crimean president and the parliament over economic issues marked the beginning of the end of the Meshkov era as the Russian movement disintegrated into several factions.

Already before Meshkov's rise to power, a draft law on privatization had been blocked by the Crimean parliament against the backdrop of rival economic interests. This draft law would have placed Bahrov, then chairman of the Crimean Supreme Soviet, in charge of the privatization process. Bahrov was closely tied to PEVK, a party representing the interests of both the Crimean nomenklatura and business structures.[37] In 1994, these forces regained strength, criticizing Meshkov's "authoritarian regime" and the "Moscow-government" in Crimea. Influential segments of the regional political elite now perceived the new privatization programs as a local sellout benefiting the interests of Russian capital.[38] As a result of this standoff, Saburov was forced to resign and the Crimean parliament imposed a moratorium on the privatization program.[39] This moratorium effectively brought the rest of the economic reform program to a halt. The breakdown of political authority allowed criminality to creep into the political void, and the failure of the regional institutions to address effectively the fundamental issues of employment, growth, law, and order meant that they lost much of their credibility in the eyes of the population.

The lack of control over Crimea's economy also contributed to clashes involving the Crimean Tatars. The Mejlis and prominent Crimean Tatar politicians routinely declared that they could not prevent violent acts if Crimean Tatar rights were not recognized. In actual fact, the number and extent of violent clashes has been limited. In June 1995 a serious incident occurred that could have spiraled out of control against the backdrop of Crimean separatism and a criminalized economy: two Crimean Tatar vendors were killed near Feodosiia by members of one of the regional mafia groups—the Bashmaki—to whom the Tatars had refused to pay protection money. When the local militia did not intervene, Crimean Tatars began to burn down businesses owned by the Bashmaki group and temporarily took hostage the head of the local militia. Crimean Tatars from other parts of Crimea immediately came to their compatriots' support. A unit of the Ukrainian special forces eventually stopped the protest. The Crimean Tatar leader Jemilev claimed that this unit had opened fire on the unarmed Tatars. Jemilev and his deputy Refat Chubarov managed to calm the Tatars in return for an investigation of the killing of the two slain Crimean Tatar vendors.

The Fall of Crimean Separatism

Political mobilization around an ethnic and territorial cleavage alone did not guarantee effective policies. Two hundred days into Meshkov's presidency, less than thirty percent of the Crimean population still supported him.[40] Consequently, as the Russia Bloc began to disintegrate, the vacuum was filled by the renascence of the political center in the Crimean parliament, which gradually emerged as the biggest faction. The open confrontation with Kyiv did not prove a success for Meshkov. The economic situation that he had promised to improve instead deteriorated further, underpinned by the region's economic dependence on Kyiv. Boycotting the Ukrainian parliamentary elections had limited Meshkov's capacity to influence decisions in Kyiv. Likewise he did not develop a sensible political program of his own. Taking advantage of Meshkov's strategic mistakes and the economic crash in the region, Kyiv gradually regained control over all of the region's power structures.

In a last-ditch effort, Meshkov issued several decrees on 5 September 1994 to dissolve the Crimean parliament and all other soviets and calling for a new Crimean Constitution to be drawn up by 9 December, to be approved by referendum in April 1995. On 8 September the Crimean Supreme Soviet amended the law on the Crimean presidency, stripping Meshkov of his power. Further regional laws also removed his second function as head of government. Meshkov was turned into a lame-duck president. The post of prime minister was reestablished, and Anatolii Franchuk appointed. Through this institutional change, the Crimean Supreme Soviet aimed to regain its control over the privatization process.

The Ukrainian presidential elections in June and July 1994 concluded a dense series of elections affecting the post-Soviet Crimean issue. The results confirmed the strength of Kyiv vis-à-vis the region.[41] The incumbent president, Leonid Kravchuk, obtained worse results in Crimea than in any other region of Ukraine. In the second and decisive round of voting on 10 July, only 8.9 percent of the participating electorate voted for him (and only 6.5 percent in Sevastopol). In Crimea, Kravchuk's name had become a synonym for Ukrainian nationalism, although a forced Ukrainization of the region had not occurred during his term in office. Moreover, he had supported the notion of Crimean autonomy early on and contributed to the momentum that maintained the dialogue with Simferopol at tense moments. In the second round of the elections, Leonid Kuchma turned Crimea into one of his regional strongholds: 89.7 percent of the voters (and 91.9 percent in Sevastopol) supported him—more than anywhere else in Ukraine.[42] In the Crimean electorate's perception, Kuchma represented a pro-Russian course. In an environment characterized by the waning cohesion of the Russia Bloc, mounting socioeconomic pressures, and the growing presence of criminal organizations creeping into regional institutions, Kuchma appeared as the better alternative. In the campaign, Kuchma had shown himself sympathetic towards the concerns of the majority of the Crimean population, advocating a platform of more local self-government, stronger links with Russia, the integration of Ukraine into CIS structures, the adoption of Russian as the second official language, greater budgetary rights for regions, and other economic reforms.[43] This campaign raised unrealistic expectations among the electorate, but Kuchma's electoral success in 1994 at least offered some relief from the chaos of the short-lived Meshkov era. By the end of 1994 Crimea's voters were so disenchanted by the Russian movement that polls showed that only about five percent of Crimeans supported Meshkov.[44]

Conclusion

The sudden surge and equally sudden retreat of support for the Russian movement in 1994 can be explained by several factors. First, the democratic and centrist regional parties were too weak to counterbalance the steady increase in ethnopolitical mobilization from 1991 to 1994. Russian nationalist political mobilization developed in symbiosis with the growth of resentment among ethnic Russians at the large-scale return of the Crimean Tatars, a return that drove a strong ethnic cleavage into regional politics and became a significant factor of conflict potential.[45] The rapid rise and fall of the Crimean separatist movement demonstrated the inherent weaknesses of this kind of mobilization. For while the widespread antagonism at Kyiv, resentment and fear of the Tatars, and insecurity arising from the economic downturn of transition impelled the regional vote towards the Russian movement in a form of self-defense, this movement lacked a coherent strategy for meeting popular expectations. The movement was programmatically shapeless, uncertain even as to whether the solution to the problems of Russians in Crimea was to be found within Ukraine or in separatism or union with Russia. The movement was also organizationally unstructured and had a number of competing leaders. It was a classic case of an umbrella movement: it could mobilize a wide spectrum of people quickly, but had major problems in delivering results once in power due to internal divisions and lack of policies.

Both ethnic Russians and Ukrainians in Crimea supported autonomy and secession, a move which highlights the regional rather than ethnic nature of Crimean separatism.[46] This "Slav" regional consensus was short-lived because the Russia Bloc became dominated by radicalized and factionalized ethnic Russian exclusivists.[47] The most serious mistake of the Russian movement, and that which ultimately led to its downfall, was the failure to develop policies that addressed the economic crisis in the region. By mid- to late 1994, the Russian movement's failure to deliver effective socioeconomic policies discredited it in the voters' eyes. Equally, the rise of the movement refocused Kyiv's attention to the Crimea question and for a time there was a reaction against any autonomy status.

The steady institutionalization of the new Ukrainian state through elections, party development, and center-regional interactions helped to contain the conflict potential inherent in the Crimean issue. Throughout the crucial period from 1991 to 1994, politics was conducted within the confines of institutions, and all but small-scale and episodic street violence was avoided. Even the more radical Russian nationalists operated through regional political institutions and organizations, and competed in the regional elections and sometimes even in national elections. It is a testament to the political maturity of the political elites at both the center and in Crimea that the Crimea question remained one that was to be resolved by political negotiation and not violence.

8 Integrating Crimea into the Ukrainian State

THE "WAR OF LAWS" OVER CRIMEA during 1994 created confusion as to who exercised legitimate authority in the region, but also demonstrated that the competing forces recognized the importance of operating through institutions and the law. This process in itself significantly reduced the potential for violent conflict. From mid-1994 the power pendulum had begun to swing back in Kyiv's favor. The next three-year period (1995–98) was dominated by attempts to resolve the Crimea question within a constitutional framework, and the adoption of the Ukrainian and Crimean constitutions reframed national and regional politics. There were four main stages in this process: the ratification of an incomplete Crimean Constitution in April 1996; the adoption of the Ukrainian Constitution in June 1996; new regional elections in March 1998; and the ratification of the final Crimean Constitution by the Ukrainian parliament in December 1998.

The Realignment of Political Forces

The implosion of the Russian movement in late 1994 opened deep fissures between the Crimean executive and legislative bodies.[1] The factions in the Crimean Supreme Soviet began to shift and regroup. The parliament's dominant faction, the Russia Bloc, began to crumble due to internal splits. By October 1994 it had fractured into three factions: Russia (*Rossiia*), Russia-Unity (*Rossiia-Edinstvo*), and Crimea (*Krym*). The faction *Sozidanie*, which formed around a core of PEVK deputies, the Crimean Tatar faction, and some of the former Russian movement deputies began to work together to find an agreement with Kyiv (see table 8.1).

This realignment reduced the ethnic political polarization and shifted Crimean politics back towards the center ground. The shift from ethnic polarization to a more differentiated politics was

Table 8.1. Factional development in the Crimean
Supreme Soviet, 1994–96 (in numbers of deputies).

Party/Faction	Summer 1994	20 Oct 1994	20 Oct 1995	18 Jan 1996	14 May 1996
Russia	44	23	9	--	--
Russia-Unity	--	17	12	10	12
Russia-Slavonic Union	--	--	--	9	9
Respublika	11	9	6	--	--
RPK	--	--	9	10	10
Agrarians and Communists	--	3	--	--	--
Agrarians	10	6	1	--	--
Union	--	--	10	11	10
Crimea	--	10	--	--	--
Reform	9	8	--	--	--
Sozidanie	--	--	24	24	21
Kurultay	14	14	13	13	13
Independents	--	5	10	19	22

Source: Analytical Center of the Crimean Supreme Soviet.
Note: Numbers frequently do not add up to the total number of 98 deputies due to the fluctuating numbers of independents. The listed "independents" are members of a faction under that name. The factions Russia, Russia-Unity, and Russia-Slavonic Union marked the first splits within the once-united Russian movement. The factions Reform and later Sozidanie and RPK became the base for PEVK supporters. The Crimean Tatar faction Kurultay was reduced to 13 deputies when Refat Chubarov became deputy parliamentary speaker in mid-1995.

a positive development for political accommodation between Kyiv and Simferopol. Following the collapse of the Russian movement, party identification among Crimea's population weakened and the divisions in the political landscape multiplied. Regional opinion surveys in 1994–96 revealed that none of the Crimean parties enjoyed the support of more than a third of the electorate. Among the three most popular parties, the Communist Party began to recover some support, and PEVK support remained stable; however, support for the various splinter groups of the Russia Bloc dropped rapidly. The decline of party identification and, by extension, the falloff in political mobilization confirmed the ethnic Russian population's skepticism about politics as a solution to their everyday problems. The collapse of the Russian movement indicated that the ethnic Russians no longer saw separatism as an answer. Polls conducted in March and June 1996, however, showed that over seventy percent of the respondents stated that they would not vote for Ukrainian independence again.[2] Thus, there was a general disappointment about regional and national politics since independence as people associated the decline in living standards with democratization. The alienation from the democratic present was matched by nostalgia for the Soviet past, especially in a highly "Sovietized" region such as Crimea.

With the regional elite politically fractured from the second half of 1994 and the population alienated from most of the political forces represented in the regional parliament, the Ukrainian parliament and President Kuchma took the opportunity to rebuild the center's authority in Crimea. Kuchma's policy was helped by the fact that both the Crimean president Meshkov and the centrist forces in the Crimean Supreme Soviet cultivated the Ukrainian president for support in their competition to dominate regional politics. In September, Kuchma attempted to build bridges between the two sides in Crimea in order to negotiate a way out of the crisis. In September and October, a number of Ukrainian delegations visited Crimea, one of them headed by Ukraine's then Deputy Prime Minister Ievhen Marchuk. Kyiv began to establish a close working relationship with the Crimean government. The newly appointed Crimean prime minister, Anatolii Franchuk, was loyal to Kyiv and, in particular, to Kuchma.[3] The moves toward political accommodation also brought the first Crimean Tatars into Crimea's executive structures.

The Ukrainian Verkhovna Rada adopted a more overtly antago-nistic approach compared to Kuchma's personnel choices. It issued an ultimatum for the Crimean parliament to change its Constitution and legislation to comply with Ukrainian norms by 1 November 1994. In the Crimean Supreme Soviet most of the Reform faction and the ethnic Crimean Tatar Kurultay faction supported this motion, whereas the Respublika, Russia, and Russia-Unity factions, which together still controlled half the seats in the regional legislature, opposed it.[4] The deadline passed, but on 10 November the Crimean parliament approved—by a small margin—a declaration to ask the Ukrainian president and the Ukrainian parliament for Crimea to be granted a voice in the national constitutional process. This was widely interpreted as a conciliatory act that could lead to discussions on the framework for a bilateral treaty between Kyiv and Simferopol. The suggestion, however, was rejected by Kyiv at this point.

In early 1995, the political conflict between the Crimean execu-tive and legislature deepened, for the most part over economic issues. The Crimean Supreme Soviet first demanded the removal of Anatolii Senchenko, Crimea's deputy prime minister in charge of privati-zation and, after achieving this goal, passed a resolution dissolving Franchuk's government. Franchuk appealed to Kyiv for political pro-tection, and the increasingly chaotic situation in the region prompted the center's direct intervention.

In March 1995, the Ukrainian parliament and president acted in unison to assert central authority over Crimea with a coup de grace to the Russian movement. On 17 March, the Ukrainian parlia-ment abolished the laws on the Crimean presidency and the office of Crimean president itself, the Constitution of 6 May 1992, and the subsequent act on its restoration, together with the Crimean laws on the regional Constitutional Court and the election of local councils. A new Ukrainian law, "On the Autonomous Republic of Crimea," affirmed the control of the central authorities over the region. It threatened to suspend the Crimean Supreme Soviet if it failed to comply with an ultimatum to draft a new Crimean Constitution with a much narrowed scope of autonomy (for example, with regard to control of regional property and land rights).[5] To demonstrate its commitment to enforce its authority, the central government signifi-cantly increased the number of regular and special troops, militia, and internal affairs (MVS) personnel stationed in Crimea.[6] Divisions resurfaced within the Ukrainian parliament, however, which weakened the center's unity in dealing with Crimea. When the Ukrainian parliament failed to invalidate the Crimean parliament's vote of no confidence in Franchuk's government, Kuchma acted to assert central control over the region through a presidential decree on 31 March 1995. The decree directly subordinated the regional government to the Ukrainian government and the Crimean prime minister to the president himself. This maneuver allowed Franchuk to stay in his post.

Kyiv's crackdown came at a convenient moment, when Russia was preoccupied with a bloody military intervention in its own troublesome separatist region: Chechnya. Consequently, when the Crimean Supreme Soviet addressed the Russian parliament and president on 18 March, asking that Russia not conclude the negotiations over the Russian-Ukrainian friendship treaty without taking Crimea's interests into consideration (see chapter 10), and Crimean parliamentary speaker Sergei Tsekov went to Moscow to appeal to the State Duma to defend Crimea's interests, these pleas were not well received. In a last-ditch effort in April 1995 the Crimean parliament tried to muster its strength by reviving the idea of a regional referendum. The aim was that the referendum would endorse the May 1992 Constitution of Crimea, provide a democratic mandate to stop the Ukrainian laws abolishing the Crimean Constitution and presidency, and support a political union of Russia, Ukraine, and Belarus. A regional political consensus had long been eroded, and once again Kyiv's pressure forced the Crimean deputies to abandon the idea of the referendum and agree to draft a new Constitution. The internal divisions within the Crimean elite had effectively cost the region the most crucial parts of its autonomy and undermined the legitimacy of the Crimean institutions vis-à-vis the Ukrainian state.

By mid-1995 the faction Sozidanie, headed by PEVK leader Volodymyr Shev´ev, established itself as the dominant force in the Crimean Supreme Soviet. In July 1995, Tsekov was removed from his post as speaker, and Meshkov, his presidency having been unceremoniously abolished by Kuchma, sought refuge in Moscow. Antiseparatist leaders assumed control of the Crimean Supreme Soviet: the centrist Ievhen Supruniuk was elected speaker, and Refat Chubarov, deputy head of the Mejlis, became deputy speaker of the Crimean parliament. Conditions were now propitious for a settlement with Kyiv and the political integration of Crimea within the Ukrainian state.

Stop-and-Go Constitution Making

The Crimean Supreme Soviet moved to comply with Kyiv's demands to draft a new Constitution that complied with Ukrainian law. On 21 September 1995, a draft Constitution was adopted in the first reading by a simple majority. This version was, in fact, a revised version of the Constitution of 25 September 1992, itself a revision of the May 1992 Constitution—and thereby hardly acceptable to Kyiv. The references to the president had been dropped, but the idea of Crimean statehood remained, Crimean citizenship and state symbols were still mentioned, and the Crimean premier was to be appointed by the Crimean parliament alone without the interference of the Ukrainian president. This draft demonstrated that even the centrist forces in Crimea aspired to a special status for the region. In October a delegation from the Crimean Supreme Soviet repeatedly traveled to Kyiv to negotiate individual clauses of the draft Constitution. By the end of October, Crimean deputy speaker Anushevan Danelian announced that agreement had been reached with Kyiv on about 130 out of 150 articles.[7] On 1 November—half a year after Kyiv's original deadline—a majority of the Crimean Supreme Soviet adopted the Constitution, including the articles not agreed to by the Ukrainian parliament and president. The vote resulted from a new consensus between the pro-Russian and centrist factions, but the Crimean Tatar faction was opposed and boycotted the vote. The Crimean deputies' attention then switched back to the attempt to get rid of Prime Minister Franchuk in an attempt to reassert control over the regional executive. The new majority in the Supreme Soviet succeeded: in late December 1995 Franchuk resigned and was replaced, with Kyiv's approval, with Deputy Prime Minister Arkadii Demydenko. The new premier, however, was as loyal to Kyiv as his predecessor.

It seemed that the new consensus among the deputies associated with the Russian movement and centrist deputies in the Supreme Soviet was driving a new confrontation with Kyiv in early 1996. Kuchma issued a presidential decree on 31 January 1996 that extended the authority of the presidential representative in Crimea to intervene in regional and local executive and legislative decisions. This decree gave Kuchma's newly appointed envoy in Crimea, Dmytro Stepaniuk, considerable powers to rein in the separatists and nationalists. His powers included securing the implementation of presidential decrees, Ukrainian laws, and decisions of local and regional government; the right to annul decisions of institutions at the local and regional levels; the coordination of the security forces in Crimea; and a consultative role with Kyiv in approval of leading appointments to all branches of central government ministries and agencies in the region. His post, defined as "an executive state organ of Ukraine" and later interpreted as equivalent to that of a Ukrainian minister or the head of a state commission, was officially placed above the executive structures of Crimea, namely the Crimean prime minister and his government.[8] Unsurprisingly, the pro-Russian parties and organizations strenuously demanded the abolition of this post.[9] Stepaniuk's appointment, the extension of his mandate, and the draft Ukrainian Constitution passed in late February 1996 all triggered new tensions in the relations between Kyiv and Crimea.

The draft Ukrainian Constitution envisaged not only a reduction of the powers to be given to Crimea, but also a normalization of its status within Ukraine. It employed the vague term "autonomy" (*avtonomiia*) when referring to Crimea, rather than the grander sounding "Autonomous Republic of Crimea." This terminology meant to indicate a break with Soviet constitutional form, as well as a downgrade in the status of Crimea. The draft gave more powers to the presidential representative, while it downgraded Crimean "laws" to "decisions and resolutions," and gave the Ukrainian parliament the authority to approve the adoption of the Crimean Constitution, now referred to as a mere "charter" (*ustav*).

In early March, the Crimean Supreme Soviet convened an extraordinary session, which provided an opportunity for deputies to protest against the draft Ukrainian Constitution. Yet again, the Crimean deputies raised the issue of holding the referendum on Crimea's status. The speaker of the Ukrainian parliament, Oleksandr Moroz, was instrumental in calming the deputies by pointing to the intermediary status of the draft Ukrainian Constitution. In response, the Crimean Soviet declared the draft in violation of both the 1991 referendum and Kyiv's international obligations, and it issued its own ultimatum to the Ukrainian parliament requiring it to adopt the Crimean Constitution by the end of March 1996. If this deadline were not met, the regional parliament reserved to itself the right to adopt the new Crimean Constitution by referendum. When the Constitutional Commission approved the draft Ukrainian Constitution on 11 March and passed it back to the Verkhovna Rada for ratification, despite the criticisms of the chapter on Crimea by Moroz and Kuchma, it seemed as if a major constitutional standoff between Kyiv and Crimea was inevitable.[10]

In the midst of the crisis the Noordwijk Roundtable, held by the OSCE High Commissioner on National Minorities on 14–17 March, gave international legitimacy to the idea of ratifying an incomplete Crimean Constitution as a compromise option. In an act of conciliation the Ukrainian parliament decided to follow this proposal. The Verkhovna Rada, however, was motivated in part by the parliamentarians' concern about the trend towards too extensive powers for the Ukrainian president vis-à-vis the legislature and, by extension, the regions. Despite the center's offer of a compromise, on 27 March 1996 the Crimean Supreme Soviet moved to internationalize the crisis by protesting about the draft Ukrainian Constitution to the OSCE, to the Council of Europe, and to the presidents and parliaments of Ukraine and Russia. This was a sensitive moment for Ukraine internationally, as its bid for membership in the Council of Europe was being decided. The Council wanted to see the constitutional disputes resolved before approving Ukraine's membership.[11]

The international pressure worked only partially, for in early April the Ukrainian parliament adopted those sections of the Crimean Constitution that it approved of, postponing clarification of controversial articles and those references that it had rejected, such as the "people of Crimea" and "state" organs of power. Crimea was defined as an "integral, autonomous part of Ukraine," the region no longer had a separate president or Constitutional Court, and the legislative powers of the Crimean Supreme Soviet were reduced. On the other hand, the Verkhovna Rada accepted the term "Autonomous Republic of Crimea," which signified a special status.[12] Reference was also still made to regional legislative powers, a provision that was in conflict with the 1996 Ukrainian Constitution, which allowed only for "normative acts" by regions.[13] The Verkhovna Rada had taken five months before considering the draft of the Crimean Constitution forwarded by the Crimean Supreme Soviet in November 1995.[14] When the Ukrainian parliament discussed the draft Ukrainian Constitution and Crimean Constitution, the Crimean deputies in the Ukrainian parliament did not act as a united bloc representing regional interests at the center, and in fact many of them were absent when the parliament approved the Crimean Constitution in early April.[15] The incomplete Crimean Constitution, adopted by the Ukrainian parliament, differed significantly from the version that was eventually adopted at the end of 1998 (see chapter 9). Importantly, the incomplete Crimean Constitution of 1996 opened the way for a new round of negotiations between Kyiv and Simferopol. The Crimean parliamentary speaker Supruniuk commented on the adoption of the incomplete Crimean Constitution:

> Given that the Ukrainian draft Constitution had already downgraded Crimea from an autonomous republic to an amorphous *avtonomiia* which would only have its *ustav* rather than its own constitution, that the majority of Ukrainian deputies accepted the existence of the "Autonomous Republic of Crimea" in the end is already a success.[16]

In late May 1996, as the Verkhovna Rada proceeded with its ratification of the Ukrainian Constitution, it returned to the issue of the name "Autonomous Republic of Crimea." The new draft Ukrainian Constitution passed in the first reading on 4 June. The Crimean parliament submitted proposals regarding the chapter on Crimea on the basis of its November 1995 Constitution. In an all-night session on 27–28 June 1996, the Ukrainian Constitution passed thanks to a strategy that cleverly packaged together the most controversial issues. The vote on the chapter on Crimean autonomy was considered in conjunction with the Ukrainian state symbols, a mixture that forced a compromise between national-democratic and communist factions in the Verkhovna Rada.[17] Ukraine now had a Constitution that guaranteed the institutionalization of Crimean autonomy and also defined the parameters of its powers.

The Ukrainian Constitution stipulates that the "Autonomous Republic of Crimea" will retain its own Verkhovna Rada ("Supreme

Soviet" or "Supreme Council," now labeled in Ukrainian), government
and Constitution.[18] The Verkhovna Rada of the Autonomous Republic of Crimea has the right to pass normative legal acts (*normatyvno-
pravovi akty*), as well as decisions and regulations (*rishennia i postanovy*).
These acts as well as the decisions of the Crimean Council of Ministers must comply with the Ukrainian Constitution, Ukrainian law,
presidential decrees, and government decisions.[19] The constitutional
terminology both upgrades and downgrades the importance of the
competences allocated to Crimea: the term Verkhovna Rada suggests
that Crimea has a proper parliament, but it does not have the right to
pass "laws," and it is repeatedly referred to as a "representative body"
(*predstavnyts'kyi orhan*) as distinct from "parliament."[20]

The Ukrainian Constitution of 1996 also reaffirms the special status of Sevastopol by defining it as a "republican city" (i.e.,
a city with special status and authority that is subordinate only to
the national government) within Ukrainian authority but outside
Crimea's administrative structures.[21] The 1996 Constitution also
established a single Ukrainian citizenship and ended the debate over
dual citizenship.[22] In March 1995, a consular group from the embassy
of the Russian Federation to Ukraine had pushed the citizenship issue
by granting Russian citizenship to Crimean residents after a draft
law providing for dual citizenship had been issued by the Crimean
parliament.[23] The controversy about dual citizenship had a regional
corollary—the idea of Crimean citizenship, which was primarily
symbolic but underscored specific political demands, such as the
right to territorial and economic assets and the right of Crimeans
to fulfill their military service in Crimea.[24] Crimean citizenship was
included in the early Crimean Constitution of 1992 and the draft of
1996, but it was rejected by the Ukrainian parliament in 1996 (and in
the revised Constitution of 1998).[25]

The Ukrainian Constitution defines Ukrainian as the only
state language and promotes its development and functioning in all
spheres throughout Ukraine.[26] The Russian language is allowed to
be freely used, but constitutionally its status is reduced to just one of
the many minority languages. The increase in the use of Ukrainian in
an overwhelmingly Russophone region such as Crimea, however, has
been very slow. In particular, the use of Ukrainian-language teaching materials at school and university levels and in Ukrainian media

broadcasts gradually raised the profile of the Ukrainian language in Crimea. By 1996, there were four Crimean Tatar schools, but only one school in Crimea offered lessons taught in Ukrainian.[27] At the university level Ukrainian language classes became compulsory, though university entrance exams were not conducted in Ukrainian.[28] Some regional media routinely trumpeted opposite views, warning that the Russian language would be curbed in Crimea and demanding that Russian become a state language.[29]

Elite Perceptions of Crimean Autonomy

By early 1996 the idea of separatism (whether in the form of independence or a union with Russia) had fallen out of fashion, and Russian nationalist demands focused on achieving strong powers for a Crimean autonomous republic within Ukraine. For the nationalists, autonomy represented the best hope for closer contacts with Russia and the protection of the Russian cultural heritage.[30] The Crimean Tatars persisted with their conception of a future national "Crimean Tatar autonomy." According to Chubarov, this could have been realized either through a bicameral regional parliament, with the upper house representing the different nationalities,[31] or through a quota system guaranteeing representation in a unicameral parliament, with "thirty percent each for the Russian, Ukrainian, and Crimean Tatar communities and ten percent for others."[32] Such a generous overrepresentation of the Crimean Tatars was unrealistic. Over time the Tatars adjusted their demands to guaranteed representation in line with their share of the Crimean population.

Representatives of the centrist PEVK as well as the Crimean premier, Demydenko, were more interested in a Crimean autonomy with strong powers over economic policy.[33] The Crimean Communist Party saw a Crimean autonomy primarily as a means of promoting reintegration trends throughout the former Soviet Union. Ukrainian nationalists and organizations on the political Right were opposed to the very notion of Crimean autonomy, but due to their minimal representation in Crimea, they had little impact on the constitutional negotiations. Mariia Ishchuk, leader of the Crimean branch of the Organization of Ukrainian Nationalists (OUN), summed up the argument: "Crimea has to be an oblast like all other regions as well. There

were and are no preconditions here to set up an Autonomous Republic of Crimea, as Crimea is not that special as often proclaimed."[34]

Thus, the overwhelming majority of the Crimean political
elites involved in the constitutional process agreed on preserving a
special status of Crimean autonomy, but there was still no consensus
on how substantive its powers should be. Moreover, there was no
agreed understanding of the term "autonomy." Kyiv exploited these
divisions, but nevertheless by 1996 had come to recognize that an
autonomy status for Crimea had to be constitutionalized.

There was a broad consensus among the Crimean elites about
the main characteristics of the Crimean region.[35] Depending on
ethnic and political background, the priority of features associated
with the region varied slightly, but not the set of characteristics as
such. The elite consensus on the region's distinctiveness hinges on
multiethnicity and related issues: multiethnicity was mentioned as
a defining feature of Crimean identity by 71.4 percent of the 42 elite
members interviewed by the author in 1996, historical and cultural
diversity by 52.4 percent, the legacy of Crimean Tatars by 45.2 percent, and the Russian majority and the role of the Russian language
by 35.7 percent. The specific elements of Crimea's economy were
singled out by 23.8 percent, the region's geopolitical context by 21.4
percent, geography and landscape by 21.4 percent, and the autonomy
status within Ukraine by 9.5 percent of the respondents.[36] The latter
suggests a disconnect between Crimea's widely recognized distinctive features, such as multiethnicity, and the institutional format of
the 1996 autonomy arrangement. A clear majority (66.7 percent)
of the interviewed Crimean elites named socioeconomic problems
as the single most important regional issue. National and cultural
issues were listed as the second and third most important issue by
52.9 percent and 62.5 percent respectively. The constitutional issue
figured as the second and third most important topic for 29.4 percent
and 25 percent, respectively. Names and labels are important means
of self-identification and the identification of "others." The term
krymchanin (Crimean) was used by most of the interviewed elite
members either as a marker of regional identity or at least as an
indicator of territorial belonging.[37]

The Crimean autonomy granted by Kyiv as a minimum compromise did not satisfy any of the regional and national actors involved.

Regionally, debates have continued up to the present day in Crimea as to whether Crimea is in fact much more exposed to Kyiv's control than other regions, as it undergoes additional checks, for example through the presidential representative and the regional branch of the Ukrainian Ministry of Internal Affairs. For pro-Russian politicians and organizations, the new status fell short of real autonomy and rendered Crimea more dependent on Kyiv.[38] Crimean elite members interviewed by the author stressed that the national and Crimean constitutions were stepping-stones that provided a constructive basis for future relations with Kyiv and for developing autonomy.

The most serious opposition to the Crimean autonomy came from the Crimean Tatars. They rejected the territorial definition of Crimean autonomy, although some saw the constitutionalization of autonomy as a first step towards their own national-territorial autonomy. The Tatars widened their cooperation with the authorities in Kyiv and Ukrainian organizations in Crimea as a means of projecting their claims. From 1996 Crimean Tatar and Ukrainian organizations in Crimea joined in opposition to the emerging Crimean autonomy status. The opposition's actual impact on the constitutional process on the Crimean side was limited, but it sent a signal to Kyiv and carried over into the Ukrainian parliamentary elections in 1998, when several Mejlis members ran on the Rukh list.[39] The electoral constituency for Rukh in Crimea was too small, however, to give the Crimean Tatars a significant role under the region's majoritarian electoral system in 1998 and 2002 (see chapter 9).

Despite debate over the "reality" of Crimea's autonomy, even symbolic autonomy can be a useful means of managing conflict.[40] With the adoption of the Ukrainian Constitution in June 1996, the framework for dealing with regional demands was established. The center-periphery conflict between Kyiv and Simferopol was institutionalized through interlocking national and regional constitutions. Crimea remains the only region of Ukraine with a constitutionally guaranteed autonomy status.[41] A constitutional system, especially a federal-type arrangement as between Ukraine and Crimea, cannot be sustained in the absence of a supportive political culture.[42] Daniel Elazar qualified this condition as a need for a "sufficiently congenial" or "sufficiently neutral" political culture or for an inherently balanced "variety of political cultures within a potential federal entity" that accept federal arrangements and make them work.[43] Some Crimean politicians have interpreted Crimean autonomy as the first step towards Ukraine's further decentralization and regionalization.[44] In Bahrov's words, "Ukraine is such a diverse state, it comprises such different regions as the Donbas, Western Ukraine, Central Ukraine, and Crimea, that the principle of federalism is effectively inscribed in its structures."[45] Aleksandr Formanchuk, analyst in the Crimean Supreme Soviet, was among the most vociferous supporters of the idea: "In the longer run, let's say after the year 2010, Ukraine will have to opt for a different state structure. A federal structure along the lines of the German model seems to be the most appropriate one."[46] Administrative elites and government officials, by definition closer to Kyiv, have always been more cautious in commenting on the prospects of a federal Ukraine, and some refused to even discuss the concept with the author, such was its sensitivity in this period.[47]

The Constitutional Endgame

In early October 1996, as the revision of the disputed articles of the Crimean Constitution got under way, a new political group emerged in Crimea out of the remnants of the Russian movement: the so-called Anti-Criminal Coalition. It dismissed the speaker of the regional Supreme Soviet, Supruniuk, and replaced him with Vasilii Kiselev, a candidate who was closer to this new coalition. In late January 1997, the Crimean Supreme Soviet dismissed the Demydenko government, a dismissal blocked by Kuchma and referred to the Constitutional Court. Kiselev was forced out because he tried to prevent the dismissal. The new speaker, Anatolii Hrytsenko, commanded a broad coalition of power in the Supreme Soviet, which eventually succeeded in overcoming Kuchma's opposition to the dismissal of the Demydenko government in early June. Under Kuchma's influence Franchuk was reappointed to the post of Crimean premier.

The political battles between Kyiv and Crimea at this time were confused by a struggle against organized crime. Kyiv had supported the Crimean political forces around Supruniuk, who were considered to be "pro-Ukrainian" or "pro-statehood" (proderzhavnyky) and thereby a counterweight to the pro-Russian or separatist groups in the region. Supruniuk and his ally Volodymyr Shev′ev (PEVK) were associated with criminal structures in Crimea, and Kuchma's support for such figures undermined his credibility in the region.[48] That Kuchma had also placed the MVS in Crimea under central control had not stopped the rise in crime. Only in the run-up to the 1998 national and regional elections did the MVS launch a crackdown on crime. Oddly, the criminal groupings around the Party of Economic Revival (PEV or PEVK for the Crimean branch), which reputedly had close links with the Ukrainian authorities and supported Kuchma, was targeted most, suggesting that the center's grip on the security structures of Crimea was more formal than actual.[49]

On 19 June 1997, the Crimean Supreme Soviet finally adopted the amendments to the regional Constitution and sent it to the Ukrainian parliament for approval. Textual changes had been made, as requested, and the articles left unapproved by the Ukrainian parliament in April 1996 had been revised.[50] The amendments nevertheless still included a number of provisions that were previously excluded by the Ukrainian parliament and thus were unlikely to be acceptable to it. The revised draft Crimean Constitution provided for the lawmaking powers of the Crimean assembly, the legislative initiative of other regional institutions, the right of the Supreme Soviet to appeal to the Constitutional Court, the right to control territorial resources and regionally raised taxes, and the equal status of the Russian, Ukrainian, and Crimean Tatar languages. The Ukrainian law "On the Verkhovna Rada of the Autonomous Republic of Crimea," presented by Kuchma to the Ukrainian parliament in mid-June, aimed to cut short a new standoff: it aimed to strip Crimean deputies of their immunity, to make their work part-time and to limit the powers of the assembly vis-à-vis the executive. The Ukrainian parliament briefly discussed suspending the Crimean Constitution altogether, in order to force the Crimean deputies to comply. In the end, however, the parliament refrained from this step.

Despite Kuchma's efforts the standoff with the Crimean Supreme Soviet continued throughout the second half of 1997. It was only on 30 January 1998 that Kuchma moved decisively to demonstrate the likely consequences of further inaction by the Crimeans. Kuchma dismissed the elected mayor of Yalta and replaced him with a presidential appointee, thus implicitly threatening the Crimean political elite with a forced closure of the Supreme Soviet.[51] The

Crimean Supreme Soviet reacted by appealing on 5 February to the Ukrainian Constitutional Court to declare the president's act unconstitutional. It also sent a complaint to the Ukrainian parliament and to the Council of Europe. Nevertheless, the Ukrainian law "On the Autonomous Republic of Crimea," proposed by Kuchma in June, was finally adopted in February 1998 in a version similar to that proposed by the president the previous year.

The Challenges for the Crimean Tatars

Although the Crimean Tatars had a stake in the constitution-making process, in particular through their one-off national quota representation in the Crimean Supreme Soviet from 1994 to 1998, the political and socioeconomic challenges they continued to face were of a different magnitude compared to those of the rest of the regional population. According to the estimates of the Ukrainian Interior Ministry, by January 1997 244,100 Crimean Tatars lived in Crimea. The flood of returnees of the early 1990s had become a steady trickle. According to Crimean Tatar official estimates, seventy-two percent of the returnees were from Uzbekistan, sixteen percent from Russia (mainly from Krasnodarskii Krai in Southern Russia, and from Moscow) and the rest from Kyrgyzstan, Tajikistan, Kazakhstan, and Ukraine.[52]

On the whole, the Crimean Tatars' living conditions have been significantly worse than those of the rest of the population. According to the State Committee for Nationalities and Migration in 1999, forty-eight percent of Crimean Tatars still were without housing,[53] and about thirty-three percent of the able-bodied population was unemployed. The rate of unemployment has been twice that of the Crimean population as a whole.[54]

Based on the shared memory of deportation, the experience of a protracted resettlement process in Crimea, and a struggle for political recognition, the Crimean Tatars—unlike the other ethnic and political groupings in the region—by and large acted as a coherent political force. While the moderate National Movement of the Crimean Tatars, the focal point of Crimean Tatar mobilization in the Soviet and early post-Soviet era, had given way to the new Mejlis, signs of factionalism within the new Crimean Tatar structures emerged more clearly at the third Kurultay in June 1996. The question whether Mejlis members should be able to combine their Mejlis duties with posts in the official governance structures of Crimea gave rise to disagreements.[55] This criticism was orchestrated largely by the OKND, which had always seen itself as the movement's radical voice. The OKND had always retained some political distance from the mainstream movement, propagating a Crimean Tatar state. The election of more OKND members to the new Mejlis in 1996—roughly half of its new members were OKND supporters—brought the divisions among the Crimean Tatar political elites to the fore.

While these disagreements were primarily political or ideological, further tensions erupted over more pragmatic socioeconomic issues. At the end of 1997, an internal split occurred when a small group of high-profile Mejlis members voiced criticism of the Mejlis leadership, including the movement's figurehead, Mustafa Jemilev. Jemilev was in charge of the Fond Krym, through which financial help for Tatar returnees had been channeled. Jemilev and the commercial Crimean Tatar Imdat-Bank, which financed economic and social programs, were accused of abusing or blocking official money earmarked for the deported peoples. The accused faction tried to limit the damage done to its image through a detailed report of the Kurultay's control commission, shedding light on the details of financial transfers and internal decision making.[56] Server Kerimov, the leader of the party Adalet, and journalist and famous poet Lilia Bujurova led a campaign of criticism against Jemilev's leadership style more generally.[57] The Kurultay, however, continued to back Jemilev.

Generational change, increasing social stratification among the Crimean Tatar population, as well as cleavages between the early and late returnees played into a new degree of factionalism inside the Crimean Tatar community. The cracks in Crimean Tatar unity emerged under the strains of resettlement and the political compromises of its moderate leadership. Additionally, radical nationalist splinter parties emerged, for instance Adalet, the Union of Crimean Tatar Officers (*Soiuz krymskotatarskikh ofitserov*) and the Union of Crimean Turks (*Soiuz krymskikh tiurkov*). These parties and groups did not rule out violence as a legitimate political means of asserting their demands. Nevertheless, the Mejlis as an institution managed to incorporate the various factions of the Tatar movement under Jemilev's moderate leadership.

The Political Economy of Crimean Autonomy

Economic interests had shaped the demands for regional autonomy from the very beginning, but intraregional elite infighting over economic assets, particularly in the context of privatization, also undermined regional unity and ultimately strengthened Kyiv's position vis-à-vis the region. Crimea's political economy was driven by actors focused on short-term rent-seeking. When regional actors saw Crimean separatism endangering their grasp on regional economic assets, as Meshkov privileged Russia-based interests, they insisted on a moratorium on privatization. The lack of a legal process of privatization, consequently, widened the scope for unofficial and criminal economic activity. The data show that Crimea clearly lagged behind all other Ukrainian oblasts in terms of privatization.[58] By the beginning of 1998, fewer state assets had been privatized in Crimea and Sevastopol than in any other region.[59] By 1 August 1998, 88.03 percent of the Crimean population had received their privatization certificates. Due to the three-year moratorium on privatization, however, only 38.8 percent of the privatization vouchers were invested in Crimea.[60] In order to combat the chronic deficit in the Crimean budget, the Crimean Stock Exchange (*Krymskaia fondavaia birzha*) made a special effort from October 1997 to intensify voucher and money privatization to refill the regional coffers.[61] The stalling of privatization due to political squabbles encouraged the criminalization of political and economic structures in Crimea.[62] By the beginning of 1997, regional security forces knew of twenty-six criminal organizations in Crimea that were deeply involved in regional politics. Allegedly as many as seventy deputies in the local and regional assemblies were associated with criminal groups. It was claimed that organized crime often laundered its capital through official channels, most notably via the newly started privatization process.[63]

The balance of political forces in Crimea from late 1994 onwards was marked by the growing competition between two strong economic "clans" that viewed political power as a means to protect and promote their economic interests: the so-called Gruppa Seilema and the Bashmaki. The former originated from the owners of a cigarette company and controlled a considerable part of Crimea's economy, including large parts of the services sector. Its political arm was PEV, registered as an all-Ukrainian rather than a Crimea-only party (PEVK). Its leader, Shev'ev, chaired the Sozidanie faction in the Crimean Supreme Soviet, which was the dominant faction from 1996 onwards. A number of high-profile politicians were associated with this group: the speaker of the Crimean Supreme Soviet, Supruniuk, and his deputy, Danelian, a deputy prime minister, and several ministers, as well as the Simferopol mayor, and an influential group of deputies in the Simferopol city council.

The Bashmaki were associated with the Respublika faction, which included some remnants of the Russian movement. The faction Russia, the Crimean Party (*Krymskaia partiia*) around Lev Mirimskii (a Crimean deputy in the Verkhovna Rada in Kyiv), and the Slavic Union (*Slavianskii soiuz*) around the deputy speaker of the Crimean Supreme Soviet, Iurii Podkopaev, were linked to this group. In the second half of 1996, this conglomerate of interrelated business interests reformulated its political efforts by founding the Anti-Criminal Coalition. Under this moralizing name it targeted its main rival, the PEV led by Shev'ev.[64] The struggle between these two clans demonstrated the fluidity of the boundaries between politics, economics, and organized crime in Crimea.[65] Informal business and criminal networks existed not in parallel to the formal institutional structures and political groups, but had effectively colonized and distorted them.

The protracted struggle for autonomy did not benefit the Crimean economy. Crimea has been among the regions worst hit by economic and social problems.[66] Crimea's industrial output in 1996 was one-fifth that of the Ukrainian average.[67] Measured against its regional contribution to Ukraine's overall industrial production, in 1996 Crimea came sixteenth (out of twenty-five).[68] By the middle of 1996, Crimea accounted for only 1.4 percent of the Ukrainian export volume.[69] Salaries in Crimea have been below the Ukrainian average, although the gap, after widening significantly towards the end of 1995, began to close throughout 1996 and stabilized at about ninety percent of the Ukrainian average throughout 1997.[70] Until January 1996, the region had attracted a total of $17 million in foreign investment, no more than 1.9 percent of the overall investment in Ukraine. By mid-1996, Crimea's share in foreign investment had increased to 5.3 percent.[71] On the initiative of Serhii Kunitsyn, mayor of Perekop, a town in northern Crimea, the idea of a free economic zone that had been discussed in the early 1990s was revived in 1995 under the name Sivash. Although a small scale experiment, Sivash became the first such zone with tax privileges in the whole of Ukraine. By 1997 Sivash had attracted over $3 million in investment, had contributed to the Crimean budget, and had created new jobs.[72] On this small scale, much-delayed national and regional economic reforms were carried out in Sivash, but the program failed to stimulate growth in the region's economy.

The question of whether regional taxes should flow immediately into the Crimean budget (one-channel system), or into a central budget from which Crimea could subsequently obtain a subsidy as in other Ukrainian oblasts remained controversial throughout the 1990s. According to its population size, Crimea was to contribute 4.3 percent of the national expenditure. Due to the ongoing politicking and the small regional tax volume, the financial relations with the center were negotiated on a yearly basis, with obligations being consistently broken by both sides. Tax collection in Crimea fell even below the notoriously low Ukrainian average.[73] That a significant number of firms, sanatoria, and other institutions belong to the center and pay their taxes centrally rather than to Crimea has additionally limited the regional tax volume. Moreover, tax privileges and exemptions were granted to many enterprises due to the infiltration by business and criminal groups of the Crimean parliament and government, as well as local councils.

Socioeconomic issues topped the list of concerns among the regional population. As discussed in chapter 7, the turn away from the Russian movement in the second half of 1994 was largely a result of its failure to deal with the region's socioeconomic problems effectively when in power. A survey conducted by the Analytical Center of the Crimean Government in June 1996 provides a representative snapshot of regional sentiment around the time of the adoption of the Ukrainian Constitution (see table 8.2). Crimea's political status and interethnic relations were overshadowed by a wide range of socioeconomic issues, thereby illustrating the reduced salience of separatism and ethnopolitics for voters at this stage.

Nevertheless, a common view of Crimea's characteristics and needs, shared by the elites and the regional population at large, was the foundation of a regional political identity.[74] Local sociological centers have conducted surveys to map the awareness of a Crimean regional identity. Not wholly free from political biases and methodological problems, these surveys nonetheless give some indication of the spread of notions of identity. For example, a poll asking specifically for the homeland identification of the Crimean population at the beginning of 1996, the year of the constitutional settlement, showed a Soviet and Crimean regional identity as almost equally strong, whereas identification with Russia or Ukraine was markedly less pronounced. When asked the question "What do you consider your homeland?" 32 percent of respondents named the USSR, 28 percent identified with Crimea, 16 percent with Russia, 11 percent with

Table 8.2. Poll results for the question, "What do you consider the main problems affecting the interests of all Crimeans?"

	Percentage of the population
Economic problems	90.3
Social security (pensions, housing, etc.)	83.7
Criminality	80.5
Decrease of moral values	69.9
Political status of Crimea	38.4
Interethnic relations	37.1
Ecological problems	20.3
Agrarian reforms	20.5

Source: Analiticheskii Tsentr Soveta Ministrov Avtonomnoi Respubliki Krym, *Opros*, June 1996. The survey was conducted among 1,000 respondents from all Crimean towns and 14 rural *raions*. Respondents were able to name several issues.

Ukraine, and 8 percent with "the whole world," while 5 percent were undecided.[75] A similar regional poll, also conducted by the Krymskii tsentr gumanitarnykh issledovanii in the spring of 1996, showed that the two main identifications—Soviet and Crimean—mark a generational gap: respondents aged thirty or younger accounted for the largest share of those putting the regional identity first, whereas respondents aged over fifty tended to define their identity primarily as Soviet. Crimean identity, in turn, was mainly defined in terms of center-periphery relations rather than in interethnic terms.[76]

Crimea in the 1998 Elections

After the "ratification in parts" of the Crimean Constitution, regional politics became embroiled in a ruthless struggle between the two competing interest groups deeply connected with criminal structures. Because both groups had representatives in the Crimean parliament, the consensus among the deputies, which had contributed to the ratification of the Crimean Constitution, fragmented. For several months, the divisions made any substantial discussion of fundamental questions impossible, and the regional parliament was in disarray. In this phase, the Communist Party, and its leader Hrach in particular, capitalized on the splits within the parliament and the rifts among different economic "clans." In 1998, the Communist Party claimed to have thirty thousand members in Crimea, a considerable reservoir of activists, and Hrach mobilized them for a major push to revive the fortunes of the Communist Party in the elections of March 1998. The results of these elections would be critical for the future of the Crimean autonomy because the new Crimean Supreme Soviet would deal with the final phase of constitution making.

In 1998, the electoral systems at the national and at the regional level were reversed. The Ukrainian Verkhovna Rada moved from a simple majoritarian system to a mixed system, with half of the 450 seats to be filled by party lists and the other half on a majoritarian basis in single-member constituencies. In contrast, the Crimean electoral system lost its elements of proportional representation and the national quotas (which favored the Tatars), switching to a simple majoritarian system. The changes to the Crimean electoral law were debated throughout the second half of 1997. On 19 June

1997 the Crimean parliament passed a normative act providing for elections via a mixed system: fifty deputies were to be elected in single-member constituencies, fifty on party lists on a proportional basis in one all-Crimean multimember constituency. Crimean Tatar representatives advocated an electoral system entirely based on proportional representation. On 13 November 1997, two different variants for Crimea were discussed in the Ukrainian parliament. President Kuchma's proposal envisaged a majoritarian system with territorial and national single-member constituencies; however, the draft put forward by a group of national deputies envisaged a mixed electoral system. The latter draft acquired more votes in the first reading and was redirected for further consideration. On 10 December 1997, a slightly revised version of this draft, tabled by the Crimean deputy Lev Mirimskii, gained the support of 226 votes. The gist of these drafts was that fifty deputies were to be elected on a majoritarian basis in single-member constituencies, and fifty on the basis of proportional representation. No mention was made of national quotas in either draft. In January 1998, Kuchma returned this law to parliament, arguing for a simple majoritarian system and presenting a mixed system as "premature" for Crimea, given that the regional political scene had not consolidated yet.[77] Eventually, the Verkhovna Rada of Ukraine approved the changes in line with Kuchma's proposals.[78]

Distinctly regional parties and movements, such as the Republican Party of Crimea, the Russian Party of Crimea, the Union in Support of the Republic of Crimea, and the Crimean Party,[79] had shaped the politics of Crimean autonomy. Even the Crimean Communist Party (*Kommunisticheskaia partiia Kryma*) maintained a special status until the 1996 Constitution entered into force: it was associated with the Communist Party of Ukraine, rather than being merely a regional branch. Crimea's party landscape was reshaped by the 1996 Ukrainian Constitution, which was designed to constrain regionalist party development. Every party has to be registered as an all-Ukrainian party in a number of oblasts. The ban on regional parties tied Crimean party politics more closely to the center, although regional specificities survived in nonparty organizations, which were often ethnically defined,[80] or electoral blocs that aligned themselves loosely with parties at the national level.

The majoritarian system in Crimea's regional elections in March

1998 weakened the representation of the various pro-Russian parties. The Communist Party overcame the barriers of a majoritarian electoral system, and independent candidates, usually local businessmen, did well. Such deputies were often linked to criminal structures, but they were also much more pragmatic compared with the more ideologically-driven Communists and Russian nationalists who were nostalgic for the Soviet past and antipathetic to Ukraine. Altogether 63.6 percent of the Ukrainian citizens in Crimea took part in the 1998 regional elections. The Communist Party, by now officially a regional branch of the Communist Party of Ukraine, became the single largest party with 35.5 percent of the vote (see table 8.3). The remnants of the former Russia Bloc were annihilated.[81] Parts of the former Russian movement survived within the Communist Party and the Union Party (*Soiuz*).[82] The 1998 Crimean election was the final confirmation of the failure of separatism, and the idea of reunion with Russia had been transformed into vague calls for a "Slavic

Table 8.3. Crimean Supreme Soviet election results, March 1998.

Party/Bloc	Percentage of votes	Seats
Communist Party of Ukraine (KPU)	35.5	33
Union Party	4.3	4
Agricultural Party of Ukraine	4.3	4
National Democratic Party (NDP)	4.3	4
Party of Economic Revival (PEV)	2.2	2
Socialist Party of Ukraine (SPU)	1.0	1
Independents	48.4	45

Source: *Krymskaia pravda*, 22 April 1998, 1.
Note: These first official results were published only about a month after the elections. In the meantime the elections were declared void in seven constituencies. The remaining seven seats were filled later. The Communist Party and NDP gained three seats each, Soiuz and the APU one each, and altogether forty-four independents were registered; see Ukraïns'kyi nezalezhnyi tsentr politychnykh doslidzhen', *Informatsiino-analitychne vydannia*, 14. For a comparative analysis of elite composition as reflected in the 1990, 1994, and 1998 elections, see appendix 3.

union." Moreover, Russia's economic crash in early 1998 undermined the belief that Russia could be an attractive alternative option for Crimea's electorate.

As the quota rule no longer applied in 1998, the political representation of the Crimean Tatars fell catastrophically. The Crimean Tatars were effectively excluded from the regional Supreme Soviet, with the exception of one Crimean Tatar Communist deputy. However, the Crimean Tatars for the first time gained national representation in the Verkhovna Rada in Kyiv. Chubarov entered the parliament as an independent candidate, and Jemilev was elected to the Verkhovna Rada on the Rukh party list. The alliance of the Tatars and Rukh boosted the regional support for Rukh to 6.75 percent.[83] The Crimean Tatars faced another serious obstacle in the elections of 1998: an estimated eighty thousand to one-hundred thousand Crimean Tatars were not able to participate in the elections, because they still had not obtained Ukrainian citizenship, primarily due to the difficulties attached to their officially renouncing their Uzbek citizenship.

On balance, the trend of political integration of Crimea into the Ukrainian state continued with the coincidence of national parliamentary elections with the regional elections. Throughout the country, support for the Communist Party was highest in Sevastopol (46 percent, as opposed to the countrywide average of 24.7 percent), closely followed by Luhansk with 45.9 percent and Crimea with 39.4 percent. While the Union Party clearly remained a regional party despite its all-Ukrainian status, Rukh emerged as the third largest party in Crimea (in terms of its voter share) as a result of Crimean Tatar support. The Crimean results for the explicitly all-Ukrainian parties, such as the Agrarian Party of Ukraine and the Green Party, came close to the countrywide average, thereby indicating the region's gradual political normalization (table 8.4, below).

Conclusion

The realignment of regional and national political actors from mid-1994 onwards, in particular the disintegration of the Russia Bloc, facilitated the gradual institutionalization of center-regional differences via a stop-go constitution-making process at the regional and national level. The representation of Crimean Tatars in the Crimean

Table 8.4. Crimean voting (in percent) in Ukrainian national elections, March 1998.

	Crimea	Sevastopol	National
KPU	39.4	46.0	24.68
Union	10.69	2.25	0.7
Rukh	6.75	1.77	9.4
Greens	5.67	5.92	5.46
NDP	4.33	6.92	5.0
APU	3.17	1.44	3.67
Hromada	2.92	2.61	4.04

Note: The table lists only the seven strongest parties in Crimea. The data, prepared by the Presidential Administration, Kyiv, list the overall support for the parties in the mixed electoral system.

Supreme Soviet from 1994 to 1998 also channeled their demands into the constitutional negotiations, although ultimately they did not see their interests adequately addressed within this framework. The sequence of constitutional arrangements from 1995 to 1998 stabilized the relationship between Kyiv and Simferopol, but it also distracted from other pressing issues, namely the region's socioeconomic problems and criminalization. By 1998, the regional parties had been integrated into the overall Ukrainian party system, a step that further reduced the political space for separatist regional mobilization. Though the constitutionalization of Ukraine and Crimean autonomy was first and foremost a domestic political process, two international developments facilitated progress on the accommodation. First, the OSCE and the Council of Europe strongly supported the adoption of the Ukrainian Constitution, including the principle of Crimean autonomy. Second, Russia's preoccupation with a separatist problem within its own boundaries—Chechnya—reduced its willingness to interfere in the negotiations between Kyiv and Simferopol. The following chapter examines the final constitutional settlement and the post-1998 "normalization" of Crimean autonomy within Ukraine.

9 Crimean Autonomy and Its Aftermath

THE POLITICAL CHANGE IN CRIMEA brought on by the 1998 elections directly preceded the final phase of constitution making. The elections led to a considerable turnover of deputies in the Crimean Supreme Soviet, with the Communists becoming the single largest faction and the remnants of the Russian movement reduced to a small rump. The new Communist-dominated Crimean leadership focused less on political autonomy and more on securing economic powers from the center. The negotiations were, in essence, conducted as a one-man show on the Crimean side by the Communist leader and new speaker of the Crimean Supreme Soviet, Hrach. He forged a consensus in the Supreme Soviet around the demand for greater economic autonomy in a new draft of the Crimean Constitution.[1] Hrach's draft Constitution, the most pro-Ukrainian Crimean constitution to date, was approved by an overwhelming majority in the Crimean Supreme Soviet on 21 October 1998.[2]

The draft still contained provisions that, if not in breach of the Ukrainian Constitution, at least required further clarification: for example, the right to regional foreign economic relations, rights to control Crimea's natural resources, the right to form and implement the budget independently (based on all taxes collected regionally and additional regional taxes), and the right of the Crimean Verkhovna Rada to dismiss the premier by a qualified majority vote and to approve appointments and dismissals—including deputy heads of interior and justice departments (but not the security services), as well as top officials of the regional tax administration and of the property fund.³ On 15 December, the new Constitution was considered by the Verkhovna Rada in Kyiv and was voted down, despite some last-minute concessions by Hrach.

Kuchma intervened to break the new deadlock. On 22 December he presided over a meeting of the key leaders on both sides: the Crimean parliamentary speaker Hrach, the Crimean premier Kunitsyn, the speaker of the Ukrainian parliament, Oleksandr Tkachenko, and the presidential representatives in Crimea and in the Ukrainain parliament. Together they forged what was later called the "constitutional compromise," allowing every party involved to save face.⁴ The Ukrainian parliament had amended some formulations, in particular references to "treaty-based" relations between Kyiv and Simferopol and to the tax system.⁵ On 23 December 1998, the Constitution was approved by the Ukrainian Rada by a slim majority. Kuchma, though opposed to some of the added provisions, decided not to veto the Constitution, probably realizing that to do so could damage his prospects in the forthcoming presidential elections in October 1999.

Hrach took credit for bringing the saga of the Crimean Constitution to an end. This triumph further boosted his image and influence in Crimea, and in the country as a whole. His popularity, and that of the Communist Party, had already risen steadily in view of its competent attempts to reverse the region's dire socioeconomic situation.⁶ The ratification of the Crimean Constitution was marked with a big celebration financed by a number of Crimean banks, though a few deputies refused to take their oath of office on the new Constitution. In line with the 1996 Ukrainian Constitution, the new Crimean Constitution defines the Autonomous Republic of Crimea as an "inseparable constituent part of Ukraine" (*neot"emlemaia sostavnaia chast' Ukrainy*). The Crimean Verkhovna Rada is referred to as a "representative organ" (*predstavitel'nyi organ*) with the right to pass normative acts only.⁷ The Supreme Soviet's listed responsibilities are limited, but the terminology left room for some interpretation and a degree of flexibility. What is new in this final Crimean Constitution is the repeatedly stated guarantee for the preservation of the autonomy status, thus blocking any future attempts by the center to downgrade Crimea to an oblast or an amorphous *avtonomiia*.

These guarantees and the acknowledgement that Crimea is a special region can be regarded as the centerpiece of this Constitution, because they reinforce the principle of Crimean autonomy by embedding it within Ukraine's overall constitutional settlement.[8] Although the regional media lamented the new Constitution's failure to protect the Russian language,[9] the 1998 Crimean Constitution specifies that parallel to the state language, Ukrainian, the use and development of Russian, Crimean Tatar, and languages of other national minorities are guaranteed. Russian as "the language of the majority of the population" and "interethnic exchange" can be used in all spheres of public life.[10] In 1997 the Crimean Supreme Soviet had passed a normative act elevating Russian to the status of an "official language," but it was revoked after the Kyiv-controlled Crimean Procuracy had voiced its criticism.[11] The Crimean assembly had thereby tested the scope of its normative acts and established that they could not conflict with the Ukrainian Constitution.

The Legal and Political Boundaries of Crimean Autonomy

Crimea's autonomy status is anchored in the Ukrainian Constitution and thereby is as insulated against revision as the fundamental law itself. Constitutional amendments need to secure the approval of a two-thirds majority in the national Verkhovna Rada. The sections on Ukraine's territorial structure and on Crimea in the Ukrainian Constitution, however, do not specifically state any further guarantees of Crimea's status. In contrast, the Crimean Constitution repeatedly refers to "state guarantees" for Crimea's autonomy. Article 3.2 of the Crimean Constitution describes the supposed guarantees of the status of the autonomous republic. Rather than defining an institutional procedure to allow for or prevent changes to Crimea's status, it consists of vague references to Crimea's self-governing powers (*samostoiatel'nost'*) in legal, organizational, financial, property-related, and resource issues as defined by the Ukrainian Constitution. The Ukrainian organs of power are asked for "consideration of the distinctive features" of the region when they are taking decisions related to the autonomous republic, to "state guarantees for the status and powers" of the autonomy and to the "legal protection of the status and powers." The final section of the Crimean Constitution deals exclusively with the guarantees for Crimea: the Ukrainian Constitution, the Crimean Constitution, and Ukrainian law are described as the triangle defining the autonomy status. The autonomous republic, the regional assembly, and government are "guaranteed by the Ukrainian state" (article 48.1). Through a regional consultative referendum, the regional assembly can propose changes to the status and powers of the autonomous republic, its Verkhovna Rada, and its Council of Ministers, in accordance with the Ukrainian Constitution and law (article 48.2 and abbreviated in article 7.2). In sum, Ukraine's "state guarantee" of Crimea's status is not defined, despite the repeated references to the Ukrainian Constitution and Ukrainian law. Ambiguity also characterizes the sections of the Crimean Constitution defining the powers of the regional authorities. The first clause of each section of the Crimean Constitution of 1998 stresses that the regional organs of power act within the jurisdiction of the Ukrainian Constitution. However, the subsequent wording of the more detailed description of the rights of the region leaves room for interpretation due to imprecision.

Consequently, the Crimean Constitution and the region's status ultimately depend on the position taken by the central authorities. The wording of the Crimean Constitution offers a symbolic but legally underdefined basis for asserting the power of the autonomy against any potential unilateral action by the center. Ukrainian legal experts have pointed to contradictions in the constitutional texts. For example, the organization of elections is defined as a national competence by Ukrainian law (Ukrainian Constitution, article 92), yet article 18.6 of the Crimean Constitution places these issues within the competences of the Crimean Verkhovna Rada. In fact, the clause in the Crimean Constitution also contains a general reference to Ukrainian law—though not to the Ukrainian Constitution. Thus, vagueness rather than an overemphasis on Crimean powers seems to be the core problem. Similarly, the powers of the Verkhovna Rada of Crimea are vaguely defined.[12] The introductory clause of article 38 of the Crimean Constitution mentions both the Ukrainian Constitution and Ukrainian law, and it refers to unspecified "boundaries of competency." It appears that here the key issue is not only the ambiguity of both constitutions, but also the long delay in passing the Ukrainian enabling laws. Article 137 of the Ukrainian Constitution briefly lists the policy areas to be governed directly by regional normative-legal acts,[13] but while the Crimean Constitution includes a more detailed list, it clarifies that acts must conform to the Ukrainian Constitution and laws (Crimean Constitution, articles 27 and 28).

As Ukrainian legal experts have also observed, the Crimean Constitution stipulates that the Crimean assembly has the right to "participate" in Ukrainian foreign policymaking (article 18.3) and to make decisions on investment, science, technology, free economic zones, licensing, and setting export quotas as well as demographic policy (article 18). The legal experts' critique does not mention that the same clause also contains the standard qualification that such rights are exercised by Crimea only so far as they are "within its competences." No such rights for Crimea in these policy areas are provided by the Ukrainian Constitution. Moreover, even the Crimean Constitution confines the scope for regional external relations to the economic sphere, science, education, and environmental and cultural issues. There are other issues about which the powers of the Crimean assembly, as stipulated in the Crimean Constitution, are not fully in accordance with the Ukrainian Constitution. Article 8 of the Crimean Constitution, for instance, states that the Verkhovna Rada of Crimea determines the special status of the regional capital Simferopol based on Ukrainian law. The Ukrainian Constitution, however, stipulates that the special status of cities is decided exclusively by Ukrainian law (article 92), and the Constitution accords a special status only to Kyiv and Sevastopol, as approved by Ukrainian law (article 133).

In democracies, constitutional ambiguities and contradictions are generally clarified by judicial review, and this process has been under way in Ukraine since 1998. The Ukrainian Constitutional Court is the ultimate arbiter of constitutional questions between the center and the region (Crimean Constitution, article 5.1). The Crimean Constitution defines the procedure by which the president of Ukraine can block normative-legal acts if they are considered to be in violation of the Ukrainian Constitution, with the Constitutional Court making the final decision (Crimean Constitution, article 5.2). Regional government acts also can be changed directly by the president of Ukraine (article 5.3). A separate article provides for the right of the Crimean assembly to address issues to the Constitutional Court in matters related to the Ukrainian Constitution and law (article 19). Since 1998 several cases related to Crimea have reached the Constitutional Court, but the Ukrainian president and the Crimean Rada have both taken the initiative. Not surprisingly, the Constitutional Court rulings have generally affirmed the center's constitutional supremacy over the region. For example, on 27 February 2001, the Constitutional Court set a precedent by declaring unconstitutional parts of four Crimean normative-legal acts that had been challenged by the president of Ukraine. This ruling clarified that only the Verkhovna Rada in Kyiv qualifies as a "parliament," whereas the Crimean Verkhovna Rada is merely the "representative organ" of the Autonomous Republic of Crimea and, therefore, cannot hold "parliamentary hearings," as stipulated in the regulations of the Crimean Rada. The same ruling defined the Crimean Constitution itself as the "key normative-legal act" among the acts adopted by the organs of the autonomous republic, a further legal downgrading of the autonomy status.[14]

Budgetary relations between Kyiv and Simferopol have been a key test ground for Crimea's powers. According to the Crimean Constitution (article 18.13), the taxes raised regionally form part of the Crimean budget. However, constitutional clauses on the budgetary relationship between Simferopol and Kyiv (article 18.13 and 18.14) are convoluted and refer to Ukrainian legislation for clarification. The Ukrainian state budget, approved by the national parliament, repeatedly provided for the transfer of value-added tax (VAT) from Crimea to the center, thereby effectively reducing Crimea's revenues.[15] The Verkhovna Rada of the Autonomous Republic initiated several Constitutional Court hearings, but in the end the Court decided in favor of the center.[16] The budgetary relations between Kyiv and Simferopol are one of only a few issues on which the interests of the Crimean government and assembly converge. Both organs of power stand for a stronger regional tax base, arguing for collecting and keeping the regionally raised taxes inclusive of VAT.

In 1998, with the chairman of the Communist Party, Hrach, elected as speaker of the Crimean assembly, and Kunitsyn (NDP) as the chairman of the regional Council of Ministers, a political balance between regional and pro-Kyiv orientations was established. From early 1999 onwards, however, there was a constant conflict between the two Crimean institutions. Until the regional elections in March 2002, Crimean politics was characterized by an internal power struggle between the two main institutions, the regional executive and the assembly, primarily revolving around the unsuccessful mutual attempts to topple Hrach and Kunitsyn. Both benefited from links with party colleagues and the authorities in Kyiv.[17] The term "Hrachism" has come to describe Hrach's dominance in 1998. A personality clash between Hrach and Kunitsyn aggravated the underlying institutional conflict, resulting from an unclear constitutional division of responsibilities.

Crimean politics were highly unstable in this period, with regional parties forming and reforming, and the coalitions in the regional assembly were often alliances of convenience. Only the well-organized and predominant Communist Party under Hrach remained a stable fixture on the political scene. The Crimean Constitution of 1998 appeared to establish a "parliamentary" autonomous republic, according to which a Rada majority determines the composition and head of the Crimean Council of Ministers. This framework has been far less stable than the constitutions suggest.[18] Neither the Crimean nor Ukrainian constitutions, nor additional laws sufficiently defined the relationship between the regional Rada and the Council of Ministers. Consequently, interpersonal and interinstitutional infighting effectively deadlocks Crimean politics. Thus, the ratification of the Crimean Constitution did little to unblock regional policymaking, especially in the economic sphere. At the same time, the ongoing executive-legislature conflict—both at the center and in Crimea—has precluded a clear-cut center-regional cleavage from reemerging. The practical scope of Crimean autonomy is not only poorly defined by the text of the regional and national constitutions, but is also shaped by an uncertain political struggle in the region and nationally.

Evidence suggests that the majority of the Crimean population has remained alienated from the constitutional settlement. A regional opinion poll conducted in March 2001 established that almost 46.6 percent of the Crimean population believed that the adoption of the Crimean Constitution had not influenced the political situation in the region. According to the same poll, 19.8 percent thought of it as having a positive influence, whereas 13.3 percent pointed to its negative impact. The respondents' list of concerns was again clearly topped by a range of socioeconomic issues, whereas the region's relations with the center was a concern for only 4.2 percent, and a lack of interaction between the regional Rada and government for only 2.7 percent.[19] These perceptions of the irrelevancy of Crimean institutions to the everyday problems of people testify to the popular disillusionment with regional politics since 1994.

The institution of Crimean autonomy per se has not fostered a positive identification with regional institutions. If, thus far, Crimea's autonomy status has had little to offer to the ethnic Russians, it has offered even less to the Crimean Tatars.[20] By the time of the ratification of the Crimean Constitution in December 1998, they had already lost their fourteen guaranteed quota seats in the Crimean assembly. The final negotiations and the ratification of the new Crimean Constitution in 1998 provided an even more definite marker of their exclusion, as the Crimean Tatars were not engaged in the process.

Despite his political clout, his broad support base, and his party apparatus, Hrach failed to make the Crimean Constitution relevant to the region's political and economic life, and to introduce much-needed structural regional reforms. Crimean autonomy, as defined in the Constitution, and as practiced under the Communist Party leader and speaker of the regional Rada from 1998 to 2002, may have reconciled Crimea with Kyiv, but it heightened the level of confrontation with the Mejlis. Neither the Ukrainian nor the Crimean Constitution recognizes the status of the Crimean Tatars as an indigenous people, nor do they guarantee their political representation in the regional institutions. There is no constitutional recognition of the Crimean Tatar political organizations, the Kurultay and Mejlis. The specific socioeconomic concerns of the Crimean Tatars—especially the question of restitution of property and land rights—tied to their return to Crimea are ignored by both constitutions. The regional Constitution refers to the Crimean Tatars only in the context of the regional language provisions: the Crimean Constitution and the regional normative-legal acts are to be published in Ukrainian, Russian, and Crimean Tatar (article 4.2). Article 10 declares that the use and development of Russian, Crimean Tatar, and other national languages will be guaranteed in addition to the state language, Ukrainian.[21] Education in national languages is specified, although whether this is to be provided for (and thus funded) by state schools or private national-cultural organizations is left open. Additionally, the possibility of having official documents issued in Crimean Tatar is singled out (article 11). Next to Ukrainian as the state language, the Russian language is privileged by being described as "the language of the majority of the population" that is "suited to interethnic communication" and "will be used in all spheres of societal life" (article 10.2).

Crimean Tatar leaders themselves are vague about the relationship of the Mejlis to the state. If it were registered as a party or NGO, it would become one among many Crimean Tatar organizations. Moreover, the demand for special recognition as a Crimean Tatar institution is itself a useful means of keeping Crimean Tatar issues on the regional and national political agenda, in recognition of the fact that the Crimean Tatars were being left out of the "normalization" process between Kyiv and Crimea. In May 1999 Kuchma established an Advisory Committee on Crimean Tatar Affairs attached to his office and chaired by Jemilev. As this consultative body comprises all thirty-three Mejlis members, it amounted to a de facto recognition of the Mejlis as the leading authoritative and representative institution of the Crimean Tatars. It may also have been an attempt to officially co-opt the moderate Crimean Tatar leaders and to constrain a radicalization of Crimean Tatar politics. Despite the vague status of the Advisory Committee, it represented an additional means for taking the Crimean Tatar demands off the streets and into institutional channels. Kuchma's decree on the Advisory Committee came on the eve of the biggest public Crimean Tatar demonstration since independence. Each year tens of thousands of Crimean Tatars combine the commemoration of the day of the deportation with a protest to demand their rights and recognition. In an attempt to preempt and undermine Kuchma's consultative body, Hrach set up the Crimea-based Council of the Crimean Tatar Elders (*Sovet aksakalov*) in April 1999 as an advisory body to the speaker of the Crimean assembly. This body brought together Crimean Tatar representatives who were critical of the Mejlis, but it failed to make an impact in regional politics.

The Elections of 2002: A Turning Point?

The Crimean elections of 31 March 2002 resulted in surprising losses for the Communist Party and gains for the Crimean Tatars, who won eight seats in the Crimean Rada despite the unfavorable majoritarian electoral system. The elections had been preceded by a lengthy debate on potential reforms to the regional electoral system to make it more representative of the minorities. A presidential commission, including Crimean deputies, members of the Crimean Council of Ministers, and Crimean Tatar representatives, tried to reach an agreement on the substance of a new law. The Verkhovna Rada of Ukraine considered various drafts, among them a mixed system (half proportional representation, half majoritarian based on single-member constituencies) and the reintroduction of national quotas. The 50-50 system without national quotas made it through the first reading in parliament, but President Kuchma once again favored the majoritarian system. That Crimea was not a separate state and that it did not have its own regional parties were among the rather nonsensical arguments used to support a majoritarian system. Hrach was also a longstanding opponent of national quotas. In mid-November 2001, the Ukrainian Verkhovna Rada failed—possibly under the president's influence—to adopt a mixed regional electoral system. Instead, cosmetic changes were made to the existing law and adopted on 17 January 2002.[22] The regional election date was fixed to coincide with the national elections on 31 March 2002.

The March 2002 elections demonstrated that the Crimean political situation continued to be in greater flux than the national political scene of Ukraine. In the elections in Crimea to the Ukrainian Verkhovna Rada five parties and blocs managed to cross the four percent threshold. The remains of the Russian movement were still represented: the Union Party participated as part of the Russian Bloc (*Russkii Blok*), which gained the support of 4.76 percent of the Crimean electorate. The ten single-member constituencies were distributed as follows: two were taken by the United Social Democratic Party of Ukraine (SDPU[o]), one by the Communist Party of Ukraine, and seven by independent candidates (see table 9.1).[23] The Communist Party lost 15.1 percent compared to 1998; the SDPU(o) gained a significant regional foothold due to the influence of the television channel Inter, which is closely tied to the SDPU(o). Without special technical equipment Crimeans received only the first Ukrainian national channel and Inter at this point. The broadcast of the main Russian channel from Moscow, ORT, had been stopped in the second half of the 1990s, sparking temporary public protests on a scale unseen since the early 1990s.

Table 9.1. Ukrainian parliamentary elections in Crimea, 2002
(party lists with results above 4 percent).

Party	Percent of votes
Communist Party of Ukraine (KPU)	33.91
United Social Democratic Party of Ukraine (SDPU[o])	12.47
Our Ukraine (*Nasha Ukraïna*)	9.77
For a United Ukraine (*Za iedynu Ukraïnu*)	5.92
Russian Bloc (*Russkii Blok*)	4.76

Source: *Kryms'ki studii, Informatsiinyi biuleten'*, no. 3–4 (15–16), May–August 2002, 14.

Crimea was one of the regions where the much talked-about "administrative resources" (*adminresurs*) were widely deployed, particularly by the Communists, the representatives of "For a United Ukraine," and the SDPU(o). The Crimean elections pitted primarily regional politicians and business elites against each other.[24] A distinctive feature of the Crimean electoral politics was that some parties could cooperate at the regional level yet remained bitter opponents at the national level. Already in the run-up to the elections, the political scene was polarized into two main groups: Hrach's "Crimean bloc," supported by Moscow-based political forces, including the leader of the Communist Party of the Russian Federation, Gennadii Zyuganov, and Moscow Mayor Iurii Luzhkov; and the so-called *kommanda Kunitsyna* (Kunitsyn's team), a loose anticommunist coalition including representatives of Labor Ukraine, the Party of Regions, the National Democratic Party, and the Agrarian Party. At the national level, all of the latter parties also formed the pro-Kuchma bloc "For a United Ukraine." The Crimean Tatars supported Viktor Yushchenko's bloc "Our Ukraine." The Communist Party remained the single biggest party represented in the Crimean Rada, but its tally of seats roughly halved. In the aftermath of the elections, the umbrella coalition of centrist and independent deputies united to form the faction "Stability" (*Stabil'nost'*), holding sixty-one seats. The subsequent vote by which the regional Rada endorsed the new Crimean Council of Ministers (ninety-four deputies voting in favor) also suggested a new atmosphere of compromise and the possibility of ending the traditional standoff between the Crimean Rada and the Council of Ministers (see table 9.2).

There was a considerable turnover of deputies: sixty-three deputies were elected to the assembly for the first time, but about half of them had at some stage occupied positions in the Council of

Table 9.2. Party membership of the deputies in the Crimean Verkhovna Rada.

Party	Deputies
Communist Party of Ukraine (KPU)	14
Agrarian Party of Ukraine (APU)	9
National Democratic Party (NDP)	6
United Social Democratic Party of Ukraine (SDPU[o])	3
Party of Regions (*Partiia rehioniv*)	3
For a United Rus (*Za iedinu Rus'*)	3
Rural Party of Ukraine (*Selians'ka partiia Ukraïny*)	1
Party of Industrialists and Entrepreneurs (*Partiia promyslovtsiv i pidpriiemtsiv*)	1
Russian-Ukrainian Union (*Rosiisko-ukraïns'kyi soiuz*)	1
Labor Ukraine (*Trudova Ukraïna*)	1
Democratic Union (*Demokratychnyi soiuz*)	1
Union Party (*Soiuz*)	1
Independents	52

Source: Data from the Analytical Center of the Crimean Assembly, October 2002. The data provided by the Ukraïns'kyi nezalezhnyi tsentr politychnykh doslidzhen' in the summer of 2002 slightly diverged from these figures: Communist Party: 15; Agrarian Party: 11; NDP: 8; For a United Rus': 2; Russian-Ukrainian Union: 1; no member of the Union Party; and 49 independents; see *Informatsiino-analitychne vydannia*, 7.

Ministers or in Crimea's local councils and administrative structures. Most of the elected deputies occupied leading positions in business and finance, and 49 percent were between 41 and 50 years of age.[25] The composition of the new Crimean Rada included forty-two Russians, thirty-five Ukrainians, eight Crimean Tatars, four Jews, two Gagauz, one Abkhaz, one Armenian, one Greek, and one Czech.[26] Local party consolidation and identification remained very low in Crimea as independents dominated the political scene: out of a total of 6,678 elected local deputies, only 1,669 were party members (425 deputies of the Agrarian Party of Ukraine, 415 of the SDPU(o), 403 of the Communist Party, 105 members of the NDP, and others).[27]

Without a national quota, just eight Crimean Tatars managed to secure seats in the regional assembly, including one Communist Party representative. At the level of local town councils, the Crimean Tatars now accounted for 13.9 percent, and in the rural *raions* for 16 percent of the deputies. Despite the lack of institutional guarantees, they managed to secure a degree of representation roughly proportional to their share of the population at the local level, thanks to a high degree of political discipline. Altogether eighty-six Crimean Tatar candidates stood in sixty-two constituencies; in over fifty constituencies, candidates proposed by the Kurultay were registered. In forty-four constituencies the Crimean Tatars put forward one candidate; in fifteen constituencies, two candidates (one supported by the Kurultay); in three constituencies, four candidates; and in thirty-eight constituencies, no Crimean Tatar candidate registered.[28]

The overall number of Crimean Tatar candidates changed little compared to the 1998 election, but the higher concentration of Crimean Tatar candidates testifies to their effective use of the electoral system. In 1998 they had put forward seventy candidates in forty-four constituencies, among them one candidate each in twenty constituencies, and two or more in twenty-four constituencies. In 2002, three candidates put themselves forward against the recommendation of the Kurultay, and a number of other candidates were not vetted by the Kurultay.[29] Thus, competition among Crimean Tatar candidates was not completely eradicated, but the Kurultay dominated the constituencies with the best electoral chances. By 15 April 2002, Crimean Tatar representation in the local organs of self-government was as follows: the Tatars accounted for 15 percent in the local councils (992 deputies)—4.9 percent in the towns of republican jurisdiction and 16 percent in the rural *raions*. By comparison, in 1998 a total of only 586 Crimean Tatar deputies had been elected. After March 2002, the Crimean Tatars were best represented in the local structures of Bilohirsk *raion* (about 38 percent); they accounted for 13 to 15 percent of the council deputies in Pervomais'ke, Chornomors'ke, Bakhchisarai, and Dzhankoi *raions*, and for 7 to 10 percent in Lenine, Saky, and Simferopol *raions*.[30]

The increase in Crimean Tatar participation and representation in 2002 is best explained by a series of contingencies. The 2002 electoral register included about thirty thousand more voters than in 1998, a figure accounted for primarily by changes in the Ukrainian legislation and bilateral Ukrainian-Uzbek agreements facilitating a steep increase in the number of Crimean Tatars obtaining Ukrainian citizenship and, thereby, the right to vote. Compared to the 1998 elections, the number of Crimean Tatar voters nearly doubled to about sixty thousand in 2002. Likewise, the Tatars' electoral strategies and voting discipline had improved. The 75 to 80 percent turnout among the Crimean Tatars was considerably higher than the Crimean average of 63 percent.[31] By 1 March 2002, a total of 259,610 Crimean Tatars were registered in Crimea. In the towns, they accounted for up to 7 percent of the population, in the rural *raions* from 13.6 to 33 percent.[32] To use the existing electoral system to its full effect, the Mejlis organizations at different levels actively intervened in the registration procedure and put forward only one candidate for most local positions to maximize the chances of success. This is a classic electoral strategy in an ethnically divided society. The Tatars are geographically concentrated, although they do not make up the majority in any constituencies. If they are united politically, they can take advantage of split votes in other local communities.

Anti–Crimean Tatar rhetoric was less prominent in the 2002 election campaign. Hrach had once again attempted to exploit the Crimean Tatar issue during the election campaign, but it did not work since the main divide was between him and the bloc of anticommunists. When a Simferopol court withdrew Hrach's registration because his personal details were incomplete, the ensuing drama completely dominated the final stage of the campaign and distracted from the anti-Tatar rhetoric. Hrach's name remained on the preprinted ballots, and he won in his constituency. Ultimately, the Ukrainian Supreme Court overruled the Simferopol court by reinstating Hrach.

The discussion about changing the regional electoral system into a system based on proportional representation continued after the 2002 elections. In October 2002, the Crimean Rada set up a working group, chaired by deputy speaker Kiselev, on the reform of the Crimean electoral system.[33] Jemilev described the political situation after the 2002 elections as "a bit better," but emphasized the need for guaranteed representation: "At the moment we are only represented due to our strong unity. But why do we have to be so united and the Russians don't have to be to have an impact?"[34] He singled out guaranteed representation, the unresolved issue of the Crimean Tatar rights in the context of the sale of land scheduled for 2005 onwards, and the status of the Crimean Tatar language as the key issues to be addressed. He demanded that there should be two state languages: Ukrainian and Crimean Tatar. In order to be adequately represented, in his view, the Crimean Tatars would need at least thirteen guaranteed seats in the regional assembly and veto rights on issues of their concern.

In the parallel national-level elections three Crimean Tatars were elected to the Verkhovna Rada in Kyiv: Jemilev and Chubarov kept their seats, this time both running on the Rukh ticket as part of the Our Ukraine bloc (28th and 60th on the list), and Zarema Katusheva was elected on the Communist Party ticket. Katusheva was born in Samarkand, had been a Communist Party member since 1978, and came to Crimea in 1990. She argued against the assumption that the Crimean Tatar people all think in unison and always agree unanimously on policy. She supported Hrach's line on opposing the national-level coalition of the Communist Party and antipresidential opposition forces around Iuliia Tymoshenko, Rukh, Socialist Party head Moroz, and Our Ukraine leader Yushchenko. Katusheva's support for Hrach's proposal to elevate Russian to an "official" language met with criticism among the Tatars and Ukraine's center-right. She interpreted her position as a stance against nationalism, and she noted that mixed marriages—she is married to a Russian—were the rule rather than the exception in Crimea.[35]

The new regime in Crimean politics after the 2002 elections

was illustrated most starkly by the removal of Hrach as speaker of the Rada. At the first session of the new Crimean assembly on 29 April, Borys Deich was elected speaker: fifty-two out of eighty-eight deputies present voted for him, while Hrach got only twenty-two votes. Kunitsyn was reelected prime minister with sixty-four votes and replaced Valerii Horbatov.[36] This vote concluded, at least temporarily, the Hrach era in Crimean politics. A majority of sixty-seven Crimean deputies asked the Ukrainian president to approve not only the Crimean prime minister, as required by the Crimean Constitution, but also the speaker of the regional Rada.[37] Thus, Kyiv was now seen as an arbiter in the intrainstitutional and interpersonal struggles in Crimea. Over a decade after the collapse of the Soviet Union, the Crimean political landscape was still shifting and developing.

The period from 2002 onwards was bound to see new disagreements between the Crimean institutions, whose responsibilities were not clearly defined—mainly with regard to the related issues of land privatization and the integration of the Crimean Tatars into Crimean society. In the autumn of 2002, the fourth meeting of the Council of Representatives of the Crimean Tatar People (*Sovet predstavitelei krymskotatarskogo naroda*) took place in Crimea in the presence of President Kuchma. The meeting provided a forum for the discussion of key issues relevant to the Crimean Tatars: the insufficiently effective use of money earmarked for settlement programs,[38] the high unemployment rate (about 20 percent), the Mejlis' concerns and proposals regarding land ownership, and the status of the Crimean Tatars as an indigenous people.[39] Local tensions involving Crimean Tatars illegally occupying land have been recurrent. In January 2003, a standoff involving Crimean Tatar settlers was avoided in a village near Sudak, where Tatar settlers, helped by the local Mejlis, started building houses on land that a Moscow-based company had acquired to build a cultural and athletic center. At first the Tatars and the company reached a compromise, but at the last moment tensions arose over the question of land ownership. The settlers were tying their protest to the Tatars' political demand to have a say in decisions regarding the commercial use of Crimean land. As on previous occasions, Crimean Tatar and Russian-speaking youth clashed, and several people were injured. A Cossack organization was said to be involved in the violence against the Tatars. An escalation was avoided through negotiations with the local community groups and militia organized by the president's representative, Oleksandr Dydenko, and Crimean Prime Minister Kunitsyn.[40] Thus, low-level interethnic violence in Crimea continued to be a cause of concern for the highest institutional levels.

Crimean Politics after the 2002 Elections

During the first session of the new Crimean Rada in May 2002, the anti-Hrach faction Stability included sixty-one deputies, including five Crimean Tatars. In contrast, the faction Prosperity in Unity (*Protsvitannia v iednosti*), dominated by a Communist Party nucleus, consisted of just twenty-three deputies. Some additional smaller groups were established, and twelve deputies abstained from any faction or group.[41] By 4 October, the balance had further tipped in favor of the majority coalition, which now had sixty-seven deputies in its ranks, while only eleven deputies had stayed in the minority Communist-dominated faction.[42] Nevertheless, the cooperation between Deich and Kunitsyn remained superficial. The economic programs of the Crimean Council of Ministers focused on the tourist sector as the first priority. Industry, which still accounted for most of the region's economy and 40 percent of its budget, was the second priority, in particular the chemical industry and shipbuilding. The third priority was agriculture, especially wine production. New regional taxes, for example an estate tax, were supposed to become operational. The capacity of the regional government to implement policies of economic management was constrained, however, by the lack of movement to clarify the budgetary relations between Kyiv and Simferopol.[43]

The political debates in Crimea showed little evidence of change. The most widely read newspaper, *Krymskaia pravda*, kept printing the column "How to Build Crimea" (*Kak nam obustroit' Krym*), which was reminiscent of the coverage in the early 1990s.[44] There was an obsession with the ethnic diversity of the region and specific historical events, such as Russia's annexation of Crimea in 1783, Crimea's unique features, and demands for special treatment of the region. Opinion polls, regularly published in the main newspapers of the Russian community (*Russkii mir, Russkaia obshchina,* a weekly supplement to *Krymskaia pravda*), demonstrated that the majority ethnic Russian regional sentiment was still in favor of closer links with Russia and felt antagonized by what was seen as the "linguistic occupation" of Crimea, hoping instead for the unification of Crimea's pro-Russian forces.[45] While *Russkii mir* was the voice of Russian nationalists like Tsekov or Luzhkov, *Krymskaia pravda* provided Hrach with a regular forum. This combination highlighted the compatibility of some of the demands put forward by the remnants of Crimea's Russian movement with those of the regional branch of the Communist Party. Thus, despite his restricted influence in the Crimean assembly, Hrach's views were still omnipresent in agenda setting for the regional political debate. Hrach has been a fervent proponent of making Russian an official or state language in Crimea and Ukraine as a whole, tying the prospects for regional interethnic peace to the status of the Russian language.[46] The demands for cultural and linguistic rights for ethnic Russians that came from leading Crimean politicians, such as the ethnic Ukrainian Hrach, were still linked to socialist-era notions of supranational integration among the Slavs.

The continuing political salience of language rights in the Crimean Rada was illustrated by its decision in October 2002, supported by an overwhelming majority (seventy-five deputies), to ask the Ukrainian parliament to reconsider the status of the Russian language in Crimea and to consider making Russian the second state language in Ukraine.[47] The salience of language and education rights in the regional political discourse underpin a permanent potential for mobilization. Aware of this potential, the Ukrainian government has managed language and cultural policy in Crimea with great sensitivity. There was no attempt to impose a rapid Ukrainization. The Tavriia National University (*Tavricheskii Natsional'nyi Universitet*) in Simferopol, for example, retained its Russian language status and, according to Pro-Rector Viktor Sharapa, there was no pressure to change this status.[48]

At the secondary school level, the diversity of languages has grown and there has been a gradual increase in the number of Crimean Tatar and Ukrainian schools. The former have especially benefited from international support for teaching facilities and materials, for example from the George Soros–funded International

Renaissance Foundation. Out of a total of six hundred schools in Crimea by 2002, there were fourteen Crimean Tatar schools and fifty-six schools with classes taught in Crimean Tatar, enabling about eleven percent of the Crimean Tatar children to learn in their native language; in addition, there were four Ukrainian schools and one polyethnic school (located in Staryi Krym and sponsored by Kyiv) with instruction in Bulgarian, Greek, Armenian, and German.[49] The data demonstrate that in language and education Crimea remains an overwhelmingly "Russian" region.

Although "normalized" constitutionally, Crimea's particularistic politics have kept it distant from the rest of Ukraine. For example, the large-scale antipresidential protests flaring up in the autumn of 2002—coordinated by the Tymoshenko bloc, the Socialist Party, and the Communist Party—largely bypassed Crimea. Despite the participation of the Ukrainian Communist Party and its leader, Petro Symonenko, the Crimean Communists did not support the protests. Hrach openly voiced his criticism of the "instrumentalization of the Communist Party" for the purposes of the protests under the slogan "Rise up, Ukraine."[50] These national and regional protests across parts of Ukraine were the precursor to the demonstrations against the falsified presidential elections of 2004—the "Orange Revolution" that brought the Kuchma era to an end.

Conclusion

By late 1998 Crimean autonomy had been constitutionalized in three steps: the incomplete Crimean Constitution passed by the Ukrainian parliament in April 1996, the Ukrainian Constitution of June 1996, and the final revision of the Crimean Constitution ratified by the Ukrainian parliament in December 1998, which anchored the Autonomous Republic of Crimea in the Ukrainian state.

During the final period of the constitutional settlement, the predominant role was played by the regional branch of the Communist Party and its leader, Leonid Hrach. He railroaded through the final draft of the Crimean Constitution, but he failed to activate the Constitution as a basis for the progression of reform in the region. The constant interpersonal and interinstitutional struggle between Hrach and Kunitsyn hampered the use of the constitutional framework to enact policies to improve the socioeconomic conditions of Crimea. Consequently, despite the stabilization of the constitutional issue voters were disillusioned by the lack of progress on socioeconomic issues; and in the elections of early 2002 they turned against the regional political elite in power. The elections not only brought to an end the era of "Hrachism," but also resulted in a significant turn-over of the deputies in the Crimean Rada. The elections temporarily brought to an end the institutional squabbles between the executive and parliament within Crimea, and paved the way for a more stable phase in regional politics without, however, bringing about a decisive shift towards effective policy implementation.

10 The International Dimensions of the Crimea Question

THE INTERNATIONAL DIMENSION OF THE CRIMEAN QUESTION consists of three principal aspects: Ukrainian-Russian relations, international involvement in mediation, and Turkey's role as an "observer" in defense of Crimean Tatar interests. The most important aspect has been the Ukrainian-Russian axis. After the breakup of the USSR in late 1991 many leading Russian politicians from across the political spectrum took a keen interest in the Crimean issue and helped to transform it into a "national" concern for Russia. The swelling tide of Crimean separatism from 1992 to 1994 came at a time when Russian nationalism within the Russian Federation was resurgent. These two movements of "Russia-firsters" complemented each other and provided the key link between regional, national, and international politics in the Crimea question.

Russian-Ukrainian relations have been crucial to the state and nation building process for both states. Ukrainian independence limits Russia's traditional sphere of influence and has forced a reassessment of the core elements of Russian national identity.[1] The process through which Russian political elites came to terms with Ukrainian independence introduced an element of instability into Russian-Ukrainian relations. Post-Soviet Ukraine has made many domestic and most foreign policy decisions with a cautious recognition of Russia's position or possible reaction. Apart from energy issues, Crimea has dominated foreign relations between the two states, whether it concerns the terms of the division of the Black Sea Fleet, the status of Sevastopol, or the status of Crimea as a whole.[2] Crimea, described by Solchanyk as "a choice piece of real estate,"[3] has been a sensitive issue in Russian politics. The Crimea question was often used instrumentally by politicians and parties in Russian domestic politics in a manner that revealed a deep uncertainty as to whether it was a domestic or foreign policy issue. Moreover, the Crimean issue illustrates the incoherence and rapidly changing nature of post-Soviet Russian foreign policy. The issues of the "Russian" diaspora and contested territories crosscut the main cleavages in Russian politics: left-right, democrat-communist, reform-antireform, liberal-nationalist. For a while different segments of the Russian political elite—especially a few vociferous politicians—put forward their claims and views, but there was no consensus on Crimea. In the early 1990s, the Russian parliament issued a series of provocative resolutions challenging the legitimacy of Ukraine's sovereignty over Crimea. Some members of the Russian government took a similar stand, but the Russian president, Boris Yeltsin, who dominated Russian foreign policymaking, took a cautious approach and refused to get drawn too deeply into the Crimean issue. He tolerated the visits of Russian officials to Crimea, but he routinely refused to support the various parliamentary resolutions on Crimea. Without his public support, these resolutions remained paper tigers. Besides, from 1992 to 1994, as the Russian nationalist wave rose over Crimea, Yeltsin was in conflict with the Russian parliament and was anxious to use any issue to distance himself from what he portrayed as its "extremism." These divisions in Russian domestic politics, consequently, weakened the leverage of Russia over Ukraine concerning the issue of Crimea.

Redefining Russian-Ukrainian Relations

The 1990 Russian-Ukrainian bilateral treaty, which committed both sides to the inviolability of borders, triggered a Russian Supreme Soviet debate in which Crimea figured prominently. The first major attempts to stake out a Russian claim to disputed territories in the "near abroad" actually came from the Yeltsin camp. Two days after the Ukrainian declaration of independence on 24 August 1991, Yeltsin's press secretary, Pavel Voshchanov, announced that Russia reserved to itself the right to revise its borders with the republics that had opted out of the negotiations over a new union treaty. In an explanatory note, Voshchanov added during a press conference on 27 August that the previous announcement referred to Crimea, the Donbas, and northern Kazakhstan. In a televised speech that day, one of Russia's leading democrats and close associate of Yeltsin in the "Democratic Russia" movement, Moscow mayor Gavriil Popov, called for local referenda to decide the status of Crimea and Odesa oblast.[4]

Yeltsin and the other leaders of successor states attempted to put an end to any challenges to post-Soviet boundaries by the agreements of 8 December 1991 establishing the Commonwealth of Independent States (CIS). The signatories proclaimed mutual respect of their territorial integrity and the inviolability of existing borders.[5] On 30 December 1991, a CIS agreement was signed according to which the successor states to the USSR could build their national armies from the Soviet military forces based on their territories. However, unspecified "strategic forces" were to remain under joint CIS control, and the question of the future of the Black Sea Fleet was not clarified. At the beginning of 1992, President Kravchuk announced the creation of the Ukrainian armed forces based on all Soviet forces on Ukrainian territory, and from 5 January onwards the Ukrainian Ministry of Defense arranged for the armed forces, the National Guard, the border troops, and eventually the Black Sea Fleet to take an oath of allegiance to the Ukrainian state.[6] This oath was implemented across Crimea quite smoothly, except in the Black Sea Fleet. Its commander, Igor' Kasatonov, refused to follow the instructions issued by the Ukrainian Ministry of Defense. His stance escalated the mobilization of public and political support against the Ukrainian "takeover" of the fleet. For the Ukrainian authorities, the protest may have come as a surprise, since there had been a heavy turnout (97 percent) of Black Sea Fleet personnel voting in the 1 December referendum on independence, of which 72 percent had voted in favor, and at least 48 percent had voted for Kravchuk as president.[7] This was a time of great uncertainty and confusion, however, and the vote was regarded more as a question of choosing democracy over communism; Russian ethnicity and the question of statehood were not the primary markers of identity for the servicemen.[8] However, the general assumption had been that the Black Sea Fleet would remain under joint CIS control. The military situation was confusing. Units of the Ukrainian National Guard—the special force formed after the

August 1991 coup—were stationed in Crimea. At the same time, the center's command of the local troops of the Ministry for Internal Affairs, which had traditionally been under the joint control of the local and national party organs and which counted many Crimeans among its staff, was uncertain. On the whole, the presence of several military units with different loyalties appears to have made all sides act with caution for fear of provoking armed conflict.

No sooner had the USSR been formally dissolved than, in January 1992, a group of Russian parliamentarians began to discuss the "legality" of the 1954 transfer of Crimea and the status of the Black Sea Fleet. This discussion was fervently pursued by the Russian media. On 23 January 1992, the Russian parliament voted by a clear majority to delegate the issue to its Committee on Foreign Affairs and Foreign Economic Relations, the Committee on Legislation, and the Ministry of Foreign Affairs, while recommending to Ukraine that it start a similar procedure. These discussions came at a time when the Russian president and parliament together with the leaders of republics and regions were negotiating a new federal treaty, which was signed in March 1992. This treaty made no claim on Crimea or Sevastopol.

According to Solchanyk the driving force behind the Russian parliament's moves on the Crimean issue was Vladimir Lukin, a leading foreign policy adviser to Yeltsin, a democrat and head of the parliamentary Committee on Foreign Affairs and Foreign Economic Relations. Lukin, Solchanyk claims, aimed to use the question of Crimea's status as Russia's bargaining chip in the ongoing negotiations over the Black Sea Fleet. According to this logic, by disputing the legal status of Crimea Russia would stimulate separatist political mobilization in Crimea and then force Ukraine to accept Russia's demands regarding the fleet and its bases in return for Russian support in containing Crimean separatism. A further means of exerting pressure on Ukraine, envisaged by Lukin, was to threaten cancellation of contracts related to Ukraine's military-industrial production.[9] This interpretation transforms the Russian concerns over sovereignty in Crimea into a cynical maneuver for the accumulation of military assets. It almost certainly underestimates the genuine Russian "national" interest in the status of Crimea. Russian sensitivity was particularly acute over the "ownership" of Sevastopol. The city was not only Russia's main naval base in the Black Sea, but had an immense cultural-historical symbolism for Russians. The Sevastopol city soviet regularly appealed to the Russian and Ukrainian presidents to implement the will of the people and allow its "return" to Russia. By mid-January 1992, however, Russia had recognized that it would have to transfer at least a part of the Black Sea Fleet to the Ukrainian armed forces.

The Black Sea Fleet has aptly been described as the world's largest "naval museum."[10] Its actual material value is debatable and is mainly confined to nuclear submarines and land-based naval installations. In 1992 the fleet comprised 300 combat ships, 14 submarines, 300 sea- and land-based planes and helicopters, and coastal infrastructure. It represented an important symbol of military power and, as such, was regarded by both Ukraine and Russia as a constituent element of statehood.[11] The fleet was based in Sevastopol, instead of Novorossiisk, for strategic and historical-symbolic reasons. In 1991, sixty-seven thousand military personnel were serving in the Black Sea Fleet, but by the end of 1995, there were only thirty-five thousand left, with further reductions pending.[12] The figures regarding the national affiliation of the staff of the Black Sea Fleet vary considerably: according to one source about 20 percent of the officer corps and about 30 percent of the sailors were Ukrainians;[13] according to another source about 30 percent of the officers and over 60 percent of the sailors were Ukrainians.[14] Whatever the correct percentages, it is clear that although nationality was initially not of primary importance, the question of the Ukrainian oath of allegiance opened deep national and ideological divisions. Kravchuk offered incentives to those who took the oath to Ukraine, such as better pay and housing, and given the climate, conditions of service and the comparatively small risk of war in Ukraine or Crimea, many sailors acted pragmatically in the choice of allegiance to Ukraine.

The negotiations about the division and bases of the aging fleet dragged on for many years.[15] The negotiations first envisaged a united fleet under joint CIS control, but the Russian demand for control of the fleet soon became predominant. Once units of the fleet took different oaths of allegiance, and with Russian and Ukrainian politicians manipulating the issue and Crimean separatism on the rise, the danger of conflict became more precarious. Since neither

Russia nor Ukraine had an interest in escalating the Black Sea Fleet issue into open armed conflict, a joint working group was set up and negotiations initiated in April 1992.

The uncertainty over Crimea was illustrated on 3–5 April 1992, when Vice President Aleksandr Rutskoi led an official Russian government delegation on a visit to Sevastopol, though it was not officially invited by the Ukrainian government. The Russian delegation included presidential adviser Sergei Stankevich and General Boris Gromov, and must have been conducted with the approval of Yeltsin.

The timing can hardly have been coincidental: Kyiv and Simferopol were in their first standoff over the Crimean constitutional issue of defining the content and boundaries of Crimean autonomy. The high-ranking Russian officials peppered their visit with numerous remarks about the illegality of the 1954 transfer; they suggested that Crimea should become part of the Russian Federation, and openly supported the controversial regional referendum that Kyiv had tried to prevent.[16] The Ukrainian authorities and media protested against the interference by the uninvited guests. The trip revealed that the political climate in Russia was shifting towards a more nationalist stance on Crimea that exhibited neo-imperial overtones. On 21 May 1992, about two weeks after Crimea's Act on State Independence, the Russian parliament nullified the 1954 transfer by an almost unanimous vote. The transfer, so went the Russian argument, had violated the Constitution of the RSFSR and Soviet legislative procedures.[17] In particular, Russians claimed that the Supreme Soviet of the RSFSR had made the decision in 1954 without the required quorum, and the Presidium—rather than the whole Supreme Soviet as required by the Constitution—had made the final decision on the matter.[18] The mutual guarantee of territorial integrity embodied in the 1990 Russian-Ukrainian treaty was now interpreted to have been valid only for as long as the Soviet Union existed, a clear divergence from Yeltsin's position at the time of ratification.[19] Equally, there was a question mark over the legality of the transfer and the Russian parliament's challenge deserved serious consideration. The Russian parliament's reassurance on 22 May that it did not intend to question Ukraine's territorial integrity did not allay Ukrainian concerns, as this seemed to leave its previous challenge over the question of Crimea's status intact.[20] The Ukrainian authorities quickly declared the status of Crimea nonnegotiable. The Ukrainian parliament accused its Russian counterpart of violating the 1990 bilateral agreement between Russia and Ukraine, the founding agreement of the CIS, and the Helsinki Final Act.[21]

Yeltsin distanced himself from the parliamentary resolution. Crimea was one of several issues related to Russian national identity and policy that began to fracture the Democratic Russia movement, of which Yeltsin was the acclaimed leader. Leading democrats such as Aleksandr Tsipko and presidential adviser Galina Staravoitova supported Ukraine's position. Prominent ministers such as Yegor Gaidar and Valerii Tishkov never questioned Ukraine's territorial integrity.[22] Conversely, the Russian Foreign Minister Andrei Kozyrev, who was generally recognized as one of Russia's leading moderates, questioned Crimea's status within Ukraine by talking about Crimea's rightful place within Russia. However, he also repeatedly warned the Russian parliament against provoking a Ukrainian-Russian confrontation over the issue. Extremist nationalist Russian politicians such as Vladimir Zhirinovskii, who paid a rabble-rousing visit to Crimea in early June 1992, were the most vocal advocates of the reassertion of Russian power and presented Crimea as a test case of Russia's status as a great power.

Kravchuk and Yeltsin began a process of personal diplomacy to negotiate on the Black Sea Fleet. The first of a series of summits was held on 23 June 1992 at the Russian Black Sea resort town of Dagomys. The agreed starting point for the negotiations was that the fleet would be divided between Russia and Ukraine. For the duration of the negotiations, the fleet would remain under joint control, with military personnel taking an oath of allegiance according to their own citizenship. The situation nevertheless became more and more complicated, with rival command structures, a lack of clear lines of command among the different units of the fleet, and a general politicization of the atmosphere in which the talks were held. According to the so-called Yalta Agreement, entering into force on 1 October 1992, joint control of the fleet was established for a three-year period, after which the Russian and Ukrainian parts of the fleet would be separated. In the interim period the joint commanders were to be appointed by the Russian and Ukrainian presidents. The lack of agreement on the eventual division of the fleet and the land-based assets hampered the implementation of this agreement. In December 1992, Admiral Kasatonov, then the Russian-appointed chief commander of the Black Sea Fleet, was promoted to First Deputy Commander in Chief of the Russian navy. The new Russian-appointed chief commander of the Black Sea Fleet was Admiral Eduard Baltin. Like his predecessor, Baltin saw himself as the defender of Russian state interests in the fleet. The Black Sea Fleet's involvement in the Georgian-Abkhaz conflict in late 1992 and early 1993, backing Russia's military support of Abkhazia, strained Ukraine-Russia relations because the Russian commanders decided unilaterally to deploy the fleet.[23] A major issue was the cofinancing of the fleet, in particular when the Ukrainian economy crashed during the transition. The gap in value between the Russian ruble and Ukraine's transitional currency widened, and the fleet personnel, whose pay was channeled through Ukraine's financial structures, saw their wages dwindling. Not surprisingly, more and more ships raised the Russian flag of St. Andrew during the first half of 1993, as sailors pragmatically decided their allegiance was to the Russian Federation and operated fully under Russian command.

The next meeting at the presidential level took place on 18 June in Zavidovo, near Moscow. The fifty-fifty division of the fleet was confirmed and Russia was granted the right to keep its base in Sevastopol. The fleet issue became increasingly tied up with Ukraine's mounting energy debt to Russia. The expectations for the next summit of the two presidents, held in mid-September 1993 at Masandra in Crimea, were low to begin with, given the increasing tensions between Ukraine and Russia. However, the summit achieved a pathbreaking agreement according to which about 30 percent of Ukraine's part of the fleet would be transferred to Russia in lieu of Ukraine's energy debts, and Ukraine would transfer its nuclear weapons to Russia.[24] The agreement came just a few days before Yeltsin used armed force to disperse the Russian parliament, paving the way for a strong presidential system.

The Status of Sevastopol

The status of Sevastopol was central to the dispute over the Black

Sea Fleet.[25] As discussed earlier, since 1948 Sevastopol had enjoyed a special constitutional status along with Moscow and Leningrad as a city of "RSFSR jurisdiction" (effectively enjoying rights similar to those of the regions of the RSFSR), a status it officially retained after the transfer of Crimea to Ukrainian administration in 1954. There was, however, no consistency in the Soviet approach to the city. For example, documentation on economic planning after 1954 often listed Sevastopol in conjunction with the Crimean and Ukrainian budgets.[26] Moreover, Sevastopol's party organization remained part of the Crimean oblast party organization and, thus, became part of the Communist Party of Ukraine in 1954.[27] In line with the 1978 Constitution of the Ukrainian SSR, the Sevastopol deputies were represented in the Supreme Soviet of the Ukrainian SSR. The command and control of the fleet, and its budgetary issues, however, were decided by the Ministry of Defense in Moscow. To make matters even more complicated, the Crimean oblast authorities were responsible for the Sevastopol branch of the Interior Ministry, the city branch of the KGB, the procuracy, the *raion* courts, tax inspection, and customs. The Sevastopol city deputies were also represented in the Crimean Supreme Soviet.[28]

Sevastopol is a distillation of the Crimean issue and of Crimea's distinctiveness. In no other place are Russian and Ukrainian historical memories and state interests so closely intertwined, as discussed in chapter 3. The fleet is a constant reminder of this historical link. According to the 1989 census, 74.5 percent of the city's population were Russians, an even higher percentage than in the rest of Crimea. The military-industrial complex accounted for the vast majority of the city's overall production and employment, and was devastated by the budgetary cuts and economic crash of the post-Soviet transition in both Ukraine and Russia. Sevastopol was a bastion of military conservatism and had even less experience with reform movements and civil society than the rest of Crimea. The city electorate followed the lead provided by other parts of Crimea and Ukraine generally by voting for a Crimean ASSR in the regional referendum in January 1991. In early 1992, the head of the Sevastopol city council met President Kravchuk in Kyiv and was granted special financial support for the city, a decision that de facto acknowledged both Kyiv's jurisdiction over Sevastopol and its special status within Ukraine.[29]

Many of the first political organizations forming in Sevastopol from 1992 onwards had links to the command structures of the Black Sea Fleet and were more pronouncedly pro-Russian than most of the all-Crimean organizations at the time. In a joint effort, some deputies from the Crimean Supreme Soviet, the Sevastopol city council, and members of different Russian parliamentary committees organized a campaign in Sevastopol and in Crimea in favor of a union with the Russian Federation.[30] This campaign helped to provide an impetus for the Russian parliament resolution on 9 December 1992 to review the legal status of Sevastopol. After many months of examination of the constitutional and legal procedures around the transfer of 1954, the Russian parliament adopted a resolution on 9 July 1993 "On the Status of the City of Sevastopol," placing the city under Russian jurisdiction.[31] The Russian Central Bank was called upon to provide funds for the city's budget, and the Russian Constitution was to be amended to include Sevastopol as a part of the Russian Federation.[32] Yeltsin and the Russian Ministry of Foreign Affairs distanced themselves from the parliament's resolution. Since Russia's federal treaty was a tripartite agreement between president, parliament and republics/regions, parliament did not have power to amend the treaty unilaterally. However, the summer of 1993 was a time of constitutional flux in Russia, as the Constitutional Assembly meeting in July was debating how to rewrite the federal treaty and form a new Constitution.

Crimea was one of many issues that contributed to the increasing standoff between the Russian parliament and the president, which reached its peak in the autumn of 1993. In response to the Russian parliament's resolution on Sevastopol, President Kravchuk appealed for support from the international community and issued a formal complaint in a letter addressed to the UN Security Council. Kravchuk referred to the Russian parliament's "wicked decisions" and "imperial thinking" in claiming Sevastopol and the Black Sea Fleet, and he sought confirmation that they were a "flagrant violation of the universally recognized norms and principles of international law."[33] The Security Council restated its commitment to Ukraine's territorial integrity and declared the Russian parliamentary resolution incompatible with both the UN Charter and the 1990 bilateral agreement between Ukraine and Russia.[34] The Security Council decision came after the receipt of a separate letter from the Russian government that condemned the Russian parliament's action as "emotional and declaratory." The Russian government undertook to resolve the differences with Ukraine through dialogue and in "strict observance" of its treaties and agreements with Ukraine and international obligations. The Russian letter did equivocate, however, by referring to the 1954 decision to transfer Crimea as an "administrative decision" of the "leaders of the former USSR." The wording also was ambivalent in its recognition of Ukrainian sovereignty over Crimea and Sevastopol as it referred to the need to maintain bases for the navy of the Russian Federation "in the territory of Ukraine, in the Crimea and in Sevastopol."[35]

Although from October 1993 the senior Russian and Ukrainian commanders were former military colleagues and had good relations, there was a considerable turnover at the level of the fleet commanders that impeded the implementation of the Russian-Ukrainian interstate agreement on the fleet. Russia continued to deploy the fleet unilaterally, as in the secret Shevardnadze-Baltin agreement of early November 1993, which led to Black Sea Fleet marines intervening in the Georgian civil war on the side of Shevardnadze to seize the port at Poti. A new crisis occurred in early April 1994 when the *Cheleken'* hydrographic vessel, equipped with expensive and sophisticated navigation instruments, tried to leave the Odesa port for Sevastopol. The Ukrainian authorities considered the ship Ukrainian property and ordered Ukrainian naval units to stop it. Russian naval commanders ordered their units to open fire if the Ukrainians did not back down. Fortunately, Ukraine did not press the matter, but the crisis demonstrated the danger of an escalation to violent conflict by decisions made by local commanders.[36] A meeting of the Russian and Ukrainian ministers of defense was held in Sevastopol on 22 April but again no final agreement could be concluded, although progress was made on how to divide the fleet, and it was envisaged that Ukraine would "sell" most of its share to Russia (in lieu of energy debts).[37]

Russian-Ukrainian Agreements and Disagreements

The year 1993 marked a turning point in the official Russian foreign policy away from Andrei Kozyrev's pro-Western so-called Atlanticist orientation, to a more nationalistic "Russia first" approach.[38] This shift accelerated after the victory of communist and extreme nationalist parties in the December 1993 Russian Duma elections. The twenty-five million Russian diaspora in the so-called near abroad, including the Russians in Crimea, became a major policy issue not only for the new Duma (as it had been for the former Supreme Soviet), but also for Yeltsin and the Russian government. But while Yeltsin publicly demanded protection for Russians in the "near abroad" as fundamental to Russia's national interest, in particular in the Baltic States, his position on Crimea remained conciliatory towards Ukraine. The Russian claims to Crimea and Sevastopol continued to be championed by politicians from across the political spectrum, including democrats associated with Yeltsin such as Yurii Luzhkov, appointed mayor of Moscow by Yeltsin in June 1992, and Ivan Rybkin, then chairman of the Duma. Certainly, much of the grandstanding by Russian politicians on the Crimea issue was for domestic "consumption" in Russia, principally for electoral gain, but we should not underestimate the strength of elite and popular sentiment on the issue.[39] The rise of nationalists to positions of power both in the Russian Duma, and in the Crimean Supreme Soviet and presidency in early 1994, placed significant pressure on Yeltsin and Kravchuk to resolve their differences over Crimea and the Black Sea Fleet. A key factor in Russian-Ukrainian relations was the constitutional transformation implemented by Yeltsin in late 1993. Yeltsin's forcible dissolution of the Russian parliament in October 1993, his imposition of a new Constitution, the recasting of parliamentary institutions, and the holding of new elections actually produced a more nationalistic and antireform Duma. Yeltsin's Constitution did, however, make foreign policy a presidential power, which Yeltsin employed to stabilize cooperative Russian-Ukrainian relations.

In a U.S.-brokered agreement on 14 January 1994, Ukraine agreed to ship all its nuclear warheads to the Russian Federation for dismantlement, and in exchange, Ukraine's territorial integrity was recognized by Russia and undersigned by the U.S.[40] This agreement appeared to finally remove any prospect of a Russian challenge to Ukraine's sovereignty over Crimea "from without." The agreement was concluded, however, at the very moment when the challenge to Ukraine "from within" was reaching its zenith through the mobilization of the Russia movement in Crimea. Meshkov's election as Crimean president in January 1994 opened a serious possibility of a separatist Crimea. The Russian government and Yeltsin refrained from openly endorsing Meshkov, but many Russian nationalists hoped that the internal momentum within Crimea would break Ukraine's hold on the region.

When the Crimean claim to independence was renewed by Meshkov and the Supreme Soviet in May 1994, the Russian parliament appealed to the Ukrainian parliament not to react with force and instead to negotiate. When Meshkov reactivated the controversial Crimean Constitution of May 1992, Kravchuk and then Foreign Minister Anatolii Zlenko approached the UN Secretary General and Security Council as well as the Conference on Security and Cooperation in Europe (CSCE), condemning the actions of the Crimean government not only as illegal but also as destabilizing and undermining the Ukrainian constitutional system and its territorial integrity. As in 1993, Ukraine resorted to the authority of international institutions and international law to block both Russian claims and Crimean demands.

When, in November 1994, Kyiv declared a long list of Crimean laws unconstitutional, the move triggered another statement by the Russian Duma, warning that a compromise between Kyiv and Simferopol was necessary in order to make progress on the Russian-Ukrainian agreement on the Black Sea Fleet and a new bilateral treaty. Konstantin Zatulin, then head of the parliamentary Committee on Cooperation with the CIS and Relations with Compatriots, and a major nationalist opponent of Russia's "retreat" from the "near abroad," was the driving force behind these moves.[41] The parameters of Russia's relations with Ukraine shifted further after the launch of the first Chechen war in December 1994, a turbulent and costly separatist challenge to Russia that distracted the attention of Russia's political forces and dampened some of the sentiment in favor of separatists generally. The Chechen conflict served as a further warning signal—to both Kyiv and Simferopol—of the violent consequences that might follow political failure. As Meshkov's support base began to crumble in Crimea, the Russian parliament renewed its nationalist claims. On 21 May 1994 Kyiv forced the Crimean parliament to rescind its resolution on independence, but the same day the Russian Duma annulled the 1954 transfer. By this stage, however, Kyiv's authority vis-à-vis the region was gradually getting stronger.

Kyiv's clampdown on Crimea in March 1995 triggered a new wave of nationalist pro-Crimean rhetoric in Russia. The Ukrainian parliament's decisions followed an address by the Crimean Supreme Soviet to the Russian president and the parliament, asking them not to pursue the Ukrainian-Russian friendship treaty. In response to the March events in Crimea, the Russian State Duma protested about Kyiv's actions and warned that they would damage the negotiations over the Black Sea Fleet.[42] On 7 April, the Duma imposed a moratorium on the division of the fleet, but it was subsequently rejected by the Council of the Federation.

Crimean parliamentary speaker Tsekov addressed the Duma on 14 April 1995, urging Russia to take a more active role in Crimea. At this point even Yeltsin, who had so far refrained from polemics, publicly stated the need for Ukraine to be more accommodating of the Crimeans' demands through dialogue. He also added that the friendship treaty could not be signed until the Crimeans' rights were guaranteed. His rhetoric was surpassed by Foreign Minister Kozyrev, who repeatedly announced on 19–20 April that, if necessary, the Russian military would be ready to protect the rights of Russians in the "near abroad." The statements caused a diplomatic uproar throughout the CIS. At the next top-level meeting in Sochi on 9 June 1995, the Ukrainian and Russian presidents attempted to bring closure to the agreement on an equal division of the fleet, with Russia "buying" parts of Ukraine's share. It was agreed that 81.7 percent of the warships and vessels would belong to the Russian Federation, and 18.3 percent to Ukraine; it was further agreed that Russia's main naval base would remain in Sevastopol.[43] This agreement settled the division of the fleet, but the details of the basing of the two separate fleets were still pending. The situation was later complicated by Ukraine's 1996 Constitution, which ruled out the stationing of foreign military units on its territory.

In the meantime, Russian parliamentarians kept up the nationalist rhetoric on the Crimean issue. Moscow mayor Luzhkov, for example, continued his regular visits to Crimea, in particular to Sevastopol,[44] to flex his "rhetorical muscles"[45] and make political capital from his image as a Russian patriot in the run-up to the Russian presidential elections. He launched a number of initiatives to assist socioeconomic development, including Moscow-subsidized housing and schools for fleet personnel. On 14 January 1996, the Russian State Duma moved to block the Sochi Agreement by passing a law halting the further division of the fleet, and a supplementary law to this effect was passed on 23 October 1996.[46] The Ukrainian parliament was asked to enter talks on the issue of the transfer of 1954, the status of Sevastopol and the division of the fleet. On 5 December 1996, the Council of the Federation followed suit, declaring Sevastopol a "Russian city."[47] It called on Yeltsin to put a moratorium on further decisions regarding the fleet, the status of Sevastopol, and Crimea as a whole. President Yeltsin, however, having won the June–July 1996 presidential elections, could afford to stamp out the Duma's more nationalistic proposals, and he vetoed both decisions.[48]

In the first months of 1997 a new atmosphere of cooperation and moderation prevailed in Russian politics. The ending of the war in Chechnya in August 1996, leading to the Russian-Chechen peace treaty of late May 1997, created a chastened mood that was conducive to the political settlement of outstanding issues. On 28 May 1997 the Russian Prime Minister, Viktor Chernomyrdin, and his Ukrainian counterpart, Pavlo Lazarenko, signed the bilateral agreements in Kyiv about the division of the fleet, including the financial details and its presence on Ukrainian territory. Based on these documents, Russia recognized Sevastopol as belonging to Ukraine and agreed to lease the base in Sevastopol and its infrastructure for 20 years, with the possibility of a renewed lease every five years after this period, provided both sides agreed on the extension. The final calculation was based on 525 warships and vessels, of which 271 went to Russia and 254 to Ukraine; of its share, Ukraine gave 117 to Russia as part of a "debt for equity" swap.[49] The annual lease was to be calculated against Ukraine's energy debt, and the bases were divided into Russian and Ukrainian sectors.[50]

This agreement marked a breakthrough for the long-awaited Russian-Ukrainian Treaty on Friendship and Cooperation. On 31 May 1997, the Russian and Ukrainian presidents signed the agreement in Moscow.[51] To come into force the treaty had to be ratified by both parliaments. The Ukrainian parliament ratified the treaty quickly, whereas its Russian counterpart dragged out the ratification process. In the meantime, Russian-Crimean economic cooperation developed.[52] In Russian nationalist rhetoric the expression "brotherly cooperation" (*bratskoe sotrudnichestvo*)[53] was coined to describe Russia's role as Crimea's main trade partner and investor. One of the most ambitious—and symbolically very significant—joint projects was the plan to construct a bridge across the Kerch strait to literally create a physical link between Crimea and Russia. Meanwhile Ukraine gradually established a closer relationship with NATO, a development that caused universal alarm in the Russian political elite. Ukraine's "Special Partnership with NATO" and, in particular, the military exercise with NATO participation off the coast of Crimea in August 1997 ("Sea Breeze 97"), accentuated Russian concerns about Ukraine's "Western" foreign policy orientation. The military exercise simulated a fight against "separatists" helped by a neighboring state: a crude and all-too-apparent reference to Crimea. The form of the exercise was designed as a clear provocation of Russia, which promptly withdrew its participation.

A Duma declaration of 23 October 1998 belatedly attempted to keep the Crimean issue alive. It protested against Ukrainian being the only state language anchored in the new Crimean Constitution. Referring to Russia's compliance with international law, the Duma criticized the "discrimination against the Russian people in Crimea, who represent the overwhelming majority of its population."[54] The new Crimean Constitution was deemed to violate the Russian-Ukrainian friendship treaty of 31 May 1997.[55] The situation in Crimea was portrayed as a dangerous precedent for worsening relations between Russians and Ukrainians throughout Ukraine. Ukrainian policies towards Crimea were defined as belonging to Ukraine's "domestic geopolitics." It further suggested that all inhabitants of Crimea born before the "arbitrary transfer" of Crimea in 1954 should be considered Russian citizens, a formulation that was bound to provoke Ukrainian anger and presidential attempts to mediate. Moreover, the Duma rejected the categorization of the over eleven million Russians in Ukraine as a national minority. This definition, in the Duma's view, should have been replaced by the recognition of "two national majorities." Since Russian is the preferred language in southern and eastern regions of Ukraine, the Duma used the draft Crimean Constitution to ask simultaneously for the recognition of Russian as the second state language in the whole of Ukraine. The Duma's protest was reinforced by a protest by the Ukrainian Communist faction in the Ukrainian parliament.[56] These declarations had clearly lost their political immediacy. Nevertheless, Russian influence in the cultural and social sphere was likely to continue and, therefore, retain some of its political overtones.[57]

The resistance of the Russian political elite to the loss of Sevastopol was profound. In the run-up to the final ratification of the Big Treaty (bol'shoi dogovor) the Russian media, and not only the nationalist and communist media but in particular the liberal *Nezavisimaia gazeta*, led a campaign to denounce it.[58] The Council of the Federation (namely, Russia's regional and republican leaders) vetoed the treaty on 27 January 1999, but after major pressure from Yeltsin the upper house finally ratified it on 17 February 1999. This end to the long saga of the Big Treaty did not silence the use of the Crimean question in Russian political rhetoric, but it was a lost cause and a closed issue for the Russian state. From now on it was confined to the political margins.

International Mediation

The end of the Cold War coincided not only with a surge in ethnic and regional conflicts but also with a new legitimacy for international mediation and intervention. Developments in Eastern Europe since the early 1990s have amply demonstrated the possibilities, complexities and limitations of international conflict regulation, the most obvious example being former Yugoslavia. The visibility and scope of international or regional organizations such as the UN or the CSCE/OSCE have increased significantly. Ukraine was admitted to the CSCE in January 1992. The triadic nexus of "soft" international mediation consists of norm setting, monitoring, and enforcement activities. In the Ukrainian case, international organizations, notably the OSCE and UN, engaged in this kind of conflict prevention. Local missions, roundtable discussions, recommendations for compromise, and self-help initiatives for the local population have been among the priorities. The success of this kind of international involvement is difficult to assess.

The OSCE High Commissioner on National Minorities

(HCNM), an innovative OSCE instrument created in 1992 as part of the security dimension of the organization, has had an impact on the developments in Crimea. The Crimean political setup appears to come closest to the ideal situation for the involvement of the High Commissioner: a preconflict situation with scope for negotiations, consensus building, and institutional mechanisms for the accommodation of diversity. The first incumbent, Max van der Stoel, was convinced that the international climate at the time facilitated his broad mandate: "only five years later, nobody would have created this position with such a far-reaching mandate to intervene in countries' domestic politics."[59] Moreover, van der Stoel was skilled at pushing the vaguely defined boundaries of his remit through a strategy of behind-the-scenes "quiet diplomacy." His involvement in Crimea is widely seen by local politicians as a significant factor in the prevention of conflict.[60] The HCNM's involvement was prompted by a letter from Ukrainian Foreign Minister Anatolii Zlenko addressed to all CSCE states on 14 July 1993, shortly after the Russian parliament had expressed its claim to Sevastopol.[61]

The HCNM was the first international actor to become involved in the political and legal aspects of the Crimean issue. In February 1994 he made his first visit to Kyiv and soon after visited Donetsk and Simferopol. On 15 May 1994, van der Stoel issued his first formal recommendation addressed to the Ukrainian foreign minister. His letter included three basic suggestions: greater clarity on nondiscrimination in language use and on linguistic rights for the Russians, Crimean autonomy, and the integration of the Crimean Tatars. He emphasized the importance of the principle of territorial integrity and the respect for Ukraine's, but stressed the importance of a constitutionally guaranteed autonomy status for Crimea, especially in economic affairs. The Crimean problem was clearly defined as an internal dispute between Kyiv and Simferopol rather than an international problem between Ukraine and Russia.[62] Zlenko replied generally positively in June 1994, indicating an interest in cooperating with the HCNM and using its constitutional and legal expertise, and with a long-term OSCE Mission that aimed to facilitate dialogue between the central government and the Crimean authorities.[63]

Van der Stoel did not interfere when the Kyiv-Simferopol confrontation reached its peak and when the intraregional institutional struggle was at its fiercest in the second half of 1994. He continued to monitor the situation but chose not to follow up immediately on his May recommendations. Locally, van der Stoel maintained relations with the moderate political forces and Kyiv. He emphasized that in contrast to Estonia and Latvia, Russia by and large did not interfere with Crimean politics, including the work of the OSCE. From autumn 1995 onwards, the OSCE gradually switched its attention from the issue of Crimean autonomy to an emphasis on what it considered to be the more complex minority-related issue of the Crimean Tatars.

Leading Ukrainian politicians deliberately used the international dimension of the Crimea question to bolster their position vis-à-vis Russia. As discussed earlier, Kravchuk obtained the support of the UN Security Council in July 1993 for Ukraine's territorial integrity. The CSCE/OSCE involvement in Crimea was followed by initiatives conducted under the auspices of the UN from 1994 and 1995 onwards, which focused on development issues, especially for the Crimean Tatars. The UN High Commissioner for Refugees (UNHCR), the International Organization for Migration (IOM), and the Council of Europe have also monitored the situation of the Tatars.

In 1994 the Crimea Development and Integration Program was initiated by the UN at the request of the Ukrainian government. Implementation of the program began in 1995 and 1996, and it was funded by the UN, bilateral funding from the Netherlands and Norway, contributions in kind from Turkey and the Crimean government, Italian humanitarian aid schemes, and Ukraine.[64] Due to the UN's focus on the resettlement of the Crimean Tatars and the overcoming of their social exclusion, many parts of the Russian Crimean community resented its work. In the early stages this kind of targeted assistance from outside was seen as privileging the Tatars, and while its motives were noble, in practice it contributed to further embedding political divisions and prejudice.[65]

Building trust between communities and fostering political consensus were key priorities in the work of the OSCE in Crimea. The OSCE Mission in Ukraine worked from November 1994 to April 1999 and had a regional office in Simferopol. As with other external assistance, the early work of the OSCE Mission in the region was met with considerable local suspicion by the Russian movement in Crimea.[66] OSCE involvement helped to establish the issue of Crimean autonomy and minority rights high on the political agenda of Ukraine. The OSCE also played a crucial mediating role in helping to restart the stalled negotiations between center and periphery.[67] The persistent involvement of the HCNM in Crimea is often singled out as one of the successful cases of conflict prevention. Mal'gin disputes this positive assessment and argues that the involvement of the OSCE actually served to raise tensions in the relationship between Kyiv and Simferopol. Similarly, Ozhiganov believes the outcome of the OSCE involvement was "disappointing," given the limited achievements on Crimean autonomy or Crimean Tatar rights.[68] Kulyk's detailed analysis of the HCNM's work in Ukraine is also ambivalent about the impact, arguing that the HCNM played a vital role in mediating compromises that helped to de-escalate crises between Kyiv and Simferopol, but ultimately the HCNM proved unable or unwilling to assert himself to ensure that the compromises were followed through in the constitutional process. This failure, Kulyk argues, favored Kyiv and ultimately undermined the Crimeans' push for autonomy.[69] In contrast to the more cautious approach of the HCNM, the then head of the OSCE Mission, Andreas Kohlschütter, was openly critical of Kyiv. For example, he publicly criticized the resolution of the Ukrainian parliament and the presidential decree of March 1995 as threats to Crimean autonomy and minority rights.[70]

The Crimean Supreme Soviet took the initiative in asking van der Stoel to act as a mediator when he visited Crimea in April 1995. Subsequently a Ukrainian Roundtable on Crimea was held in Locarno, Switzerland, on 11–14 May 1995, and co-chaired by the HNCM and the Head of the OSCE Mission in Ukraine. Van der Stoel claims that the Locarno talks "took the sting out of the issue," for they forced both Kyiv and Simferopol to step back from the increasingly tense confrontational politics over the status issue.[71] The Locarno Roundtable brought together sixteen key actors from Ukraine and Crimea outside their usual environment, promoted dialogue among the conflicting parties, and advanced the more conciliatory approach of the Ukrainian parliament speaker Moroz.[72]

In mid-May the HCNM presented the OSCE roundtable's recommendations to the Ukrainian foreign minister, who forwarded them to both the Ukrainian and the Crimean parliaments. These recommendations suggested defining the autonomy's economic powers, revisiting the law on demarcating powers (which had never been implemented) in return for Crimea's giving up its claim to statehood, and introducing an appeals procedure by which the Crimean parliament could directly approach the Constitutional Court of Ukraine or another interim "organ of conciliation" while the Constitutional Court was being set up.[73] Kyiv, however, saw in Locarno a useful tool to apply international leverage to compel the Crimeans to comply with Ukrainian law and sidestepped the HCNM's recommendations.[74]

Nevertheless, the phrase "the spirit of Locarno" echoed in Crimean politics for the remainder of the constitutional struggle. The Crimean and Ukrainian parliaments exchanged incompatible proposals in May 1995, but they returned to dialogue and toned down their respective demands and rhetoric. Harking back to Locarno, the Ukrainian parliament passed a resolution, masterminded by parliamentary speaker Moroz, requesting the Crimean parliament to revoke its decision on the referendum and to submit a draft of the new Constitution based on the demarcation law. This conciliatory step opened up a new pathway for the Crimean parliamentarians. The OSCE's Kohlschütter attended a sitting of the Verkhovna Rada in Kyiv and was invited by the Presidium of the Crimean Supreme Soviet to address directly the session of the Supreme Soviet in order to remind the deputies of what had been achieved at Locarno. Continuing their initial opposition to the demarcation law in 1992, the Crimean Tatar faction and the Mejlis reacted negatively to this speech.[75] Despite the criticism Kohlschütter earned from the Tatars and from some national-democratic factions in the Ukrainian parliament, the Locarno talks helped to achieve a breakthrough in the deadlock.

Violent clashes involving Crimean Tatars refocused the HCNM's work on Tatar issues. The HCNM's recommendations of May 1994 had stressed the importance of addressing the concerns of the Crimean Tatars and supported the establishment of their quota of fourteen reserved seats in the regional parliament.[76] The OSCE sponsored another roundtable in Yalta on 20–22 September 1995 to discuss the problems of the deported peoples and explore ways to improve their integration into society. On 12 October 1995 the HCNM

sent Foreign Minister Hennadii Udovenko a new set of recommendations. In furtherance of the Locarno recommendations, van der
Stoel referred to the demarcation law as a basis for compromise, and
again proposed that Crimea be given autonomy on some economic
and cultural matters, called for the cancellation of the demand for
Crimean citizenship, pushed for a Crimean share of the revenues of
Ukrainian property and natural resources in Crimea, and suggested
closer integration of Sevastopol with the rest of Crimea.[77]

A subsequent roundtable held in Noordwijk, Netherlands, on
14–17 March 1996 with participants from Ukraine and Crimea coincided with the last tense period of constitution making (see chapter
8), when the Ukrainian parliament was discussing a draft state Constitution that would have reduced Crimea's status to that of a vaguely
defined "autonomy" (avtonomiia). This roundtable had a moderating
effect and helped to recover some of the mood for compromise by
once again putting economic rights before the political and legal
aspects of autonomy. On the basis of these discussions, the HCNM's
new set of recommendations of 19 March 1996 urged the Verkhovna
Rada to seek a partial ratification of the Crimean Constitution, while
asking the Crimean parliament to reconsider the disputed articles
of the Crimean draft.[78] This clever idea of a ratification-in-parts
proved successful.[79] During a visit of the HCNM to Kyiv—and after
a last-minute consultation of parliamentary speaker Moroz with van
der Stoel—the Ukrainian parliament approved parts of the Crimean
Constitution on 4 April 1996. The HCNM kept up the momentum
by sending further recommendations to Foreign Minister Udovenko,
including specific suggestions regarding the pending articles of the
Crimean Constitution. These recommendations no longer referred
to the demarcation law.[80]

In April van der Stoel took part in a donor conference organized
by the UNDP in Geneva to raise funds for humanitarian aid for the
returnees.[81] His recommendation of 14 February 1997, addressed as
usual to Udovenko, had noted the lack of international legal consensus on the notion of "indigenous peoples" and had proposed protecting national minorities, using Russian, Tatar, and other languages,
and easing the citizenship procedure for the Crimean Tatars.[82] Of
the 105,000 Crimean Tatars who were without Ukrainian citizenship, about twenty-three thousand lacked any citizenship, while the

remainder were mainly Uzbek citizens. The procedure by which they could obtain Ukrainian citizenship was lengthy and costly: they had to appear in person at the embassy in Kyiv to give up Uzbek citizenship and pay at least $100 (several months' salary) for a procedure that took up to a year.[83] The HCNM's recommendation of 14 February 1997 also included the proposal to set up a consultative body that would ensure a regular dialogue between the Ukrainian executive structures and the Crimean Tatars in the absence of the official recognition of the Crimean Tatar organizations. This body was eventually established by Kuchma in 1999 (see chapter 9).

On 20 May 1997 the Ukrainian citizenship law was amended. People who were born in Ukraine or whose children and grandchildren were residents could now acquire Ukrainian citizenship simply by applying, provided they were not citizens of another country. Bilateral Ukrainian-Uzbek negotiations and appeals by the HCNM and UNHCR partly facilitated an intergovernmental agreement in September 1998, and an Uzbek presidential decree on 31 July 1998 that introduced a simplified procedure for canceling the citizenship of the deportees. Initially, the deadline for this procedure was the end of 1999. By then 86.2 percent of those Crimean Tatars who were Uzbek citizens used the procedure (which was extended during Kuchma's visit to Uzbekistan in October 2000). In May 2000, a similar agreement was reached with Kazakhstan. Ukraine's new citizenship law of 18 January 2001 went one step further by focusing more on the issue of statelessness and replacing the obligatory proof of the cancellation of a person's former citizenship with a simple declaration of renunciation.[84]

Overall, van der Stoel issued six recommendations between May 1994 and February 1997, followed by further visits to Ukraine and a further recommendation in January 2001, concerning the right of parental choice and improvements in the educational and linguistic facilities for Russians in Ukraine and Ukrainians in Russia.[85] The HCNM recommendation of 15 May 1994 had already cautioned against developing the Ukrainian language at the expense of Russian. The violent clashes in April 2000 in Lviv over public language use, which resulted in the death of a Ukrainophone composer, renewed the HCNM's involvement in the area of language and educational policies. After visiting Lviv, Kyiv, and other cities, van der Stoel held a seminar on education and languages in Odesa on 13–14 September 1999 to discuss the standards enshrined in the general Recommendations of the HCNM (that is, the 1996 Hague Recommendations regarding the Education Rights of National Minorities, the 1998 Oslo Recommendations regarding the Linguistic Rights of National Minorities, and the 1999 Lund Recommendations on the Effective Participation of National Minorities in Public Life). His subsequent Ukraine-specific recommendation of 12 January 2001 concentrated on the protection of Russian as a minority language. But despite Zlenko's promise that there would be a "comprehensive and thorough elaboration" of the recommendations in Ukrainian policy, they were ignored.

Kulyk's conclusion about the HCNM's involvement in Crimea is persuasive. He describes the HCNM's role as "less proactive and more mediating," and emphasizes van der Stoel's role in the de-escalation of crises rather than in substantive policy change and his attraction of international attention to the concerns of the Crimean Tatars and funding for their humanitarian needs.[86] Van der Stoel personally does not recall negative reactions to his involvement at the time, compared to that of the mission. As elsewhere, however, the relationship between the mission and the HCNM was not clearly defined. Van der Stoel remembers having used economic arguments, such as Crimea's water dependency and tourism value, to remind politicians of the need for regional stability. He had favored an electoral mechanism guaranteeing the Tatars' representation in regional politics and their involvement in a consultative body. But mostly in the first years of his involvement he concentrated on mediating a constitutional compromise on the autonomy issue. According to van der Stoel "it was not clear initially what the minimum consensus was" that would facilitate and sustain a settlement in Crimea.[87] Whereas he continually commented on the details of citizenship and language provisions in Estonia and Latvia, in Crimea his proposals were of a more general kind and his follow-up was less detailed and persistent.

The next HCNM, Rolf Ekeus, who took over from van der Stoel in 2001, expressed his support for both the Council of Representatives of the Crimean Tatar People (set up in 1999) and guaranteed representation of the Tatars in the Crimean Rada. However, his approach was much more standoffish than van der Stoel's, and he did not visit

Ukraine or Crimea during the crucial phase of the discussions about changes to the regional electoral law at the end of 2001. Overall, the formal settlement of the constitutional issue, the closure of the OSCE Mission in 1999 (followed by the establishment of an OSCE Project Coordinator based in Kyiv), and the reduced presence of the current HCNM in Ukraine and Crimea have radically reduced OSCE influence on Ukraine.

The Crimean Supreme Soviet was also instrumental in drawing in the mediation of another international body, the Council of Europe. In the autumn of 1995 the Supreme Soviet asked the Council of Europe to help settle the autonomy issue before admitting Ukraine as a member. But Ukraine's membership application was not affected and was approved in November 1995. As part of its application Ukraine had signed the Framework Convention for the Protection of National Minorities in September 1995, thereby signaling its general commitment to minority rights (the Framework Convention was later ratified by the Ukrainian parliament in December 1997). The Framework Convention provides the legal basis for a continuous external and internal evaluation process of government policy on minority issues. In Ukraine, the monitoring process by definition includes the question of Crimea's status, language rights, and the position of the Crimean Tatars. The Council of Europe organized a first roundtable on the Crimean Tatars in 1999. The Parliamentary Assembly of the Council of Europe (PACE) then commissioned Lord Ponsonby to monitor the Crimean Tatar situation. Despite dissatisfaction among the Crimean Tatars (apparently Ponsonby offended the Tatars when he did not meet with their political leaders while visiting Crimea in the autumn of 1999), Ponsonby's report initiated PACE Recommendation No. 1455 in 2000, which called for international support for the Crimean Tatars, including financial support from the EU and other donors, and urged Ukraine and Crimean authorities to move on "restoring and securing the rights of the Crimean Tatars to education in the Crimean Tatar language, and the use of their language in all private and public affairs."[88] According to a later PACE report of 2000, about 25 percent of Crimean Tatar settlements lack electricity, 70 percent lack water, 90 percent lack paved roads, 96 percent lack gas, and 100 percent lack sewers.[89]

Both the Council of Europe and the OSCE tended to approach

the Crimean Tatar issue as a question of "national minority" status rather than an "indigenous people" status, as this kept the issue within their remit and the Framework Convention and was less controversial within Ukraine. Van der Stoel advised the Crimean Tatars not to insist on the label "indigenous" and to accept the label "national minority" instead, because the latter term was already sufficiently ambivalent.[90] This could be regarded as a sign of his lack of sensitivity to Crimean Tatar concerns and identity. Article 92 of the Ukrainian Constitution refers both to "indigenous people" and "national minorities" (without specifying which groups meet the criteria), and both groups' rights are left to be delineated by Ukrainian legislation. That legislation has been stalled for many years in the Ukrainian parliament—a testament to the failure of the OSCE and Council of Europe to advance policy on multiethnic rights in Ukraine.

The "Turkish Factor"

In Crimean Russian political discourse, the terms "Turkish influence" (*vliianie Turtsii*) and "the Islamic factor" (*islamskii faktor*) are regularly manipulated to elicit fears among the Slav population and to marginalize the Crimean Tatars. Numerous pseudoscholarly accounts have been produced in Crimea since the early 1990s that wildly stress Crimea's geopolitical vulnerability to Islamic radicalism.[91] Ukraine's relationship with Turkey is an important dimension of its Black Sea regional policy, but this relationship is effectively mediated by how Ukraine is perceived by Turkey to address the concerns of the Crimean Tatars. That Crimean Tatar delegations have been received at the highest state level in Turkey symbolically affirms the close historical, cultural and contemporary political links between Turkey and Crimea. In 1996, for example, Mejlis leader Jemilev accompanied a delegation headed by then Crimean Prime Minister Demydenko during which Jemilev was greeted as if he were a co-leader of Crimea. However, the Turkish authorities have to date offered only symbolic, moral, and humanitarian support for the Crimean Tatars and have refrained from interfering in the Crimean struggle over autonomy. The Turkish government's only official act was the promise to build a thousand houses for the Crimean Tatars—an as-yet incomplete project entrusted to the Turkish International Cooperation Agency.[92]

The sizable Crimean Tatar diaspora in Turkey, which has seen a gradual revival over the last decade in close connection with the Tatars' return to Crimea, has been more active than the Turkish government. Its private initiatives have focused on humanitarian aid, education, cultural matters, and symbolic appearances at public events. By 1996, official Turkish government statistics listed only three schools set up by private Turkish companies in 1993 and 1994 and comprising altogether about three hundred pupils.[93] According to Kirimli, the General Center of the Crimean Turkish Associations has supported six schools, one university, several libraries, a printing house, a children's hospital, and a clinic in Crimea. Moreover, the Turkish government funded the education of about five hundred Tatar students from Crimea at Turkish universities.[94]

Popular opinion in Crimea tends to overestimate the relations between the Crimean Tatars and Turkey, and the "Islamic factor" more generally. A common rumor going the rounds of the Russia movement in the 1990s was that the former Turkish President, Suleiman Demirel, advised Kyiv to welcome back into Crimea all Turks of Crimean Tatar origin in return for Turkish economic assistance and diplomatic backing in world politics.[95] Crimean Russians often exaggerate the numbers of Tatar students going to Turkey, and there are unsubstantiated claims that the students receive military training in Turkey. By contrast, the Kurultay has repeatedly condemned any attempts by foreign Islamic missionaries to intervene in the Crimean Tatars' traditions and political outlook.[96] The fact that Wahhabism has had virtually no impact among the Crimean Tatars even after the global "war on terror" started in late 2001 is sufficient disproof of the presence of an "Islamic factor" in the sense of Islamist radicalism.

The Russian Federation, Ukraine, and Turkey are the three major players in the Black Sea region.[97] In contrast to Ukrainian-Turkish relations, those between Russia and Turkey in the post-Soviet period have been strained, not least over their respective spheres of influence in Central Asia, the Caucasus, and the Black Sea region. The Black Sea Economic Cooperation, formally initiated by Turkey in 1992 and involving all Black Sea states, provides an institutional forum in which Russia's influence is diluted. While this form of regional cooperation, focusing on economic matters, could potentially contribute to political stability in the region, it has played no significant role in Crimean politics.[98] In sum, despite its historical and cultural ties with the Crimean Tatars, Turkey has not made any serious attempt to become a mediator or power broker.

Conclusion

There were moments during the early 1990s when the potential for a conflict between Russian and Ukraine was high. Both states were dealing with the traumas of the transition, including redefining their national identity and state building. Russian involvement did not escalate beyond the heightened nationalist political rhetoric that infected much of its political class, from democrats to fascists, over Crimea. From 1993 the Yeltsin administration marginalized the Crimean autonomy issue and concentrated on the negotiations over strategic bilateral agreements with Ukraine concerning nuclear weapons and the Black Sea Fleet, which required an acceptance of Ukraine's territorial integrity. By prioritizing Russia's strategic military interests, Yeltsin sacrificed the nationalist sentiment about Russian sovereignty over Crimea, and in particular over Sevastopol. In the final phase of the Crimean constitution-making process from 1995 to 1998, Russia's influence in the region was further reduced. The Chechen war distracted Russia's attention and made the issue of separatism highly unattractive. The agreement on the Black Sea Fleet and the Ukrainian-Russian Friendship Treaty in 1997 drastically limited the scope for the Russian parliament or individual Russian politicians to mobilize around the Crimean issue.

The Ukrainian leadership managed the Crimea question shrewdly. There was an acceptance that Crimea was a constitutional problem that required an institutional compromise. Ukraine persistently accepted the principle of an autonomy status for Crimea, while prolonging any definition of it until it had the upper hand in the negotiations. Ukraine also manipulated international opinion by its work with the UN, OSCE, and HCNM. In particular, the latter's mediation was used to de-escalate crises with Crimea and to mollify and moderate Crimean separatism. While Ukraine welcomed the HCNM's recommendations, it implemented them only patchily. Kyiv's approach was to make tactical compromises in order to win the longer strategic game of state building. This approach was evident in the mutual balancing of concessions over the various Russian-Ukrainian treaties, especially the Big Treaty of 1997. It epitomized Kyiv's successful management of the international dimension of the Crimea question.

Conclusion: Autonomy and the Process of Accommodating Diversity

CRIMEA ILLUSTRATES THE DISJUNCTURE between state boundaries and historically constructed identities in the aftermath of the Soviet collapse. It is an example of a contested territory with multiple deeply embedded cultural, historical, and institutional memories. Over the *longue durée* imperial rulers, travelers, poets, writers, artists, and historians of different national backgrounds have created and shaped deeply rooted images and memories tied to Crimea. Crimea's location, its multiethnicity, and diverse history are the common markers of these imaginings. Under the conditions of regime change and of weak statehood, selective memories may provide a source of historical legitimacy and be a potent basis of political mobilization. The manner in which territory and ethnicity overlap in these cultural, historical, and institutional legacies, in particular, shapes the potential for and the dynamics of conflict. Both elements are powerful forces in political symbolism and are the building blocks of lasting myths. As such, they also provide key layers in the foundations of mobilization around issues of identity.

Post-Soviet political mobilization in Crimea drew on the region's multiethnicity and diverse history. Short-lived or only half-realized visions of a "Ukrainian Crimea" or Crimean autonomy created powerful images in the contemporary political discourse. The historical precedents of a Crimean autonomy status in the aftermath of the 1917 revolutions and in the early Soviet period, discussed in chapter 4, shaped the perceptions and raised the expectations of the regional political actors of different ethnic and political backgrounds. They provided a starting point for political mobilization, as seen in chapter 6. Crimean autonomy, in particular the Crimean ASSR, has been interpreted either as a territorial autonomy status or as a Crimean Tatar national autonomy. In a context of democratization and state building, the popular mandate for autonomy in a historically contested region was difficult for the Ukrainian state to resist.

The transfer of Crimea to the Ukrainian SSR in 1954 and arguments about the legality of the transfer also impelled the post-Soviet debates over Crimea's status. The details and rationale of the transfer remain vague, but the archival evidence presented in chapters 4 and 5 allows us to go beyond the crude descriptions of the transfer as Khrushchev's "gift" in celebration of the 300th anniversary of Pereiaslav. Khrushchev can be considered the initiator of the idea, but his own political position did not allow him unilaterally to orchestrate a boundary change of this sort in 1954. The transfer accorded with the Soviet economic and nationality policy at the time and was integrated into the celebrations of the Pereiaslav Treaty and into Soviet mythmaking only in an ad hoc fashion at the last moment. It is evident that the decision to transfer Crimea was not simply one of Khrushchev's erratic decisions. The possibility of a transfer had been discussed several years earlier in 1944 by Khrushchev himself, and it was part of an economic rationale for integrating Crimea and Ukraine, including the resettlement of Ukrainians in the region after the end of World War Two. Khrushchev appears to have played a central role in the timing of the transfer, but this was the era of "collective leadership" and the decision must have been a collective one for the party Presidium. The transfer occurred during a period of infighting and a power struggle after Stalin's death, yet the transfer was not an explicit issue in this struggle.

The transfer of Crimea to Ukraine could easily be interpreted as a symbolic affirmation of the "Slavic Brotherhood" of Russia and Ukraine, but Crimea became a part of the powerful Pereiaslav myth only retrospectively. Obviously, the idea that Crimea could become a part of an independent Ukrainian state was beyond the horizon of the decision-makers in 1954. Regardless of all deadlocked legalist and historicist arguments prevailing in post-Soviet Russian-Ukrainian discussions about 1954, the salience of geographical factors and economic reasoning put forward at the time of the transfer are difficult to dispute. Some forty years after the transfer, Ukraine accumulated its own stock of vested interests in the region. Crimea's water and energy dependence, channeled through Soviet Ukrainian structures, and the inherited responsibility for the mass return of the Crimean Tatars, have reinforced Ukraine's post-Soviet claim to the region.

Crimea was a latecomer in terms of political mobilization in the era of perestroika. Apart from a short-lived ecological movement and a feeble democratic group, the issue of Crimean autonomy provided the first major issue of contestation. The regional institutions and elites proved too weak, inexperienced, and divided to control the autonomy movement. What started as a territorial question within the USSR developed into a demand for territorial autonomy within the new Ukrainian state and culminated in the Russian nationalist and separatist movement in 1994. By then a distinct regional party system had developed that was skewed towards ethnopolitical mobilization. Successive waves of political mobilization in Crimea in the late 1980s and early 1990s produced a highly factionalized political elite. Embryonic political party development during the first years of democratic transition tended towards political extremes. Crimean political mobilization did not occur along clear-cut ethnic cleavages, nor can it be subsumed adequately under the label "separatism." Separatist slogans were widely used by Meshkov in the 1994 election campaigns, but even those advocating the idea never seriously tried to implement it. Paradoxically, the majority of the Crimean population appeared simultaneously to oppose Crimea's exit from Ukraine while favoring Crimea's reintegration with Russia. These ambivalent attitudes are the result of Crimea's strong Soviet identity and reflect the difficulties of coming to terms with the end of the USSR. The movement for Crimean autonomy was not confined only to the upper echelons of regional and national politics but developed both at elite and mass level.

Ethnopolitical mobilization is difficult enough to control in stable, mature democracies. In conditions of postcommunist transition, when the new states lacked strong institutions and democratic experience, the potential for political instability and conflict was all the greater. Given Ukraine's many political and economic problems and its inexperience with independent statehood, its handling of the Crimean issue has been quite successful. Though not yet part of a fully functioning democratic political system, Crimea confirms that democracy is possible in deeply divided societies with a "narrow margin of consensus," as Nordlinger suggested.[1] In Crimea, a potential for Russian nationalism still exists, but there is no apparent outlet for large-scale mobilization.

As for ethnopolitical mobilization, the historical animosities between Russians and Crimean Tatars were more pronounced than the distinctions between Russians and Ukrainians in Crimea.[2] Even at its peak, the regional Russian movement mobilized against the Ukrainian center in Kyiv rather than against ethnic Ukrainians (mostly Russophones) living in Crimea. After all, the amorphous Russian movement had ethnic Ukrainians in its midst. A territorial cleavage couched in ethnic and national terms, consequently, was at the center of political mobilization. The quick rise and fall of the *Meshkovshchina* was a dialectical phenomenon, demonstrating how easily a dormant ethnic factor can be politically mobilized—and how fickle it can prove in the presence of crosscutting divisions, shifting alliances, and changing interests. This crosscutting complexity of the Crimean issue has been the major source of weakness in the ethnopolitical mobilization in the region.

The Crimean case is a good demonstration of the weakness of Russian nationalism as an effective and long-term means of political mobilization among the Russophones of the FSU. The Russian movement failed to combine ethnopolitical mobilization with effective socioeconomic policies and remained too internally divided to address the concerns of the regional population. Political failure to cope with bread and butter issues quickly deflated the mass support for the Russian movement, pointing to the pragmatic nature of identities.

The contrast between the failed Russian movement in Crimea and the strongly resurgent Crimean Tatar national movement is particularly striking. The intense political activity of well-organized Crimean Tatars presents a sharp counterpoint to the loosely organized and fragmented Russian movement. While the experience of ethnocide and current ethnic discrimination has kept the Crimean Tatars united across different social strata and political and economic interests, the Russian national movement was constructed around a confused Soviet-Russian identity with blurred political goals.

Although Soviet nostalgia was often couched in the rhetoric of Russian nationalism, the Russian movement lacked symbolic figureheads or leaders who could articulate a coherent ethnopolitical project. In Crimea, Russian nationalism was a default option of political mobilization, but given its underlying contradictions, its political success was fleeting.

The Crimean case provides a corrective for some basic assumptions in the conceptual debates about nationalism and conflict. Ethnic nationalism is not the single most important post-Soviet issue, particularly not in regionally diverse countries like Ukraine where it can temporarily disguise more deeply rooted cleavages, interlocking identities, or issues of concern. While the language issue and foreign policy orientation provided regional political actors with their rhetoric, the socioeconomic dimension emerged as a decisive undercurrent of regional concern. As a case of conflict prevention, Crimea demonstrates the limits of the East-West categorization of nationalism, with the East being more prone to conflict and violence.

The "Russian idea" in Crimea has always remained vaguely reflected in a plethora of "Russian" organizations that came and went without forming a cohesive bloc. While there has never been a significant support base for Crimean independence, Crimean Russians have been in favor of improved links or integration with Russia. The majority of Crimean Ukrainians have revealed a similar orientation, though no majority support for integration with Russia, while only the Crimean Tatars have been consistently opposed to close ties with Russia.[3] Once the pro-Russia movement self-destructed in Crimea due to its ineffectiveness in government, Kyiv took advantage and with a policy of institutional compromise stabilized the region.

Kyiv has played a long game with Crimea. What seems in hindsight to have been Kyiv's clever strategy of moderation was actually a case of pragmatism and ad hoc decisions. The principle of autonomy was conceded but not elaborated. By the time the status was finally inscribed in the Ukrainian Constitution, the regionalist and separatist movement had withered and fragmented. Despite claims that "the Crimean peninsula has...faced a bewildering array of options with regard to its future position in the post-Soviet world,"[4] Crimea's realistic political options were clearly limited from the outset. It received fewer rights than, for example, the Russian or Spanish autonomies,

Quebec, Scotland, or Northern Ireland. By comparison, its status poses less of a threat to the Ukrainian state, and is therefore less likely to be contested or eroded by the center.

Managing the Crimean issue has been an integral part of the making of the new Ukrainian state and, to an extent, a test of its democratic credentials. Finding a solution to this regional challenge required domestic and international political compromises. Internationally, Crimea has been a focal point for the assertion of Ukrainian sovereignty against Russian populist neoimperial tendencies. The agreements with Russia have been bolstered by other international actors and organizations. Domestically, the establishment of Crimea's territorial autonomy status—however feeble the institutional result may have been—was an exercise in consensus-building politics driven by the constant search for compromises among different political and national orientations.

Domestic and foreign policy issues are inextricably linked in Crimea, since the region is the hub of the geopolitical triangle of Russia, Ukraine, and Turkey. The foreign policy aspect provided a backdrop against which the whole Crimean issue and the Russian movement, in particular, unfolded. Apart from the actual disputes between Ukraine and the Russian Federation over the Black Sea Fleet, the status of Sevastopol and the legality of the 1954 transfer, the sheer presence of the Russian neighbor does provide a check on Ukraine's regional policy. Crimea's status has also been manipulated—though not very successfully—in Russian domestic politics. Ukraine's policy was helped by foreign policy, with Russia's bitter lesson of failed military intervention in Chechnya confirming Yeltsin's restrained stance on Crimea. OSCE and UN mediation and integration programs internationalized the Crimean issue. Western involvement, especially that of the OSCE and the HCNM, helped to maintain the momentum for a constitutional settlement and to overcome the frequent stalemates along the protracted path of negotiation.

Conflict has been avoided in Crimea not so much because of the institution of autonomy as such, but because of the lengthy elite bargaining process involving national and regional elites that preceded the constitutional settlement. Constitution making at the state level, in particular the endless struggles between the president and the parliament, also left an imprint on the way in which the

Crimean issue was managed, for a divided center kept open the political space for Crimean autonomy to be institutionalized. The center proved unable to expunge the principle of autonomy that had defined a minimum consensus among the most influential regional political forces from the early 1990s.

Transitions are multilevel processes; when the state is weak, the subnational level gains in political importance. It is at this level that the decisions about political and economic change must be implemented and embedded, if transition is to move on to a consolidation phase. Consequently, elite configurations and behavior at the subnational level have a crucial impact on transition generally and on conflict potential and state building in particular (see appendix 3). The emphasis of the transition literature on elite pacts and institutional design at the national level can be extended to the regional level. Crimean politics, especially the interaction between Kyiv and Simferopol, provides for a textbook illustration of elite negotiations trying to foster a minimal consensus: an "elite pact." Tracing the key actors and issues throughout the period from 1991 to 1998 in chapters 6, 7, and 8 has revealed the importance of the parallel national and regional constitution-making processes. These processes involved fluctuating regional and center-regional elite coalitions and a loosely defined regional elite pact: a minimum consensus among the politically influential elites on the preservation of a regional autonomy status as part of Ukraine's democratic state building.

Four mitigating background conditions underscored the importance of the institution-making process from 1991 to 1998. First, Crimea's multiethnicity, enhanced by historical and institutional legacies, has prevented a clear-cut ethnopolitical cleavage, mobilization, and polarization. Second, Russian nationalist mobilization proved unsustainable. The Russian movement, based on a blurred Soviet-Russian identity, failed mainly because of its inability to manage regional socioeconomic problems, and because disunity and poor leadership hobbled its political effectiveness. Third, the political elites at the center proved more sensitive to cultural and linguistic concerns than the 1990 Ukrainian language law suggested. They allowed for a more gradual change and regional differentiation in the implementation of Ukrainization. Fourth, regional political mobilization lacked an active external prop, since both Russia and Turkey pursued a cautious approach to their ethnic kin groups and did not offer significant political or economic support for the stricken region.

Institutional linkages between central and regional elites were forged by participation in democratization. A total of ten regional and national elections plus a regional and a national referendum were held during the period from 1991 to 2002. This series of elections had a clear impact on regional political mobilization. It shifted legitimacy back and forth between the regional and the national level of government and contributed to Crimea's gradual political integration into the Ukrainian polity. Although Crimean voter participation in national elections remained below the national average, the decision of the majority of the Crimean electorate to participate in national elections conferred an important degree of legitimacy to the Ukrainian state and its key institutions. Thus, the interaction between Ukrainian and Crimean elections and referenda shows that the Linz-Stepan hypothesis, which states that the destabilizing effect of an electoral sequence in which the regime's "founding elections" take place at the regional rather than the national level, captures no more than a very general correlation.[5] Instead of the one-off correlation of electoral sequencing, the interconnection of regional and national elections over time has a less clear-cut effect on producing instability than the original analysis by Linz and Stepan suggested. Moreover, the sequence of multiple elections can have the opposite effect from what they concluded: it can actually lock a region into the state-building process.

Through the regional referendum in January 1991—rather than an election—Crimea forced itself onto Kyiv's political agenda before the central institutions of the emerging Ukrainian state had a chance to develop a regional policy approach. Two factors set the stage for the region's political integration: a statewide referendum on Ukrainian independence in 1991, which achieved at least a small majority in Crimea; and concurrent Ukrainian presidential elections, in which the overall winner, Leonid Kravchuk, obtained an equally slim majority in Crimea. The Crimean presidential elections in January 1994 tipped the balance of power in favor of regional political actors and increased the distance between the center and the periphery. The elections to the Crimean Supreme Soviet in spring 1994 reinforced this shift. The Ukrainian parliamentary and presidential elections in summer 1994, in turn, counterbalanced it. The parliamentary elections were boycotted by the pro-Russian movement and led to a majority of communist and independent deputies with moderate views about Crimea's position. In the presidential elections, the candidacy of Leonid Kuchma, a Russian-speaker from the east of Ukraine, allowed for Russian nationalist and regionalist sentiment to be channeled into national-level politics.

After the Russian movement fragmented, the next elections—the first post-Soviet local elections—in 1995–96 shifted the balance of power further away from the regionalist-separatist platform, extending the political base for communists and independent candidates who were generally oriented towards Kyiv. In the period from 1998 to 2002, regional election outcomes and the regional results in national elections were primarily a slight variation on the national-level trends. Crimean electoral politics has, thus, been much more complex than a one-off sequencing event, and the region has increasingly become locked into the overall Ukrainian electoral and party-building processes.

As the national and regional electoral dynamics demonstrate, the Crimean issue has been tied up with the overall transition process in Ukraine. The emerging political system and the constant struggle between the president and the national parliament, in particular, left their imprint on the drawn-out constitutional process. The struggle between Ukraine's executive and legislature had a dual function: in the early stage, it inhibited the center's political capacity to deal with the challenge emanating from Crimea. It ruled out a radical approach on the center's part and reinforced the need for negotiation in the absence of an evident political consensus. While the majority of Crimea's politically influential elites agreed on the need for a special status of some kind, fracture lines emerged along ethnopolitical cleavages once the principles of Crimean autonomy were to be defined.

Crosscutting of central and regional differences has been the key to political stability in Ukraine. Moreover, the protracted institutionalization of Crimean autonomy has strengthened the civic definition of the new Ukrainian state and, paradoxically, it has contributed to political stability. The Crimean case demonstrates that regional diversity, even when politicized, does not necessarily destabilize a state and that in a regionally diverse country ethnicity is just one cleavage among many others available for political mobilization. However, while the process of autonomization has contributed to the prevention of conflict, it has rendered the regional political economy of transition more complicated. Political mobilization and the attempts to defuse it have distracted reform and acted as a vehicle for the criminalization of Crimea's economy.

The Crimean question substantiates the claim that institutions and elites play a significant role in transition and conflict prevention. We should be more cautious, however, about the role of institutional *design*. Horowitz noted the difficulty of distinguishing between cause and effect when he asked whether moderated and flexible cleavages have been the result of consociational arrangements or whether the low intensity and fluidity of conflicts has made consociationalism possible.[6] In Crimea we are confronted with a similar dilemma: has Crimean autonomy prevented conflict in the region, or has autonomy been the outcome because separatism and nationalism were weak? This question cannot be answered straightforwardly, but the analysis presented in this book emphasizes the regional and national political processes of constitution *making*, involving a changing set of actors and institutional compromises, as a key determinant of conflict prevention rather than the actual institutional outcome—Crimea's autonomy status, which is symbolically significant but pragmatically weak in terms of powers. This finding should be of relevance to other preconflict situations as well as attempts to manage hot conflict through institutions.[7] However, the tensions between cause and effect and between structure and agency cannot entirely be resolved.

Ukrainian state and nation building is an inherently regionalized process. The literature on regionalism tends to equate it with substate nationalism and assumes a fixed center-periphery polarization. Crimea's defining features are multiethnicity and the interaction of ethnic with other socioeconomic, historical, and territorial cleavages, as well as a network of center-periphery linkages at the elite level. It can be considered a strength, not a weakness, that both national and regional identities in Ukraine are still in the making. The interface of confrontation is, consequently, not strictly delimited and, thus, gives flexibility to the political process. What appears to be destabilizing in the short term—the struggle between center and periphery—may not hinder but rather promote democratic development in the long term, so long as institutions, elites, and identities continuously interlock. Tracing the attempts to achieve or destroy consensus identifies the key agents involved in this process—primarily political elites—and their rationale: the preservation of status and of access to power resources. Along the same lines of consensus and dissent, the linkage between the different layers of regional and national identity crystallizes. The interlocking of regional and national identities signifies that multiple identities can coexist as long as the necessary and often delicate balance between them is conditioned on the political will of elites and on compliance by society. Contrary to widespread fears of their consequences for state unity, regional identities can thus contribute to state integration and the construction of a civic national identity, as long as they are guaranteed a political voice through regional and/or central institutions and networks securing the stake regional elites have in the transition processes. Once this interaction is interrupted by a clash between or among the different identities, regional actors can capitalize on underlying cleavages and dormant regional identities. A failure to accept the de facto polycentric nature of the Ukrainian state would strengthen regionalist movements in different parts of the country.

Ukraine is experiencing processes similar to those that occurred in Western Europe a century or more ago, yet its institutional solutions and its time frame resemble those of some of the advanced West European democracies where regional and substate national consciousness have resurfaced in recent years. Ukraine, in contrast, also has the multiple burdens of simultaneously building independent statehood and national identity, democratizing, attempting to implement fundamental marketizing economic reforms, and accommodating regional, cultural, and political diversity. It seems an impossible task, but by comparison with most other regional and ethnic conflicts in postcommunist transitions, in which coercion and imposition have been the norm, Ukraine's management of the Crimean issue has a model character.

This book started from the premise that Crimea's situation is "a conflict that did not happen." It is important to qualify this statement at the end. Altogether three potential conflicts have been avoided: a potential clash between Ukraine and Russia, ethnic strife within the region (including within the divided Russian or Russian-speaking majority), and, most important, a center-periphery conflict within Ukraine. The Crimean Tatar issue is, however, still to be resolved. The question of permanent minority representation has still to be tackled, since political representation and societal integration of the Crimean Tatars is a key to future regional stability.

Crimean regional autonomy, although severely limited in practice, is part of an asymmetric arrangement in Ukraine that de facto perforates the unitary state set out in the 1996 Constitution. Although there is still a fair amount of skepticism about Crimean autonomy at the center, in particular among right-wing parties, there is a significant consensus that the removal of the constitutionally guaranteed status would be destabilizing.[8] Consequently, for the foreseeable future Ukrainian politics will continue to operate in the political space between a unitary and a federal state.

Epilogue

UKRAINE'S 2004 "ORANGE REVOLUTION" by and large bypassed Crimea, and apart from a series of personnel changes its aftermath did not mark a substantive change in Crimean politics. The final confirmation of this trend came with the March 2006 elections. In the first round of the presidential elections on 31 October 2004 Viktor Yushchenko, the leader of the anti-Kuchma opposition, obtained a mere 12.79 percent in Crimea (and 5.97 percent in Sevastopol), while his rival Viktor Yanukovych, a protégé of both Kuchma and Russian President Putin, secured the support of 69.17 percent in Crimea and 73.54 percent in Sevastopol. In the rigged second round standoff between Yanukovych and Yushchenko on 21 November, which set off the mass protests in the streets of Kyiv and regional cities, Yushchenko obtained 14.59 percent in Crimea (7.61 percent in Sevastopol), while Yanukovych improved his share of the regional vote to 81.99 percent (88.97 percent in Sevastopol). In a landmark decision, Ukraine's Supreme Court overturned the result of the second round of voting due to electoral fraud on Yanukovych's behalf. In the repeated second and decisive round of the elections on 26 December Yushchenko only slightly improved his Crimean result to 15.41 percent (7.96 percent in Sevastopol), whereas Yanukovych won 81.26 percent of the Crimean vote (and 88.83 percent in Sevastopol).[1] Crimea clearly stayed one of Yanukovych's strongholds as the dramatic events were unfolding.[2] This result was as much an anti-Yushchenko vote, nurtured by old fears that western Ukraine would dominate the rest of the country, as a vote for Yanukovych as a political leader and in support of his program (which mentioned an enhanced status of the Russian language and the importance of good relations with Russia).[3] The Russian Community of Crimea (*Russkaia obshchina Kryma*), an umbrella organization linked to the Crimean branch of the party Russian Bloc (*Russkii blok*), was the main driving force behind the regional campaign for Yanukovych.[4] The leading figures in this movement, among them well-known regional politicians of the Russian movement such as Crimean deputy Sergei Tsekov, were keen to project an image of unity within the disparate Russian movement in the run-up to the elections in 2006.[5] The reaction to the Orange Revolution helped to bolster this image, at least temporarily.

The election results effectively pitted the Crimean Tatars against the Russian-speaking regional majority. It was the clearest split of the regional electorate ever and threatened a potential reopening of the ethnic splits of the early 1990s.[6] The Crimean Tatars were the main base for the pro-Yushchenko forces in the 2004 elections (and the 2006 parliamentary elections).[7] The Tatars had no other electoral option. For the regional media and Russian organizations, the close association between the Crimean Tatars and the pro-Yushchenko vote provided a rationale for reverting back to their familiar political rhetoric of interethnic tension.

Yushchenko's election victory did little to counter this regional tension. The Crimean Tatars feared that while the Ukrainian government as a whole was gaining in international support, the cause of the Crimean Tatars would find it even harder to attract the attention of Western governments and donors than before. Moreover, the fear of growing Islamic fundamentalism in the region in the form of Wahhabism and Hizb ut-Tahrir—so far a fear rather than a political reality—could further sideline the political and cultural claims of the Tatars in an international climate dominated by the "war on terror." The Crimean Tatar leadership has distanced itself from foreign-sponsored Islamic groups and seeks to limit their activities. The Law on the Rehabilitation of Peoples Deported on Ethnic Grounds, adopted by the national parliament but vetoed by Kuchma owing to disagreements about the words "deportation" and "the Crimean Tatar people" as well as the issue of land rights, has not come unstuck, and the recognition of the Crimean Tatars as an "indigenous people" is still pending. The Crimean Tatar leadership has been pushing for an official status of the Crimean Tatar language and a mechanism for ensuring proportional representation of the Tatars in the regional branches of power. The entitlement and allotment of land remains particularly controversial in Crimea, mostly in connection with the Crimean Tatars' claims as an indigenous people and their occupation of land in the absence of proactive regional or national policymaking. An ongoing moratorium on land distribution has postponed an official policy and contributed to de facto seizure of land as well as the shadow economy in the region.[8] After a meeting with Mustafa Jemilev and Refat Chubarov in February 2005, Yushchenko set up a commission to examine and map the current situation, but no viable solution has been found or implemented.[9]

Ukraine emerged from the presidential elections with its regional political elite divided. The fact that the elections had revived the polarization between the Crimean Tatars and the Russian movement in Crimea made this regional challenge more difficult for Yushchenko. The incoming Orange regime moved quickly to exchange the pro-Kuchma executive leadership in key regions and rein in corruption, and on 20 April 2005 Anatolii Matvienko, the head of the Sobor Party that was a member of Iuliia Tymoshenko's bloc in the 2002 parliamentary elections, was confirmed as Crimea's new prime minister.[10] His predecessor Serhii Kunitsyn, a member of the pro-Kuchma People's Democratic Party, initially refused to resign, but a combination of pressure over corruption charges and the offer of a post as presidential adviser "convinced" him otherwise. Yushchenko's ultimately unsuccessful attempt to win over southern and eastern Ukraine ahead of the 2006 parliamentary elections was initially helped by the pragmatic approach of formerly pro-Kuchma or pro-Yanukovych parliamentarians at the national and regional level, many of whom continue to shift their affiliations in line with the political climate. Less than four months into Yushchenko's presidency, a slight majority in the 100-seat Crimean assembly had come out in support of Yushchenko, among them the formerly pro-Kuchma faction Stability and the newly created pro-Yushchenko Power in Unity. Though the composition of the regional factions continued to fluctuate, the

2004 elections and their aftermath brought about the fragmentation of the majority faction Stability, which had dominated the Crimean assembly since the 2002 elections.

This majority faction had consisted of a fairly stable group of about eighty deputies backing the speaker Borys Deich and Crimea's premier Kunitsyn. Both belonged to parties close to Kuchma, namely the Party of Regions and the People's Democratic Party, respectively. At the national level both parties formed part of the pro-Kuchma or pro-government majority in parliament. That majority consisted of diverse economic and political interests, which were united by their pragmatic support for Kuchma and the victory of a loyal successor, then Prime Minister Yanukovych. Sustained cooperation between these groups at the national level underpinned a calm period in center-region politics, as well as the pragmatic cooperation between the Crimean government and the Crimean assembly. However, by the end of the Kuchma era the stabilizing effect on Crimean politics had turned into complete political stagnation, an effect heightened by the personal links between individuals in the executive and legislature.

The Orange Revolution reshuffled the cards of Crimean politics through executive personnel changes and realignments in the assembly—without, however, breaking through the continuity of familiar names dominating the Crimean assembly and the regional public discourse. The disintegration of the majority in the Crimean assembly in the aftermath of the 2004 presidential elections was hastened by the partial revival of the once powerful political Left in the form of a loose group of deputies from the Union Party and the Communist Party, which rallied around the need to turn Crimean institutions into an effective instrument of control over the Crimean government.[11] Matvienko's first attempts at restructuring and downsizing the administrative structures in Crimea were met with resistance by the regional assembly.[12] Its speaker, Deich, encouraged cooperation with the new Crimean government, though the interests within the assembly and vis-à-vis the regional government quickly became fractured and made for a return to ad hoc coalition building.[13] In a climate of political uncertainty, regional politicians and commentators close to the Russian movement foresaw a long struggle over Crimea's autonomy status,[14] although there was no evidence that the center had any intentions to rock the boat by eliminating the current weak status that the regional authorities have still not managed to exploit fully.[15]

Matvienko's term in office proved short-lived; he resigned in September 2005 ahead of a vote of no-confidence in the Crimean assembly. Anatolii Burdiuhov, an ally of Yushchenko and the regional representative of the National Bank of Ukraine, replaced Matvienko as the next interim prime minister. His cabinet increased the number of Crimean Tatar representatives to six (two deputy prime ministers, two ministers, two heads of committees).[16]

In April 2004 Kuchma had signed a law approved by the Verkhovna Rada to change the electoral system for subnational elections. According to this law, all local councils (with the exception of the smallest rural councils) and the Crimean Verkhovna Rada were to move from a majoritarian electoral system to a fully proportional one. Initially, the Crimean Verkhovna Rada interpreted the new electoral law as a violation of its prerogatives as a regional authority. This protest reflected the as yet undefined nature of the regional party political scene, where many deputies owed their seat in the assembly to personal factors rather than to party identification and a coherent program. The majoritarian regional electoral system was arguably more amenable to this than a system of proportional representation based on party affiliations. Due to their relative advantage in party organization and profile, the Crimean branch of the Communist Party of Ukraine and the United Social Democratic Party of Ukraine (SDPU[o]) were the most vociferous supporters of a proportional system in Crimea. Similarly, the Crimean Tatars pinned their hopes for greater representation on proportional representation.[17]

In the 2006 parliamentary elections Yanukovych could once again rely on Crimea as one of his strongholds, thereby making for continuity from 2004. Nationwide, Yanukovych's Party of Regions emerged as the strongest party with 32.14 percent. In Crimea 58.01 percent endorsed Yanukovych's party (64.26 percent in Sevastopol). The distance in voter support between the Party of Regions and Yushchenko's Our Ukraine and Tymoshenko's bloc was much greater than the national average: only 7.62 percent of Crimea's voters supported Our Ukraine (2.4 percent in Sevastopol) and 6.54 percent Tymoshenko's bloc (4.53 percent in Sevastopol). The Nataliia Vitrenko bloc, built around the Progressive Socialist Party, obtained its best result in Crimea (6.18 percent and 10.09 percent in Sevastopol) based on its aggressive pro-Russian rhetoric, but failed to cross the national threshold, and the Communist Party gained 4.53 percent in the region (4.76 percent in Sevastopol).[18]

In the Crimean assembly elections Yanukovych's Party of Regions obtained 32.55 percent of the vote (as part of a bloc including the Russian Bloc)—the same as his overall national-level result. Regional predictions had put Yanukovych's electoral support even higher. Nevertheless, the distance between his party and other parties was much more pronounced than at the national level. The bloc Union won the support of 7.63 percent; the bloc headed by former premier Kunitsyn 7.56 percent; the Communist Party 6.55 percent; the People's Movement of Ukraine Rukh, which formed part of the Our Ukraine bloc, 6.26 percent (almost entirely based on the Crimean Tatar vote); the Tymoshenko bloc 6.08 percent; Vitrenko's bloc National Opposition (based on the Progressive Socialist Party of Ukraine) 4.87 percent; and the opposition bloc "Ne tak!" (including the United Social Democratic Party) 3.09 percent.[19] Following the March 2006 elections, the For Yanukovych bloc—based on the Party of Regions—secured 44 of the 100 seats in the Crimean assembly, Kunitsyn's bloc and Union 10 seats each, the Communist Party 9 seats, Tymoshenko's bloc and Rukh (Our Ukraine) 8 seats each, Vitrenko's bloc 7 seats, and the anti-Yushchenko bloc "Ne tak!" 4 seats.[20]

In its regional alliance with the Progressive Socialist Party and smaller explicitly pro-Russian groups, the pro-Yanukovych bloc elected Anatolii Hrytsenko to replace Deich as parliamentary speaker in May with over 70 deputies voting in favor.[21] Hrytsenko is one of many familiar political figures in Crimea resurfacing depending on the political climate; he occupied the post of speaker already in 1997–98. The region's institutional structures were notably less dysfunctional than those at the national level. The postelection limbo at the national level, caused by the protracted and farcical coalition talks between the former Orange partners (Yushchenko's Our Ukraine, Tymoshenko's bloc, and the Socialist Party), however, reopened space for the politicization of Ukraine's regional divisions—in particular, the Russian language issue and the tension between Crimean Tatars and Russians.[22]

Regional and local opposition to NATO was another outlet

for political discontent, channeled into local street protests in late May against the landing of US marines and military equipment in preparation of the annual bilateral Ukraine-US military exercise, in which other countries participate within NATO's Partnership for Peace framework. The Crimean assembly followed suit in early June with a resolution declaring the peninsula a NATO-free zone. Although such a resolution can easily be overruled by the center, it highlighted that the Ukrainian parliament had not authorized the exercise involving foreign troops on Ukrainian territory and that the issue of Ukraine's NATO membership is far more controversial in the east and south of Ukraine than Yushchenko's foreign policy suggests. The reemergence of several issues associated with regional, national, and international identities demonstrated that only a comparatively strong center can effectively control regional diversity. Despite the absence of such control, however, Crimean politics did not spiral out of control, thereby highlighting more than a minimum consensus on the established institutional parameters of political interaction.

Following the 2006 elections on a proportional representation basis, the Crimean Tatars are represented in the Crimean assembly with 8 deputies (and with 2 deputies in the Verkhovna Rada in Kyiv). The Kurultay session of December 2005 had decided almost unanimously to renew its electoral alliance with Narodnyi Rukh Ukraïny, which guaranteed the inclusion of Crimean Tatar candidates in the passing part of the electoral lists of the Our Ukraine bloc. The Kurultay and the most prominent Crimean Tatar politicians, Jemilev and Chubarov, once again appealed to the Crimean Tatars to opt for voting discipline and vote for the political parties of Our Ukraine at the national level and for the Crimean branch of Rukh in the Crimean regional and local elections. Mainstream parties, such as the the Party of Regions and the United Social Democratic Party, paid greater lip service than before to Crimean Tatar concerns in order to attract votes. Moreover, a rival Crimean Tatar party, the Crimean Tatar Bloc, was set up to split the Tatar vote. Under the leadership of Edip Gafarov, who was expelled from the Kurultay, this bloc switched allegiance to the Union Party and attracted about 3 percent of the Crimean Tatar vote. These various maneuvers contributed to Crimean Tatar representation in the regional assembly staying below the target figure of 10–13 deputies.[23]

After the elections of 2004 Yushchenko had to counter rumors that he might end the agreement according to which Russia leases its bases in Sevastopol until 2017. He pointed out that the current agreement does not reflect the situation on the ground adequately; for example, with regard to the land use of the Russian Black Sea Fleet. In his view, these issues should be settled on the basis of additional agreements as soon as possible. A change to the basic principles of the current lease agreement were (and still are) not expected. At a ceremony introducing the new commander of the Russian Black Sea Fleet in early March 2005, Russian Defense Minister Sergei Ivanov reconfirmed that although Russia was building a second navy base for the fleet in Novorossiisk, it had no immediate intention of moving the command and core of its Black Sea Fleet, not least due to the costs involved in such a move. Contrary to widespread predictions, Russia has not openly meddled in Ukraine's postelection politics, including Crimea. President Putin's open support for Kuchma and Yanukovych in 2004, even when the manipulation of the elections was evident, put the Russian leadership on the defensive in his first contacts with the new Ukrainian president. On the whole, Russian-Ukranian relations have remained businesslike. The temporary agreement on a gradual increase in Russian gas prices for Ukraine in January 2006, confirmed by Yanukovych and Putin until the end of 2006, is part of this attempt to put Ukrainian-Russian relations on a different footing. Given Ukraine's dependency on Russian oil and gas and Yanukovych's concern for good relations with Russia the redefinition of Ukrainian-Russian relations is ongoing.

Throughout the Orange Revolution and the 2006 elections Ukraine's Constitutional Court remained nonoperational, as the parliament repeatedly failed to approve and appoint new judges to fill vacant posts. However, the process of judicial review with regard to Crimea's status had continued into the late Kuchma era, further clarifying the relationship between the Ukrainian and Crimean constitutions. Ukraine's most senior judges have repeatedly reinforced the constitutional basis of the Crimean autonomy within Ukraine's constitutional and legal framework. The most important judicial ruling came in a case that involved an appeal by fifty deputies of the Ukrainian parliament questioning the congruence between the

Ukrainian Constitution, on the one hand, and the Crimean Constitution and the Ukrainian law On the Adoption of the Constitution
of the Autonomous Republic of Crimea of December 1998, on the
other. The Constitutional Court of Ukraine ruled in January 2003
that the disputed provisions of the Crimean Constitution were in
conformity with the Ukrainian Constitution, specifically those concerning the definition of the "territory of the Autonomous Republic of Crimea" and prospective changes in its territorial boundaries
(article 7), Crimea's right to decide upon its emblem, flag, and the
music and text of its anthem, as well as the use of these symbols
by normative-legal acts of the Crimean Verkhovna Rada (article 8),
and Crimea's right to collect taxes and duties on its territory and to
experiment with regional tax regimes (article 18).[24]

The judgment emphasized that none of the above provisions
conflicted with the Ukrainian Constitution, thereby legally reinforcing both the superiority of the Ukrainian Constitution and the
hierarchical relationship between it and the Crimean Constitution.
The Court called the Crimean Constitution "organically linked" to
the law of the Ukrainian Verkhovna Rada on the adoption of the
Crimean Constitution in December 1998. Only in one instance did
the Court openly criticize the Crimean Constitution, namely in its
use of the term "capital" (*stolytsia*) with reference to Simferopol. In
the Court's opinion the reference was "incorrect," as only Kyiv was
entitled to this status.[25] Representations were made to the Court
by the Ukrainian president and the speakers of the Ukrainian and
Crimean Verkhovna Rada. Their views tended to underpin the constitutional status quo by denying contradictions between the national
and regional constitutions. The Court's detailed references to their
arguments make it clear that the process of judicial review is based on
a dialogue between the different branches and levels of institutional
authority.

A further ruling in April 2003 declared parts of the Ukrainian
law on the Crimean elections unconstitutional, namely the provision
that required representatives of the Ukrainian army and security
services, judges, procurators, and civil servants in general who were
candidates in the regional elections to lay down their professional
duties for the duration of the electoral campaign.[26] This decision
replicated an earlier ruling according to which candidates belonging

to these groups and running for a seat in the national parliament had the right but not the obligation to stand down for the election period. In May 2004 the Constitutional Court ruled that the post of head of a local administration was incompatible with a mandate as a deputy of the Verkhovna Rada in Kyiv or the Verhkovna Rada of the Autonomous Republic of Crimea because they were all "representative organs."[27] The ruling was a reaction to the fact that several Crimean deputies in the Verkhovna Rada were also local government officeholders.

The overall image of the Constitutional Court of Ukraine has been tainted by a number of controversial rulings, most importantly its endorsement of Kuchma's constitutional referendum of 2000, the outcome of which was never implemented, and the Court's ruling of late 2003 that cleared the legal path for Kuchma to seek a third term in office—an option Kuchma refrained from. Despite these controversial Constitutional Court decisions, its rulings on the Crimean Constitution were balanced. They contributed to the consolidation of Ukraine's constitutional system by reaffirming the legitimacy of Crimea's autonomy status and clarifying some of the ambiguities between the national and the regional constitutions.

The ruling of 16 January 2003 also engaged with the status of the Crimean referendum of January 1991 that paved the way for the establishment of the Crimean ASSR a month later. With hindsight the Court declared the 1991 referendum consultative and nonbinding. Moreover, it asserted that based on the 1978 Constitution of the Ukrainian SSR and the 1990 Declaration of Sovereignty, only the Supreme Soviet of the Ukrainian SSR was entitled to take a decision on the establishment of a Crimean ASSR within the Ukrainian SSR.[28] The Court also drew on international norms to inform its judgment. In its interpretation of the provisions for changes to the "territory of the Autonomous Republic of Crimea," the ruling includes an explicit reference to the Council of Europe's European Charter of Local Self-Government, which was ratified by Ukraine in 1997 and entered into force in 1998. It thereby introduced a "soft" international safeguard for Crimea's status, as article 5 of the charter requires any changes to local territorial boundaries to be based on prior consultation with the local self-government bodies and possibly a referendum. Referring to the European Charter as well as Ukrainian constitutional law, the ruling gave article 7.2 of the Crimean Constitution, which stipulates that any changes to the "territory of the Autonomous Republic of Crimea" have to take into account the results of a local referendum (i.e., at the level of the autonomy) and a decision by the Crimean Verkhovna Rada, a legal bolster from two ends. A headline in the Ukrainian weekly *Zerkalo nedeli*—"The Constitution of Crimea is constitutional. Almost…"—captured both the importance of the Court's ruling and the remaining constitutional ambiguity that has become synonymous with Crimea's autonomy status.[29]

Of the three main conflict dimensions discussed in this book—the relationship between Kyiv and Simferopol, relations between Russia and Ukraine, and the Crimean Tatar issue—it is the latter that poses the most serious challenge to political stability in Crimea. Recent clashes between Crimean Tatars and Russian groups in the coastal village of Partenit demonstrate that an underlying tension finds itself outlets through unnecessarily provocative politics over symbols. The construction of a local market on the ground of a Crimean Tatar holy site and the prominent placement of Russian Orthodox crosses at the entry to towns or on sites closely associated with a Crimean Tatar legacy, such as Bakhchisarai or Feodosiia (Kefe), are the best examples in this context.[30] As Crimea's landscape once again exhibits a distinctive Crimean Tatar identity—embodied in the many Crimean Tatar settlements, the progressive construction of mosques and sites celebrating the Crimean Tatar heritage, and the new Tatar-language television station Atlant—intraregional identity politics has acquired new outlets for mobilization.

The confrontation of cultural symbols and myths is part of the process of state building and region building in transition. At times it appears unnecessarily provocative and conflict-prone, but within a sufficiently flexible institutional and political context this type of identity politics does not have to disintegrate into a scenario of violence. The politics of identity and transition require a constant active engagement of the key political elites with the management of diversity. Although none of the key regional players is satisfied with Crimea's current autonomy status, as they are projecting their expectations and fears onto it,[31] it has continued to frame an over-arching climate of dialogue and compromise. Just as the process of autonomy making proved more important than the final institutional shape of the autonomy in conflict prevention, the autonomy status cannot resolve the region's political and economic issues. However, it provides the basic parameters within which to address these issues. Compared to many postconflict situations or frozen conflicts, this is not a bad starting point.

As for the international dimension of the Crimea question, over time Russian-Ukrainian relations have become more businesslike, and the pool of Russian politicians who visibly gain from employing the Crimean card has dwindled. The Orange Revolution led to a partial and temporary rearrangement of political alignments in Crimea, but Crimea's strong pro-Yanukovych vote in the 2006 parliamentary elections and the overwhelming support for his expanded party base in Crimea's regional elections demonstrate a considerable degree of continuity in Crimean politics. If anything, the experience of the Orange Revolution has helped to galvanize a new unity among Crimea's centrist politicians and the various parts of the former Russian movement. However, the support for Yanukovych, whose postelection rhetoric has been moderate on issues such as federalism and an enhanced status for the Russian language, does not lend itself to ethnopolitical tensions similar to those of the early 1990s. Recent political and legal developments demonstrate that despite the ambiguities and weaknesses of the constitutional settlement, the autonomy arrangement provides an institutional foundation for integrating and moderating the behavior of regional and national-level elites. Against a background of dramatic national-level political events it has served as a stabilizing device and an institutional reminder of the importance of bargaining, compromise, and tolerance in the construction of a democratic Ukraine beyond the Orange Revolution.

August 2006

Appendix 1
The Crimean Population, 1897–2001

Changes in ethnic composition of the Crimean
population (percent in parentheses).

	1897	1921	1939	1979	1989	2001
Russians	274,724 (45.3)	370,888 (51.5)	558,481 (49.6)	1,460,980 (68.4)	1,629,542 (67.0)	1,180,400 (58.5)
Ukrainians			154,123 (13.7)	547,336 (25.6)	625,919 (25.8)	492,200 (24.4)
Crimean Tatars	186,212 (34.1)	184,568 (25.9)	218,879 (19.4)	5,422 (0.3)	38,365 (1.6)	243,400 (12.1)

Note: No distinction was made between Russians and Ukrainians in 1897 and 1921.
Source: Data for 1897–1989 are from *Naselenie Krymskoi oblasti po dannym perepisi* (Simferopol, 1989), 7–10, cited in Yevtoukh, "Dynamics of Interethnic Relations in Crimea," 73; data for 2001 are from http://www.ukrcensus.gov.ua/results/general/nationality/crimea (accessed 16 May 2007). It should be noted that figures for 1989 also appear on the website, and differ slightly from those found in Yevtoukh.

Appendix 2
Elite Interviews in April and September–October 1996

Note: The institutional affiliations are listed as of spring 1996. The constitution of 1996 necessitated the reorganization of regional parties into branch offices of all-Ukrainian parties. During the second phase of the elite interviews this process was ongoing.

Vasvi Abduraimov, head of the National Movement of the Crimean Tatars (*Natsional'noe dvizhenie krymskikh tatar*)

Mykola Bahrov [Nikolai Bagrov], parliamentary speaker 1991–94, then pro-rector of Simferopol State University (now Tavriia National University)

Boris Balaian, head of the Culture Fund (*Fond kul'tury*)

Larisa Barzut, deputy in Simferopol city council and school director (the only school at that time with Ukrainian classes)

Valerii Bocherov, member of the political council of the Labor Party (*Partiia truda*)

Refat Chubarov, deputy parliamentary speaker and deputy head of the Mejlis

Anushevan Danelian, deputy parliamentary speaker and head of the Armenian organization

Arkadii Demydenko, Crimean prime minister

Anatolii Filatov, leader of the Democratic Party of Crimea (*Demokraticheskaia partiia Kryma*)

Aleksandr Formanchuk, analyst at the Analytical Center of the Crimean Supreme Soviet

Iurii Gorbunov, lecturer, Simferopol State University (now Tavriia National University)

Petr Harchev, head of the regional office of Prosvita

Leonid Hrach [Grach], Crimean deputy and leader of the Crimean Communist Party (*Kommunisticheskaia partiia Kryma*)

Volodymyr Iehudin, Crimean deputy in the Verkhovna Rada (Agrarian faction)

Vladislav Iermakov, leader of the regional branch of the Ukrainian Republican Party (*Ukraïns'ka respublikans'ka partiia*)

Mariia Ishchuk, leader of the regional office of the Organization of Ukrainian Nationalists (*Orhanizatsiia ukraïns'kykh natsionalistiv*)

Mustafa Jemilev, leader of the Mejlis

Server Kerimov, leader of the Crimean Tatar party Adalet

Iurii Komov, Crimean deputy until 1994, leader of the regional office of the Interregional Bloc of Reforms (*Mezhrehional'nyi blok reform*)

Valerii Kucharenko, deputy in Simferopol city council, head of the city committee of the Communist Party

Aleksandr Loevskii, Crimean deputy and editor-in-chief of *Krymskie izvestiia*

Andrei Mal'gin, Crimean local history museum and journalist for *Tavricheskie vedomosti*

Lev Mirimskii, Crimean deputy in the Ukrainian parliament and enterprise director

Andrei Nikiforov, lecturer, Simferopol State University (now Tavriia National University) and analyst at the Crimean Center of Humanitarian Research (*Kryms'kyi tsentr humanitarnykh doslidzhen'*)

Alla Petrova, head of the Taras Shevchenko Ukrainian Language Society (*Tovarystvo ukraïns'koï movy im. T. Shevchenka*)

Leonid Piluns'kyi, journalist and leader of the regional office of Rukh

Nataliia Pimenova, Crimean deputy in the Verkhovna Rada (Communist faction)

Iurii Podkopaev, deputy parliamentary speaker and leader of the Party of Slavic Unity (*Partiia slavianskogo edinstva*)

Aleksandr Pol'chenko, head of the Social Service of Ukraine (*Suspil'na sluzhba Ukraïny*)

Iurii Polkanov, researcher and head of the Association of the Karaim (*Assotsiatsiia Karaimov*)

Volodymyr Prytula, journalist and head of the Independent Crimean Center for Political Research

David Rebi, head of the Association of the Krymchaks (*Assotsiatsiia Krymchakov*)

Vladimir Renpening, deputy and leader of the Association of Crimean Germans (Wiedergeburt)

Viktor Sharapa, pro-rector, Simferopol State University (now Tavriia National University)

Volodymyr Shev'ev, leader of the Party of the Economic Revival of Crimea (*Partiia ekonomicheskogo vozrozhdeniia Kryma*) and the parliamentary faction Sozidanie

Sergei Shuvainikov, leader of the Russian Party of Crimea (*Russkaia partiia Kryma*)

Dmytro Stepaniuk, presidential representative in Crimea

Ievhen Supruniuk, speaker of the Crimean Supreme Soviet

Sergei Tsekov, deputy and leader of the Republican Party of Crimea (*Respublikanskaia partiia Kryma*)

Vladimir Zaskoka, Crimean deputy and head of the Control Commission for Privatization Issues

Al'bert Zhumykin, Crimean deputy in the Verkhovna Rada (Communist faction)

Vladimir Zubarev, lawyer at the Crimean College of Lawyers (*Krymskaia kollegiia advokatov*)

Appendix 3
Regional Elite Turnover and Profile, 1990–98

G IVEN THE SIMULTANEITY OF DEMOCRATIZATION, marketization, and state building, a variety of elites has a stake in the decisions being taken during transition, and an overlap between interests leaves the boundaries between different elite segments blurred and difficult to demarcate. In addition to the common horizontal distinction based on occupational criteria (political, economic, administrative, and cultural elites) the distinction between old and new elite, based on a cutoff point of 1991, tries to capture the scale of turnover and adaptation of post-Soviet elites. The category "new elites," however, is not always correlated with a willingness to reform. Coalitions between old and new elites, on which peaceful transition hinges, are seen as conducive to the functioning of the state and a smoother transition. Fractured elites and the circulation of elites embody the danger of competition, instability, and conflict. Integrated elites, on the contrary, sharing interests and attitudes or complementing each other are generally seen as conducive to political stability. The underlying assumption has been for the most part that post-Soviet transitions have been characterized by a substantial recirculation of the old Communist nomenklatura into new political and economic bodies. The so-called nomenklatura privatization, for example, enabled the old elite to reposition itself as the new "party of power" in what Sergei Kordonskii called the "administrative market."[1] Post-Soviet elite studies have tried to quantify these kinds of elite developments and behavior, mostly with reference to Russia's regions.[2] As the Crimean Supreme Soviet has been the most important regional institution over time, the elected deputies provide a good insight into regional elite turnover, the elite's sociological profile, and party identification. A comparison of the three consecutive elections to the regional Supreme Soviet in March 1990, April 1994, and March 1998 conveys a longitudinal picture of elite recruitment patterns and turnover.[3]

In the Soviet period the nomination and election of regional deputies were controlled by the Communist Party. Predetermined quotas for the representation of gender, age, education, occupation, nationality, and party membership had to be fulfilled. Real political power rested with the party organs, so that this manufactured extreme pluralism of representation in the elected state bodies was little more than a symbolic function of the system's ideological claims to be a "state of the whole people." Gorbachev's reforms shifted political power from the party to the state bodies. At the subnational level, power was transferred from the regional party *obkoms* to the regional soviets. Accordingly, the elections of March 1990, generally referred to as the founding elections of post-Soviet democracy, initiated an elite adaptation process at all political levels. Political, administrative, and economic leaders, the main pillars of the old party elite, repositioned themselves and shifted to the state institutions as the new nucleus of real power.

In Crimea, the longitudinal data demonstrate massive turnover of individual deputies. In the 1994 and 1998 elections the reelection rate was below 10 percent. A total of 13 individuals who were elected to the regional soviet in 1990 and lost their mandate in 1994 managed to achieve a political comeback in 1998. Only a handful of deputies, such as Communist leader Hrach, who had immense regional political clout, were continuously represented in the regional soviet of 1990, 1994, and 1998.[4] The high turnover in personnel underscores the fact that the regional political space has been in flux. This volatility, however, was accompanied by a parallel trend for consolidation in the sociological background of the elected deputies. On the whole, the deputy cohort became slightly younger in the period from 1990 to 1998. In 1990 the largest group of regional deputies fell into the age cohort 50–59 years (42.9 percent), followed by the 40–49-year-old cohort (33.5 percent) and the 60–69-year-old cohort (19.3 percent). The elections of 1994 reversed the two largest age groups: the age group of 40–49 years emerged as the single largest category (40.8

percent), followed by the category 50–59 years (30.6 percent) and 60–69 years (15.3 percent). The trend of 1994 was reinforced by the 1998 elections. An even clearer majority of deputies was drawn from the cohort 40–49 years (44.1 percent), followed by a further reduced proportion of 50–59-year-olds (29.0 percent). The previously third largest group of 60–69-year-olds (10.8 percent) was for the first time overtaken by the younger group of deputies 30–39 years of age (12.9 percent). Moreover, the first two deputies under 30 years old were represented in parliament.

The 1990 regional soviet elections brought a surge in representation of all four elite segments, mainly economic leaders (25.5 percent), followed by members of the professional elite (18.0 percent) and political leaders (14.9 percent). In 1994 economic leaders were still the single largest elite group elected to the Crimean Supreme Soviet (22.4 percent). Specific developments in Crimea, namely the profile of the temporarily predominant pro-Russian and separatist movement, explain the expansion of the cohorts of elite and non-elite professionals (16.3 percent and 21.4 percent respectively). Compared with Russian regions, professionals were much more active in politics in Crimea at this point. The influx of people without any specific experience in politics belonged to the early postcommunist phase in Crimea. In terms of political mobilization, Crimea was a latecomer, with no significant stake in the democratic and national movement before 1991. The election outcomes of 1994 can be seen as a reaction to the events of 1991 and their consequences, essentially in the form of a belated regional grassroots movement. By 1998 the recruitment patterns of the Crimean political elite were stabilizing and reflected the postcommunist trend identified in Russian regions. The proportion of economic leaders rose to 45.2 percent, followed by members of the administrative elite (14 percent) and the professional elite (12.9 percent). The decreasing significance of the professionals, in particular the non-elite professionals, resulted from the backlash against the Russian movement in Crimea. It had discredited itself in the eyes of the population due to ineffectiveness, so that the electorate voted for deputies with experience and, even more importantly, with the financial means to deliver on election promises. The most striking trend is the predominance of economic managers in the regional parliament. While this process of interlocking between political and economic structures is traditionally of a more covert nature in Western societies, postcommunist transitions, and the Crimean example in particular, exhibit open and direct links between political and economic interests. There is no distinction between formal and informal networks; the same individuals and groups are influential in politics and business alike and, given Crimea's high crime rate, often linked with criminal structures as well.

Engineers (18.4 percent), teachers (11.2 percent), and doctors (10.2 percent) dominated the Supreme Soviet in 1994. By 1998 the proportion of those professions that recruit economic leaders had risen considerably: 38.7 percent of the regional deputies were engineers, 12.9 percent agricultural specialists (mostly directors of former kolkhoz farms), and economists (10.8 percent).[5] In general, intellectuals and professionals were more likely to secure parliamentary seats in the immediate aftermath of the breakup of the USSR. Professionals represent the highly educated segments of society, their jobs are often closely linked to public affairs and, therefore, provide an outlet and the necessary means and skills for political activity. Their legal, academic, or journalistic training and capacity for articulation, for example, can prove extremely helpful for purposes of political mobilization. During the early stages of transition, intellectuals and professionals benefited from an image of being outside the previous regime. It was easier for them to put forward new, anti-Soviet and nationalist ideas without their credibility being called into question. As transition progressed, however, it became obvious that while intellectuals and professionals may provide the ideology and the program of political change, they have neither the financial means nor the political skills to ensure the implementation of policies. In the Crimean case, the influx of intellectuals and professionals into the regional parliament came to a halt when they proved incapable of fulfilling their promises and effecting change due to their lack of experience, financial means, and political-economic networks.

For the post-Soviet Crimean political elite, party affiliation has been considerably less important than in Soviet times. In 1990, as the Communist Party disintegrated, it was still able to secure an overwhelming majority of the seats in the regional Supreme Soviet (83.2 percent and 1.9 percent Komsomol). In 1994 82.7 percent of the regional deputies (data available for 95.9 percent of deputies) were elected on party platforms. The explanation for the comparatively high percentage in comparison with Russian regional assembly elections in 1994 (8.2 percent party affiliation) lies in the domestic and foreign-policy dimensions of the Crimean issue.[6] Crimean regionalism and separatism was channeled into the Russia Bloc, a loose conglomerate of pro-Russian and Russian nationalist parties (56.1 percent). What looks statistically like a strong party affiliation was in fact the expression of support for a vague notion of "Russianness" personified by an umbrella movement. The quota guaranteeing the parliamentary representation of the deported peoples accounted for another 18 seats altogether (16.3 percent). These seats were in practice tied to political and cultural national organizations. Crimea is therefore comparatively unusual in that national-cultural and political identity, enhanced by the quota system, boosted the showing of party blocs and organizations.

Despite Crimea's distinct regional electoral patterns, in 1994 and 1998 "independents" accounted for the single largest cohort of elected deputies (17.3 in 1994 and 48.4 percent in 1998.). These figures underscore a general trend towards high numbers of independents in the early stages of transition. A plausible explanation is that in a constantly changing political environment, in which parties come and go and are often little more than support groups for certain individuals with indistinguishable programs, the regional political elite has learned to "maintain the manoeuvrability gained from a publicly declared independent posture in the shifting sands of (an) unstable transitional political landscape."[7] In the aftermath of regional elections, so-called independents often revealed closeness to certain parties or parliamentary factions. Political "independence," if real or simply declared, was an elite strategy for political survival and appeals to a considerable part of the electorate. This attitude, an elite response to widespread party skepticism, presented a formidable obstacle to political party development, made the outcome of elections less clear-cut, and turned politics into a bargaining game on the basis of personal interests. The outcome on the one hand became more unpredictable, but on the other hand extremist political or ideological positions were also less viable. In the Crimean context independents were less likely to engage in separatist or nationalist mobilization.

After a near-exclusion of the Communist Party in 1994 (2.0 percent), the party managed to reestablish itself as the largest party represented in the Crimean parliament in 1998 (34.4 percent). Despite this strong showing, however, it failed to secure a majority and remained dependent on building coalitions with independent candidates to pursue its policies. The abolishment of the quota system for the 1998 elections prevented the regional representation of any of the deported nationalities, most notably the Crimean Tatars. Just one Crimean Tatar was elected, and that was on the Communist platform. All the other parties gained no more than marginal representation.

The new Ukrainian Constitution of 1996 set up a new institutional framework to prevent regional party deviation by a special clause requiring the registration of every party at the national level. This change had a number of effects. It weakened the distinctly Crimean parties, especially the pro-Russian ones. It also contributed to a resurgence in support for the Communist Party in the regional elections. It also opened the way for all-Ukrainian parties, such as APU and NDP, to gain a foothold in the Crimean parliament. The PEV, the Ukrainian-wide version of the Crimean PEVK, the most influential Crimean party in the parliament from 1994 to 1998, almost disappeared, mainly due to a thorough anticriminal campaign by the Ukrainian police in the run-up to the elections in March 1998 that forced many prominent PEV leaders into hiding. The only party with a distinctly regional profile despite its registration as an all-Ukrainian party was Union, which emerged from the rubble of the Russian Bloc. The main reason for the regional "Communist comeback" lies in the prolonged and painful economic transition process in Ukraine and the fact that Crimea lagged behind most other Ukrainian regions. In 1998 Crimea's regional outlook rejoined the political profile of the southern and eastern regions of Ukraine in general.

While the representation of deputies from rural areas gradually decreased, from 36.0 percent in 1990 to 28.6 percent in 1994 before stabilizing at 28.0 percent in 1998, the proportion of deputies living in Simferopol increased significantly: in 1990 25.5 percent of the deputies lived in the capital, 30.6 percent in 1994 and 34.4 percent in 1998. Accordingly, the Crimean Supreme Soviet increasingly became linked to Simferopol itself, and the distinction between regional and local politics blurred. In 1994 the representation of deputies from Sevastopol soared to 12.2 percent as part of regional political developments. Residence in Sevastopol was then a good indicator for pro-Russian party affiliation and the occupational backgrounds tied to the army and the Black Sea Fleet. By 1998, the Ukrainian Constitution had clarified that Sevastopol is administered separately from the rest of Crimea and has its own administration like the city of Kyiv. The city of Sevastopol was no longer officially represented in the Crimean Supreme Soviet, although its delegates attended its sessions.

The Crimean Deputies in the Ukrainian Parliament

A seat in the Ukrainian parliament comes with a higher political profile and immunity, an important incentive for business elites in a transition state.[8] Although in principle Crimea's deputies in Kyiv represent the region and its political elite at the higher level, recruitment patterns and elite circulation follow a different dynamic at the interface between regional and national politics. Individual turnover was more significant at the national than at the regional soviet level. From 1990 to 1994, only a single Verkhovna Rada deputy from Crimea managed to retain his seat. Only in conjunction with the occupational background of the deputies can this fact generate conclusions about elite change. In the 1998 elections, altogether seven deputies stayed in their posts. This considerable stability in personnel indicates the significance of formal and informal networks safeguarding this segment of the political elite. The power of incumbency is part of the explanation, since this is often greater at the national level due to the higher profile of politicians. It is also a further indication that different election criteria were at work during regional and national elections. The extreme shifts in regional politics in 1994 and after were not mirrored at the national level, partly due to Meshkov's boycott of the national elections. In 1994 the proportion of economic leaders among the Crimean deputies in Kyiv increased dramatically from 9.5 percent to 34.8 percent, and the proportion of administrative officials rose in similar terms from 9.5 percent to 30.4 percent. The sudden rise of economic leaders, in particular, has to be linked to the advantages tied to the immunity that is granted to parliament members in Kyiv, guaranteeing greater freedom for business activities in the semiofficial sphere. By 1998 almost equal representation of political, economic, and administrative leaders was achieved. Professional recruitment patterns were comparable to those in the regional parliament.

In 1990 all Crimean deputies in the Ukrainian Supreme Soviet were members of the Communist Party. Although independent candidates were deliberately chosen to fill lower-level positions, for example in the regional soviet, higher positions in the political hierarchy were often reserved for party members. Despite a clear drop in its influence in the aftermath of the USSR, the Communist Party has remained the single most important party affiliation among Rada deputies during the first decade of post-Soviet transition. (43.5 percent in 1994, 29.4 percent in 1998). In 1998 the proportion of independents was for the first time above the communists, reflecting Crimean regional and all-Ukrainian voting patterns. Similar to the regional soviet deputies, all-Ukrainian parties, Soiuz, APU and in 1998 NDP, Hromada, and even Rukh secured between one and two seats each.

Local Elites and Elections in Crimea

Comparative data from the local elections in Crimea, held in 1995–96 and 1998, reveal that local politics in Crimea have persistently followed a different path than regional politics. Simferopol is the exception in many ways, as local and regional politics are conflated and similar political forces compete for both representative bodies. The events, personalities, and scandals in the Crimean parliament have overshadowed the developments on the ground, but the local level has maintained its own profile in the Crimean *raions*. In 1995 the local level proved more resistant to political and economic change. At the level where face-to-face contact matters and decisions are actually being implemented, personal knowledge of the candidates and residual fears of change, as well as the temporal sequencing of the regional and local elections, explain the discrepancy in outcome between the regional and local parliaments. Familiar independent candidates and Communists proved strongest in 1995, indicating the loss of confidence in the Russian movement at the regional level and the fact that practical rather than ideological choices dominate in local elections.

Altogether 1,482 candidates had been deputies in the outgoing local soviets.[9] The first round of voting on 25 June 1995 and further rounds on 9 July and 29 October filled all but nine councils. Altogether 4,280 deputies had to be elected for 311 councils at different levels.[10] Of the elected deputies, 3,064 held no seat in the previous election period, a figure which amounts to an individual turnover of 71.5 percent. Only 11.8 percent of the elected deputies had a party affiliation, as opposed to 87.8 percent independents. Communist Party affiliation accounted for 85.1 percent of the deputies with party affiliation, followed by 12.1 percent for PEVK, and 0.6 percent each for the Union in Support of Crimea and the Crimean branch of the Ukrainian Republican Party. Six parties secured only one or two seats, among them the RPK (0.4 percent of the deputies with party affiliation). Of the elected deputies, 52.3 percent were Russian nationals, 37.9 percent Ukrainians, and only 4.1 percent Crimean Tatars.[11] In 1998, however, the recruitment patterns changed. With the Simferopol city council being the exception, the Communists failed to achieve the electoral victory they had expected.[12] Business-related people stood a much better chance of getting elected at the local level.

In the 1998 elections 11,773 candidates registered for the 6,663 seats in local councils.[13] Competition was particularly strong for the city councils. In the overwhelming majority of constituencies the seats were filled in the first round of voting. *Raion* and city councils were substantially renewed: only 24 percent of the previous city council deputies and 19 percent of the *raion* deputies were reelected. At the city level considerably more deputies were associated with political parties (47 percent as opposed to only 20 percent at the *raion* level). While teachers and medical staff were now well represented in city councils (20–30 percent), at the *raion* and village level representatives of agricultural firms were elected. About 56 percent of the deputies in the Simferopol *raion* council were the directors and/or main specialists of the important firms and factories in the area. Out of 6,429 elected deputies, only 518 were Communists, 232 were members of the APU, 23 were members of the NDPU, eight were members of the SDPU, and five were members of the SPU (*Selians'ka partiia Ukraïny*). The majority of deputies were independents (88 percent). Therefore, no single party dominated the local elections. Among 777 city council deputies there were no more than 100 Communists. The Simferopol city council, where 35 out of 50 deputies were Communists, was a notable exception. The 1998 local elections also exchanged a considerable number of mayors (heads of soviets). In towns of *raion* subordination only one former mayor stayed on; out of 11 towns of republican subordination seven elected a new head. In contrast, about 70 percent of mayors at the village level retained their position. Among the 15 elected city mayors there were eight independents, four Communists, and two representatives of the NDP. Out of 37 elected in settlements only four were Communists with 30 independents, while there were 12 Communists among the 243 heads of village councils. Despite considerable overall turnover, in the election of the city, town, and village heads the electorate went for well-known candidates who had previously held other positions.

Table 1. Comparison of 1995 and 1998 Crimean parliamentary elections (results in percentages unless otherwise noted).

	End of 1995 (three rounds)	1998 (first round)
Party members	11.8	12.2
Communist Party members	10.1 (429 seats)	8.1 (518 seats)
Independents	88.2	87.8
Individual turnover	71.9	76 (city level) 81 (*raion* level)
Total	99.5 (4,260 deputies)	96.5 (6,429 deputies)

Source: Author's calculations on the basis of the data provided by the Supreme Soviet for 1995 and 1998.

The Simferopol city council deserves special mention, as its role is enhanced through its location and involvement in regional politics. In 1995 all 50 city deputies were elected in two rounds on 25 June and 10 September 1995. The biggest group by far, 37 deputies (74 percent), were independents. The Communist Party became the single largest party represented with 12 deputies (24 percent), followed only by

one member (2 percent) of the Union in Support of the Republic of Crimea. There has been great continuity at the head of the
city council, who was for the first time publicly elected in 1995. The
incumbent, Valerii Iermak, was elected in 1995 and reelected in 1998
despite his non-Communist affiliation. The Simferopol city council
witnessed a considerable turnover of individuals: only 8 out of 50
deputies were reelected in March 1998: 13 independent candidates, 34
Communists, and one member of the Party of the Protectors of the
Fatherland (*Partiia zashchitnikov Otechestva*).[14] For the first time since
1994, intensive cooperation between the large Communist factions
in both local and regional soviets was possible. The beginning of a
new Communist wave had already manifested itself in the support for
Hrach as the new speaker of the Crimean parliament in April 1998.

Table 2. Party membership in the Simferopol
City Council, 1990–98.

	1990–95	1995–98	Since 1998
Communist Party	67%	24%	68%
Independents	26%	74%	26%
Number of deputies	150	50	50

Source: Central Election Commission; data were available only for the 104 deputies elected
in the first two rounds of the elections in March 1990. As the percentage of Communists
among those 104 was 67.31 percent, this makes for a good overall estimate.

In 1998 the Ukrainian parliamentary elections coincided with
the elections to the Crimean parliament and the local councils.
National and regional elections followed a similar pattern, which in
turn resembled the outcome of the local elections in the Crimean
capital Simferopol. The other local constituencies diverged from the
overall pattern in not enlarging the Communists' strongholds. At
the local level independent businessmen with the necessary financial
means, who are believed to secure effective policies, proved more
successful than the appeal of old ideologies.

The considerable reduction in the size of the regional parliament from 163 in 1990 to 100 in 1998 (98 in 1994) was accompanied by a narrowing of recruitment patterns for the elected deputies. While significant changes in party affiliation are expected in the volatile realm of postcommunist electoral politics, the sociological profile of the elected deputies underwent significant change. The regional deputy corps of 1994–98 was characterized by great numbers of professionals, a finding that correlates well with the strong showing of the pro-Russian movement. By contrast, over time the majority of deputies represented the regional economic elite. Independent from one another, economic leadership position and Communist party membership were the two main pull factors in the 1998 regional elections, roughly representing the division between "old" and "new" elites. The Crimean case provides ample evidence to illustrate the influx of economic leaders into political positions and the resulting interlocking of political and economic elites. As Deutsch put it, "wealth, influence, and power come in clusters" among the elites at the local, regional, and national level.[15] This influx of new people, or the repositioning of old elite segments, does not guarantee the emergence of an innovative, pro-reform elite, but it widened the scope for cooperation with Kyiv and a workable autonomy framework. The original near-disappearance of Communists from the regional political scene and their belated comeback in 1998 was linked to the specific dynamics of Crimean political development. The instability in the Supreme Soviet translated into frequent personnel change in the regional executive structures, in particular in the leadership of the Council of Ministers.

While in 1994 pro-Russian sentiment, borne mainly out of socioeconomic insecurity and a fear of Ukrainization, led to a sweeping victory of the Russia Bloc, the elections of 1998 reflected the subsequent disappointment with this movement. Protest and nostalgia were channeled into a strong Communist vote at the regional level, although it remained short of a clear majority. The Communists' victory was offset by a large number of independents and influential businessmen. The implications of the narrowing recruitment patterns for the regional political elite are difficult to predict. In the post-Soviet context, where assets and influence are being redistributed, it can hardly be a guarantee for increasing political stability and / or reform progress. While this interlocking of political and economic segments of the elite and the consequential crosscutting of cleavages have assisted in the marginalization of ethnopolitics in Crimea, it has not so far translated into much-needed economic structural reforms.

Notes

Introduction

1. See Sasse, "The 'New' Ukraine."
2. *The Guardian*, 25 May 1994.
3. *The Economist*, 17 July 1993, 38.
4. See, for example, Kuzio, "Russia-Crimea-Ukraine"; or Kuzio, "The Crimea and European Security."
5. It is more appropriate to call these conditions "risk factors" rather than causes of conflict. See Zürcher and Koehler, "Introduction," 6; Koehler and Zürcher, "Institutions and the Organisation of Stability and Violence," especially 243.
6. William Zimmerman had still excluded Crimea from his evidence for the emergence of a political community in Ukraine; see Zimmerman, "Is Ukraine a Political Community?" 54.
7. For a survey of this literature see Hughes and Sasse, "Comparing Ethnic and Regional Conflicts."
8. Beissinger, *Nationalist Mobilization*, 35.
9. Through one detailed case study this book hopes to demonstrate what Beissinger has shown statistically: the same structural conditions are correlated with violent and nonviolent mobilization. See ibid., 280–81.
10. Garnett, *Keystone in the Arch*, 22. Garnett sees Ukraine's biggest internal dividing line between Crimea and the rest of the country and thereby explicitly calls the stereotypical East-West divide into question.
11. Ascherson, *Black Sea*, 10.
12. Between 18 May and 4 June Soviet documentation recorded a total of 225,009 deported people, among them 183,155 Crimean Tatars,

15,040 Greeks, 12,422 Bulgarians, 9,621 Armenians, 1,119 Germans, and 3,652 others. Of Crimean Tatars, 151,604 were reported to have been resettled to Uzbekistan and 31,551 to the RSFSR; altogether 38,802 Armenians, Bulgarians, Germans, and Greeks had been deported to the Bashkir ASSR, Mariiskaia ASSR, several oblasts in the RSFSR, and Gurevskaia oblast in Kazakhstan; see Bugai, *Iosif Stalin—Lavrentiiu Berii*, 129–50. For eyewitness accounts and a description of the special settlement regime in Central Asia, see Williams, *Crimean Tatars*, 386–99.

13.   Luther, *Die Krim unter deutscher Besatzung*. Kirimal (*Der Nationale Kampf der Krimtürken*, 304–22) estimates that between 8,000 and 20,000 Crimean Tatars fought in voluntary battalions under the German army at different times. These battalions were deployed primarily in the fight against the Soviet partisans.

14.   According to the 2001 Ukrainian census, Crimea has 2,024,000 inhabitants in total. The 377,200 inhabitants of Sevastopol are listed separately (*Vseukraïns'kyi perepys naselennia 2001*, http://www.ukrcensus.gov.ua/results/general/nationality [accessed 23 March 2007]). The return of deportees, mainly the Crimean Tatars, disguises the decrease of the regional population. By 1 January 1998 247,728 Crimean Tatars, 2,215 Greeks, 596 Germans, 416 Bulgarians, and 324 Armenians were officially registered in Crimea. See data from the State Commission on Nationalities Questions and Migration, 1998.

15.   By comparison, the last Soviet census in 1989 still recorded 67 percent Russians, 25.8 percent Ukrainians, and only 1.6 percent Crimean Tatars. See Yevtoukh, "The Dynamics of Interethnic Relations in Crimea," 79.

16.   In fact, the number of pensioners in Crimea lies just under the Ukrainian average. In 1995, 284 in 1000 inhabitants were pensioners in Ukraine, as compared to 256 in 1000 in Crimea and 250 in Sevastopol. With a share of 3.9 percent of the total number of pensioners in Ukraine, Crimea lies clearly behind the regions with the highest numbers of pensioners, Donetsk (10.9 percent) and Dnipropetrovsk (7.5 percent) (see Administratsiia Presydenta Ukrainy, Upravlinnia z pytan' ekonomiky, *Ukraïna ta ïï rehiony*, 4. The census data of 1989 also puts Crimea clearly behind the eastern regions in terms of absolute numbers of pensioners. One of the regions that is most comparable to Crimea in 1989 is Lviv. Payments for veterans, however, accounted for a larger share of regional expenditures in Crimea than in most other Ukrainian regions. Thus, the distinctive feature

has been the type of pensioners concentrated in Crimea. See data compiled by the Ukrainian Ministry of Finance, 1996. In 1989, 15.2 percent of Crimea's population were over 60 years old. By 2001, the share of Crimean inhabitants aged 60 and over had increased to 20.1 percent. In 1989, 18.2 percent of the population were pensioners; in 2001 their share had risen to 22.5 percent (21.3 percent and 23.9 percent respectively in Ukraine as a whole). For the 1989 and 2001 data, see *Vseukraïns'kyi perepys naselennia 2001*, http://www.ukrcensus.gov.ua/results/general/age (accessed 23 March 2007).

17. This finding is in line with M. Steven Fish's conclusion that "the origins of most institutional development and innovation are found in the competition for the right to rule, rather than in ruling itself"; see Fish, "The Dynamics of Democratic Erosion," 84.

18. Beissinger's seminal study on nationalist mobilization in the late Soviet Union starts from a similar premise: the phenomenon that has to be explained—the upsurge of nationalism—becomes part of the actual explanation of a "tide of nationalism" and, ultimately, the collapse of the Soviet Union. Nationalism, thus, becomes both "a structured and a structuring phenomenon" (9), a cause of action as well as a product of action (11). Beissinger makes a convincing case for detailed analytical narratives tracing events through a period of "thickened history" in order to bridge this methodological dilemma. See Beissinger, *Nationalist Mobilization*, 1–34.

19. For a recent reexamination of the early period of Soviet nationality policies, see Martin, *The Affirmative Action Empire*.

Chapter 1

1. Horowitz, *Ethnic Groups in Conflict*, 190; Snyder, *From Voting to Violence*, 15–16, 20–21, 27–42.

2. Horowitz concentrates on opportunity structures during transition and institutional mechanisms enabling "democracy in divided societies," whereas Snyder—in line with traditional liberal thinking—displays skepticism about institutionalized power sharing. See Horowitz, "Democracy in Divided Societies," 18–38; and Snyder, *From Voting to Violence*, 40.

3. This definitional ambiguity has been summarized best by Connor, "A Nation Is a Nation," 379–88.

4. See Gellner, *Nations and Nationalism*, 68.

5. Renan, "Qu'est-ce qu'une nation?" 17–18.

6. For the distinction between Eastern and Western nationalism, see Kohn, *Idea of Nationalism*. The distinction between Eastern and

Western patterns also remains central to Gellner's European map of nationalism, although there are several in-between zones that blur the boundary between the two ideal types. See Gellner, *Nationalism*, 50–58.

7. A. Smith, *National Identity*, 13. This is reflected in his definition of a nation "as named human population sharing an historic territory, common myths and historical memories, a mass, public culture, a common economy and common legal rights and duties for all members" (14).

8. Breuilly, *Nationalism and the State*, 390.

9. Gellner, *Nations and Nationalism*, 1; Gellner, *Nationalism*, 72.

10. See, for example, Geyer, "Der Nationalstaat im postkommunistischen Mittel- und Osteuropa."

11. Gellner, *Nationalism*, 11.

12. O'Leary, "On the Nature of Nationalism."

13. Breuilly, *Nationalism and the State*, 25.

14. Gellner, *Nations and Nationalism*, 43.

15. For an overview of this literature and the key issues of Russian federalism, see Hughes, "Managing Secession Potential," 36–68; Stepan, "Russian Federalism in Comparative Perspective"; Cashaback, "Accommodating Multiculturalism in Russia and Canada."

16. Holdar, "Torn Between East and West."

17. Lipset and Rokkan, "Cleavage Structures, Party Systems, and Voter Alignments," 1–64.

18. Rokkan and Urwin, *Economy, Territory, Identity*; Keating, *State and Regional Nationalism*; Keating, *New Regionalism in Western Europe*.

19. Rokkan and Urwin, *Economy, Territory, Identity*, 3.

20. For the term "triple transition," see Offe, *Varieties of Transition*.

21. See Huntington, *Third Wave*; McFaul, "Fourth Wave of Democracy and Dictatorship."

22. The comparability of these three regions of transition gave rise to a heated debate in the early 1990s. For an overview of the debate, see Bunce, "Regional Differences in Democratization." For a concise discussion of the false dichotomy between area studies and comparative politics, see Anderson et al., "Conclusion: Postcommunism and the Theory of Democracy," 153–54.

23. For the pessimistic view that democracy in an ethnically diverse state is next to impossible, see Mill, *Considerations on Representative Government*, 389–90.

24. Rustow, "Transitions to Democracy," 351.

25. Offe, *Varieties of Transition*, 50–81.

26. Linz and Stepan, *Problems of Democratic Transition and Consolidation*.

The authors single out two institutional means with a stabilizing effect: consociationalism and electoral sequencing. The record of consociationalism is mixed when it comes to conflict management, and the sequencing of national and regional elections, when applied to the FSU, seems less clear-cut than they suggest. See Linz and Stepan, "Political Identities and Electoral Sequences."

27. Beissinger and Young, "Effective State," 467. This volume suggests that postcolonial Africa makes for the best regional comparison with post-Soviet Eurasia because of a shared experience of "state crises."

28. Whether or not the political elites were united before the onset of change—either in favor of or in opposition to reforms—has proven a more reliable indicator of democratization in the early phase of postcommunism than the existence of elite pacts. See Roeder, "The Rejection of Authoritarianism," 11–53.

29. Stepan, "Federalism and Democracy." In this piece Stepan advocates federalism as a stabilizing institution in divided societies undergoing democratization.

30. Whitehead, "Three International Dimensions of Democratization," 3–25; Schmitter, "Influence of the International Context," 26–54.

31. The relationship between the making of one nation and the unmaking of another has systematically been traced by Roman Szporluk in "Ukraine: From an Imperial Periphery to a Sovereign State."

32. For a discussion of the two breakups of the Russian state in the twentieth century, see Szporluk, "Fall of the Tsarist Empire and the USSR."

33. See Snyder, "Reconstructing Politics," 1–13; Motyl, "After Empire," 14–33; for a comparative historical overview of the dynamics of imperial collapse and its aftermath, see Lieven, *Empire*; Dawisha and Parrott, *End of Empire*.

34. Forsberg, "Collapse of the Soviet Union," 3–20. This book primarily deals with historic border changes during and in the aftermath of World War II.

35. Beissinger and Young, "Introduction," 47.

36. Zürcher and Koehler, "Introduction," 1.

37. One of the best known taxonomies is the one by McGarry and O'Leary, which distinguishes between four "methods for eliminating differences" (genocide, forced mass population transfers, partition/secession, integration/assimilation) and "methods for managing differences" (hegemonic control, arbitration, cantonization/federalization, consociationalism/power sharing); see McGarry and O'Leary, "Introduction," 1–40.

38. Gurr and Harff, *Ethnic Conflict in World Politics*, 83–84.

39. Carment and James, "Ethnic Conflict at the International Level," 2.

40. Beissinger, *Nationalist Mobilization*, 259–70.

41. Lijphart, *Democracy in Plural Societies*; Horowitz, *Ethnic Groups in Conflict*; Rothschild, *Ethnopolitics*; Nordlinger, *Conflict Regulation in Divided Societies*.

42. Conflicts and conflict potential are defined by their sustained nature and potential for violence beyond sporadic episodes of rioting.

43. Carment and James, "Ethnic Conflict at the International Level," 2. Paradoxically, this trend has been accompanied by a surge in internationally sanctioned interventionism.

44. Rubin, "Conclusion," 166–68.

45. See Lapidus, "Ethnicity and State Building," 325–27. Lapidus sees the potential for future conflict "from the Crimea to the Caucasus to Kazakhstan" as being high (353–55).

46. See Szporluk, *National Identity and Ethnicity*; Bremmer and Taras, *New States, New Politics*; A. Smith et al., *Nation-Building in the Post-Soviet Borderlands*; Drobizheva et al., *Ethnic Conflict in the Post-Soviet World*; Arbatov, *Managing Conflict in the Former Soviet Union*. For the four key studies on the Russians or Russian-speakers in the FSU, see Kolstø, *Russians in the Former Soviet Republics*; Melvin, *Russians Beyond Russia*; Chinn and Kaiser, *Russians as the New Minority*; Laitin, *Identity in Formation*.

47. Roeder, "Peoples and States after 1989," 873–76.

48. For a discussion of these trends of "deinstitutionalization" and "reinstitutionalization," see Hughes and Sasse, "Conflict and Accommodation in the FSU," 231–33.

49. Leonid Kravchuk's answer to the author's question at the conference "From Soviet to Independent Ukraine," University of Birmingham, 13 June 1996. Despite the vehement denial of its relevance among high-ranking Ukrainian politicians and constitutional lawyers, the idea of a federal Ukraine resonates with historical experiences in Mykhailo Drahomanov's writings and a number of short-lived institutional experiments in the period 1917–21. See Sasse, "The 'New' Ukraine," 78–79.

50. See Zolotarev, "Federativnoe ustroistvo Ukrainy," 70.

51. See *Perturbantsii* (Warsaw), no. 1 (Autumn 1989): 70–76, quoted in a profile on Chornovil prepared by the Ukrainian Center for Independent Political Research (*Ukraïns'kyi nezalezhnyi tsentr politychnykh doslidzhen'*), Kyiv 1996. In this article Chornovil is even said to have supported the idea of Crimean independence. Volodymyr Hryn'ov, Adviser to the Ukrainian President on Regional Issues, con-

firmed Chornovil's early views on federalism in an interview with the author (Kyiv, 25 October 1996).

52. See *Mizhrehional'nyi Blok Reform: Prohramni partiini dokumenty.*

53. In the Crimean context see Zolotarev, "Federativnoe ustroistvo Ukrainy," 70–75. As Zolotarev phrased it: "Federalism is for Ukraine the opportunity to colonize regional specificities, among them the stereotypes about patriotism" (73). See also Miroshnik et al., *Regional'noe razvitie Ukrainy*; and the article by the Kharkiv regional council deputy Evgenii Solov'ev, "Ukraina v kontekste vsemirnogo protsessa detsentralizatsii," 14–15. The issue of the journal *Biznes Inform* containing Solov'ev's article came out under the title "Federativnaia Respublika Ukraina?" and collects a number of articles about the advantages of political and economic decentralization. For a detailed account of regional decentralization and interregional links, see also Nemyria, "Regional Identity and Interests," 303–23; idem, "Regionalism," 72–90.

54. Kravchenko, *Terytorial'nyi ustrii*, 33–37.

55. Hryn'ov, *Nova Ukraïna*. For Hryn'ov, Crimea's autonomy anchors the idea of regionalization in Ukraine's constitutional and political reality (author's interview with Hryn'ov, Kyiv, 25 October 1996).

56. Evans, Rueschemeyer, and Skocpol, *Bringing the State Back In*. See, in particular, Skocpol, "Bringing the State Back In," 3–37; and Evans, Rueschemeyer, and Skocpol, "On the Road," 347–66.

57. Skocpol, "Bringing the State Back In," 8.

58. Ibid., 28.

59. Hanson, "Defining Democratic Consolidation," 94.

60. Gellner, *Nationalism*, 86.

61. Brubaker, *Nationalism Reframed*, 23.

62. A notable exception to this rule is the study by Valerie Bunce, which puts forward a parallel explanation of the breakup of socialist federations and the collapse of the socialist system by demonstrating how socialist institutions gradually undermined what they were designed to uphold; see Bunce, *Subversive Institutions*.

63. These are the additional elements framing the communist-era conflict potential reflected in the analyses by Brubaker and Bunce. Holloway and Stedman singled out three related reasons for state weakness in the FSU: arbitrary boundaries, ineffective bureaucracies and the "transition trap," the fact that partially implemented economic and political reforms impede state-building. See Holloway and Stedman, "Civil Wars and State-Building," 180.

64. Beissinger, *Nationalist Mobilization*, 26–33.

65. Ibid., 14. This definition of "institutions" as a key element of a political process is close to the one employed by O'Donnell. See Guillermo O'Donnell, "Delegative Democracy," 96–98.
66. See North's famous definition of institutions as "formal" and "informal" constraints: North, *Institutions*, 4.
67. See Hughes and Sasse, "Conflict and Accommodation in the FSU," 231–33.
68. For the term "nationalizing state," see Brubaker, *Nationalism Reframed*, 63–66.
69. See Subtelny, *Ukraine: A History*; Magosci, *History of Ukraine*.
70. One prominent example per theme will suffice in this context: Wilson, *Ukrainian Nationalism in the 1990s*; Wolczuk, *The Moulding of Ukraine*; Birch, *Elections and Democratization in Ukraine*; D'Anieri et al., *Politics and Society in Ukraine*; Wittkowsky, *Fünf Jahre ohne Plan*; Kubicek, *Unbroken Ties*; Prizel, *National Identity and Foreign Policy*.
71. Wilson, *Ukrainian Nationalism in the 1990s*, 25, 117–46; Wilson, *Ukrainians: Unexpected Nation*, 207. For a similar emphasis on ethnolinguistic criteria, see also Arel and Khmelko, "Russian Factor," 81–91.
72. Ukraine's dramatic overall population decline, emigration, and the fading bias towards Russian self-identification, a common practice in the Soviet Union, account for the decrease in the ethnic Russian population. However, blurred ethnic and linguistic identities still preclude clear-cut self-identification patterns. The 2001 census further records a rise in the number of people considering Ukrainian their mother tongue. See also Arel, "Interpreting 'Nationality.'"
73. See note 45 above.
74. Smith and Wilson highlight that Russian mobilization in the Donbas proved limited due to the fact that socioeconomic interests and regional political interests do not necessarily coincide with ethnolinguistic identities; see Smith and Wilson, "Rethinking Russia's Post-Soviet Diaspora."
75. Kuzio, *Ukraine: State and Nation Building*, 75–79.
76. Kuzio, "National Identity in Independent Ukraine," 603–4.
77. Liber, "Imagining Ukraine," 204.
78. Nevertheless, he uses the terms "Ukrainian" and "Russian" as distinct ethnic categories. See Shulman, "Competing versus Complementary Identities."
79. Solchanyk, *Ukraine and Russia*, 136.
80. See Pirie, "History, Politics and National Identity"; and "National Identity and Politics"; Jackson, "National Identity in Ukraine";

and Jackson, "Identity, Language and Transformation in Eastern Ukraine."

81. See Hesli, "Public Support," 91–115; Hesli et al., "Political Party Development in Divided Societies"; Kubicek, "Regional Polarisation in Ukraine."

82. For a summary of the survey results in Kyiv, Lviv, and Simferopol, see Bremmer, "Politics of Ethnicity." Bremmer distinguished between a limited sense of interethnic dislike between the two ethnic groups and significant differences in their political sentiments, notably in Crimea.

83. Barrington, "Views of the 'Ethnic Other' in Ukraine."

84. See Arel and Wilson, "Ukrainian Parliamentary Elections"; Bojcun, "Ukrainian Parliamentary Elections."

85. In an unpublished paper Albert Diversé put forward the then unusual argument that the presidential elections in 1994 were characterized by distinctly regional rather than ethnic voting patterns ("Regional Voting Behavior in Ukraine").

86. Birch, "Party System Formation," 139–60.

87. Craumer and Clem, "Ukraine's Emerging Electoral Geography," 4; Birch, "Interpreting the Regional Effect."

88. Prizel (*National Identity and Foreign Policy*, 404–27) has analyzed the triangle of perceptions and historically grounded conceptions of national interests between Ukraine, Russia and Poland.

89. For a general overview of all four issues, see Drohobycky, *Crimea: Dynamics, Challenges, and Prospects*. On the Crimean Tatars, see Fisher, *Crimean Tatars*; Allworth, *Tatars of Crimea*; Williams, *Crimean Tatars*; Guboglo and Chervonnaia, "Crimean Tatar Question"; Guboglo and Chervonnaia, *Krymskotatarskoe natsional'noe dvizhenie*.

90. Ozhiganov, "Crimean Republic," 83. A notable exception to this trend is an article by the Crimean scholar Andrei Mal'gin, who discussed Crimea as an example of post-Soviet regionalism in comparison with Transdnistria and Transcarpathia. See Mal'gin, "Pridnestrov'e, Krym, Zakarpat'e." For a description of Crimea as an ethnic conflict that did not erupt see Ozhiganov, "Crimean Republic"; Guboglo and Chervonnaia, "Krymskotatarskii vopros," 88–120; Kuzio, *Ukraine: State and Nation Building*, 75; Dawson, "Ethnicity, Ideology and Geopolitics in Crimea."

91. Kuzio, "Russia-Crimea-Ukraine"; Kuzio, "Crimea and European Security." Comparing the attitudes of ethnic Russians and Ukrainians in Kyiv, Lviv, and Simferopol, Bremmer ("Ethnic Issues in Crimea," 24–28) demonstrated a considerable gap between a limited sense of

interethnic dislike in Simferopol on the one hand and markedly different political interests between the two groups. He concluded with a cautious note about the potential for conflict between Russians and Ukrainians in Crimea. Belitser and Bodruk ("Krym kak region potentsial'nogo konflikta") put the emphasis on the Crimean Tatar issue as the key to potential conflict.

92.   For a comprehensive overview of the Crimean issue from 1989 to 1994, emphasizing its domestic dimensions, see Shevchuk, "Krym." For a description of the unfolding political events, see Wilson, "Crimea's Political Cauldron"; Wilson, "Elections in the Crimea"; Solchanyk, "Crimea's Presidential Election"; Bukkvoll, *Ukraine and European Security*, 45–60; Garnett, *Keystone in the Arch*, 26–28; Kuzio, *Ukraine under Kuchma*, 67–89.

93.   See Usov, "Status of the Republic of Crimea," 59–72.

94.   Among the first studies were Solchanyk, "Crimean Imbroglio"; D. Clarke, "Saga of the Black Sea Fleet," 45–49; Nahaylo, "Massandra Summit and Ukraine"; Malek, "Krim im russisch-ukrainischen Spannungsfeld"; Solchanyk, "Russia, Ukraine, and the Imperial Legacy"; Marples and Duke, "Ukraine, Russia, and the Question of Crimea."

95.   For a then exceptional emphasis on the local political nature of the Crimean conflict potential and the assessment that "there is no serious outside support," see Popadiuk, "Crimea and Ukraine's Future," 31. Ozhiganov ("Crimean Republic," 83–85) also prioritizes the political rivalries among the Crimean authorities and the Crimean Tatars and those between the Ukrainian authorities in Kyiv and pro-Russian leaders as explanations of the conflict, while the influence of Russia and Turkey are additional aggravating factors.

96.   Chase, "Conflict in the Crimea."

97.   Stewart, "Autonomy," 138.

98.   Tarlton, "Symmetry and Asymmetry as Elements of Federalism," 868.

99.   Ukraine can be described as a "federalized society." For the concept, see Livingston, "Note on the Nature of Federalism."

Chapter 2

1.   Anderson wrote about this community: "It is imagined because the members of even the smallest nation will never know most of their fellow-members, meet them or even hear of them, yet in the minds of each lives the image of their communion." See Anderson, *Imagined Communities*, 7.

2. Deutsch (*Nationalism and Social Communication*, 107, 178) aptly defines symbols as the "community of complementary habits of communication" which lies at the basis of nations and nationalism.
3. Smith, *Ethnic Origins of Nations*, 77.
4. Schöpflin, "Functions of Myth," 20.
5. See Overing, "Role of Myth," 1–18.
6. See Schöpflin, "Functions of Myth," 28–35; Smith, *Ethnic Origins of Nations*, 192.
7. Plokhy, "City of Glory," 370.
8. Schama, *Landscape and Memory*, 61.
9. Smith, "Culture, Community and Territory," 453–54.
10. Hirsch, "Landscape," 2.
11. According to the French historian Jules Michelet, "history is…geography" (quoted in Caval, "France," 42).
12. Kaufmann and Zimmer, "In Search of the Authentic Nation," 486–87.
13. Ibid., 483–510.
14. Ascherson, *Black Sea*, 17–21.
15. See Brückner, "Die Reise Katharinas II." Brückner described the journey as both a cunning political activity and imperial leisure: "Die Reise war eine politische Action und zugleich eine Lustpartie von Fürsten und Staatmännern, ein diplomatischer Congress von Schöngeistern und Salonmenschen, Scherz und Ernst vereinigend, ein Feuerwerk zur Erheiterung und zugleich eine Gewitterwolke, die den nahenden Sturm verkündete, der launige Einfall einer geistreichen und liebenswürdigen Fürstin und zugleich der gewaltige Ausdruck jener eroberungssüchtigen stolzen Politik, welche Russland und insbesondere die Regierung Katharinas auszeichnete und schon so oft den Westen in Bestürzung versetzt hatte" (2).
16. Catherine II stopped at Perekop, Bakhchisarai, Sevastopol, Karasubazar, and Kafa. Perekop was still called Orkapısı; Sevastopol was locally still known as Akyar and Kafa as Kefe; see Fisher, *Russian Annexation of the Crimea*, 155.
17. Ibid. For Potemkin it was a welcome occasion to triumph over his enemies, who had spread rumors in St. Petersburg about his incapability and mismanagement of Crimean affairs. See Brückner, "Die Reise Katharinas II.," 5–6.
18. This quote has been attributed to Joseph II, who accompanied Catherine II on her trip. See Barkobets and Zemlynichenko, *Romanovy i Krym*, 10. Conversely, the less favorable description of Crimea as "the wart on Russia's nose" is attributed to Potemkin; see

Reid, *Borderland*, 187. The term "jewel in the crown" was later used by the British to describe their colonial possession of India.

19. Schlögel, *Die Promenade von Jalta*, 214.
20. Ibid., 216.
21. See, for example, Ena, *Zapovednye landshafty Kryma*.
22. Hooson, "Ex-Soviet Identities and the Return of Geography," 134–40.
23. Dawson, *Eco-Nationalism*, 143–59.
24. For Anderson (*Imagined Communities*, 173–75) the three main tools behind the imagining of communities are the map, the census, and the museum.
25. See Bourdieu, *Outline of a Theory of Practice*, 2.
26. Allworth, "Renewing Self-Awareness," 5–9.
27. Williams, *Crimean Tatars*, 17–19.
28. Ibid., 71–72.
29. Kirimal (*Der Nationale Kampf der Krimtürken*, 2) wrote about "Russia's lack of knowledge and information about the social, economic, and political life, as well as the customs, of this hostile and completely alien land." The reports by P. S. Pallas also demonstrate this need for information; see Pallas, *Bemerkungen auf einer Reise*.
30. The first study of Crimea was prepared by Deputy Governor K. I. Gablits in 1785. His study *Fizicheskoe opisanie Tavricheskoi oblasti po vsem trem tsarstvam prirody* was published under Catherine II and translated into German, French, and English; see Andreev, *Istoriia Kryma*, 193. The traveler Maria Guthrie, writing in 1795, already refers to new Russian maps of the region on the basis of surveys done after 1783. See Guthrie, *Tour Performed in the Years 1795–6*, 54.
31. See Kulakovskii, *Proshloe Tavridy*.
32. Some later travelers pointed to what they called "topographical errors," the revival of old names in the wrong places. Sevastopol, for example, is seen as being derived from "Sebastopolis," a seaport of the Eastern empire; see Tefler, *Crimea and Transcaucasus*, 19.
33. See Koch, *Crimea and Odessa*, 51.
34. Hosking, *Russia*, 11. See also Riasanovsky, *History of Russia*, 232.
35. Kirimal, *Der Nationale Kampf der Krimtürken*, 4.
36. Ibid.
37. See Allworth, "Renewing Self-Awareness," 9.
38. Bobrovitsa, "Iazyk zemli...ili ukaza?" *Zerkalo nedeli*, 14 December 1996, 4.
39. *Bol'shaia Sovetskaia Entsiklopediia*, 3rd ed., s.v. "Krymsko-Tatarskii iazyk."

40. See Allworth, "Renewing Self-Awareness," 13–14.
41. For a comprehensive list of the old Crimean Tatar names and their (Soviet-)Russian equivalents, see ibid., 16. For the post-Soviet discussion on the return to the old toponymy, see Bobrovitsa, "Iazyk zemli," 4.
42. Clarke, *Travels in Various Countries*, 173 (as cited in Williams, *Crimean Tatars*, 87).
43. Pallas, *Bemerkungen auf einer Reise*, 8–12. See Demidoff, *Travels in Southern Russia*.
44. Ibid.
45. Craven, *Journey through the Crimea*, 143.
46. Guthrie, *Tour Performed in the Years 1795–6*, 195–96.
47. Ibid.; Craven, *Journey through the Crimea*, 161.
48. Craven, *Journey through the Crimea*, 167. A Russian traveler, commissioned by Nicholas I, spreads an even stronger image of regional peace and harmony under the "generous" conqueror. See Demidoff, *Travels in Southern Russia*, 1:305–6.
49. Koch, *Crimea and Odessa*, 40.
50. Craven, *Journey through the Crimea*, 187; Guthrie, *Tour Performed in the Years 1795–6*, 91.
51. Holderness, *Journey from Riga to the Crimea*, 214.
52. Kohl, *Russia*, 452, 461.
53. Seymour, *Russia on the Black Sea*, 76.
54. Neilson, *Crimea*, 11.
55. See, for example, Guthrie, *Tour Performed in the Years 1795–6*, 117.
56. The reputation of Crimea as a prime resort comparable to Italy is aptly described by Demidoff, *Travels in Southern Russia*, 1:294. The direct connection between the beauty of the scenery and landscape painting is made: "Italy itself is surpassed—surpassed by the Crimea: landscape painters must allow it" (ibid., 1:339).
57. Seymour, *Russia on the Black Sea*, 198. A German traveler referred to Crimea as "the promised land of the Russians"; see Koch, *Crimea and Odessa*, 1.
58. Maria Guthrie's report of 1802, for example, was dedicated to Alexander I; see Guthrie, *Tour Performed in the Years 1795–6*, vi.
59. Kohl, *Russia*, 450.
60. Seymour, *Russia on the Black Sea*, 211.
61. Neilson, *Crimea*, 2–4.
62. Guthrie, *Tour Performed in the Years 1795–6*, 72, 117. For a more informative and favorable account of Crimean Tatar life, see Baye, *Chez les Tatars de Crimée*.

63. Guthrie, *Tour Performed in the Years 1795–6*, 120.
64. Ibid., 223; see also Tefler, *Crimea and Transcaucasus*, 170.
65. Holderness, *Journey from Riga to the Crimea*, 205.
66. Neilson, *Crimea*, 4–5.
67. Holderness, *Journey from Riga to the Crimea*, 243. Holderness presents one subgroup of the Crimean Tatars, the Nogai Tatars populating the north of the peninsula, in a much more negative light by pointing to their lack of morals and mischief (ibid., 141).
68. Seymour, *Russia on the Black Sea*, 57.
69. Demidoff, *Travels in Southern Russia*, 6.
70. Holderness, *Journey from Riga to the Crimea*, 270.
71. Tefler, *Crimea and Transcaucasus*, 191.
72. Neilson, *Crimea*, 62. Interestingly, the author of this otherwise apolitical account sees the honest character of the Tatars changing due to the bad influence of the Russian settlers.
73. For one of the most respectful accounts, see Markov, *Ocherki Kryma*, 210–11.
74. Holderness, *Journey from Riga to the Crimea*, 92, 107, 155; Tefler, *Crimea and Transcaucasus*, 167; Demidoff, *Travels in Southern Russia*, 341; Koch, *Crimea and Odessa*, 40.
75. Neilson, *Crimea*, 33.
76. Guthrie, *Tour Performed in the Years 1795–6*, 214.
77. Holderness, *Journey from Riga to the Crimea*, 243.
78. The Khan's Palace was reconstructed under the Russian authorities according to their taste, and official guest rooms were added. Tefler (*Crimea and Transcaucasus*, 188) points to the "strange incongruity" resulting from alterations made to the palace under Catherine II. Moreover, a monument was erected at the palace entrance to commemorate the visit of the empress in 1787; see Koch, *Crimea and Odessa*, 72.
79. Neilson, *Crimea*, 56.
80. Seymour, *Russia on the Black Sea*, 57.
81. See Clarke, *Travels in Various Countries*, 145, 173; Hommaire de Hell, *Travels in the Steppes*, 423 (as cited in Williams, *Crimean Tatars*, 107).
82. Koch, *Crimea: From Kertch to Perekop*, 23–24 (as cited in Williams, *Crimean Tatars*, 134).
83. Williams, *Crimean Tatars*, 118–19.
84. Markov, *Ocherki Kryma*.
85. Markov, *Ocherki Kryma*, 21.
86. Ibid., 90.
87. Ibid., 121–22.

88. Ibid., 332. The image of a Tatar squatting under a tree smoking his pipe became a standard illustration in the travel literature; see Demidoff, *Travels in Southern Russia*, 344; Neilson, *Crimea*, 5. See also the reference to the Tatars working only from May to August in their gardens after which "they remain idle and enjoy themselves as best they can"; in Tefler, *Crimea and Transcaucasus*, 210.

89. See Markov, *Ocherki Kryma*, 53.

90. Markov's aristocratic family background must have been an additional obstacle to Soviet historiography.

91. Markov, *Ocherki Kryma*, 91, 93, 104, 115, 127, 130.

92. Quoted in the introduction to Voloshin, *Koktebel'skie berega*, 14.

93. The journal *Brega Tavridy*, a late Soviet creation, took up this idea and transformed itself into a forum for Crimean writers of all nationalities, but it has constantly been hampered by a lack of financial means. See *Literaturnaia gazeta*, 24 January 1996, 7.

94. See, for example, Belousov, *Skazka starogo Aiu-Daga*; Belousov, *Skazka o volshebnom iakore*; Belousov, *Kak chelovek v Krymu zdorov'e nashel*.

95. See, for example, Filatova, *Legendy Kryma*; Solodovnikova, *Legendy Kryma v pereskaze Eleny Krishtof*.

96. Basirov et al., *Fairytale Echo*. Complementary material includes colorful illustrations of each legend and methodological recommendations for teachers.

97. Kotsiubinskii, *Skazki i legendi Tatar Kryma*. The famous Crimean Tatar variant of the Ayu-Dag legend, for instance, ends on a misplaced note about the Soviet pioneer camp "Artek," which was built in the neighborhood of the "bear-mountain" (326–34).

98. See Pushkin's poems "Pogaslo dnevnoe svetilo…" (1820), "Kto videl krai…" (1821), "Tavrida" (1822); in Pushkin, *Sochineniia v trekh tomakh*, 1:224–25, 1:247–48, and 1:275–77, respectively. The most emphatic poem, summing up the different elements of Pushkin's image of Crimea, is "Kto videl krai…." The nature (*roskosh' prirody*), the surrounding sea (*Gde veselo shumiat i bleshut vody; i mirnye laskaiut berega*), the mild climate (*Gde na kholmy pod lavrovye svody / Ne smeiut lech' ugriumye snega*), and the variety of fruit (*Iantar' visit na lozakh vinograda*) are praised with devotion. The poem remains apolitical, but reflects typical Russian views of that period: he draws an overtly optimistic picture of harmony, referring to the "simple but hospitable Tatars" (*Gde v tishine prostykh tatar sem'i / Sredi zabot i s druzhboiu vzaimnoi / Pod krovleiu zhivut gostepriimnoi*) and their gardens. Moreover, a reference to Elizaveta Vorontsova, the Russian governor's wife, leaves no doubt about rightful Russian rule in

Crimea (*liubimyi krai Elviny*). One of Pushkin's major works, the poem *Evgenii Onegin*, also draws on these Crimean images.

99. The Polish poet Adam Mickiewicz wrote a similarly well-known cycle of poems about Bakhchisarai and the palace.

100. Pushkin, *Sochineniia v trekh tomakh*, 2:48–61.

101. Chekhov, *Rasskazy i povesti*, 430–45.

102. See Voloshin, *Koktebel'skie berega*. For examples of Voloshin's literary and personal reception, see Losev, *Obraz poeta*.

103. Voloshin took part in the mythmaking around his biography. He traced his own surname "Kirienko-Voloshin" back to the Zaporizhzhia region, more specifically to a blind bandura player, Matvei Voloshin, in the sixteenth century. A different account links the name "Voloshin" with a young man from Kishinev called Kirienko-Voloshin, who knew Pushkin. For Voloshin's own biographical account, see Voloshin, *Koktebel'skie berega*, 9–10.

104. See, for example, Marina Tsvetaeva's poem "Nad Feodosiei ugas..." (Naumenko, *M. Tsvetaeva i Krym*, 23–24).

105. Poem "Dneval'nyi," in Naumenko, *M. Tsvetaeva i Krym*, 37–38; for interpretation see 72–73.

106. See Tsvetaeva's poem "Vetkhozavetnaia tishina..." (1932), which refers to Voloshin's preeminent grave on top of a mountain near his house and ends with the link between place and memory: "Mesto otkupleno do kontsa / Pamiati i planety"; see Naumenko, *M. Tsvetaeva i Krym*, 29–30.

107. His novels and short stories include *Alye parusa, Begushchaia po volnam, Zolotaia tsep', Doroga v nikuda, Kapitan Dyuk*; see Grin, *Sobranie sochinenii v 6-ti tomakh*.

108. A good example is the famous line by Voloshin: "Eti predely sviashchenny uzh tem, chto odnazhdy pod vecher Pushkin na nikh pogliadel s korablia, po doroge v Gursuf..."; see Voloshin, *Koktebel'skie berega* (1927), quoted in Rudiakov and Kazarin, *Krym: Poeticheskii atlas*, 120. One of Tsvetaeva's poems, "Vstrecha s Pushkinym" (1913), ponders an encounter with Pushkin in Crimea, referring to landmarks such as the Ayu-Dag and "lyrical places" (*liricheskie mesta*) in general. Moreover, Crimea appears as, above all, Pushkin's place; literary symbols are deeply ingrained and inextricably linked with Crimea as a whole and specific places in the peninsula. See Naumenko, *M. Tsvetaeva i Krym*, 15–17.

109. See Voloshin's poem "Dom poeta," which describes the crossing of different cultures: "Sarmatskii mech i skifskaia strela, / Ol'viiskii gerb, sleznitsa iz stekla, / Tatarskii glet zelenovato-busyi / Sosedstvuiut s venetsianskoi busoi"; see Voloshin, *Koktebel'skie berega*, 200.

110. Aksenov, *Ostrov Krym*. All quotes are taken from Aksenov, *Island of Crimea*.
111. See Degtiarev, *Krymskaia palitra*.
112. This criticism was voiced by the Ukrainian historian Vasyl' Dubrovs'kyi already in the 1920s. He rightly pointed out that the Crimean Tatar figured as only part of the Crimean landscape (*kryms'kyi peizazh*). He points to one exception, the turn-of-the-century Ukrainian writer and revolutionary M. Kotsiubins'kyi, without however mentioning his contributions to typically Soviet literature; see Dubrovs'kyi, *Ukraïna i Krym v istorychnykh vzaemynakh* (based on the typescript of a talk at an academic congress in Kharkiv, 2 November 1929, that was later banned), 19. Dubrovs'kyi provides a long list of examples drawn from Russian literature of the eighteenth and nineteenth centuries to prove his point. For a compendium of Russian and Soviet-Russian poetry on Crimea, see Rudiakov and Kazarin, *Krym: Poeticheskii atlas*.
113. For a good example of the strong sense in Russia of Crimean writers such as Voloshin being "Russian poets" (*russkii poet*) whatever their nationality, see *Literaturnaia gazeta*, 24 January 1996, 4.
114. Hubar, *Chornomors'ka khvylia*.
115. See, for example, poems by Dmytro Cherevychnyi in ibid., 12–13. His poem "Pryïzhdzhaite v Krym" (23–24) reads like a perfect example of Soviet propaganda for Crimea's qualities as a holiday resort or a postcommunist advertisement slogan ("Khto ne buv shche u Krymu, / Toi, mabut', ne znaie, / Shcho prekrasnishoho kraiu / Na zemli nemaie. / V Krymu hori, more, pliazh, / Protsedury i masazh…"). For a Ukrainian-language reproduction of the Sevastopol myth, see Valentyna Nevinchana, "Parad na hrafs'kii prystani v Sevastopoli" in ibid., 45.
116. *Literaturnaia gazeta*, 24 January 1996, 4.
117. The author had to restrict herself to translated or Russian-language examples of Crimean Tatar poetry. This short section cannot do justice to Crimean Tatar literature and simply hopes to provide a flavor of the themes and intensiveness reflected in this work.
118. Williams, *Crimean Tatars*, 308.
119. The eulogy above the entrance gate reads: "Kırım Giray Khan, son of his excellency Devlet Giray, the source of peace and security, wise sovereign, his imperial star rose above the glorious horizon. His beautiful Crimean throne gave brilliant illumination to the whole world"; see translation in Fisher, *Russian Annexation of the Crimea*, 1. The inscription above the portal of the royal mosque at Bakhchisarai reads: "The person of Selim Giray is comparable to a rose garden;

the son who is born to him is a rose. Each in his turn has many honors in his palace. The rose garden is ornamented by a new flower; its unique and fresh rose has become the Lion of the padishah of Crimea, Selamet Giray Khan"; cited in Reid, *Borderland*, 169.

120. For more details on these different cultural expressions and their meaning see Gülüm, "Rituals," 84–98.
121. Williams, *Crimean Tatars*, 129, 168–70.
122. For the English translation of one of his stanzas, see ibid., 283–84.
123. Ibid., 256.
124. Bujurova, "Kak pakhnet rodina?" (*Nekuplennyi bilet*, 32). The poem was written in Russian and is an expression of the generation that was born in Central Asia and knew about Crimea only through personal stories and literature. Cited in translation in Allworth, "Renewing Self-Awareness," 3–4.
125. Bujurova, "My segodnia vernulis'" (*Avdet*, no. 15–16, 2 July 1991, 8; cited in translation in Allworth, *Tatars of Crimea*, 4).
126. Bujurova's poem "Govori" (Speak) centers on this experience of growing up hearing the stories about Crimea. The poignant lines "Speak father speak, speak until the dusk" frame the beginning and end of this poem. For the English translation of the poem, see Williams, *Crimean Tatars*, 415.
127. For a detailed anthropological account of the discourse about the self-immolation of Musa Mamut in the late 1970s in response to Soviet repression and the function of various speech patterns, see Uehling, "Squatting."
128. See Aradzhioni and Laptev, *Etnografiia Kryma*. For an "ethnopolitically correct," though somewhat stale and simplistic, introduction to Crimea's diverse history addressed at schoolchildren, see Diulichev, *Rasskazy po istorii Kryma*.

Chapter Three

1. Shils, *Center and Periphery*, 186.
2. Billig, *Banal Nationalism*, 10.
3. For an extension of this argument in the Ukrainian context, see Szporluk, "Ukraine," 93.
4. Anderson, *Imagined Communities*, 22.
5. For the graphic phrase "biography of the nation," see ibid., 204. Duara (*Rescuing History from the Nation*) has put the equally poignant call to "rescue history from the nation" against the typically linear and evolutionary history of nation-states. His idea of a "bifurcated" history that stresses how the present shapes the past, developed with a view to modern China, also applies to Ukraine.

6. For a thought-provoking discussion on the nature of Ukrainian history, focusing on questions of continuity, see von Hagen, "Does Ukraine Have a History?" and Grabowicz, "Ukrainian Studies," and the replies by Andreas Kappeler, Iaroslav Isaievych, Serhii M. Plokhy, and Yuri Slezkine (*Slavic Review* 54, no. 3 [1995]: 691–719). For an overview of the reinterpreted topics in Ukrainian school books, see Kuzio, "History, Memory and Nation-Building," 253–54.

7. See Billig, *Banal Nationalism*.

8. The Crimean flag depicts a broad white band across the middle, flanked by thin blue and red horizontal stripes at the top and bottom respectively. The Pan-Slavic flag consists of three equal-size bands in the same order. The flag of the Russian Empire and today's Russian Federation is white, blue, and red (from the top).

9. Diulichev, *Rasskazy po istorii Kryma*, 8–9.

10. For this graphic expression see Shapovalova et al., *Krym: Pamiatniki slavy i bessmertiia*, 6. Shapovalova lists about 300 monuments in Crimea linked to the October Revolution and the Civil War alone (10).

11. See, for example, Solov'ev, *Istoriia Rossii*, 31, 34; Kliuchevskii, *Kurs Russkoi Istorii*, 2:196 (lecture 31).

12. Velychenko, "Origins of the Official Soviet Interpretation," 238.

13. *Bol'shaia Sovetskaia Entsiklopediia*, 1st ed., s.v. "Krymskaia Avto-nomnaia Sovetskaia Sotsialisticheskaia Respublika."

14. Williams, *Crimean Tatars*, 30.

15. For details on this Soviet rewriting of history to make Crimea "an integral part of Slavdom," see Tillet, *Great Friendship*, 290–91.

16. See *Bol'shaia Sovetskaia Entsiklopediia*, 2nd ed., s.v. "Krymskaia oblast'."

17. See, for example, Formanchuk, *Krym mnogonatsional'nyi*.

18. Pioro, *Krymskaia Gotiia*, 30–34.

19. Andreev, *Istoriia Kryma*. Andreev dates the arrival of "Russian tribes" in the Black Sea region to the eighth century. They are said to have dominated this area for the next two hundred years (83).

20. Barkobets i Zemlynichenko, *Romanovy i Krym*.

21. Losev, *Krymskii al'bom*.

22. Luzhkov, "Russkaia Palestina." The title of the preface highlights that these books are not published without a political agenda. In a second preface Andrei Bitov even describes Crimea as the "amazing artery of Russian life"; see Bitov, "K chitateliam 'Krymskogo al'boma.'"

23. A rare exception is an essay by the historian Sergei Korolev in the 2001 edition. The fact that this piece deals with the decades just

before the Russian annexation of Crimea, and concentrates on the links between some of the khanate's elites and the Russian Empire, does not change the focus of this series; see S. Korolev, "Tretii Krym."

24. Subtelny, *Ukraine: A History*, 585.
25. Ascherson, *Black Sea*, 42.
26. Anderson, *Imagined Communities*, 178. Anderson stressed that both the museums and "museumizing imagination" are intrinsically political.
27. See Bolotina, "Sevastopol'," 134–41.
28. Shapovalova et al., *Krym: Pamiatniki slavy i bessmertiia*, 49.
29. Plokhy, "City of Glory," 372.
30. Markevich, *Tavricheskaia guberniia*, 246–48.
31. The late General Todleben gave his house to the city in order to make it into a museum commemorating the siege. For a reference to this private initiative, see Michel, *Handbook for Travellers*, 281.
32. Plokhy, "City of Glory," 375–76.
33. For an example of such a personal story, see Stetsenko, "Chernomorskii flot i Sevastopol," 142–53.
34. Tolstoi, *Sevastopol'skie rasskazy*.
35. Contemporary guidebooks for Western travelers to Russia list the monuments and museum of Sevastopol among the most significant sights in Crimea. See Michel, *Handbook for Travellers*, 279–81.
36. Plokhy, "City of Glory," 376.
37. Tarle, *Gorod russkoi slavy*. For a discussion of this work, see Plokhy, "City of Glory," 379–81.
38. Williams, *Crimean Tatars*, 154.
39. Markov, *Ocherki Kryma*, 122.
40. According to Aleksandr Herzen, Russian and Greek land speculators deliberately spread these rumors to benefit from the Tatars' plight; see Williams, *Crimean Tatars*, 152.
41. Williams provides interesting evidence to show that the image of the traitor proved so strong that in the Western diaspora Crimean Tatars preferred not to call themselves "Crimean Tatars" for fear of being labeled "Nazis"; see ibid., 407.
42. See Solzhenitsyn, *Russkii vopros*, 29, 96–97.
43. See *Literaturnaia Rossiia*, 8 January 1993.
44. See "Obrashchenie potomkov geroev Sevastopolia k Prezidentu, pravitel'stvu i Federal'nomu Sobraniiu Rossii," *Krymskoe vremia*, no. 116, 1996.
45. *Krymskaia pravda*, 3 March 1992.

46. The author had to restrict herself to Russian- and Ukrainian-language sources and can only glean some elements from the quickly expanding Crimean Tatar historiography, published in Crimean Tatar, from secondary literature.

47. See Williams, *Crimean Tatars*, 2, 9, 30, 75, 173, 177, 227.

48. Ibid., 333.

49. Ibid., 419–39.

50. The publication of new editions of Crimean Tatar history accounts by foreign scholars underscores this trend. See, for example, Tunmann, *Krymskoe khanstvo*.

51. Scott, *Baltic*, 207 (as cited in Williams, *Crimean Tatars*, 52).

52. For the different approaches put forward by representatives of the Russian imperial system and Gaspıralı, see Tuna, "Gaspirali v. Il'minskii."

53. Thereafter, the khanate was partly mythologized as a state based on popular participation and legitimacy. See Kirimal, *Der Nationale Kampf der Krimtürken*, 99 (also n. 421), 174 (n. 25). The semihistorical, semifictitious work of the nineteenth-century French orientalist David-Léon Cahun, particularly his *La bannière bleue*, which was translated into Turkish, became an influential source of inspiration. The color turquoise was named after Turkey itself and was widely accepted as the national color of the Turks.

54. Speech cited in German translation; see Kirimal, *Der Nationale Kampf der Krimtürken*, 86.

55. Vozgrin, *Istoricheskie sud'by krymskikh tatar*.

56. Ibadullaev, *Zabveniiu ne podlezhit*.

57. Bugai, *Iosif Stalin*, 129–50.

58. For an example see Kudusov, *Istoriia formirovaniia krymskotatarskoi natsii*. Kudusov downplays the links between the Crimean Tatar links and the Golden Horde.

59. See Sevdiiar, *Etiudy ob etnogeneze krymskikh Tatar*, 1–2.

60. Williams, *Crimean Tatars*, 67.

61. A recently published introduction to the history and relics of Crimean Tatar architecture in Crimea may be a step in this direction; see Krykun, *Pam'iatnyky kryms'kotatars'koï arkhitektury*. The preface by Leonid Hrach, the leader of the Crimean Communist Party and speaker of the Crimean assembly at the time of publication, looks out of place, given Hrach's political position on the Crimean Tatars. In his preface he follows a typical Soviet line, emphasizing that Crimea has to be a "common house" for all nationalities based in the region. On the effort to teach Crimean Tatar children about

Tatar traditions, values, and sociolinguistic patterns of behavior, see Khairuddinov and Useinov, *Etiket krymskikh tatar* (published in Russian with the financial help of the International Renaissance Foundation).

62. Guboglo and Chervonnaia, *Krymskotatarskoe natsional'noe dvizhenie*.

63. See Drahomanov, *Hromada*, 5–8, and the map in Reclus, *L'Europe Scandinavie et Russe*, 488. Drahomanov assisted his friend Reclus in editing this volume, so that the map is most certainly his conception. The author is grateful to Albert Diversé for the reference to this map.

64. For the census results, see Saunders, "Russia's Ukrainian Policy (1847–1905)," 190.

65. Rudnyts'kyi, *Ukraine: The Land and Its People*, 140.

66. Hrushevs'kyi, *Istoriia Ukraïny-Rusy*, vols. 4, 8, 10.

67. Elsewhere Hrushevs'kyi is quoted as referring to the early settlers of Crimea as proto-Ukrainians; see Chumak, *Ukraïna i Krym*, 4.

68. Rudnyts'kyi, *Chomu my khochemo samostiinoï Ukraïny*, 46, 78, 101, 103–4; Dubrovs'kyi, *Ukraïna i Krym*.

69. See, for example, Ivanchenko, "Ukraïns'kyi Krym."

70. Butkevych, "Pravo na Krym," 7–52. References are made to the 1897 census listing a substantial number of Ukrainians in Crimea (24).

71. Ivanchenko, "Ukraïns'kyi Krym," 14.

72. See, for example, Knysh, "Crimean Roots," 295; Dashkevych, *Ukraïna vchora i nyni*, 100–15; and Chumak, *Ukraïna i Krym*.

73. "Iak kozaky Chorne More zdobyvaly," *Holos Ukraïny*, 14 February 1992, 13; Chumak, "Kryms'ke khanstvo i Zaporozhzhia: shliakh vid vorozhnechi do vzaemorozuminnia," *Holos Ukraïny*, 13 June 1992, 12. For a later, more moderate version, see Chumak, "Krym—fenomen na mezhi Evropy ta Azii," *Uriadovyi kur'er*, 17 February 1996, 7.

74. See Hrytsak, *Istoriia Ukraïny*, 342–43.

Chapter Four

1. Torbakov ("Russian-Ukrainian Relations") gives examples of the views put forward by historians and contemporaries regarding a Ukrainian Crimea prior to 1991.

2. For a collection of primary sources on Crimean Tatar political activity in this period, see Bokov, *Voprosy razvitiia Kryma*.

3. The Crimean Tatar activist Edige Kirimal distinguishes between three distinct phases in 1917: the preparatory phase of cultural autonomy (25 March/7 April–mid May 1917), the struggle for territorial autonomy (mid-May–mid-November 1917) and the realization of national independence (mid-November 1917–mid January

1918). For details on each phase, see Kirimal, *Der Nationale Kampf der Krimtürken*, 35–164.

4. Williams, *Crimean Tatars*, 339.

5. Ibid., 340.

6. Ibid., 341.

7. Kirimal, *Der Nationale Kampf der Krimtürken*, 104.

8. Williams, *Crimean Tatars*, 342.

9. For the Crimean Tatar National Constitution, 13 (26) December 1917, see Guboglo and Chervonnaia, *Krymskotatarskoe natsional'noe dvizhenie*, 2:22–40.

10. For the detailed sources and maps of this administrative-territorial change see Kirimal, *Der Nationale Kampf der Krimtürken*, 87n367.

11. Torbakov, "Russian-Ukrainian Relations," 681.

12. Ibid., 682.

13. Fedyshyn, *Germany's Drive to the East*, 196, 239.

14. For the Crimean Tatar address to the German government (21 July 1918), see Guboglo and Chervonnaia, *Krymskotatarskoe natsional'noe dvizhenie*, 2:175–76.

15. Kirimal, *Der Nationale Kampf der Krimtürken*, 195–98.

16. Zarubin and Zarubin, "*Krymskoe pravitel'stvo.*"

17. Kirimal, *Der Nationale Kampf der Krimtürken*, 205.

18. Kirimal (ibid., 125–26) reports about a subsequent incident worsening mutual relations: in July 1917 a Crimean Tatar delegation in Kyiv was confronted with an ethnographic map of Ukraine produced in Lviv that included the northern part of Crimea (above the line Evpatoriia–Feodosiia) in the sphere of Ukrainian culture and customs. The Crimean Tatars took this map as a political construct, foreboding a possible Ukrainian expansion into Crimea. Kirimal refutes the validity of the map. It seems, however, to be linked to nineteenth-century maps drawn on the basis of the 1897 census.

19. Ibid., 126, 210–42.

20. Torbakov, "Russian-Ukrainian Relations," 683–84.

21. Ibid., 683.

22. Skoropads'kyi, *Spohady*, 262. Skoropads'kyi's memoirs provide a vivid insight into the turbulent events in Crimea. He tends to focus on the pragmatic issues, namely Crimea's economic dependence on Ukraine, its cultural ties to the rest of Ukraine, the presence of ethnic Ukrainians in Crimea, and the strategic importance of Sevastopol as a naval base. Politically, he wanted to prevent Crimea from turning into the base for a new one-and-indivisible Russia. Complex historical figures such as Skoropads'kyi, who crosscut ethnic and political fault lines, illustrate Ukraine's historical dilemmas

and choices, although they prove difficult to integrate into national historiography. Post-Soviet Ukrainian historiography has tried to rehabilitate Skoropads′kyi as a Ukrainian patriot and state builder, but the Crimean issue has not attracted special attention. See Pyrih and Prodaniuk, "Skoropads′kyi."

23. See Skoropads′kyi's letter to the German ambassador, published in Skoropads′kyi, *Spohady*, 222–23.
24. Doroshenko, *History of Ukraine*, 632–34.
25. Fedyshyn, *Germany's Drive to the East*, 170.
26. Ibid., 195–97. See also V. A. Obolenskii's memoirs, "Krym pri nemtsakh," 14–18.
27. Torbakov, "Russian-Ukrainian Relations," 686.
28. Ibid., 688.
29. Roeder, "Soviet Federalism and Ethnic Mobilization," 150.
30. See section 35 of the 1936 Constitution of the USSR and section 110 of the 1977 Constitution of the USSR.
31. For the resolution signed by Lenin and Kalin, see Broshevan and Formanchuk, *Krymskaia Respublika*, 113–15.
32. *Konstitutsiia RSFSR*, 10 July 1918, article 11. The 1924 Soviet Constitution refers to the status of an ASSR, but only the 1936 Soviet Constitution (article 22) lists all the ASSRs of the RSFSR, including Crimea.
33. *Konstitutsiia Krymskoi Sotsialisticheskoi Sovetskoi Respubliki*, pt. 1, article 3, from *Sobranie Uzakonenii i Rasporiazhenii Pabochego i Krest′ianskogo Pravitel′stva Krymskoi Sotsialisticheskoi Respubliki*, 1 February 1922, GAARK, fond SIF.NSB.
34. Ibid., article 2.
35. Ibid., 1.
36. Ibid., pt. 5, articles 31 and 32.
37. See the revised *Konstitutsiia Krymskoi Avtonomnoi Sotsialisticheskoi Sovetskoi Respubliki* of 5 May 1929, GAARK, fond SIF.NSB, pt. 1. This Constitution referred back to the resolution of the All-Russian Central Executive Committee and the Soviet of People's Commissars of the RSFSR of 18 October 1921, "On the Autonomy of Crimea," as defining Crimea's status within the RSFSR (article 2). Russian and Tatar were now simply referred to as "commonly used languages" (*obshcheupotrebitel′nye iazyki*) rather than "state languages" (article 6).
38. Williams, *Crimean Tatars*, 337.
39. Kirimal, *Der Nationale Kampf der Krimtürken*, 288–89, 334, 352.
40. Sagatovskii, "Tavrida internatsional′naia," 33–37.
41. See Fisher, *Crimean Tatars*, 147.
42. In his speech Stalin said, "Take the Crimean Autonomous Republic,

for example. It is a border republic, but the Crimean Tatars do not constitute the majority in that Republic; on the contrary, they are a minority. Consequently, it would be wrong and illogical to transfer the Crimean Republic to the category of Union Republics." For the English translation see Stalin, *Problems of Leninism*, 826–27.

43. *Vsesoiuznaia perepis' naseleniia 1939 goda*, 67; cited in Allworth, "Renewing Self-Awareness," 11–12.

44. The 1939 census data remained unpublished at the time. See *Vsesoiuznaia perepis' naseleniia 1939 goda*, 66; cited in Allworth, "Renewing Self-Awareness," 12.

45. *Konstitutsiia Krymskoi Avtonomnoi Sovetskoi Sotsialisticheskoi Respubliki* (Gosudarstvennoe Izdatel'stvo Krymskoi ASSR, 1938), pt. 2, articles 13 and 16, GAARK, fond SIF.NSB.

46. Ibid., article 15.

47. Ibid., pt. 10, articles 111, 112. One year later the Tatar alphabet, including the inscription on the flag, was changed one more time, this time from the Latin to the Cyrillic script.

48. Ibid., pt. 3, article 24.

49. Ibid., pt. 4, article 78.

50. *Ukaz Verkhovnogo Soveta SSSR*, 30 June 1945, in *Sbornik zakonov SSSR*, 54. In the early 1980s the Soviet authorities planned to turn two sparsely populated Uzbek raions south of Samarkand and Bukhara into a new Crimean Tatar homeland. Not surprisingly, this idea was never realized. See Williams, *Crimean Tatars*, 430.

51. The benefit of hindsight has sneaked an element of "dramatic change" into some references to the events of 1954, although only the long-term implications of this transfer could have this effect. See, for example, Dawson, "Ethnicity, Ideology and Geopolitics," 431.

52. Even a study by a regional analyst, which sets out to undo numerous myths surrounding Crimea, does not raise the question whether Khrushchev in 1954 was in a position to decide about the transfer. Instead the image of Khrushchev as the "Soviet leader" making the decision is being reinforced. Khrushchev is accused of a lack of historical knowledge, which led him to underestimate the historical symbolism of Crimea's link with Russia; see Formanchuk, *Mify sovetskoi epokhi*, 415–16.

53. See Luzhkov's preface in Losev, *Krymskii al'bom*.

54. Taubman, *Khrushchev*, 186. Subtelny, *Ukraine: A History*, 499–500.

55. Subtelny, *Ukraine: A History*, 500.

56. Magocsi, *History of Ukraine*, 22–23, 653–54. A real loosening of political control occurred only in 1957 with the introduction of decentralized regional economic planning bodies (*sovnarkhozy*).

57. Wilson, *Ukrainian Nationalism in the 1990s*, 17.
58. Williams, *Crimean Tatars*, 408.
59. Ozhiganov, "Crimean Republic," 93.
60. Motyl, *Dilemmas of Independence*, 10.
61. Fisher, *Russian Annexation of the Crimea*, 173; see also Potichnyj, "Struggle of the Crimean Tatars," 307.
62. Bilinsky, *Second Soviet Republic*, 94. Bilinsky dates the resettlement to the 1950s. Fisher (*Russian Annexation of the Crimea*, 174) refers to a first migration wave in 1944–49, during which the deported Crimean Tatars were replaced with Russian settlers from the regions of Voronezh, Kursk, Briansk, Rostov, and Tambov, and a second wave from early 1950 to August 1954 involving Ukrainian settlers from Western Ukraine. See also chapter 5 in this book.
63. Solchanyk, *Ukraine and Russia*, 4, 160.
64. Ibid., 165–66.
65. The event apparently had a bigger echo in other communist countries, for example in China and Poland.
66. The *Ukrainian Bulletin*, published by the Ukrainian Congress Committee of America, compiled an overview of Western media reports from early 1954 in its 1–15 April issue, 3. The chosen excerpts reflect criticism of Moscow's great power policies towards Ukraine.
67. For an overview of the Western discussions about the 1654 agreement see Tsybul's'kyi, "Pereiaslavs'ka Rada 1654 roku."
68. Salisbury, "Soviet Transfers Crimea to the Ukrainian Republic."
69. McCormick, "Russia's Indifference."
70. Rudnytsky, "Letter to the Editor."
71. A brochure on Crimea, published in New York in 1954, aptly illustrates this pro-Ukrainian view on the transfer, according to which the Soviet government had rightfully returned an integral part of "state and political independence" to Ukraine. See Sychyns'kyi, *Istorychnyi narys*, 31. This brochure offers a blend of pro-Ukrainian feelings, anti-Tatar and anti-Polish tendencies without being overtly anti-Soviet or anti-Russian. For a strong anti-Moscow view on the "Pereiaslav legend," which was successfully shaped throughout the centuries, and a "rehabilitation" of Khmel'nyts'kyi as a Ukrainian national hero, see Bzhes'kyi, "Pereiaslavs'ka umova."
72. Editorial, "Moscow's Struggle for the Soul of Ukraine," *Ukrainian Bulletin*, 1–15 April 1954, 8.
73. Fisher, *Russian Annexation of the Crimea*, 173–74.
74. In contrast to the Crimean Tatars, the Chechens were rehabilitated and regained an ethnoterritorial status shortly after Stalin's death.

Comparatively speaking, the Chechens had put the Soviet authorities under greater pressure early on due to the higher number of deportees and the persistent attempts to return to their former territory, which was more accessible than Crimea. See Nekrich, *Punished Peoples*, 137; and Williams, *Crimean Tatars*, 399.

75. N. Khrushchev, *Khrushchev Remembers*; Burlatsky, *Khrushchev and the First Russian Spring*; Medvedev and Medvedev, *Khrushchev and the Years in Power*; Kaganovich, *Pamiatnye zapiski rabochego*.

76. See S. Khrushchev, *Khrushchev on Khrushchev*.

77. Among the most recent biographies see Tompson, *Khrushchev: A Political Life*; and Aksiutin, *Nikita Sergeevich Khrushchev*.

78. *Izvestiia*, 19 February 1954; *Pravda*, 27 April 1954.

79. See, for example, *Proekt postanovleniia TsK KPSS o 300-letii vossoedinenii Ukrainy s Rossiei*, prepared by Suslov and others on the basis of recommendations of the TsK KP Ukrainy and forwarded to Khrushchev on 18–19 August 1953: Rossiiskii gosudarstvennyi arkhiv noveishei istorii (RGANI) (formerly Tsentr khraneniia sovremennoi dokumentatsii), f. 5, op. 5, d. 9, pp. 51–60; or Kyrychenko's letter to Khrushchev (14 December 1953) with the details about the festivities and a special session of the Supreme Soviet of the UkrSSR to take place in Kyiv in May 1954: RGANI, f. 5, op. 5, d. 490, pp. 87–88. The draft speeches and draft proposals prepared by the Agitprop and the Science and Culture sections of the Central Committee of the KPSS mention the "reunification of all Ukrainian lands," after which "the Soviet Ukraine became one of the biggest states in Europe" (referring to the incorporation of Transcarpathia in 1945). Evidently, Crimea was not considered an essential part of Ukraine; see RGANI, f. 5, op. 30, d. 52, pp. 1–39; for quotes see p. 23. In the supplement listing the planned events in each region, the Crimean oblast is still missing. For further documents planning the celebrations without mentioning Crimea, see TsDAHO, f. 1, op. 24, no. 3505. For details about the anniversary session of the Supreme Soviet of the Ukrainian SSR, without a mention of Crimea, see TsDAHO, f. 1, op. 24, no. 3506. Similarly, Kyrychenko in January 1954 does not yet include Crimea in his schedule of regional party conferences for 1954, which comprises all other oblasts of the Ukrainian SSR; see TsDAHO, f. 1, op. 24, no. 3536.

80. Osipov, *Velikaia druzhba*, 3, 20–21.

81. Ibid., 26.

82. For an example of how the Crimean region could be incorporated without specific references to the transfer, see the draft formulation

by the Ukrainian Central Committee submitted to the Supreme Soviet of the USSR, the USSR Council of Ministers, and the TsK KPSS in May 1954: "From the Carpathian heights to the Donetsk steppes, from the woodlands to the shores of the Black Sea—through the expanses of the native Ukrainian land, as everywhere in our country, creative work is gushing forth, which multiplies the might of the Soviet Union"; RGANI, f. 5, op. 30, d. 50, p. 162.

83.   Sevastopol as the historical symbol of Russian glory continued to enjoy a special status in Soviet memory as the "Russian-Soviet" city. See Semin, *Sevastopol': Istoricheskii ocherk*, 3–4. The decree of 1948 that subordinated Sevastopol directly to central Soviet jurisdiction played no visible role in the transfer of Crimea, a fact which contributed to the future confusion about its relationship with the rest of Crimea.

84.   Lialikov, *Sovetskaia Ukraina*; Virnyk, *Ukrainskaia SSR*; Nesterenko, *Ocherki razvitiia narodnogo khoziaistva Ukrainskoi SSR*. All these publications paint a highly optimistic picture of the potential of the Crimean economy.

85.   Anecdotal evidence suggests that the limited Ukrainian edition of *Krymskaia pravda* was largely ignored by the local population.

86.   Ivan Rudnytsky in his introduction to Basarab, *Pereiaslav 1654*, xxi.

87.   Ibid., xxi–xxii.

88.   Kargalov, *Na stepnoi granitse*. This book concentrates on the struggle between the Russian Empire and the Crimean Khanate.

89.   This sentiment was summed up as follows: "This is Crimea—the beauty and pride of the Ukrainian Soviet Socialist Republic, the southern forepost of our country"; see Gerasimov, *Oblast', v kotoroi my zhivem*, 5. Five years after the transfer of Crimea this publication emphasizes that Ukraine has fulfilled its promise to foster development in Crimea (ibid., 91). For a good example of Soviet Crimean history, see Nadinskii, *Krym v periode Velikoi Oktiabr'skoi Sotsialisticheskoi Revoliutsii*. The idea of a Soviet Black Sea Region, as propagated in Riazantsev, *Sovetskoe Chernomor'e*, becomes part of the Soviet multinational integrative myth that also functions as an assertion against Turkish claims.

90.   Grabovskii, *Pereiaslav-Khmel'nitskii*, 5.

91.   See Bilets'kyi, *Braterstvo kul'tur*.

92.   Lewytzkij, *Politics and Society in Soviet Ukraine*, 164–66.

93.   For an explicit anti-Polish standpoint see Osipov, *Velikaia druzhba*, 3, 20–21.

94.   A concrete hint at the underlying anti-Polish argument can be found in Sychyns'kyi, *Istorychnyi narys*, 30. The author explicitly refers to

statist Polish projects to unite the peoples between the Black Sea and Baltic Sea. Crimea is seen as a key to these plans. Reference is made to Sejdament, a Crimean Tatar living in Warsaw, who prepared a memorandum for the League of Nations in the 1930s asking for Crimea to be turned into a Polish protectorate.

95.   Velychenko, *Shaping Identity*, 63.
96.   Bilinsky, *Second Soviet Republic*, 18.
97.   See, for example, *Ukraïns'kyi istorychnyi zhurnal* or *Otechestvennaia istoriia* from 1990 onwards.
98.   This is indirectly reflected in the fact that no special role was envisaged for Polish representation during the celebrations. M. Zamiagin, the head of the European section of the Foreign Ministry of the USSR, calls Polish participation not a bad idea "if the Polish comrades consider it necessary," and stresses the need for them to celebrate the union of Ukraine and Russia in view of "that friendship, which characterizes the relations of the new, people's democracy of Poland with the Soviet Union"; see RGANI, f. 5, op. 30, d. 50, p. 115.
99.   Ohloblyn, *Dumky pro Khmel'nychchynu*.
100.   Horobets', "Pereiaslavs'ko-Moskovs'kyi dohovir 1654 r.," 17.
101.   Basarab, *Pereiaslav 1654*.
102.   *Uriadovyi kur'er*, 23 December 1995, 4–5.
103.   See the similar argument in Bzhes'kyi, *Pereiaslavs'ka umova*; Apanovich, *Ukraïns'ko-rosiis'kyi dohovir 1654 r.*

Chapter Five

1.   Volobueva and Iofis, "Iskliuchitel'no zamechatel'nyi akt bratskoi pomoshchi." The documents are assembled from the Arkhiv Prezidenta Rossiiskoi Federatsii (APRF) and the Gosudarstvennyi Arkhiv Rossiiskoi Federatsii (GARF), formerly known as the Tsentral'nyi Gosudarstvennyi Arkhiv Oktiabrskoi Revolutsii (TsGAOR).
2.   See RGANI, f. 2, op. 1, dok. 46, 61, 62, 89, 90. Speeches at the Plenum meeting of the Central Committee of the KPSS at the end of February 1954 simply reflect the transfer as a new administrative reality ("*na iug Ukrainy, v Krym*") and highlight the region's agricultural problems; see dok. 89, p. 56. The Politburo is another organ, which might have been involved in the decision about the transfer, but the Politburo minutes were not accessible to the author at RGANI.
3.   Volobueva and Iofis, "Iskliuchitel'no zamechatel'nyi akt bratskoi pomoshchi," 39–40.
4.   The fact that a second meeting of the Presidium took place on the

same day is an unusual coincidence. In the period 1951–55 this is the only occasion where two meetings were held on the same day. This may be an indication that all did not proceed as normal at the meeting.

5. The nine members were Nikolai Bulganin, Lazar Kaganovich, Khrushchev, Malenkov, Anastas Mikoian, Viacheslav Molotov, Mikhail Pervukhin, Aleksandr Saburov, and Voroshilov. The candidates were Kyrychenko, Panteleimon Ponomarenko, and Nikolai Shvernik. The Ukrainian Party Secretary Kyrychenko had replaced Leonid Mel'nikov at a Central Committee plenary session in early summer 1953. See Schapiro, *Communist Party of the Soviet Union*; Kraus, *Composition of Leading Organs*, 2–5.

6. Evgenii Ambartsumov (interview in *Novoe vremia*, no. 6 [1992]: 18) sees Khrushchev's own initiative behind this note, because he needed a reason to raise the issue at the Politburo.

7. The euphemistic terms used in the resolutions and speeches are *obshchnost' ekonomiki, khoziaistvennaia tselesoobraznost', istoricheski slozhivshiesia kul'turnye sviazi mezhdu naseleniem Krymskoi oblasti i Ukrainskoi SSR*, and *territorial'noe tiagotenie Krymskoi oblasti k Ukrainskoi SSR*. The Crimean oblast is even described as the "natural continuation of the southern steppes of Ukraine." See *Istoricheskii arkhiv*, no. 1, 1992, 41, 43, 46, 48.

8. Butkevych confirms that this procedure was in accord with general Soviet legal practice, based on article 15b of the Constitution of the Ukrainian SSR and article 16a of the Constitution of the RSFSR. Butkevych ("Pravo na Krym," 46–47), however, calls the exchange of Presidium resolutions a "gentlemen's agreement," leaving room for disputes.

9. *Izvestiia*, 28 May 1954, 8; *Natsional'ni vidnosyny v Ukraïni u XX st.*, 328.

10. This information was provided by Valerii Vasilev, historian at the Tavria National University, in an interview with the author, Simferopol, 3 May 1998.

11. Ambartsumov, interview in *Novoe vremia* (see n. 6), 18–20.

12. Ozhiganov, "Crimean Republic," 92–93.

13. Ambartsumov, interview in *Novoe vremia* (see n. 6), 19.

14. *Konstitutsiia SSSR*, 1936, articles 14, 18, 31.

15. *Konstitutsiia RSFSR*, 13 March 1948, pt. 2, article 19.

16. Ibid., pt. 2, article 16.

17. TsDAHO, f. 1, op. 24, no. 3753, pp. 12–20.

18. TsDAHO, f. 1, op. 24, no. 3758, pp. 15–16.

19. For a concise summary of these events see Dunlop, *Russia Confronts Chechnya*, 40–84; and Bugai, "Truth about the Deportation."

20. Dunlop (*Russia Confronts Chechnya*, 73) graphically described the consequences of Soviet policy: "The Chechen-Ingush ASSR simply disappeared into a memory hole...."

21. RGANI, f. 89, d. 8, p. 61. For the details on the transfer of the districts to the newly created ASSR, see the archival evidence presented in Dunlop, *Russia Confronts Chechnya*, 78–79. In contrast to the majority they had held before the war, the Chechens and Ingush accounted for only 41 percent of the population of the new ASSR.

22. According to popular history accounts Khrushchev was born into a Russified family which was descended from the Zaporizhzhian Cossacks and had settled in the Kursk district in the seventeenth century. See Alexandrov, *Khrushchev of the Ukraine*, 9–11.

23. Adzhubei, "Kak Khrushchev Krym Ukraine otdal."

24. This alleged arbitrariness on Khrushchev's part was most poignantly expressed by the former chairman of the Russian Supreme Soviet, Ruslan Khazbulatov: "Khrushchev must have either suffered from a hangover or a bad case of sun-stroke when he gave Crimea away"; cited in Markus, "Black Sea Dispute Apparently Over," 31.

25. Around the time of the transfer of Crimea, however, Soviet historiography began to acknowledge the existence of the Crimean Tatars as a separate people. See Gimadi, "Ob upotreblenie nazvaniia 'Tatary,'" 116.

26. Pavel Knyshevskii, "Shtrikhi k portretam kremlevskoi galerei," *Novoe vremia*, no. 9, 1994, 52–54.

27. Ibid., 54. According to this account, Khrushchev emphatically described Ukraine as "*tonka kishka*," a reference to its lack of strength.

28. TsDAHO, f. 1, op. 23, spr. 636. The author is grateful to Prof. Yurii Shapoval for his advice on the location of these documents.

29. See, for example, Ozhiganov, "Crimean Republic," 83–84.

30. See *Informatsiia zamestitelia predsedatelia Sovnarkoma USSR V. Starchenko i sekretaria TsK KP(b)U D. Korotchenko v GKO V. Molotovu*, TsDAHO, f. 1, op. 24, spr.1318, p. 2. The 9,000 people were to come from the regions of Vinnytsia, Podil, Zhytomyr, Kyiv, Chernyhiv, Sumy, and Poltava. According to Crimean archival evidence the ambitious plan for 1944 envisaged the resettlement of altogether 17,040 families or 62,104 people from the Krasnodar, Stavropol, Voronezh, Kursk, Orlovsk, Tambov, Rostov, Kyiv, Vinnytsia, Zhytomyr and Podil oblasts; see Derzhavnyi Arkhiv Krymskoi Oblasti, f. P-2888,

op. 1, spr. 12, ark. 1, cited in Maksimenko, "Pereselennya v Krym sil's'koho naselennia," 53.

31. Maksimenko, "Pereselennia v Krym sil's'koho naselennia," 53.

32. This link to the deportation of the Crimean Tatars is directly addressed in a letter to the State Commission in charge of the resettlement of peasants in Crimea, headed by D. Korotchenko, the deputy head of the *Sovnarkom* of the RSFSR; see TsDAHO, f. 1, op. 23, spr. 1319, p. 11 (16 August 1944). The resettlement plans at the *raion* level initially envisaged replacing the Crimean Tatar workforce one to one. For the example of Kuibysheve *raion*, see TsDAHO, f. 1, op. 23, spr. 1318, p. 3.

33. Ibid., 10, 148.

34. TsDAHO, f. 1, op. 23, spr. 1318, letter by the deputy head of the Sovnarkom USSR, V. Starchenko to L. M. Kaganovich, pp. 141–44. For further documentation about the methods of resettlement from different regions in 1953, see TsDAHO, f. 1, op. 24, no. 3088, pp. 1–10, 11–17, 24–30, 32–33.

35. TsDAHO, f. 1, op. 23, spr. 1318, pp. 7–8. In January 1945, for example, the deputy head of the agricultural section of the Ukrainian Central Committee, T. S. Mal'tsev, wrote to his colleague A. N. Itskov in the KPSS Central Committee in Moscow, referring to the letters written by a resettled peasant from Zhytomyr, complaining that in Crimea the new settlers were treated like deported criminals. See TsDAHO, f. 1, op. 23, spr. 1320, p. 118.

36. TsDAHO, f. 1, op. 23, spr. 1318, pp. 9–12: letter by the secretary of the Ukrainian Central Committee D. S. Korotchenko to the Central Committee of the All-Union Communist Party (Bolsheviks), TsK VKP(b), G. M. Malenkov, *O vypolnenie postanovleniia Gosudarstvennogo Komiteta Oborony ot 12 avgusta 1994 g. "O pereselenie kolkhoznikov v raiony Kryma,"* October 1944.

37. In March 1953, for example, a plan was issued according to which another 1,200 families were to be moved to Crimea from the Ukrainian regions of Sumy and Chernihiv. See information provided by the deputy head of the Resettlement Department of the Ukrainian Council of Ministers, A. Mohila, addressed to L. G. Mel'nikov, 10 March 1953; TsDAHO, f. 1, op. 24, spr. 2804, p. 41.

38. TsDAHO, f. 1, op. 24, spr. 2804, p. 225. As of 1 December 1953 1,270 families, as compared to the envisaged figure of 1,150 families, had been moved to Crimea. Overall, 10,406 families, as compared to an envisaged total of 12,350 families, had been moved from or within the Ukrainian SSR.

39. TsDAHO, f. 1, op. 24, spr. 3587, p. 18: *O neotlozhnykh merakh po pereseleniiu v Ukrainskoi SSR*, letter by V. Bacherikov, deputy head of the department in charge of the resettlement of the Ukrainian, Belarusian, and Moldovan *raions*, to Kyrychenko (13 February 1954). The letter lists the numbers for peasants that were resettled in 1953, but they are not broken down by region and thereby conceal the number of new arrivals in Crimea.

40. Only 542 families, or 2.4 percent, of the target figure for 1954 had been moved to the southern regions of the Ukrainian SSR by March 1954; TsDAHO, f. 1, op. 24, no. 3587, pp. 15–16.

41. See, for example, Suslov's letter of 21 May 1953 addressed to Khrushchev: RGANI, f. 5, op. 39, d. 6, pp. 11–19.

42. In the period 1949–54, altogether 108,400 families were resettled in the southern regions of the Ukrainian SSR, including Crimea. By March 1954, 26,800 of these families had already left their new farms to go home. In the first two months of 1954 alone, 3,900 families left, among them 319 families settled in Crimea. See TsDAHO, f. 1. op. 24, no. 3587, pp. 41–42. Further correspondence between Ukrainian and Soviet party organs, kept in the same files, reflect the party's efforts (on paper) throughout 1954–55 to improve the settler's living conditions and provide them with housing, food, and money (ibid., 67–69).

43. See evidence from the Crimean Party Archive, cited in Maksimenko, "Pereselennia v Krym sil's'koho naselennia," 53. To compensate for the new loss of badly needed workforce in Crimea, another 13,000 families were to be settled in Crimean *kolkhozes* between 1950 and 1954; see archival evidence cited in ibid., 54–55.

44. This important point is also raised by Adzhubei in his eyewitness account of Khrushchev's personal input into the decision. See Adzhubei, "Kak Khrushchev Krym Ukraine otdal," 21.

45. Pistrak, *Great Tactician*, 250.

46. For a collection of materials on Khrushchev's rise to leadership see Swearer, *Politics of Succession in the USSR*.

47. Medvedev, *All Stalin's Men*, 46.

48. Medvedev and Medvedev, *Khrushchev: The Years in Power*; Rush, *Rise of Khrushchev*, 1–3; Aksiutin, *Nikita Sergeevich Khrushchev*, 44.

49. Ambartsumov, interview in *Novoe vremia* (see n. 6), 18.

50. Rush, *Rise of Khrushchev*, 63.

51. Subtelny, *Ukraine: A History*, 502–3. See also Applebaum, *Gulag: A History*.

52. Rush, *Rise of Khrushchev*, 43.

53. TsDAHO, f. 1, op. 24, spr. 3595, pp. 91–99.

54. Ibid., 19.

55. For a good description of Soviet nationality policy after World War II see Rudnytsky's introduction to Basarab, *Pereiaslav 1654*, xix–xx; and Rudnytsky, "Pereiaslav: History and Myth."

56. Khrushchev launched his party campaign against inefficiency at the February 1954 Plenum of the Central Committee of the KPSS. In response to this decree, the Crimean Party Conference, held in March 1954, provides ample evidence for the bad state of the Crimean economy, agriculture, and party organization—the three pillars of Khrushchev's program. See the letter by Kyrychenko addressed to Khrushchev (31 March 1954), summarizing the main results of the Crimean, Odesa, and Cherkasy party conferences on the February Plenum; RGANI, f. 5, op. 30, d. 50, pp. 66–74. Another historical institutional memory was revived by the division of Ukraine into three economic regions: *Iugo-Zapadnyi raion* (Southwestern district), *Donetsk-Pridneprovskii raion* (Donetsk-Dnepr district) and *Iuzhnyi raion* (Southern district), which included the oblasts of Crimea, Mykolaïv, Odesa, and Kherson and thereby resembled the old province of Novorosiia. For the territorial divisions, see Tsentral'noe statisticheskoe upravlenie pri Sovet Ministrov SSSR, *Itogi vsesoiuznogo perepisi naseleniia 1959 goda*.

57. Crimean archival evidence cited in Tsentral'noe statisticheskoe upravlenie pri Sovet Ministrov SSSR, *Itogi vsesoiuznogo perepisi naseleniia 1959 goda*, 56–57.

58. Maksimenko, "Pereselennia v Krym sil's'koho naselennia," 58.

59. Lewytzkyj, *Politics and Society in Soviet Ukraine, 1953–1980*, 7; and Bilinsky, *Second Soviet Republic*, 57.

60. Statisticheskoe upravlenie Krymskoi oblasti, *Narodnoe khoziaistvo Krymskoi oblasti*, 228 (note that the years are not printed in the right order in this report). For example, the results in most school subjects fell below the average scores of the Ukrainian SSR. The worse performance of Russian language classes was highlighted, which may be connected to the influx of Ukrainophone settlers; ibid., 151. In this context, the lack of access to Ukrainian-language newspapers and periodicals was criticized.

61. TsDAHO, f. 1, op. 24, spr. 3672, p. 1. This material includes a draft letter addressed to Malenkov and Khrushchev to be signed by Kyrychenko; see ibid., 2.

62. TsDAHO, f. 1, op. 23, no. 3672, pp. 31–32.

63. Though its status under "republican authority," which Sevastopol had been granted in 1948 within the RSFSR, was not referred to

during the 1954 transfer of the Crimean oblast, article 77 of the Ukrainian Constitution of 1978 declared Sevastopol unilaterally a city under republican authority of the UkrSSR; see Ozhiganov, "Crimean Republic," 123n73.

64. The Sevastopol *gorkom*, for example, had to ask the Ukrainian Central Committee and the Council of Ministers of the Ukrainian SSR for money to organize the celebrations of the 100th anniversary of the 1854–55 siege of Sevastopol and involved the Ukrainian Ministry of Culture in the preparation of the event; see TsDAHO, f. 1, op. 24, no. 3505, spr. 1–2, pp. 68–70. On another occasion Kyrychenko sent a draft resolution to the Central Committee in Moscow to consider a speedier restoration of Sevastopol; see TsDAHO, f. 1, op. 24, no. 3668, pp. 1–2.

65. From 1953 to 1956 the number of Crimean enterprises managed at these levels increased by almost 100 percent to altogether 81.7 percent of all enterprises in the region. See Statisticheskoe upravlenie Krymskoi oblasti, *Narodnoe khoziaistvo Krymskoi oblasti*, 23. Even in Sevastopol there is a considerable increase, from 24 percent in 1953 to 45 percent in 1956; ibid., 23.

66. TsDAHO, f. 1, op. 24, spr. 3672, p. 5.

67. Ibid., 26–28. In the sphere of education, references are made to the insufficient numbers of schools. There is, however, no indication of the language of instruction.

68. TsDAHO, f. 1, op. 24, spr. 3540, pp. 141–55: *O nekotorykh nedostatkakh v rabote partiinykh i sovetskikh organov Krymskoi oblasti*, 7 September 1954.

69. Ibid., 142.

70. Ibid., 143.

71. Statisticheskoe upravlenie Krymskoi oblasti, *Narodnoe khoziaistvo Krymskoi oblasti*, 25–30.

72. *Spravka ob ob"emakh kapitalovlozhenii po Krymskoi oblasti*, see TsDAHO, f. 1, op. 24, spr. 3672, p. 4.

73. Statisticheskoe upravlenie Krymskoi oblasti, *Narodnoe khozyaistvo Krymskoi oblasti*, 143. The figures compare with a drop from 806.8 to 801.3 from 1951 to 1952 and an increase to 877.1 in 1954.

74. TsDAHO, f. 1, op. 23, spr. 3664, pp. 8–23, letter by the head of the Main Division of Water Affairs at the Council of Ministers of the Ukrainian SSR, P. Matsui to Kyrychenko, TsK KPSS of Ukraine, including *Proekt Postanovleniia Soveta Ministrov SSR*.

75. The construction plans of the South-Ukrainian and Northern-Crimean canal date back to a resolution of the Council of Ministers of the USSR of 20 September 1950; see TsDAHO, f. 1, op. 24, spr.

3476, pp. 103–4. For more detailed plans which illustrate that all-union organs controlled the construction process, see TsDAHO, f. 1, op. 24, spr. 2893, pp. 33–49, 50–54, 77–81, 109, 124–26, 147–156.

76. See, for example, Kyrychenko's letter to the TsK KPSS, September 1954, TsDAHO, f. 1, op. 24, spr. 3672, pp. 231–32.

77. *Proekt: Postanovlenie Soveta Ministrov SSSR i TsK KPSS O meropri-iatiiakh po uluchsheniiu vodosnabzheniia, kanalizatsii i blagoustroistva kurortnykh gorodov Krymskoi oblasti Ukrainskoi SSR*, TsDAHO, f. 1, op. 24, spr. 3672, pp. 233–38.

78. TsDAHO, f. 1, op. 23, spr. 3664, pp. 5–7, Autumn 1954.

79. TsDAHO, f. 1, op. 24, spr. 3614, p. 6.

80. TsDAHO, f. 1, op. 23, spr. 3614, p. 2.

Chapter Six

1. See Shevchuk, "Krym," 52.

2. According to the personal account by the then head of the Crimean Supreme Soviet (and former *obkom* secretary), Mykola Bahrov, the coup was staged with the help of Gorbachev himself and elements of the regional party elite in Crimea. Bahrov tried to prove that he had nothing to do with the coup and retained close links with Leonid Kravchuk instead. See Bahrov, *Krym: vremia nadezhd i trevog*, 155–91. His position remained cautious though, and he did not support the proposal discussed in the Crimean Supreme Soviet to declare the coup illegal, a decision he justified with an emphasis on the need for regional stability, given the number of people in Crimea at the height of the tourist season (ibid., 170).

3. For a detailed account of the movement's development, see Dawson, *Eco-Nationalism*, 143–59.

4. Ideas about completing the nuclear power station were nevertheless still floated in 1990.

5. Sergei Shuvainikov, since 1994 known as one of Crimea's most notorious Russian nationalists, was among the most vociferous opponents of the Crimean nuclear power station. He chose to declare himself leader of the Crimean branch of the Ukrainian movement Zelenyi Svit rather than the predominantly Russian and Moscow-based Ekologiia i Mir. See Dawson, *Eco-nationalism*, 154–55.

6. The Crimean anti-nuclear campaign differed from the protest in Tatarstan against the nuclear power station that neared completion there in the late 1980s. In the Tatar ASSR environmental concerns became intertwined with nationalist mobilization. For a comparison of the Tatar and Crimean cases see ibid., 124–61.

7. According to Kuzio, three-quarters of Crimea's population arrived in the peninsula after 1945; see Kuzio, *Ukraine: State and Nation Building*, 87. Guboglo and Chervonnaia ("Crimean Tatar Question," 38) state that after World War II 90 percent of the Crimean population did not have historical roots in the region, but they do not cite any evidence for this figure. Based on these Soviet settlers, Formanchuk (*Mify sovetskoi epokhi*, 418) described Crimea's population as an "artifical conglomerate of different ethnic groups."

8. The party committee of the Black Sea Fleet, for example, issued a statement on 21 June 1991 addressed to the Central Committee of the KPSS voicing its "dissatisfaction with the passive position of the Central Committee of the KPSS with regard to the deformation of the country's socialist order" and calling for a special party congress. See RGANI, f. 89, p. 8, dok. 3.

9. Author's interview in Simferopol, 5 April 1996.

10. Guboglo and Chervonnaya, *Krymskotatarskoe natsional'noe dvizhenie*, 3:67–68.

11. Usov, "K voprosu o statuse Respubliki Krym," 68.

12. *Krymskaia pravda*, 11 January 1991, 2. In an interview with the author on 1 April 1996, Leonid Hrach, the leader of the Crimean Communist Party, confirmed that this view prevailed in Communist Party circles at the time. For another vivid impression of the perception of the Crimean Tatars' return posing a "threat" to the regional elite at the time, see Formanchuk, *Mify sovetskoi epokhi*, 507.

13. For the decree of 1989 and subsequent decrees of the Supreme Soviet, see Guboglo and Chervonnaya, *Krymskotatarskoe natsional'noe dvizhenie*, 2:77–78.

14. See, for example, *Krymskaia pravda*, 5 August 1990, 2; 9 August 1990, 1.

15. For one of the frequent references to the democratic principles on which Crimean autonomy was to be erected, see *Krymskaia pravda*, 20 February 1991, 2.

16. For an excerpt from Ivashko's speech, see Solchanyk, *Ukraine and Russia*, 187.

17. Bahrov, *Krym: vremia nadezhd i trevog*, 99. A first declaration was issued by the *obkom* of the party in January 1990; ibid., 95. Mal'gin (*Krymskii uzel*, 62) has argued that the issue of Crimean autonomy had already been widely discussed in society before it was addressed by the Communist Party. However, the Communist Party undoubtedly acted as a catalyst to intensify and channel the sentiment.

18. *Krymskaia pravda*, 23 June 1990, 3; 30 August 1990, 1; Bahrov, *Krym: vremia nadezhd i trevog*, 99.

19. See *Krymskaia pravda*, 29 July 1990, 2.
20. *Krymskaia pravda*, 5 September 1990, 1; 18 September 1990, 2; 5 April 1990; 19 June 1990, 2.
21. For the discussion of the unconstitutional transfer and possible options concerning the future status of Crimea by a party and committee member, see *Krymskaia pravda*, 19 August 1990, 3.
22. *Krymskaia pravda*, 12 June 1990, 1.
23. *Pravda Ukrainy*, 14 November 1990.
24. Mal'gin, *Krymskii uzel*, 63.
25. See *Krymskaia pravda* throughout January 1991; see in particular 17 January 1991, 2.
26. *Krymskaia pravda*, 17 May 1990, 2; 9 June 1990, 2; 26 June 1990, 2; 27 June 1990, 1, 3.
27. *Krymskaia pravda*, 1 June 1990, 1; 16 January 1991, 2; 19 January 1991, 1.
28. *Krymskaia pravda*, 10 January 1991, 1–2. Crimea was presented as a "bureaucratic colony" (*vedomstvennaia koloniia*); see *Krymskaia pravda*, 10 January 1991, 2.
29. For Arel ("Language Politics in Independent Ukraine," 597), "Language politics is the politics of threatened identity."
30. Ministerstvo Statystyky Ukrainy, *Natsional'nyi sklad naselennia Ukraïny*, ch. 2.
31. Dawson, *Eco-nationalism*, 158. By 2001 59.5 percent of the Ukrainians in Crimea considered Russian their native language. According to the 2001 census 77 percent of the Crimean population considered Russian its native language, 11.4 percent Crimean Tatar, and 10.1 percent Ukrainian (see Vseukraïns'kyi perepys naselennia, "Movnyi sklad naselennia").
32. See the interview with Bahrov in *Krymskaia pravda*, 30 January 1991, 1.
33. For the exact formulation of the referendum question, see *Krymskaia pravda*, 5 January 1991, 1. For the official announcement of the result, see *Krymskaia pravda*, 22 January 1991, 1. Only 5.6 percent of those participating voted no. Sevastopol had simultaneously supported the notion of union-republic status for the city as the main base of the fleet by 93 percent of the votes; see Mal'gin, *Krymskii uzel*, 33.
34. *Krymskaia pravda*, 22 February 1991, 2. For the stenogram of the discussion in the Ukrainian Supreme Soviet, see *Krymskaia pravda*, 13 February 1991, 1; 23 February 1991, 1–2; 26 February 1991, 1–2.
35. *Krymskaia pravda*, 14 June 1991, 2. In the end, 303 out of 389 present deputies in the Verkhovna Rada voted in favor of the constitutionalization of Crimea's status. Early conceptions of a Crimean Constitution devised by the Crimean Communist Party and the working group of the Crimean Supreme Soviet confusingly spoke

of Crimea's independent and democratic statehood within both the Ukrainian SSR and a new Union of Sovereign States emerging from the USSR; see *Krymskaia pravda*, 16 May 1991, 1–2; 17 May 1991, 1–2.

36. *Krymskaia pravda*, 23 March 1991, 1.
37. According to Bahrov (*Krym: Vremia nadezhd i trevog*, 112–18), their relations worsened shortly after Hrach's election.
38. *Krymskaia pravda*, 20 March 1991, 2.
39. Ozhiganov, "Crimean Republic," 99. In June 1991 the Ukrainian Supreme Soviet had asked the Crimean parliament to come up with suggestions regarding the delimitation of powers by 1 September, but the August coup changed the parameters of the interaction between center and periphery.
40. See the pamphlet *Deputatskaia Fraktsiia "Respublikanskaia Partiia Kryma": Zaiavlenie o piatiletnei godovshchine referenduma 20 ianvaria 1991 goda*, 17 January 1996.
41. Meshkov also entertained links with the Crimean organization of the Don Cossacks, a radicalized splinter group advocating reintegration with Russia; see Ozhiganov, "Crimean Republic," 100.
42. Mal'gin, *Krymskii uzel*, 66.
43. Data are from the Central Electoral Commission, Simferopol, 1991.
44. Mal'gin, *Krymskii uzel*, 66–67.
45. Formanchuk, *Mify sovetskoi epokhi*, 389–90.
46. For a brief summary of events, see Ukraïns'kyi nezalezhnyi tsentr politychnykh doslidzhen', *Crimea*.
47. For pseudohistorical accounts of Stepan Bandera, see *Krymskaia pravda*, 3 January 1991, 3; 4 January 1991, 3. The term *banderovtsy* became a standard derogatory label for the nationalists of western Ukraine.
48. Mal'gin, *Krymskii uzel*, 67.
49. *Pravda Ukrainy*, 25 April 1992.
50. For a draft law to this effect, prepared by the Verkhovna Rada on 29 April 1992, see *Holos Ukraïny*, 5 May 1992, 2. For a discussion about the lost opportunity, see Mal'gin, *Krymskii uzel*, 68.
51. Author's interview with Mykola Bahrov, Simferopol, 5 April 1996.
52. Author's interview with Iurii Komov, Simferopol, 5 September 1996. Komov in 1992 belonged to the same parliamentary faction as Meshkov (Demokraticheskii Krym).
53. See *Konstitutsiia Respubliki Krym*, 6 May 1992, preamble, pt. 1, articles 1 and 10.
54. Markus, "Crimea Restores 1992 Constitution," 9–12.

55. *Konstitutsiia Respubliki Krym*, compare section 1, articles 1 and 9.

56. Ibid., pt. 1, articles 2, 4, 103. According to both constitutions of 1992 the Republic of Crimea has an independent judiciary, including a Constitutional Court and a High Court (articles 135 and 139, respectively). All judges were to be elected by the Crimean Supreme Soviet. While the Constitution of May 1992 envisaged the Crimean prosecutor to be elected by the Crimean Supreme Soviet, the Constitution of September 1992 specified that the prosecutor would be appointed and dismissed by the Ukrainian General Prosecutor in agreement with the Crimean Supreme Soviet (articles 148 and 152, respectively). Formanchuk (*Mify sovetskoi epokhi*, 522) described this Constitution as a strategic move by the Supreme Soviet under Bahrov's leadership to stabilize the increasingly precarious regional situation. Bahrov may well have hoped to avoid both an intraregional clash and a clash with Kyiv, but Kyiv's reaction was not unexpected.

57. In an interview with the author, Simferopol, 5 April 1996, Bahrov explained this move as a form of leverage to extract specific economic rights from Kyiv.

58. Bahrov, *Krym: Vremia nadezhd i trevog*, 265–75.

59. Bahrov's speech is reprinted in ibid., 268–75.

60. Ukraïns'kyi nezalezhnyi tsentr politychnykh doslidzhen', *Crimea*, 26–27, 31.

61. Kulyk, "Revisiting a Success Story," 31.

62. Bahrov, *Krym: Vremia trevog i nadezhd*, 275–76.

63. *Konstitutsiia Respubliki Krym* (approved by the Crimean Supreme Soviet on 6 May 1992 and amended on 25 September 1992).

64. *Konstitutsiia Respubliki Krym*, 25 September 1992, article 1.

65. See Williams, *Crimean Tatars*, 419–43.

66. Ibid., 430.

67. See Formanchuk, *Mify sovetskoi epokhi*, 501.

68. Mal'gin, *Krymskii uzel*, 123.

69. *Krymskaia pravda*, 24 July 1990, 1.

70. Mal'gin, *Krymskii uzel*, 124.

71. *Krymskaia pravda*, 27 June 1991, 1–2.

72. According to Bahrov (*Krym: Vremia nadezhd i trevog*, 294), who was not in Crimea at the time, this incident brought the region to the brink of "civil war." He interprets the outcome as a rethinking of strategy on the part of the Tatars who subsequently increased the scope for dialogue.

Chapter Seven

1. For a comprehensive overview of Ukrainian and Crimean parties

from 1989 to 1996 and after reregistration in 1997, see V. Korolev, *Politicheskie partii Ukrainy i Kryma*.

2. The DPK actively cooperated with Crimean Tatar organizations before the 1994 regional parliamentary elections; see *Nezavisimaia gazeta*, 6 October 1993.

3. "Ekonomika i politika perekhodnogo perioda: Programmnye dokumenty Partii ekonomicheskogo vozrozhdeniia Kryma (PEVK)," *Krymskaia pravda*, 16 March 1993, 2.

4. There has been a tendency in Crimea for all regional parties to call themselves "centrist," including the Russian movement and Communist Party. For a discussion of the absence of a real centrist ideology and policy see Zarechnyi, "Kontury tsentrizma."

5. Wilson, "Crimea's Political Cauldron."

6. Ukraïns'kyi nezalezhnyi tsentr politychnykh doslidzhen', *Crimea*, 70.

7. For brief historical accounts of the deported Crimean nationalities, including the two smaller indigenous peoples, the Karaim and Krymchaks, see Nikolaenko, *Skvoz' veka*; Broshevan and Renpening, *Krymskie nemtsy*; Khadzhiiski, *Bŭlgari v Tavriia*; Polkanov, *Krymskie Karaimy*; Khazanov, *Krymchaks*.

8. *Krymskaia pravda*, 13 January 1994, 2.

9. The other three candidates failed to develop a distinct profile: Shuvainikov tried to occupy the same spectrum as Meshkov, while Iermakov and V. A. Verkoshanskii disappeared behind Bahrov's profile.

10. For the official election results of the first round of voting, see *Krymskaia pravda*, 18 January 1994, 1; *Krymskie izvestiia*, 19 January 1994, 1.

11. For opinion poll data reflecting the electorate's ambivalence and majority support for "Crimean independence within Ukraine" rather than within Russia, see Solchanyk, *Ukraine and Russia*, 191.

12. See Mal'gin, *Krymskii uzel*, 81.

13. Ibid., 192.

14. The Crimean president led the executive, and there was no longer a Crimean prime minister.

15. Arel's claim that the victory of the "Block Russia" was mainly the result of the proportional representation electoral system at the regional level is, therefore, untenable. See Arel, "Ukraine," 4.

16. For the phrasing of the referendum questions, see *Krymskaia pravda*, 13 March 1994, 1; for Kravchuk's decree downgrading the referendum to an opinion poll, see *Krymskaia pravda*, 17 March 1994, 1.

17. Data from the Central Electoral Commission, April 1994.

18. Ozhiganov ("Crimean Republic," 112) described Crimea as the "most militarized zone in Europe after Bosnia."
19. For the decree, see Ukraïns´kyi nezalezhnyi tsentr politychnykh doslidzhen´, *Crimea*, 75–76.
20. Mal´gin, *Krysmkii uzel*, 85.
21. Ozhiganov, "Crimean Republic," 113.
22. Mal´gin, *Krymskii uzel*, 85.
23. Ukraïns´kyi nezalezhnyi tsentr politychnykh doslidzhen´, *Crimea*, 84.
24. *Krymskaia pravda*, 3 January 1991, 1.
25. See Mal´gin, *Krymskii uzel*, 73–74.
26. Kudriatsev and Shumskii, "Rekratsionnoe khoziaistvo Kryma," 114–15.
27. *Zerkalo nedeli*, 14 June 1997.
28. Crimean gas resources account for about 40 percent of the regional gas needs; see Kudriatsev, "Toplivno-energeticheskaia baza," 207.
29. United Nations Development Programme (UNDP), *Crimea*, 6. For further details about Crimea's water resources and management, see *Voprosy razvitiia Kryma*.
30. UNDP, *Crimea*, 6. According to Shevchuk ("Krym," 52), who relies on internal data of a USSR State Committee (1985), 25.7 percent of the Crimean workforce was involved in the military-industrial complex, compared to the Ukrainian average of 18.6 percent.
31. 95 percent of the Crimean machine building sector were dependent on Russia and the rest of the USSR; see Amelchenko, "Mashinostroenie Kryma," 212.
32. Economic development programs such as the one developed by Crimean Prime Minister Demydenko in 1996 and a big investment fair in Yalta had hardly any effect.
33. Confirmed in the author's interview with Yurii Komov, Simferopol, 5 September 1996. The unrealistic idea of an economically self-sufficient Crimea was still floated in regional politics several years later, for example as a rationale behind the economic program of then Crimean premier Demydenko; author's interview with Demydenko, Simferopol, 17 September 1996.
34. Author's interview with Mykola Bahrov, Simferopol, 5 April 1996.
35. See Mal´gin, *Krymskii uzel*, 75–77.
36. Ibid., 87.
37. Confirmed in author's interview with Vladimir Zaskoka, regional deputy and head of the Privatization Control Commission of the Supreme Soviet, 9 September 1996.

38. *Moskovskie novosti*, 18–25 September 1994, 6.

39. On this conflict of interests under Saburov, see Wittkowsky, "Politische Eliten der Ukraine," 374–75.

40. Opinion poll conducted by "Laboratoriia sotsiologii Krymskogo tsentra gumanitarnykh issledovanii," *Krymskaia pravda*, 30 August 1994, 1.

41. In June 1994 the Ukrainian parliament had begun to prepare legislation to annul Crimean laws, and by the end of July Kyiv had reestablished its control over the local police.

42. Kravchuk won only 8.9 percent of the votes in Crimea; see *Krymskaia pravda*, 12 July 1994, 1. For a clear example of the regional media campaign for Kuchma, see "Pomozhem bratskomu narodu Ukrainy osvobodit'sia ot Kravchuka!" *Krymskaia pravda*, 8 July 1994, 1.

43. *Krymskaia pravda*, 18 June 1994, 1; 23 June 1994, 1.

44. Mal'gin, *Krymskii uzel*, 92.

45. For the most systematic analysis of the Crimean Tatar national movement from their deportation up to the 1990s, including key documents, see Guboglo and Chervonnaia, *Krymskotatarskoe natsional'noe dvizhenie*. See also Adnyliuk, *Kryms'ki tatary 1944–1994 rr.*; Kuras, *Kryms'ki tatary*; and Viatkin and Kul'pin, *Krymskie tatary*.

46. For evidence of the similar support of ethnic Russians and Ukrainians, see Dawson, *Eco-nationalism*, 159 and the survey she refers to in n. 62.

47. Dawson ("Ethnicity, Ideology and Geopolitics in Crimea," 442) claims that the failure of Blok Rossiia lies in its attempt to mobilize the population around a nonexistent Russian-Ukrainian cleavage in society. In fact, pro-Russian parties and organizations have continually made use of the anti-Tatar feelings among the Crimean Slav population. The Russian-Ukrainian cleavage was never solely perceived of or mobilized as a regional ethnic issue, as Dawson assumes (ibid., 443), but rather as an opposition movement of a Russified regional population against the Ukrainian government and in favor of closer links with Russia. The shorthand "Russian-Ukrainian conflict," used to describe the developments in Crimea, oversimplifies the conflict.

Chapter Eight

1. The struggle between Crimean president Meshkov and speaker Tsekov to some extent paralleled the standoff between the Russian president and parliament. See *Moskovskie novosti*, 11–18 September 1994, 1, 4; *Komsomol'skaia pravda*, 13 September 1994, 1, 2; *Krymskaia pravda*, 15 September 1994, 1; *Rossiiskaia gazeta*, 15 September, 1, 6.

2. According to surveys conducted by the Analytical Center of the Crimean government in March and June 1996, 71.2 percent and 73.7 percent of the respondents said they would not vote for Ukrainian independence again. Only 5.7 percent and 5.5 percent, respectively, said they would support Ukrainian independence.

3. Franchuk was the father-in-law of Kuchma's daughter.

4. Mal'gin, *Krymskii uzel*, 91.

5. Verkhovna Rada Ukraïny, *Zakon vid 17.03.1995 No. 92/95-VR "Pro skasuvannia Konstitutsiï i deiakykh zakoniv Avtonomnoi Respubliky Krym"* and *No. 95/95-VR "Pro Avtonomnu Respubliku Krym"*; see http://zakon.rada.gov.ua; see also Lapychak, "Crackdown on Crimean Separatism." For a collection of documents and reactions, see Ukraïns'kyi nezalezhnyi tsentr politychnykh doslidzhen', *Chy rozhoryt'sia kryms'ka kryza?*

6. Mal'gin, *Krymskii uzel*, 94.

7. Kulyk, "Revisiting a Success Story," 49, 51.

8. *Predstavnytstvo Prezydenta Ukraïny v Respublitsi Krym: Ukrepliaia vlast' i zakonnist'*, and *Pres-sluzhba, Predstavnytstvo Prezydenta Ukraïny: Spravka*, 5 February 1996. For the original description of the post, see Tabachnyk, *Polozhennia pro Predstavnytstvo Prezydenta Ukraïny.*

9. *Krymskaia pravda*, 23 March 1996, 2.

10. Kulyk, "Revisiting a Success Story," 54–55.

11. See Parliamentary Assembly of the Council of Europe, *On the Application by Ukraine for Membership.* In this document the Council of Europe set Ukraine the deadline of 8 June 1996 to finalize its Constitution, including the scope of Crimea's autonomy. Based on conditions such as this one, Ukraine joined the Council of Europe in November 1995.

12. *Holos Ukraïny*, 9 April 1996, 5.

13. In the Constitution of 1996, which was in part accepted by the Ukrainian parliament, references are still made to the lawmaking responsibilities of the Crimean Supreme Soviet, whereas they were omitted in the final version ratified in 1999.

14. Author's interview with Ievhen Supruniuk, Simferopol, 8 April 1996.

15. In an interview with the author (Simferopol, 5 April 1996) Bahrov complained: "How is it possible that the Crimean deputies were absent when the Crimean Constitution was discussed in the Ukrainian parliament? The electorate has to know about these facts...."

16. Author's interview with Ievhen Supruniuk, Simferopol, 8 April 1996.

For evidence showing that the status of Crimea was still unclear a month before the adoption of the Crimean Constitution, see *Krymskoe vremia*, 26 March 1996, 7.

17. Author's interview with Volodymyr Iehudin, Crimean deputy in the Verkhovna Rada in Kyiv, Simferopol, 7 October 1996.

18. *Konstitutsiia Avtonomnoi Respubliki Krym* (draft of April 1996), esp. articles 98, 105–22, 123–24; and *Konstytutsiia Ukraïny*, 1996, article 10.

19. See *Konstytutsiia Ukraïny*, 1996, articles 135, 136. In practice, these decisions themselves may be in contradiction to each other.

20. The term *Verkhovna Rada*, used to describe both the Ukrainian parliament and the Crimean "representative organ," does not make for a clear distinction. To reflect the downgrading of the regional legislative powers the term "regional assembly" will be used in the remainder of the book.

21. *Konstytutsiia Ukraïny*, 1996, article 133.

22. *Konstytutsiia Ukraïny*, 1996, pt. 1, article 4.

23. "Rossiiskoe grazhdanstvo zhitelyam Kryma!" *Krymskaia pravda*, 22 March 1995 and Interfaks, in *Krymskaia pravda*, 24 March 1995.

24. Similar developments have taken place in Russia, for instance in the Republic of Tatarstan, which introduced its own citizenship in the Tatarstan Constitution of 1994 to exist alongside Russian Federation citizenship.

25. *Konstitutsiia Respubliki Krym* (6 May 1992 and April 1996), articles 17 and 15. The compromise Constitution of September 1992 and the final version of December 1998 did not envisage Crimean citizenship.

26. *Konstitutsiia Ukraïny*, 1996, pt. 1, article 10.

27. Author's interview with Larisa Barzut, deputy in the Simferopol city council and director of the 21st school, the only school at that time with classes taught in Ukrainian, Simferopol, 13 September 1996; and with Vladimir Kavraiskii, Crimean deputy minister for education, Simferopol, 8 October 1996. By 1998 the Crimean ministry of education listed just one Ukrainian grammar school, though Ukrainian language had become an obligatory subject in Crimean schools; see *Krymskaia pravda*, 14 April 1998.

28. Viktor Sharapa, prorector of Simferopol State University (now Tavriia National University), recalled meetings in Kyiv at which the complete switch of the Crimean university to Ukrainian was considered; author's interview, Simferopol, 26 March 1996.

29. *Krymskaia pravda*, 31 January 1998, 2; 28 April 1998.

30. Author's interview with Sergei Tsekov, leader of the PPK, Simferopol, 5 September 1996.

31. Jemilev proposed a more radical version of a bicameral regional parliament, one chamber of which would be controlled by the Crimean Tatars (plus Krymchaks and Karaims); author's interview with Mustafa Jemilev, Simferopol, 19 September 1996.

32. Author's interview with Refat Chubarov, Simferopol, 8 April 1996.

33. Author's interview with Ievhen Shev'ev, Simferopol, 15 April 1996; interview with Demydenko, 17 September 1996.

34. Author's interview with Mariia Ishchuk, Simferopol, 18 September 1996.

35. A total of 42 interviews were conducted; they comprised 16 representatives of Crimean political institutions, 21 leaders of parties or organizations at the local or regional level, and 10 "opinion makers." The interviews are judged by the author to be a fair representation of the views of the most prominent decision makers at the time. The interviews were conducted in two stages in April and October–November 1996, during a period when the adoption processes for the regional and national constitutions were peaking. For a complete list of the interviewees see appendix 2. That the interviews included the leading political decision makers was confirmed by the fact that a ranking, produced by the respectable Kryms'kyi nezalezhnyi tsentr politychnykh doslidzhen' in Simferopol, listed 9 of the interviewees among the top 10 most influential elite members in early 1996 (this list was a composite of rankings given by about 100 Crimean, Ukrainian, and foreign media representatives), and 8 were ranked among the top 10 at the end of 1995.

36. The categories capture the formulations of the interviewees. They are not mutually exclusive; in most cases the interviewees listed several components of Crimean regional identity.

37. In an interview with the author in Simferopol, 8 April 1996, the journalist and analyst Andrei Mal'gin distinguished between three identities: a Russian versus Ukrainian identity tied up with the respective ethnic core; a state identity, allowing for political integration into the Ukrainian state; and, thirdly, he sees a genuine regional identity emerging. Mal'gin used a very open definition of regionalism as "the population's concern for their territory." This definition lends itself to a shared concern for the region's economic and political crisis. The regional analyst Andrii Nikiforov predicted a growing awareness of a common Crimean regional identity: "It will take one generation for the Crimean regional identity to fully come to the fore. Right now this dead capital is trembling somewhere at the bot-

tom of people's souls"; author's interview in Simferopol, 9 October 1996.

38. Author's interview with Sergei Tsekov, 5 September 1996; and Sergei Shuvainikov, head of the Russian Party of Crimea, Simferopol, 5 September 1996.

39. At a personal level these links between Crimean Tatar and Ukrainian activists dates back to the dissident movement in the Soviet Union. In particular, Jemilev, leader of the Mejlis and figurehead of the Crimean Tatar national movement, and V'iacheslav Chornovil, leader of Rukh, are linked by their gulag memories. They were imprisoned in neighboring camps; author's interview with Jemilev, Simferopol, 19 September 1996.

40. Coakley, *Territorial Management of Ethnic Conflict*, 14.

41. Elazar, for example, although not a specialist on the region, views the further federalisation of both Ukraine and Georgia positively; see his *Federalism and the Way to Peace*, 74, 81. At the same time, however, he overestimates the likelihood of a confederalization of the CIS.

42. Wildavsky, *Federalism and Political Culture*, 40. At the mass level Hesli conducted surveys in 1992, confirming support for the idea of devolution, particularly in the East and South of Ukraine; see Hesli, "Public Support," 91–121.

43. Elazar, *Federalism and the Way to Peace*, 165.

44. Author's interview with Ievhen Supruniuk, Simferopol, 8 April 1996.

45. Author's interview with Mykola Bahrov, Simferopol, 5 April 1996.

46. Author's interview with Aleksandr Formanchuk, Simferopol, 1 April 1996.

47. Crimean prime minister Demydenko, for example, refused to speculate at all on the development of federalism in an interview with the author, Simferopol, 17 September 1996.

48. *Krymskoe vremia*, 14 November 1998, 5.

49. *Krymskaia pravda*, 14 February 1998, 1–2.

50. For details on these amendments, see Kulyk, "Revisiting a Success Story," 63–64.

51. *Krymskaia pravda*, 5 February 1998, 1–2.

52. Williams, *Crimean Tatars*, 454.

53. Mal'gin, *Krymskii uzel*, 135. From 1992 to 1997 the Ukrainian state built five thousand (and bought another four hundred) houses and flats for the Crimean Tatars, amounting to housing for about twenty thousand people.

54. Figures quoted in Solchanyk, *Ukraine and Russia*, 200.

55. *Kratkaia khronika deiatel'nosti Medzhlisa*; and speeches and resolutions of the third Kurultay, 1996.

56. *Avdet*, 27 January 1998, 2. For a collection of primary sources on this internal split, see Kryms'kyi tsentr nezalezhnykh politychnykh doslidnykiv i zhurnalistiv, *Kryms'ko-tatars'ke pytannia*, Simferopol, 1998.

57. Mal'gin, *Krymskii uzel*, 144.

58. *Chas*, 6 December 1996, 7. By 1996 only 3.76 small firms were privatized per 10,000 inhabitants in Crimea, as compared to an average of 17.46 in western regions, 10.35 in southern regions, 9.41 in northern regions, 9.05 in central regions, and 7.52 in eastern regions; see *Chas*, 22 November 1996. By the autumn of 1997 altogether 1,760 objects had been privatized, though the functioning of these privatized firms was questionable (see *Krymskoe vremia*, 1 October 1997, 7). The head of the Crimean Property Fund, Aleksei Golovizin, voiced his criticism of these firms and struggled for a quick and controlled process of privatization that would include the sanatoria. Golovizin's assassination in 1997 indicated the strong opposition of business clans to attempts to regulate privatization; see *Region*, 24 May 1997, 11.

59. Tomenko, *Abetka ukraïns'koï polityky*, 99.

60. *Otchet predsedatelia Fonda imushchestva ARK Shimina Iuriia Vladimirovicha o rabote fonda v 2003 godu*, http://www.kfp.com.ua/fondim/dokl_shimin_2003.php (accessed 17 April 2007).

61. *Krymskaia pravda*, 12 September 1998, 1.

62. The fact that the 1998 Crimean Constitution no longer envisages legal immunity for deputies, as was the case in the earlier constitutions and drafts of 1992 and 1996, can be seen as a reaction to the criminalization of the regional parliament.

63. *Finantsova Ukraïna*, 11 February 1997, 9; for further details on criminal activities in Crimea see "Kriminal'nyi feodalizm," *Moskovskie novosti*, 19–26 May 1996, 8; *Region*, 1 February 1997, 14.

64. Author's interview with Volodymyr Prytula, Crimean Independent Center of Political Research, Simferopol, 6 September 1996.

65. At that time at least 22 regional deputies out of a total of 98, and some of the representatives of the Council of Ministers, were strongly linked to criminal elements; author's interview with Iurii Komov, Simferopol, 5 September 1996, and with Vladimir Zaskoka, 9 September 1996.

66. *Statystychnyi biuleten' za 9 misiatsiv 1996 roku*, October 1996, 8.

67. *Finantsova Ukraïna*, 11 February 1997.

68. Administratsiia Prezydenta Ukraïny, *Ukraïna ta ii rehiony*, 25.

69. Administratsiia Prezydenta Ukraïny, *Monitoring makroekonomichnoho ta rehional'noho rozvitku Ukraïny, 63.*

70. Administratsiia Prezydenta Ukraïny, *Ukraïna ta ïï rehiony,* 38–39. In December 1995 Crimea reached a low, with its average monthly salary at 85 percent of the Ukrainian average. By the middle of 1996 the gap had narrowed to 94.8 percent of the Ukrainian average. These figures, however, do not indicate the delays in payment. In December 1997 monthly salaries in Crimea stood at 91.5 percent of the Ukrainian average.

71. Administratsiia Prezydenta Ukraïny, *Ukraïna ta ïï rehiony,* 60.

72. *Zerkalo nedeli,* 31 May 1997; *Region,* 8 February 1997, 11.

73. In the first half of 1996 Ukraine reportedly raised 65.3 percent of the taxes envisaged in the budget, whereas Crimea only raised 36.7 percent of its share. See *Uriadovyi kur'er,* 21 September 1996.

74. See Sochor, "No Middle Ground?"

75. The poll was conducted by the Krymskii tsentr gumanitarnykh issledovanii and published in *Krymskaya pravda,* 20 January 1996, 1. Comparative survey data from the eastern and southern regions of Ukraine confirm this trend; see *Political Portrait of Ukraine,* no. 9 (1994): 45.

76. Results of a poll conducted by the Krymskii tsentr gumanitarnykh issledovanii published in *Krymskie izvestiia,* 2 April 1996, 1.

77. Ukraïns'kyi nezalezhnyi tsentr politychnykh doslidzhen', *Informatsiino-analitychne vydannia,* 20.

78. *Krymskaia pravda,* 11 February 1998, 1. See also *Verkhovna Rada Ukraïny, zakon vid 03.03.1998, no. 134/98-VR "Pro vnesennia zmin do Zakonu Ukraïny 'Pro vybory deputativ Verkhovnoï Rady Avtonomnoï Respubliky Krym,'"* http://zakon.rada.gov.ua (accessed 6 March 2007).

79. See *Deklaratsiia Krymskoi Partii,* Simferopol, 1996.

80. See, for example, the program and materials of the founding session of the Kongress russkogo naroda, Simferopol, 5 October 1996. Shortly after the Russian Assembly, the Crimean Germans followed with their Volkstag in November 1996. It is ironic that the most vociferous Russian nationalist, Sergei Shuvainikov, adopted the organizational principles for his assembly from the Crimean Tatar Kurultay.

81. Tsekov, "Ia—ne separatist i ne vrag Ukrainy," *Region,* 17 May 1997, 9.

82. The Ukrainian media described the Communist Party and Union Party jointly as a "collective Meshkov," as they combined some of the goals of the 1994 movement, such as the striving for a Slavic

Union, the position of Russian as the first language in Crimea, and for strong self-governing rights for the region; see *Zerkalo nedeli*, 24 January 1998.

83. This is the overall share of votes in the mixed Ukrainian electoral system, according to data obtained from the Presidential Administration, Kyiv, April 1998.

Chapter Nine

1. Formanchuk aptly described him as a "communist statist" (*kommunist-gosudarstvennik*); see Formanchuk, *Mify sovetskoi epokhi*, 570.
2. *Zerkalo nedeli*, 6 February 1999, 4; Kulyk, "Revisiting a Success Story," 65.
3. *Konstitutsiia Avtonomnoi Respubliki Krym*, 23 December 1998.
4. *Krymskaia pravda*, 25 December 1998, 1–2.
5. *Krymskoe vremia*, 1 December 1998, 6.
6. He explicitly tried to enhance his role as Crimean parliamentary speaker by raising the question of whether his constitutionally defined role did not equal presidential functions. See *Krymskaia pravda*, 25 December 1998, 2. In fact, the Crimean Constitution gives him the right only to suggest the deputy heads of the two key security posts, the regional branches of the Ukrainian Ministry of Internal Affairs and the Ukrainian Ministry of Justice; see *Konstitutsiia Avtonomnoi Respubliki Krym*, 23 December 1998, article 29.10.
7. *Konstitutsiia Avtonomnoi Respubliki Krym*, 23 December 1998, article 1.
8. Ibid., articles 2.2 and 48.
9. *Krymskoe vremia*, 1 December 1998, 6.
10. *Konstitutsiia Avtonomnoi Respubliki Krym*, 23 December 1998, articles 10.1, 10.2, 11.
11. Mal'gin, *Krymskii uzel*, 101–2.
12. See the journal *National Security and Defence* 4, no. 16 (2001): 14–16.
13. They include agriculture and forestry, trade and industry, construction and housing, tourism, cultural institutions, transport, hunting and fishing and medical services (*Konstytutsiia Ukraïny*, 28 June 1996, article 137).
14. Ruling of the Constitutional Court of Ukraine, case no. 1-20/2001, 27 February 2001, especially clause 2.2. A further ruling, case no. 1-7/2001 (21 December 2001) followed the same procedure and declared that the Crimean Assembly's definition of the deputies' status was unconstitutional. Rulings can be found on the Court's website: http://www.ccu.gov.ua/ (accessed 9 March 2007).
15. For more details see *National and Security Defence* 4, no. 16 (2001): 16.

16. Ruling of the Constitutional Court of Ukraine, case no. 2-28/2002, 18 April 2002.
17. See Formanchuk, *Mify sovetskoi epokhi*, 573.
18. This arrangement can also strengthen the power of the Council of Ministers over regional policy in the absence of a stable majority in the Crimean Assembly.
19. See the Crimean poll conducted by the Ukrainian Center for Economic and Political Studies, 14–28 March 2001; results published in *National Security and Defence* 4, no. 16 (2001): 16.
20. For a detailed analysis of the Crimean Tatars' exclusion from the autonomy see Stewart, "Autonomy," 125–38.
21. The Russian language is described as "the language of the majority of the population" that is "suited to interethnic communication" and "will be used in all spheres of societal life" (article 10, clause 2).
22. Ukraïns'kyi nezalezhnyi tsentr politychnykh doslidzhen', *Informatsiino-analitychne vydannia*, 20–21. The gist of the amendments concerned the temporal synchronization of the national and regional electoral process.
23. Ibid., 29.
24. Ukraïns'kyi nezalezhnyi tsentr politychnykh doslidzhen', *Informatsiino-analitychne vydannia*, 4.
25. Ibid. According to this source at least 42 deputies work in business or financial institutions, 14 work for security structures, and 10 head civil society organizations. As for the age structure of the deputies, 12 percent of deputies are 31–40 years old, 49 percent 41–50 years, 28 percent 51–60 years, 10 percent 61–70 years, and 1 percent is over 70 years old; see *Russkii mir*, 19 April 2002, 2.
26. Chubarov, "Vybory 31 bereznia 2002 roku," 25. The figures reflect the composition of the assembly as of 15 April 2002 and do not include the disputed seats.
27. Data from the Analytical Center of the Crimean Supreme Soviet, October 2002.
28. Chubarov, "Vybory 31 bereznia 2002 roku," 24.
29. Ibid.; Ukraïns'kyi nezalezhnyi tsentr politychnykh doslidzhen', *Informatsiino-analitychne vydannia*, 36.
30. Ukraïns'kyi nezalezhnyi tsentr politychnykh doslidzhen', *Informatsiino-analitychne vydannia*, 37–38. On the whole, participation in Crimea declined somewhat, thereby indicating that the participation among the Slav population dropped; see ibid., 25.
31. Ibid., 38, 42.
32. Ibid., 44.
33. *Krymskie izvestiia*, 8 October 2002, 1. The proposals and positions

were confused. Under the pressure of considerable antipresidential opposition Kuchma changed his mind: in August 2002 he came out in favor of a national-level system entirely based on proportional representation (PR). The regional public discourse on the issue was also confused; see *Krymskaia pravda*, 16 October 2002, 2. After having suffered an electoral defeat, Hrach himself then became an opponent of the majoritarian system, calling it "undemocratic." Following on from Kuchma's proposals, he proposed a draft law on regional elections along similar lines; see *Krymskaia pravda*, 5 October 2002, 1. The arguments put forward against a mixed or a PR system were as unconvincing as the pseudoarguments for the majoritarian system; see *Krymskoe vremia*, 11 October 2002, 3.

34. Author's interview with Jemilev, Simferopol, 5 October 2002.
35. See the portrait of Katusheva in *Krymskaia pravda*, 29 January 2003, 2.
36. A Crimean Tatar, Edip Gafarov, became deputy prime minister.
37. Ukraïns´kyi nezalezhnyi tsentr politychnykh doslidzhen´, *Informatsiino-analitychne vydannia*, 16.
38. The 2002 state program for the settlement and sociocultural development of the deported peoples earmarked 55.1 million *hryvnias*; 39.8 million were to come from Ukraine's state budget and 15.3 million from the Crimean budget. About 70–75 percent of the sums were actually spent; see *Krymskaia pravda*, 23 January 2003, 2.
39. *Krymskoe vremia*, 5 November 2002, 3. The coverage in this newspaper is generally biased against the Crimean Tatars. See, for example, the criticism of proposals about national quotas, indigenous peoples, and changes to the current format of Crimean autonomy, resulting from a monitoring exercise coordinated by Iurii Bilukha, the Crimean representative of the Ukrainian High Commissioner on Human Rights, a post created in April 1999; see *Krymskoe vremia*, 14 December 2002, 3.
40. The regional media voiced fears that the widespread bribes for bureaucrats and officials could soon be complemented by bribes for local Mejlis structures in return for not opposing the business activities of non-Tatars; see *Krymskoe vremia*, 18 January 2003, 3; and 28 January 2003, 1–2.
41. Ukraïns´kyi nezalezhnyi tsentr politychnykh doslidzhen´, *Informatsiino-analitychne vydannia*, 45–46.
42. *Krymskie izvestiia*, 4 October 2002.
43. *Krymskoe vremia*, 18 January 2003, 3.
44. Originally the official Communist Party newspaper, *Krymskaia pravda* turned itself into a strong support base for the Republican

Movement, Meshkov, and the Russia Bloc; in 1994 it backed Kuchma's bid for the presidency, and by 1998 it had come round to a communist-friendly line with strong Russian nationalist overtones.

45. *Krymskaia pravda*, 17 January 2001, 1; 4 October 2002, 1; 25 January 2003.

46. *Krymskaia pravda*, 7 April 2000, 2; 10 October 2002, 2.

47. *Krymskaia pravda*, 19 October 2002, 1.

48. Author's interview with Viktor Sharapa, prorector of Tavriia National University, Simferopol, 10 October 2002. In the autumn of 2002 there were 14,000 students enrolled at this university. At this point it shared its level of accreditation with only 14 other universities across Ukraine. In 2001 a presidential decree had turned the university into one of three universities in Ukraine with a somewhat higher degree of self-government and funding.

49. Author's interview with Safure Kadmametova, head of the Association of Crimean Tatar Educational Sector, Simferopol, 5 October 2002. In 2001 there were 4 schools with Ukrainian as the language of instruction, 9 Crimean Tatar schools, 33 bilingual schools (Russian and Crimean Tatar), and 81 Russian-language schools offering some classes in Crimean Tatar; see *National Security and Defence* 4, no. 16 (2001): 21, 24.

50. *Krymskaia pravda*, 2 October 2002, 1, and 4 October 2002, 1.

Chapter Ten

1. For a collection of views and statements of prominent Russian politicians, reflecting the difficulties to accept Ukraine's independent statehood, see Ukraïns´kyi nezalezhnyi tsentr politychnykh doslidzhen´, *A Russia That We....* For an extreme neoimperialist view see Dugin, *Osnovy geopolitiki*, a book that calls itself the first Russian textbook on geopolitics for diplomats, lawyers, bankers, and political scientists. The "Ukrainian problem" is defined as the most serious question Moscow has to deal with (ibid., 382). Ukrainian sovereignty is presented as a danger for Russian geopolitics and the whole Eurasian region (348). Ukraine is not accepted as an independent state: "Ukraine as a state does not make any geopolitical sense. She lacks a particular culture of universal significance, geographical distinctiveness and a clear ethnic feature" (377). As for Crimea, a complete integration with Russia is deemed unrealistic due to the extreme nationalism of the *malorossy*, but regional autonomy under Moscow's strategic control and respect for Ukraine's socioeconomic interests and the Crimean Tatars' ethnocultural demands are pre-

sented as the only sensible solution to the Crimean question (380). In contrast to this view, the Russian daily *Nezavisimaia gazeta* started a more rational exchange of views on Russian-Ukrainian relations in a special supplement (December 1996, 1–5). The necessity to accept Ukrainian independence and the fact that Crimea and Sevastopol belong to the Ukrainian state, although their history remains closely associated with the Russian and Soviet empires, underpins these articles.

2. For a description of the different Russian-Ukrainian dimensions of the Crimean issue, see V. Savchenko, "Sevastopol'skii sindrom," *Moskovskie novosti*, 25 February–3 March 1996.

3. Solchanyk, *Ukraine and Russia*, 160.

4. Ibid., 56–57.

5. The UN Charter explicitly refers to the prohibited use of force against the territorial integrity or political independence of any state. The agreement establishing the CIS of December 1991 is even more precise: all the signatories agreed to "the principles of equality and non-intervention in internal affairs, of abstention from the use of force and from economic or other means of applying pressure and of settling controversial issues through agreement, and other universally recognized principles and norms of international law"; cited in Chase, "Conflict in the Crimea," 241.

6. Mal'gin, *Krymskii uzel*, 17–18.

7. Ibid., 19.

8. Simonsen, "'You Take Your Oath Only Once,'" 311.

9. For a detailed account of Lukin's reasoning, including primary evidence, see Solchanyk, *Ukraine and Russia*, 166–69. Lukin was appointed ambassador to the US in February 1992, and later cofounded the social-democratic Iabloko bloc with Grigorii Iavlinskii.

10. Konstantin Pleshakov, "Krym: Kuda nas tolkaiut glupye nationalisty," *Novoe vremia*, 31 July 1993, 6. For the assets of the Black Sea Fleet see Ozhiganov, "Crimean Republic," 120.

11. Tilly's thoughts about the link between military and state building reverberate in post-Soviet politics; see Tilly, "War Making and State Making."

12. Mal'gin, *Krymskii uzel*, 40.

13. The figures given by Admiral Igor' Kasatonov in January 1992 listed 19 percent of the officers and 30 percent of the sailors and lower-ranking officers; see *Izvestiia*, 7 January 1992.

14. *Izvestiia*, 10 January 1992, 2. According to yet another estimate, by January 1992 under 30 percent of the 70,000 sailors were Ukrainians; see Simonsen, "'You Take Your Oath Only Once,'" 302.

15. Lepingwell, "Black Sea Fleet Agreement"; Markus, "Ukrainian Navy and the Black Sea Fleet"; Markus, "Black Sea Fleet Dispute Apparently Over."

16. Mal'gin, *Krymskii uzel*, 10–11.

17. *Nezavisimaia gazeta*, 22 May 1992; *Izvestiia*, 25 May 1992, 4. The article also indicates concern about a possible regional conflict between Russia and Ukraine voiced in the French, American, and German press. For sharp replies in the Ukrainian media, see *Pravda Ukraïny*, 27 May 1992, 1–2.

18. This argument was, for example, used by Evgenii Ambartsumov, then deputy head of the Committee on Foreign Affairs and External Economic Ties, when pushed to justify the change in direction; see Solchanyk, *Ukraine and Russia*, 162.

19. For an indicative quote by Yeltsin shortly after signing the treaty, demonstrating that the bilateral treaty was not tied to the future of the Soviet Union or the union treaty, see ibid., 164.

20. Mal'gin (*Krymskii uzel*, 11) points to this second resolution to show that the Russian parliament advanced a moral rather than a political claim. This distinction remains unclear, but Mal'gin is right in highlighting the ambivalence of the Russian position and the lack of a clear policy towards Crimea and Ukraine as a whole.

21. *Vidomosti Verkhovnoï Rady Ukraïny*, 12 May 1992, 554–55.

22. Tolz, "Conflicting 'Homeland Myths,'" 283.

23. For more details on this issue, see Mal'gin, *Krymskii uzel*, 25.

24. Ibid., 28–29.

25. For different views on the status of Sevastopol, see *Nezavisimaia gazeta*, 18 December 1996, 5.

26. See archival materials quoted in chapter 5, which include Sevastopol in the budget of the Ukrainian SSR. Moreover, the chairman of the Sevastopol *ispolkom* was invited to the meeting of the USSR Presidium on 19 February 1954 concerning the transfer of Crimea. The territorial-administrative status of Sevastopol also remained ambiguous. The handbook *SSSR: Administrativno-territorial'noe delenie soiuznykh respublik* lists Sevastopol as a city under republican jurisdiction within the RSFSR (71), while the same collection, published in 1954, refers to Sevastopol as a city under republican jurisdiction within the Ukrainian SSR (209). The editions of 1947, 1949, and 1954 give the exact same size for the territory of the Crimean oblast without indicating a change of the administrative borders. The RSFSR Constitution of 12 April 1978 lists only Moscow and Leningrad as cities under republican jurisdiction (article 71), whereas the Constitution of the Ukrainian SSR of 20 April 1978 lists

Kyiv and Sevastopol (article 77). Sevastopol also remained a constituency of the Ukrainian SSR in Soviet elections (*Ukaz Presidiuma VS SSSR*, 22 March 1966, *Vedomosti VS SSSR*, no. 12 (1036), p. 190). For a detailed summary of the Ukrainian legal position on Sevastopol, see *Uriadovyi kur'er*, 4 January 1997, 4. Interestingly, the mayor of Odesa, Eduard Hurvits, came out as a strong supporter of the Ukrainian arguments, referring to most of the documents quoted above; see his article "Sevastopol'skie skazki," *Izvestiia*, 6 November 1996.

27. Usov, "Status of the Republic of Crimea," 72. Bahrov (*Krym: Vremia nadezhd i trevog*, 303–4) recalls that in Soviet times no one questioned the fact that Sevastopol was part of Crimea.

28. See Mal'gin, *Krymskii uzel*, 32–33.

29. Ibid., 34. On 20 March 1992 Iermakov became Kravchuk's first official presidential representative in Sevastopol.

30. For more details on this campaign, see Mal'gin, *Krymskii uzel*, 34–36.

31. Crow, "Russian Parliament Asserts Control."

32. Solchanyk, *Ukraine and Russia*, 173.

33. Letter dated 13 July 1993 from the Permanent Representative of Ukraine to the United Nations addressed to the President of the Security Council; see document S/26075, http://www.un.org/Depts/dhl (accessed 19 March 2007).

34. Note by the President of the Security Council dated 20 July 1993, document S/26118, http://www.un.org/Depts/dhl (accessed 19 March 2007); see also van Ham, *Ukraine, Russia, and European Security*, 26–27.

35. Letter dated 19 July 1993 from the Permanent Representative of the Russian Federation to the United Nations addressed to the President of the Security Council; see document S/26109 at http://www.un.org/Depts/dhl/ (accessed 4 April 2007).

36. Mal'gin, *Krymskii uzel*, 30–31; Markus, "Ukrainian Navy and the Black Sea Fleet," 35–36.

37. Simonsen, "'You Take Your Oath Only Once,'" 292. At this meeting it was agreed that Ukraine would receive only 18 percent of the whole fleet (around 164 operational vessels out of a total of 833), with the option to sell to Russia the rest of its 50 percent entitlement, previously agreed in 1992, and Russia would retain control of the main navy bases in Sevastopol, Kerch, and Balaklava.

38. For the most detailed discussion on the changes in Russian foreign policymaking, see Malcolm et al., *Internal Factors in Russian Foreign Policy*; see, in particular, Light, "Russian Foreign Policy Thinking."

39. Luzhkov, for example, once claimed, "Sevastopol is ready to become Moscow's 11th district"; see *Argumenty i fakty: Ukraina*, no. 50 (72), 1996, 3.

40. This agreement was reinforced by the *Memorandum pro harantiï bezpeky u zv'iazku z pryiednanniam Ukraïny do Dohovoru pro nerozpovsiudzhennia iadernoï zbroï*, Budapest, 5 December 1994. This memorandum was signed by representatives of Ukraine, Russia, the United States, and Britain.

41. See Solchanyk, *Ukraine and Russia*, 175–76. Zatulin was a classic example of "Soviet" Russian nationalism in the Duma. He had been born in Batumi, Georgia, but was an ethnic Russian, and was a Duma deputy for a single mandate constituency in Krasnodarskii Krai. As recently as June 2006 Zatulin, along with LDPR leader and Duma Vice Speaker Zhirinovskii, was banned from entering Ukraine to join anti-NATO protests in Crimea.

42. *Izvestiia*, 21 April 1995, 1.

43. Mal'gin, *Krymskii uzel*, 39; Ozhiganov, "Crimean Republic," 126.

44. Luzhkov frequently invokes the historic image of Sevastopol as the "city of Russian glory"; see *Literaturnaia gazeta*, 22 January 1997, 3.

45. Mal'gin, *Krymskii uzel*, 16.

46. *Nezavisimaia gazeta*, 18 October 1996, 1, 3. See also Gosudarstvennaia Duma, *Postanovlenie*.

47. Sovet Federatsii, Postanovlenie Federal'nogo Sobraniia Rossiiskoi Federatsii, *Zaiavlenie*.

48. *Rossiiskie vesti*, 30 November 1996, 3.

49. Mal'gin, *Krymskii uzel*, 45–46.

50. For details on the BSF agreement of May 1997, according to which Russia leases the Sevastopol bases for a period of twenty years, and the possibility of a renewed agreement, see *Den'*, 29 May 1997, 1; *Zerkalo nedeli*, 31 May 1997, 4; *Uriadovyi kur'er*, 6 June 1997, 2.

51. *Nezavisimaia gazeta* closely followed the final preparations and delays of the Black Sea Fleet agreement and the friendship treaty; see, for example, 23 October 1996, 1, 3; 5 November 1996, 3; 10 November 1996, 3; 15 November 1996, 3; 28 November 1996, 3; 30 November 1996, 1, 3. For regional reactions to the treaty, see *Krymskoe vremia*, 24 May 1997, 4; 31 May 1997, 4.

52. *Krymskaia pravda*, 11 June 1997, 1–2. Then Crimean Prime Minister Franchuk estimated the potential Crimean profit from economic links with Russia as adding a minimum of at least 20 percent to the regional budget.

53. *Krymskaia pravda*, 11 June 1997, 1–2.

54. *Krymskoe vremia*, 5 November 1998, 6. The Russian government did little more than provide humanitarian aid; for example, schoolbooks to the Russian Community of Crimea through the organization Moskva-Krym.

55. The friendship treaty had not yet been ratified by the Russian side.

56. *Krymskoe vremia*, 14 November 1998, 3.

57. *Den'*, 21 January 1997, 1.

58. See Zatulin's hateful article calling the treaty the "deception of the century" (*"obman veka"*) in *Nezavisimaia gazeta*, 26 January 1999, 1, 8. Apart from *Nezavisimaia gazeta*, Ostankino TV, the news agencies ITAR-TASS and Interfax, the press center of the Black Sea Fleet and *Izvestiia* have been singled out as regularly reporting unverified and biased material on Ukrainian-Russian affairs, for example on Ukrainian troop movements in Crimea or Turkish weapon supplies. See Tulko, "Conflicting Reports Fuel Crimean Tension."

59. Author's interview with Max van der Stoel, The Hague, 16 April 2002.

60. See, for example, Mychaijlyszyn, "OSCE and Regional Conflicts in the FSU." Ozhiganov's characterization of the OSCE involvement as "disappointing" and biased is not widely shared among analysts; see Ozhiganov, "Crimean Republic," 133.

61. Kulyk, "Revisiting a Success Story," 24–25.

62. Letter from the CSCE High Commissioner on National Minorities to the Minister for Foreign Affairs of Ukraine dated 15 May 1994; see reference no. 2415/94/L, CSCE communication no. 23/94, http://www.osce.org/hcnm/documents.html (accessed 20 March 2007).

63. Ibid.

64. United Nations, *Crimea Integration and Development Programme.*

65. *Russkii mir*, a supplement to *Krymskaia pravda*, for example, alleged that a substantial part of the almost five million dollars earmarked for 1995–2000 was channelled through Imdat-Bank by the Crimean Tatar elite without directing it towards the intended projects; see *Russkii mir*, 12 July 2002.

66. Author's interviews with representatives of the OSCE Mission in Simferopol, April and October 1996.

67. John Packer, "Autonomy within the OSCE," 306.

68. Mal'gin, *Krymskii uzel*, 95; Ozhiganov, "Crimean Republic," 133.

69. Kulyk, "Revisiting a Success Story," 129–30.

70. Ibid., 42.

71. Author's interview with Max van der Stoel, The Hague, 16 April 2002.

72. Kulyk, "Revisiting a Success Story," 43.

73. "Letter of Mr. Max van der Stoel to Hennady Udovenko, Minister of Foreign Affairs of Ukraine, 15 May 1995," http://arts.uwaterloo. ca/MINELRES/count/ukraine/950515r.htm (accessed 19 March 2007).

74. See the 30 June 1995 "Reply of the Minister of Foreign Affairs of Ukraine, Mr Udovenko, to the letter of Mr. Max van der Stoel, dated 15 May 1995"; see reference number HC/4/95, http://www.osce. org/documents (accessed 20 March 2007).

75. Kulyk, "Revisiting a Success Story," 44–45.

76. Ibid., 74.

77. Ibid., 49–51. See "Letter of Mr. Max van der Stoel to the Minister of Foreign Affairs of Ukraine, Mr. Hennady Udovenko," dated 12 October 1995; see reference no. HC/10/95, 15 November 1995, http://www.osce.org (accessed 20 March 2007).

78. Letter of Mr. Max van der Stoel to the Minister of Foreign Affairs of Ukraine, Mr. Hennady Udovenko, dated 19 March 1996; see reference no. HC/7/96, 15 May 1996, http://www.osce.org/documents/ (accessed 20 March 2007).

79. For the details on the exchanges between Kyiv and Simferopol, see Kulyk, "Revisiting a Success Story", 56–58.

80. "Letter of Mr. Max van der Stoel to the Minister of Foreign Affairs of Ukraine, Mr. Hennady Udovenko," dated 5 April 1995; see reference number 500/R/L at http://www.osce.org/documents (accessed 20 March 2007).

81. Together with the UNHCR, UNDP, and the OSCE Mission, van der Stoel was also involved in the organization of follow-up donor conferences focusing on the Crimean Tatars that took place in Kyiv in June 1998 and December 2000.

82. Letter of Mr. Max van der Stoel to the Minister of Foreign Affairs of Ukraine, Mr. Hennady Udovenko, dated 14 February 1997, and the reply of Mr. Udovenko, dated 15 March 1997; see reference no. HC/4/97, 14 April 1997, http://www.osce.org/documents (accessed 20 March 2007).

83. Kulyk, "Revisiting a Success Story," 90.

84. Verkhovna Rada Ukraïny, "Pro hromadianstvo Ukraïny," zakon vid 18.01.2001 2235-III, http://zakon.rada.gov.ua (accessed 20 March 2007).

85. Letter of Max van der Stoel to the Minister for Foreign Affairs of Ukraine, Anatoly Zlenko, dated 12 January 2001, and the reply of Zlenko, dated 6 April 2001; http://www.osce.org/documents/ html/pdftohtml/2761_en.pdf.html (accessed 20 March 2007).

86. Kulyk, "Revisiting a Success Story," 127, 130–31.

87. Author's interview with Max van der Stoel, The Hague, 16 April 2002.
88. Parliamentary Assembly Council of Europe, "Repatriation and Integration of the Tatars of Crimea," recommendation 1455, 5 April 2000, http://assembly.coe.int (accessed 20 March 2007).
89. Parliamentary Assembly of the Council of Europe, Committee on Migration, Refugees and Demography. Rapporteur Lord Ponsonby, UK, Socialist Group. "Repatriation and Integration of the Tatars of Crimea," document no. 8655, 18 February 2000, http://assembly.coe.int/ASP/Doc/DocListing_E.asp (accessed 20 March 2007).
90. Author's interview with Max van der Stoel, The Hague, 16 April 2002.
91. See, for example, Kiselev and Kiseleva, *Razmyshleniia o Kryme i geopolitike*.
92. See Kirimli, "Turko-Ukrainian Relations," 6.
93. Two of the schools were set up by the company Cag Education, the latter by the ASR Foreign Trade company. The author is grateful to Yasemin Kilit for providing this information.
94. Kirimli, "Turko-Ukrainian Relations," 5–6.
95. See Ozhiganov, "Crimean Republic," 85.
96. Shved, "Islamic Factor," 250.
97. For a conventional, but detailed, security analysis in the Black Sea region, see Sezer, "Balance of Power."
98. Connelly, "Black Sea Economic Cooperation."

Conclusion

1. Nordlinger, *Conflict Regulation in Divided Societies*, 2.
2. For surveys proving this point, see Bremmer, "Politics of Ethnicity." For a notable study on the Donbas, demonstrating that ethnicity is not the sole marker of identity and that regional diversity can foster state integration, see Nemyria, "Regional Identity and Interests"; and Nemyria, "Regionalism."
3. For opinion poll data from 1996, see Solchanyk, *Ukraine and Russia*, 198–99.
4. Dawson, "Ethnicity, Ideology and Geopolitics in Crimea," 431.
5. For a similar point in the context of the 1994 elections, see Wilson, "Presidential and Parliamentary Elections in Ukraine."
6. Horowitz, *Ethnic Groups in Conflict*, 571–72.
7. Mal'gin (*Krymskii uzel*, 110) put forward the argument that Crimean autonomy has prevented a conflict scenario similar to that in Transdnistria.

8. For the consensus among the factions in the Ukrainian parliament regarding the status issue, see *National Security and Defence* 4, no. 16 (2001): 40–42.

Epilogue

1. For the breakdown of the elections results see http://www.cvk.gov. ua (accessed 22 March 2007) .

2. The predominant regional media wrote about the "orange pseudo-revolution" (*Krymskaia pravda,* 16 December 2004) and ran an anti-Yushchenko campaign, calling the repeat elections unfair and unconstitutional; see, for example, *Krymskaia pravda,* 28 December 2004, 1. In the aftermath of the elections opinion polls were published according to which, for example, over 93 percent of Crimean students thought the repeated second round of the elections had been unfair. Whether or not these figures were correct, the regional media actively tried to keep the politicization of the population alive beyond the elections. See *Krymskaia pravda,* 11 January 2005.

3. See regional academic Andrei Nikiforov, according to whom Crimea currently still lacks in political leadership and in the ability to articulate its own claim or political program; *Krymskaia pravda,* 28 January 2005.

4. *Krymskaia pravda,* 10 December 2005.

5. *Krymskaia pravda,* 1 April 2005.

6. See Statements of the Head of the Mejlis of the Crimean Tatar people, 31 December 2004 and 25 January 2005, http://qurultay.org (accessed 22 March 2007).

7. See Mustafa Jemilev in *Krymskoe vremia,* 3 March 2005.

8. *Zerkalo nedeli,* 7 May 2005, 3.

9. In the meantime prominent regional media outlets continue to blame the Crimean Tatars for having complicated the land issue, not least through their occupation of valuable land along Crimea's south coast; see, for example, *Krymskaia pravda,* 18 March 2005.

10. *Zerkalo nedeli,* 7 May 2005, 1.

11. *Krymskoe vremia,* 3 March 2005.

12. *Zerkalo nedeli,* 7 May 2005, 3.

13. *Krymskaia pravda,* 20 May 2005.

14. *Krymskaia pravda,* 28 January 2005.

15. A number of Crimean analysts still interpret Crimean autonomy as a protection against the center (*Krymskaia pravda,* 29 December 2004); either on its own or within a wider southeastern region that could include other smaller autonomies.

16. International Committee for Crimea, *ICC News Digest*, no. 3 (Fall 2005), http://www.iccrimea.org/news/newsdigest3.html (accessed 22 March 2007).

17. In the pre-election context the latest figures of Crimean Tatar educational representation were highlighted by Crimean Tatar groups. According to the Audit Committee of the Crimean Tatar Education, there were 22 Crimean Tatar groups in Crimean kindergardens, 14 recognized Crimean Tatar National Schools with Crimean Tatar language instruction, 5 Russian schools with Crimean Tatar language courses (classified as bilingual schools), 70 Russian schools offering Crimean Tatar classes (without being classified as bilingual schools), and courses in Crimean Tatar language at the Tavrida National University and the Crimean Engineering and Pedagogical University; see "The State of the Crimean Tatar Education in Crimea," News Digest Special Report, *ICC News Digest*, no. 4 (Winter 2006), http://www.iccrimea.org/news/newsdigest4.html (accessed 22 March 2007).

18. For the official election results, see http://www.cvk.gov.ua/ (accessed 22 March 2007).

19. *Krymskaia pravda*, 20 April 2006, 1.

20. Ibid. See also International Committee for Crimea, *ICC News Digest*, no. 5 (Spring 2006), http://www.iccrimea.org/news/newsdigest5.html (accessed 22 March 2007).

21. *Jamestown Monitor 3*, issue 96, 17 May 2006.

22. For an example of this rhetoric of an imminent conflict, see *Segodnia*, 13 May 2006.

23. Jemilev referred to Crimean Tatar deptuties not elected from the lists approved by the Kurultay as "random Crimean Tatars"; see "Mustafa Dzemilev about Election 2006," Crimea-L, 20 March 2006, http://www.iccrimea.org/cl.html (accessed 22 March 2007). For the strong appeal to Crimean Tatars to vote for the approved lists, see "Refat Chubarov about Election 2006," Crimea-L, 20 March 2006, http://www.iccrimea.org/cl.html (accessed 22 March 2007). Chubarov bases his calculations on a total number of 160,000 Crimean Tatar voters, of whom 100,000 were expected to take part in the elections. The target figure for representation in the Crimean assembly was 13 deputies.

24. Rishennia Konstytutsiinoho Sudu Ukraïny, no. 1-rp vid 16.01.2003, http://www.ccu.gov.ua/pls/wccu/p0062?lang=0&rej=0&pf5511=3 3823 (accessed 22 March 2007).

25. Additionally, the official website of the Constitutional Court has also

posted the opinion of one of the Constitutional Court Judges, Viktor Skomorokhy, who disagrees with the Court's overall judgment; see "Okrema Dumka," http://www.ccu.gov.ua/pls/wccu/p0062?lang =0&rej=0&pf5511=33823&pf5921=658 (accessed 22 March 2007). Skomorokhy not only diverges from the Court's decision on the constitutionality of the provisions detailed above, but also points to the basic tension between the concept of a unitary state and an autonomous republic, as embodied in the Ukrainian Constitution, and implies that the Court's critique of the word "capital," used with reference to Simferopol in the Crimean Constitution, is the result of a political rather than a legal assessment.

26. Rishennia Konstytutsiinoho Sudu Ukraïny, no. 9-rp vid 17.04.2003, http://www.ccu.gov.ua/pls/wccu/p0062?lang=0&rej=0&pf5511=3 3831 (accessed 22 March 2007).

27. Rishennia Konstytutsiinoho Sudu Ukraïny, no. 12-rp vid 20.05.2004, http://www.ccu.gov.ua/pls/wccu/p0062?lang=0&rej=0&pf5511=6 1296 (accessed 22 March 2007).

28. Rishennia Konstytutsiinoho Sudu Ukraïny, no. 1-rp vid 16.01.2003, http://www.ccu.gov.ua/pls/wccu/p0062?lang=0&rej=0&pf5511=3 3823 (accessed 22 March 2007).

29. Mykola Semena, "Konstitutsiia Kryma konstitutsionna? Pochti...," *Zerkalo nedeli*, 1–7 February 2003.

30. E. Morgan Williams, *Action Ukraine Report*, nos. 697 and 698, 15–16 May 2006.

31. For an assessment of the failure of the autonomy status based on these expectations, see Mikita Kasianenko's comment on the 15th anniversary of the Autonomous Republic of Crimea, *Den'*, 21 January 2006 (as cited in International Committee, *ICC News Digest*, no. 4 [Winter 2006], http://www.iccrimea.org/news/newsdigest4. html [accessed 22 March 2007]).

Appendix Three

1. Kordonskii, "Structure of Economic Space."

2. Kryshtanovskaia and White ("From Soviet Nomenklatura to Russian Elite") concluded that a "bifurcated elite" had emerged with distinct political and economic segment, whereas Hughes demonstrated that these segments are intrinsically locked and reminiscent of Mill's model of a "power elite"; see Hughes, "Sub-national Elites." For the empirical analysis of "old" versus "new" elites, see Hughes et al., "From Plan to Network."

3. Personal background information about the deputies is taken from

their electoral briefs in the regional newspapers. Only deputies elected in the first and second round of voting have been included. The data are treated as a whole population rather than a sample, as the data cover the overwhelming majority of deputies (depending on the variable, either the total or over 90 percent) has been included. The analysis was complicated by the fact that the amount of information provided on each variable differed from year to year. The Communist Party background was no longer highlighted from 1994 onwards, and information from 1998 excluded the educational and national background of the candidates. With the exception of the clearly recognizable Crimean Tatar names, nationality could no longer be assessed with certainty. The time of the election represents the cutoff point for the data; subsequent changes in the deputy corps or the deputies' party affiliation are not accounted for until the next election. For the election year 1998 data were only accessible for the deputies elected in the first round of the regional elections, which filled 93 percent of the seats.

4. For his background see Krymskii tsentr gumanitarnykh issledovanii, *Leonid Grach.*

5. For 1990 the information about the deputies' professional background was not included in the election lists. The most complete information (97.8 percent) was available for 1998 (as compared to 74.5 percent in 1994).

6. For party affiliation among Russian regional deputies see Hughes, "Sub-national Elites," 1025.

7. Ibid. Hughes' conclusions are exemplified by the Crimean case.

8. Twenty-one, twenty-three, and seventeen deputies respectively have been included in the statistical analysis of the three election years 1990, 1994, and 1998.

9. See Otdel po robote s mestnymi sovetami i territoriiami Sekretariata Verkhovnogo Soveta Kryma, *Informatsiia o khode podgotovki vyborov deputatov.*

10. Author's calculations based on the data provided in Verkhovna Rada Kryma, *Statystychnyi zvit.*

11. Data were available for 4,260 out of 4,280 deputies.

12. Crimea, therefore, does not fit a pattern of Communist strongholds at the local level observed by analysts in the aftermath of the 1998 elections.

13. For the following details see the interview with Ivan Maistrenko, head of the Supreme Soviet department on local self-government, published in *Krymskaia pravda*, 28 April 1998, 1, 3.

14. The total amounts to 48 deputies, as two deputies won an additional mandate to the Crimean Soviet. In these two constituencies the elections had to be repeated. For the statistical information, see *Krymskaia pravda*, 25 April 1998, 1.

15. Deutsch, *Nationalism and Social Communication*, 36.

Works Cited

Archives

APRF	Arkhiv Presidenta Rossiiskoi Federatsii
GAARK	Gosudarstvennyi arkhiv Avtonomnoi Respubliki Krym
RGANI	Rossiiskii gosudarstvennyi arkhiv noveishei istorii (RGANI) (formerly Tsentr khraneniia sovremennoi dokumentatsii)
RGASPI	Rossiiskii gosudarstvennyi arkhiv sotsial′no-politicheskoi istorii (formerly Rossiiskii tsentr khranenii i izucheniia dokumentov sovremennoi noveishoi istorii)
TsDAHO	Tsentral′nyi derzhavnyi arkhiv hromads′kykh ob'iednan′ Ukraïny
TsGAOR	Tsentral′nyi gosudarstvennyi arkhiv Oktiabr′skoi Revoliutsii
TsGARF	Tsentral′nyi gosudarstvennyi arkhiv Rossiiskoi Federatsii

Newspapers

Argumenty i fakty. Ukraina
Avdet
Biznes Inform
Chas
Den′
Economist
Finantsova Ukraïna
The Guardian
Holos Ukraïny
Izvestiia
Komsolmol′skaia pravda

Krymskaia pravda
Krymskie izvestiia
Krymskoe vremia
Literaturnaia gazeta
Literaturnaia Rossiia
Moskovskie novosti
New York Times
Nezavisimaia gazeta
Novoe vremia
Pravda
Pravda Ukrainy
Region
Rossiiskaia gazeta
Russkii mir
Ukrainian Bulletin
Uriadovyi kur'er
Zerkalo nedeli

Internet Resources

http://aspects.crimeastar.net
http://crimea.vlasti.net
http://www.analytik.org.ua
http://www.ccu.gov.ua
http://www.iccrimea.org
http://www.pfond.crimea.ua
http://www.ukrcensus.gov.ua/results/

Other Sources

Administratsiia Presydenta Ukraïny, *Monitoring makroekonomichnoho ta rehional'noho rozvitku Ukraïny:Ukraïna ta iï rehiony.* Kyiv, 1996–1997.
Administratsiia Presydenta Ukraïny, Upravlennia z pitan' ekonomiki. *Ukraïna ta iï rehiony: Ekonomichnyi ohliad 1 pivrichchia 1996 r.* No. 4, March 1996.
Adnyliuk, Iu. Z., ed. *Kryms'ki tatary 1944–1994 rr.: Statti, dokumenty, svidchennia ochevidtsiv.* Kyiv: Ridnyi krai, 1995.
Adzhubei, Aleksei. "Kak Khrushchev Krym Ukraine otdal: Vospominaniia na zadannuiu temu." *Novoe vremia,* no. 6, 1992, 20–21.
Aksenov, Vasilii. *Ostrov Krym.* Ann Arbor: Ardis, 1981; reprinted Simferopol: Redotdel Krymskogo upravleniia po pechati, 1992.

Aksenov, Vasilii. *The Island of Crimea*. Translated by M. H. Heim. London: Hutchinson, 1985.

Aksiutin, Iu. V. *Nikita Sergeevich Khrushchev: Materialy k biografii*. Moscow: Izdatel'stvo politicheskoi literatury, 1989.

Alexandrov, Victor. *Khrushchev of the Ukraine: A Biography*. Translated by Paul Selver. London: Victor Gollancz, 1957.

Allworth, Edward. "Renewing Self-Awareness." In Allworth, *Tatars of Crimea*, 1–26.

———, ed. *The Tatars of Crimea: Return to the Homeland*. 2nd rev. ed. London: Duke University Press, 1998.

Amelchenko, M. R. "Mashinostroenie Kryma." In Fomin et al., *Krym: nastoiashchee i budushchee*, 212–17.

Anderson, Benedict. *Imagined Communities: Reflections on the Origin and Spread of Nationalism*. 6th ed. London: Verso, 1990.

Anderson, Richard D., et al. "Conclusion: Postcommunism and the Theory of Democracy." In Anderson et al., *Postcommunism and the Theory of Democracy*, 152–68.

———, eds. *Postcommunism and the Theory of Democracy*. Princeton: Princeton University Press, 2001.

Andreev, A. P. *Istoriia Kryma: Kratkoe opisanie proshlogo Krymskogo poluostrova*. Moscow: Izdatel'stvo Mezhregional'nyi tsentr otraslevoi informatiki Gosatomnadzora Rossii, 1997.

Apanovich, Olena. *Ukraïns'ko-rossiis'kyi dohovir 1654 r.: Mify i real'nist'*. Kyiv: Varta, 1994.

Applebaum, Anne. *Gulag: A History*. New York: Doubleday, 2003.

Aradzhioni, M. A., and Iu. N. Laptev, eds. *Etnografiia Kryma XIX–XX vv. i sovremennye etnokul'turnye protsessy: Materialy i issledovaniia*. Simferopol: KEM, filial KRKM, 2002.

Arbatov, Alexei, et al., eds. *Managing Conflict in the Former Soviet Union: Russian and American Perspectives*. Cambridge, Mass.: MIT Press, 1997.

Arel, Dominique. "Language Politics in Independent Ukraine: Towards One or Two State Languages?" *Nationalities Papers* 23, no. 3 (1995): 597–622.

———. "Ukraine: Renewed Paralysis at the Center, and New Trouble in Crimea?" *Analysis of Current Events* 10, no. 5 (1998).

———. "Interpreting 'Nationality' and 'Language' in the 2001 Ukrainian Census." *Post-Soviet Affairs* 18, no. 3 (2002): 213–49.

Arel, Dominique, and Valerii Khmelko. "The Russian Factor and Territorial Polarization in Ukraine." *The Harriman Review* 9, no. 1–2 (1996): 81–91.

Arel, Dominique, and Andrew Wilson. "The Ukrainian Parliamentary Elections." *RFE/RL Research Report* 3, no. 26 (1 July 1994): 6–17.

Ascherson, Neal. *Black Sea*. New York: Hill & Wang, 1995.

Bahrov, Mykola [Nikolai Bagrov]. *Krym: Vremia nadezhd i trevog*. Simferopol, 1996.

Barkobets, A. I., and M. A. Zemlynichenko. *Romanovy i Krym*. Moscow: Krik, 1993.

Barrington, Lowell W. "Views of the 'Ethnic Other' in Ukraine." *Nationalism and Ethnic Politics* 8, no. 2 (2002): 83–96.

Basarab, John. *Pereiaslav 1654: A Historiographical Study*. Edmonton: The Canadian Institute of Ukrainian Studies Press, 1982.

Basirov, V. M., et al., eds. *Fairytale Echo*. Simferopol: Dolia, 2001.

Baye, J., Baron de. *Chez les Tatars de Crimée: Souvenirs d'une Mission*. Paris: Libraire Nilsson, 1906.

Beissinger, Mark R. *Nationalist Mobilization and the Collapse of the Soviet State*. Cambridge: Cambrige University Press, 2002.

Beissinger, Mark R., and Crawford Young. "The Effective State in Postcolonial Africa and Post-Soviet Eurasia: Hopeless Chimera or Possible Dream?" In Beissinger and Young, *Beyond State Crisis?* 465–87.

———. "Introduction: Comparing State Crises across Two Continents." In Beissinger and Young, *Beyond State Crisis?* 3–18.

———, eds. *Beyond State Crisis? Postcolonial Africa and Post-Soviet Eurasia in Comparative Perspective*. Washington, D.C.: Woodrow Wilson Center Press, 2002.

Belitser, Nataliia, and Oleg Bodruk. "Krym kak region potentsial'nogo konflikta." In *Rossiia, Ukraina, Belorussiia: Etnicheskie i regional'nye konflikty v Evrasii*, edited by A. P. Fomenko, bk. 2, 83–113. Moscow: Ves' mir, 1997.

Belousov, Evgeni. *Skazka starogo Aiu-Daga*. Simferopol: Tavriia, 1994.

———. *Kak chelovek v Krymu zdorov'e nashel*. Simferopol: Tavriia, 1995.

———. *Skazka o volshebnom iakore i slavnom goroda Feodosii*. Simferopol: Tavriia, 1995.

Bilets'kyi, O. I. *Braterstvo kul'tur: Zbirnyk materialiv z istorii rosiis'ko-ukrains'koho kul'turnoho iednannia*. Kyiv, 1954.

Bilinsky, Yaroslav. *The Second Soviet Republic: The Ukraine after World War II*. New Brunswick: Rutgers University Press, 1964.

Billig, Michael. *Banal Nationalism*. London: Sage, 1995.

Birch, Sarah. "Party System Formation and Voting Behaviour in the Ukrainian Parliamentary Elections of 1994." In Kuzio, *Contemporary Ukraine*, 139–60.

———. "Interpreting the Regional Effect in Ukrainian Politics." *Europe-Asia Studies* 52, no. 6 (2000): 1017–42.

———. *Elections and Democratization in Ukraine*. Basingstoke: Macmillan, 2000.

Bitov, Andrei. "K chitateliam 'Krymskogo al'boma.'" Preface to Losev, *Krymskii al'bom 1999*, 6.

Bojcun, Marco. "The Ukrainian Parliamentary Elections of March–April 1994." *Europe-Asia Studies* 47, no. 2 (1995): 229–49.

Bokov, V. A., ed. *Voprosy razvitiia Kryma: Nauchno-prakticheskii diskussionno-analiticheskii sbornik*. Pt. 3. Simferopol: Tavriia, 1996.

Bolotina, Natal'ia. "Sevastopol', gde nyne Akhtiiar...." In Losev, *Krymskii al'bom 1999*, 134–41.

Bol'shaia Sovetskaia Entsiklopediia. 1st ed. Moscow: Sovetskaia entsiklopediia, 1926–47.

———. 2nd ed. Moscow: Bol'shaia sovetskaia entsiklopediia, 1949–58.

———. 3rd ed. Moscow: Sovetskaia entsiklopediia, 1970–81.

Bourdieu, Pierre. *Outline of a Theory of Practice*. Cambridge: Cambridge University Press, 1977.

Bremmer, Ian. "Ethnic Issues in Crimea." *RFE/RL Research Report* 2, no. 18 (30 April 1993): 24–28.

———. "The Politics of Ethnicity: Russians in the New Ukraine." *Europe-Asia Studies* 46, no. 2 (1994): 261–83.

Bremmer, Ian, and Ray Taras, eds. *New States, New Politics: Building the Post-Soviet Nations*. Cambridge: Cambridge University Press, 1997.

Breuilly, John. *Nationalism and the State*. 2nd ed. Manchester: Manchester University Press, 1993.

Broshevan, V. M., and A. A. Formanchuk. *Krymskaia Respublika—god 1921-i: kratkii istoricheskii ocherk*. Simferopol: Tavriia, 1992.

Broshevan, V. M., and V. Renpening. *Krymskie nemtsy: Kratkii istoricheskii ocherk*. Simferopol: T-vo nezavisimykh istorikov-kraevedov, 1996.

Brubaker, Rogers. *Nationalism Reframed: Nationhood and the National Question in the New Europe*. Cambridge: Cambridge University Press, 1996.

Brückner, A. "Die Reise Katharinas II. nach Südrussland im Jahre 1787." *Russische Revue, Monatsschrift für die Kunde Russlands* 2 (1873): 1–33.

Bugai, N. F. "The Truth about the Deportation of the Chechen and Ingush Peoples." *Soviet Studies in History*, Fall 1991, 67–77.

———, ed. *Iosif Stalin—Lavrentiu Berii: "Ikh nado deportirovat": Dokumenty, fakty, kommentarii*. Moscow: Druzhba narodov, 1992.

Bujurova [Budzhurova], Lilia. *Nekuplennyi bilet: Sbornkik stikhov*. Simferopol: Krymizdat, 1990.

Bukkvoll, Tor. *Ukraine and European Security*. London: Royal Institute of International Affairs, 1997.

Bunce, Valerie. "Regional Differences in Democratization: The East Versus the South." *Post-Soviet Affairs* 14, no. 3 (1998): 187–211.

———. *Subversive Institutions: The Design and the Destruction of Socialism and the State*. Cambridge: Cambridge University Press, 1999.

Burlatsky, Fedor. *Khrushchev and the First Russian Spring: The Era of Khrushchev through the Eyes of his Adviser*. New York: Maxwell Macmillan International, 1988.

Butkevych, Volodymyr. "Pravo na Krym; khto ioho maie: Rosiia? Ukraïna?" In *Krym—ne til'ky zona vidpochynku*, edited by Volodymyr Butkevych et al., 7–52. Lviv: Memoriial, Poklyk sumlinnia, 1993.

Bzhes'kyi, Roman. *Pereiaslavs'ka umova v plianakh Khmel'nyts'koho ta "Pereiaslavs'ka lehenda."* Toronto: Z druk. vyd-choï spilky "Homonu Ukraïny," 1954.

Cahun, David-Léon. *La bannière bleue: aventures d'un musulman d'un chrétien et d'un païen à l'epoque des croisades et de la conquête mongole*. Paris: Hachette, 1877.

Carment, David, and Patrick James. "Ethnic Conflict at the International Level: Causation, Prevention, and Peacekeeping." In *Peace in the Midst of Wars: Preventing and Managing International Ethnic Conflicts*, edited by David Carment and Patrick James, 1–29. Columbia , S.C.: University of South Carolina Press, 1998.

Cashaback, David P. "Accommodating Multiculturalism in Russia and Canada: A Comparative Study of Federal Design and Language Policy in Tatarstan and Quebec." PhD dissertation, London School of Economics and Political Science, 2006.

Caval, Paul. "France: From Michelet to Braudel." In Hooson, *Geography and National Identity*, 39–57.

Chase, Philip. "Conflict in the Crimea: An Examination of Ethnic Conflict under the Contemporary Model of Sovereignty." *Columbia Journal of Transnational Law* 34, no. 1 (1996): 219–54.

Chekhov, A. P. *Rasskazy i povesti*. Moscow: Pravda, 1984.

Chinn, Jeff, and Robert Kaiser. *Russians as the New Minority: Ethnicity and Nationalism in the Soviet Successor States*. Boulder: Westview Press, 1996.

Chubarov, Refat. "Vybory 31 bereznia 2002 roku v Avtonomnii Respublitsi Krym." *Kryms'ki studiï*, no. 3–4 (2002): 12–27.

Chumak, Vasyl'. *Ukraïna i Krym: Spil'nist' istorychnoï doli: Fenomen na mezhi Evropy ta skhodu*. Kyiv: Fotovideoservis, 1993.

Clarke, Douglas L. "The Saga of the Black Sea Fleet." *RFE/RL Research Report* 1, no. 4 (24 January 1992): 45–53.

Clarke, Edward. *Travels in Various Countries of Europe and Asia, Part One: Russia, Tahtary and Turkey*. London: T. Cadell and W. Davies, 1816.

Coakley, John, ed. *The Territorial Management of Ethnic Conflict*. Regions and Regionalism 2. London: Frank Cass, 1993.

Connelly, Daniel A. "Black Sea Economic Cooperation." *RFE/RL Research Report* 3, no. 26 (1 July 1994): 31–38.

Connor, Walker. "A Nation Is a Nation, Is a State, Is an Ethnic Group, Is a...." *Ethnic and Racial Studies* 1, no. 4 (1978): 379–88.

Craumer, Peter R., and James Clem. "Ukraine's Emerging Electoral Geography: A Regional Analysis of the 1998 Parliamentary Elections." *Post-Soviet Geography and Economics* 40, no. 1 (1999): 1–26.

Craven, Elizabeth. *A Journey through the Crimea to Constantinople in a Series of Letters from the Right Honourable Elizabeth Lady Craven to His Serene Highness the Margrave of Brandebourg, Anspach and Bareith Written in the year 1789.* 2nd ed. London: G. G. J. & J. Robinson, 1789.

Crow, Suzanne. "Russian Parliament Asserts Control over Sevastopol." *RFE/RL Research Report* 2, no. 31 (30 July 1993): 37–41.

D'Anieri, Paul et al., eds. *Politics and Society in Ukraine.* Boulder: Westview Press, 1999.

Dashkevych, Iaroslav. *Ukraïna vchora i nyni: narysy, vystupy, ese: do II Mizhnarodnoho konhresu Ukraïnistiv, Lviv, serpen 1993 r.* Kyiv: Instytut ukraïnskoï arkheohrafiï AN Ukraïny, 1993.

Dawisha, Karen, and Bruce Parrott, eds. *The End of Empire? The Transformation of the USSR in Comparative Perspective.* Armonk, N.Y.: M. E. Sharpe, 1997.

Dawson, Jane I. *Eco-nationalism: Anti-nuclear Activism and National Identity in Russia, Lithuania and Ukraine.* Durham: Duke University Press, 1996.

———. "Ethnicity, Ideology and Geopolitics in Crimea." *Communist and Post-Communist Studies* 30, no. 4 (1997): 427–44.

Degtiarev, P. A., ed. *Krymskaia palitra: Rasskazy. Ocherki. Glavy iz romanov i povestei.* Simferopol: Tavriia, 1982.

Demidoff, Anatole de. *Travels in Southern Russia and the Crimea; Through Hungary, Wallachia and Moldavia during the year 1837.* 2 vols. London: John Mitchell Royal Library, 1853.

Derzhavnyi Komitet Statystyky Ukraïny. *Statystychnyi shchorichnyk Ukraïny za 1996 rik.* Kyiv: Vydavnytstvo "Ukraïns´ka entsiklopediia" imeni M. P. Bazhana, 1997.

Deutsch, Karl W. *Nationalism and Social Communication: An Inquiry into the Foundations of Nationality.* 2nd ed. Cambridge: MIT Press, 1966.

Diulichev, V. P. *Rasskazy po istorii Kryma.* 5th rev. ed. Simferopol: Biznes-Inform, 2002.

Diversé, Albert. "Regional Voting Behavior in Ukraine." *Mimeo*, Harvard University, 1997.

Doroshenko, D. *History of Ukraine.* Reprint of 1939 edition. Edmonton: University of Alberta.

Drahomanov, M. *Hromada: Ukraïns´ka Zbirka.* Geneva, 1878.

Drobizheva, Leokadia, et al., eds. *Ethnic Conflict in the Post-Soviet World: Case Studies and Analysis.* Armonk, N.Y.: M. E. Sharpe, 1996.

Drohobycky, Maria, ed. *Crimea: Dynamics, Challenges, and Prospects*. Lanham, Md.: Rowman and Littlefield Publishers, 1995.

Duara, Prasenjit. *Rescuing History from the Nation: Questioning Narratives of Modern China*. Chicago: University of Chicago Press, 1995.

Dubrovs'kyi, Vasyl', *Ukraïna i Krym v istorychnykh vzaemynakh*. Geneva: Ukraïns'kyi Mors'kyi Instytut, 1996.

Dugin, Aleksandr. *Osnovy geopolitiki: Geopoliticheskoe budushchee Rossii*. Moscow: Arktogeia, 1997.

Dunlop, John B. *Russia Confronts Chechnya*. Cambridge: Cambridge University Press, 1998.

Elazar, Daniel J. *Federalism and the Way to Peace*. Kingston, Ont.: Institute of Intergovernmental Relations, Queens University, 1995.

Ena, V. G. *Zapovednye landshafty Kryma: Nauchno-populiarnyi ocherk*. Simferopol: Tavriia, 1983.

Evans, Peter B., Dietrich Rueschemeyer, and Theda Skocpol, eds. *Bringing the State Back In*. Cambridge: Cambridge University Press, 1985.

———. "On the Road toward a More Adequate Understanding of the State." In Evans, Rueschemeyer, and Skocpol, *Bringing the State Back In*, 347–66.

Fedyshyn, Oleh. *Germany's Drive to the East and the Ukrainian Revolution 1917–1918*. New Brunswick: Rutgers University Press, 1971.

Filatova, M., ed. *Legendy Kryma*. Simferopol: Biznes-Inform, 1996.

Fish, M. Steven. "The Dynamics of Democratic Erosion." In Anderson et al., *Postcommunism and the Theory of Democracy*, 54–95.

Fisher, Alan W. *The Russian Annexation of the Crimea 1772–1783*. London: Cambridge University Press, 1970.

———. *The Crimean Tatars*. Stanford: Hoover Institution Press, 1978.

Fomin, F. M., et al. *Krym: Nastoiashchee i budushchee*. Simferopol: Tavriia, 1995.

Formanchuk, O. A., ed. *Krym mnogonatsional'nyi*. Simferopol: Tavrida, 1988.

———. *Mify sovetskoi epokhi*. Simferopol: Tavriia, 2002.

Forsberg, Tuomas. "The Collapse of the Soviet Union and Historical Border Questions." In *Contested Territory: Border Disputes at the Edge of the Former Soviet Empire*, edited by Tuomas Forsberg, 3–20. Aldershot: Edward Elgar, 1995.

Garnett, Sherman W. *Keystone in the Arch: Ukraine in the Emerging Security Environment of Central and Eastern Europe*. Washington, D.C.: Carnegie Endowment for International Peace, 1997.

Gellner, Ernest. *Nations and Nationalism*. 5th ed. Oxford: Blackwell Publishers, 1988.

———. *Nationalism*. London: Weidenfeld & Nicolson, 1997.

Gerasimov, D. *Oblast', v kotoroi my zhivem: Ocherk o Kryme*. Simferopol: Krymizdat, 1959.

Geyer, Dietrich. "Der Nationalstaat im postkommunistischen Mittel- und Osteuropa." *Osteuropa* 48, no. 7 (1998): 652–60.

Gimadi, Kh. G. "Ob upotreblenie nazvaniia 'Tatary.'" *Voprosy istorii*, no. 8 (1954): 116.

Goble, Paul, and Gennadii Bordiugov, eds. *Mezhnatsional'nye otnosheniia v Rossii i SNG: Seminar moskovskogo tsentra Karnegi*. Pt. 1, *Doklady 1993–1994 gg*. Moscow: AIRO-XX, 1994.

Gosudarstvennaia Duma. *Postanovlenie "Ob obrashchenii Gosudarstvennoi Dumy Federal'nogo Sobraniia Rossiiskoi Federatsii k Verkhovnomu Sovetu Ukrainy" v sviazi s priniatiem Gosudarstvennoi Dumoi zakona "O prekrashchenii razdela Chernomorskogo flota."* Moscow, 24 October 1996.

Grabovskii, I. A. *Pereiaslav-Khmel'nitskii: Arkhitekturno-istoricheskii ocherk*. Kyiv: Izd-vo Akad. arkhitektury Ukrainskoi SSR, 1954.

Grabowicz, George G. "Ukrainian Studies: Framing the Contexts." *Slavic Review* 54, no. 3 (1995): 674–90.

Grin, A. S. *Sobranie sochinenii v 6-ti tomakh*. Moscow: Pravda, 1980.

Guboglo, M. N., and S. M. Chervonnaia. "The Crimean Tatar Question and the Present Ethnopolitical Situation in Crimea." *Russian Politics and Law* 33, no. 6 (1995): 31–60.

Guboglo, M. N., and S. M. Chervonnaia, eds. *Krymskotatarskoe natsional'noe dvizhenie*. 4 vols. Moscow: Rossiiskaia Akademiia Nauk, 1992–97.

———. "Krymskotatarskii vopros i sovremennaia etnopoliticheskaia situatsiia v Krymu." In Goble and Bordiugov, *Mezhnatsional'nye otnosheniia v Rossii i SNG*, 88–120.

Gülüm, Riza. "Rituals: Artistic, Cultural and Social Activity." In Allworth, *Tatars of Crimea*, 84–98.

Gurr, Ted Robert, and Barbara Harff. *Ethnic Conflict in World Politics*. Boulder: Westview Press, 1994.

Guthrie, Maria. *A Tour Performed in the Years 1795–6 through the Taurida, or Crimea, the Ancient Kingdom of Bosphorous, the Once Powerful Republic of Tauric Cherson, and All the Other Countries on the North Shore of the Euxine, Ceded to Russia by the Peace of Kainardgi and Jassy, Described in Letters to Her Husband, Matthew Guthrie*. London: Nichols & Son, 1802.

Ham, Peter van. *Ukraine, Russia, and European Security: Implications for Western Policy*. Chaillot Paper 13. Paris: Institute for Security Studies, West European Union, 1994.

Hanson, Stephen E. "Defining Democratic Consolidation." In Anderson et al., *Postcommunism and the Theory of Democracy*, 126–51.

Hesli, Vicki L. "Public Support for the Devolution of Power in Ukraine: Regional Patterns." *Europe-Asia Studies* 47, no. 1 (1995): 91–121.

Hesli, Vicki L., et al. "Political Party Development in Divided Societies: The Case of Ukraine." *Electoral Studies* 17, no. 2 (1998): 235–56.

Hirsch, Eric. "Landscape: Between Place and Space." In *The Anthropology of Landscape: Perspectives on Place and Space*, edited by Eric Hirsch and Michael O'Hanlon, 1–30. Oxford: Oxford University Press, 1995.

Holdar, Sven. "Torn Between East and West: The Regional Factor in Ukrainian Politics." *Post-Soviet Geography* 36, no. 2 (1995): 112–32.

Holderness, Mary. *Journey from Riga to the Crimea with Some Account of the Manners and Customs of the Colonists of New Russia*. 2nd ed. London: Sherwood, Gilbert & Piper, 1827.

Holloway, David, and Stephen John Stedman. "Civil Wars and State-Building in Africa and Eurasia." In Beissinger and Young, *Beyond State Crisis?* 161–88.

Hommaire de Hell, Xavier. *Travels in the Steppes of the Caspian Sea, the Crimea and the Caucasus*. London: Chapman and Hall, 1847.

Hooson, David. "Ex-Soviet Identities and the Return of Geography." In Hooson, *Geography and National Identity*, 134–40.

———, ed. *Geography and National Identity*. Oxford: Blackwell Publishers, 1994.

Horobets', V. M. "Pereiaslavs'ko-moskovs'kyi dohovir 1654 r.: Prychyny i naslidky istoriohrafychnoï traditsiï istorychnoï realiï." In Smolii et al., *Ukraïns'ko-rosiis'kyi dohovir 1654 r.*, 45–56.

Horowitz, Donald L. *Ethnic Groups in Conflict*. Berkeley: University of California Press, 1985.

———. "Democracy in Divided Societies: The Challenge of Ethnic Conflict." *Journal of Democracy* 4, no. 4 (1993): 18–38.

Hosking, Geoffrey. *Russia: People and Empire 1552–1917*. London: HarperCollins Publishers, 1997.

Hosking, Geoffrey, and George Schöpflin, eds. *Myths and Nationhood*. London: Hurst & Co, 1997.

Hrushevs'kyi, Mikhailo. *Istoriia Ukraïny-Rusy*. Vols. 4, 8, 10. Reprint. Kyiv: Naukova dumka, 1993.

Hryn'ov, V. B. *Nova Ukraïna: Iakoiu ia ïï bachu*. Kyiv: Arbis, 1995.

Hrytsak, Iaroslav. *Istoriia Ukraïny*. Lviv: Svit, 1996.

Hubar, Oleksandr, ed. *Chornomors'ka khvylia*. Donetsk: Donets'kyi ukraïns'kyi kul'turolohichnyi tsentr, 1995.

Hughes, James. "Sub-national Elites and Post-communist Transformation in Russia: A Reply to Kryshtanovskaya and White." *Europe-Asia Studies* 49, no. 6 (1997): 1017–36.

Hughes, James. "Managing Secession Potential in the Russian Federation." In Hughes and Sasse, *Ethnicity and Territory in the Former Soviet Union*, 36–68.

Hughes, James, et al. "From Plan to Network: Urban Elites and the Postcommunist Organizational State in Russia." *European Journal of Political Research* 41, no. 3 (2002): 395–420.

Hughes, James, and Gwendolyn Sasse. "Comparing Ethnic and Regional Conflicts in the Former Soviet Union." In Hughes and Sasse, *Ethnicity and Territory in the Former Soviet Union*, 1–31.

———. "Conflict and Accommodation in the FSU: The Role of Institutions and Regimes." In Hughes and Sasse, *Ethnicity and Territory in the Former Soviet Union*, 220–40.

———, eds. *Ethnicity and Territory in the Former Soviet Union: Regions in Conflict*. London: Frank Cass, 2002.

Huntington, Samuel P. *The Third Wave: Democratization in the Late Twentieth Century*. Norman, Okla.: University of Oklahoma Press, 1991.

Ibadullaev, Nariman, ed. *Zabveniiu ne podlezhit: Iz istorii krymskotatarskoi gosudarstvennosti i Kryma*. Kazan': Tatarskoe Knizhnoe Izdatel'stvo, 1992.

Informatsionno-analiticheskii Tsentr Pravitel'stva Avtonomnoi Respubliki Krym. *Naselenie Kryma o svoem obraze zhizni: Analiticheskaia spravka ob osnovnykh itogakh sotsiologicheskogo issledovaniia*. Simferopol, 1996.

Ivanchenko, Raïsa. "Ukraïns'kyi Krym." *Ukraïns'ka kul'tura*, no. 6 (1997): 12–14.

Jackson, Louise. "Identity, Language and Transformation in Eastern Ukraine: A Case Study of Zaporizhzhia." In Kuzio, *Contemporary Ukraine*, 99–113.

———. "National Identity in Ukraine: A Regional Perspective." PhD dissertation, University of Birmingham, 1999.

Kaganovich, Lazar' Moiseevich. *Pamiatnye zapiski rabochego, kommunista-bol'shevika, profsoiuznogo, partiinogo i sovetsko-gosudarstvennogo rabotnika*. Edited by I. V. Sakharov. Moscow: Vagrius, 1996.

Kairuddinov, M. A., and S. M. Useinov. *Etiket Krymskikh Tatar*. Simferopol: Sonat, 2001.

Kargalov, V. V. *Na stepnoi granitse: Oborona "Krymskoi Ukrainy" russkogo gosudarstva v pervoi polovine XVI stoletiia*. Moscow: Nauka, 1974.

Kaufmann, Eric, and Oliver Zimmer. "In Search of the Authentic Nation: Landscape and National Identity in Canada and Switzerland." *Nations and Nationalism* 4, no. 4 (1998): 483–510.

Keating, Michael. *State and Regional Nationalism: Territorial Politics and the European State*. New York: Harvester, 1988.

Keating, Michael. *The New Regionalism in Western Europe: Territorial Restructuring and Political Change*. Northampton, Mass.: Edward Elgar, 1998.

Khadzhiiski, Misho. *Bŭlgari v Tavriia*, Veliko Tŭrnovo: Univ. izd-vo "Sv.sv. Kiril i Metodii," 1992.

Khairuddinov, M. A., and S. Useinov. *Etiket krymskikh tatar*. Simferopol, 2001.

Khazanov, Anatoly. *The Krymchaks: A Vanishing Group in the Soviet Union*. Research Paper no. 71. Jerusalem: The Center, 1989.

Khrushchev, Nikita S. *Khrushchev Remembers*. Edited and translated by Strobe Talbott. 2 vols. London: Deutsch, 1974.

Khrushchev, Sergei. *Khrushchev on Khrushchev: An Inside Account of the Man and his Era*. Boston: Little, Brown & Co., 1990.

Khto ie Khto v ukraïns'koi politytsi. Vols. 3–5. Kyiv: TOV K.I.S., 1996–98.

Kirimal, Edige. *Der Nationale Kampf der Krimtürken mit besonderer Berücksichtigung der Jahre 1917–1918*. Emsdetten, Westf.: Verlag Lechte, 1952.

Kirimli, Hakan, "Turko-Ukrainian Relations and the Crimean Tatars." http://www.iccrimea.org/scholarly/tuarel-hakan.html. Posted 20 October 2003; accessed 18 April 2007.

Kiselev, S. N., and N. V. Kiseleva. *Razmyshleniia o Kryme i geopolitike*. Simferopol: Krymskii arkhiv, 1994.

Kliuchevskii, V. O. *Kurs Russkoi Istorii*. Vol. 2. Reprint. Moscow: Mysl', 1988.

Knysh, George. "The Crimean Roots of Ancient Ukrainian Statehood." *The Ukrainian Quarterly* 49, no. 3 (1993): 294–317.

Koch, Charles. *The Crimea and Odessa: Journal of a Tour, with an Account of the Climate and Vegetation*. Translated by J. B. Horner. London: John Murray, 1855.

———. *The Crimea: From Kertch to Perekop*. London: Routledge, 1855.

Koehler, Jan, and Christoph Zürcher. "Institutions and the Organisation of Stability and Violence." In Zürcher and Koehler, *Potentials of Disorder*, 243–66.

Kohl, J. G. *Russia: St. Petersburg, Moscow, Krakoff, Riga, Odessa, the German Provinces, on the Baltic, the Steppes, the Crimea and the Interior of the Empire*. London: Chapman and Hall, 1842.

Kohn, Hans. *The Idea of Nationalism: A Study in Its Origins and Background*. New York: Macmillan, 1945.

Kolstø, Pål. *Russians in the Former Soviet Republics*. London: Hurst & Co., 1995.

Konstitutsiia Avtonomnoi Respubliki Krym. [Draft.] Simferopol, April 1996.

Konstitutsiia Avtonomnoi Respubliki Krym. Simferopol, December 1998.

Konstitutsiia Respubliki Krym. Simferopol, 6 May 1992.

Konstitutsiia Respubliki Krym. Simferopol, 25 September 1992.

Konstitutsiia Rossiiskoi Sovetskoi Federativnoi Sotsialisticheskoi Respubliki, 10 July 1918. http://www.hist.msu.ru/ER/Etext/cnst1918.htm. Accessed 22 November 2006.

Konstitutsiia Rossiiskoi Sovetskoi Federativnoi Sotsialisticheskoi Respubliki, 13 March 1948. Moscow: Izdanie Verkhovnogo Soveta RSFSR.

Konstitutsiia SSSR. Moscow, 1936.

Konstytutsiia Ukraïny. Kyiv, 1996.

Kordonskii, Sergei. "The Structure of Economic Space in Post-Perestroika Society and the Transformation of the Administrative Market." In *Post-Soviet Puzzles,* ed. Klaus Segbers and Stephan de Spiegeleire, 1:157–204. Baden-Baden: Nomos Verlagsgesellschaft, 1995.

Korolev, Sergei. "Tretii Krym: Sud'by tatarskoi nezavisimosti v tret'ei chetverti XVII veka." Preface to *Krymskii al'bom 2001,* edited by Dmitrii Losev, 10–25. Feodosiia and Moscow: Izdatel'skii dom Koktebel', 2000.

Korolev, V. I. *Politicheskie partii Ukrainy i Kryma v XX stoletii.* Simferopol: V. I. Korolev, 1998.

Kotsiubinskii, S. D., ed. *Skazki i legendi Tatar Kryma.* Simferopol: Gosizdat Krymskoi ASSR, 1936; reprinted Moscow: Novosti, 1992.

Kratkaia khronika deiatel'nosti Medzhlisa krymskotatarskogo naroda: iiul' 1991 g.–iiun' 1996 g. Simferopol: n.p., 1996.

Kraus, Herwig, ed. *The Composition of Leading Organs of the CPSU (1952–1982).* Supplement to the *Radio Liberty Research Bulletin,* 1982.

Kravchenko, V. I. *Terytorial'nyi ustrii ta mistsevi orhany vlady Ukraïny.* Naukovi Dopovidi 43. Kyiv: Natsional'nyi Instytut Stratehichnykh Doslidzhen', 1995.

Krykun, Iukhym. *Pam'iatnyky kryms'kotatars'koï arkhitektury.* Simferopol: Tavrida, 2001.

Krymskii tsentr gumanitarnykh issledovanii. *Leonid Grach: Politicheskii portret na fone sobytii.* Simferopol: Tavriia, 1995.

Kryms'kyi tsentr nezalezhnykh politychnykh doslidnykiv i zhurnalistiv. *Kryms'ko-tatars'ke pytannia.* Simferopol, 1998.

Kryshtanovskaya, Olga, and Stephen White. "From Soviet Nomenklatura to Russian Elite." *Europe-Asia Studies* 48, no. 5 (1996): 711–34.

Kubicek, Paul. "Regional Polarisation in Ukraine: Public Opinion, Voting and Legislative Behaviour." *Europe-Asia Studies* 52, no. 2 (2000): 273–94.

———. *Unbroken Ties: The State, Interest Associations, and Corporatism in Post-Soviet Ukraine.* Ann Arbor: University of Michigan Press, 2000.

Kubijovyc, Volodymyr, and Danylo Husar Struk, eds. *Encyclopedia of Ukraine*. Toronto: University of Toronto Press, 1984–1993.

Kudriatsev, V. B., "Toplivno-energeticheskaia baza—odna iz vedushchikh i prioritetnykh otraslei." In Fomin et al., *Krym: nastoiashchee i budushchee*, 207–12.

Kudriatsev, V. B., and V. M. Shumskii. "Rekratsionnoe khoziaistvo Kryma." In Fomin et al., *Krym: nastoiashchee i budushchee*, 114–25.

Kudusov, Ernst. *Istoriia formirovaniia krymskotatarskoi natsii*. Simferopol: Kasavet, 1996.

Kulakovskii, Iulian´, ed. *Proshloe Tavridy: Kratkii istoricheskii ocherk*. 2nd rev. ed. Kyiv: S. V. Kul´zhenko, 1914.

Kulyk, Volodymyr. "Revisiting a Success Story: Implementation of the Recommendations of the OSCE High Commissioner on National Minorities to Ukraine, 1994–2001." *CORE Working Paper 6*. Hamburg: Centre for OSCE Research (CORE), 2002.

Kuras, I., ed. *Kryms´ki tatary: istoriia i suchasnist´ (do 50-richchia deportatsiï kryms´kotatars´koho narodu). Materialy mizhnarodnoï naukovoï konferentsiï, Kyiv 13–14 travnia 1994 r.* Kyiv: Instytut Natsional´nykh Vidnosyn i Politolohiï NAN Ukraïny, 1995.

Kuzio, Taras. "The Crimea and European Security." *European Security 3*, no. 4 (Winter 1994): 734–74.

———. "Russia-Crimea-Ukraine: Triangle of Conflict." *Conflict Studies 267* (January 1994): 1–35.

———. "National Identity in Independent Ukraine: An Identity in Transition." *Nationalism and Ethnic Politics 2*, no. 4 (1996): 582–608.

———. *Ukraine under Kuchma: Political Reform, Economic Transformation and Security Policy in Independent Ukraine*. London: Macmillan Press, 1997.

———. *Ukraine: State and Nation Building*. London and New York: Routledge, 1998.

———, ed. *Contemporary Ukraine: Dynamics of Post-Soviet Transformation*. Armonk, N.Y.: M. E. Sharpe, 1998.

———. "History, Memory and Nation-Building in the Post-Soviet Colonial Space." *Nationalities Papers 30*, no. 2 (2002): 241–64.

Laitin, David. *Identity in Formation: The Russian-speaking Population in the Near Abroad*. Ithaca: Cornell University Press, 1998.

Lapidus, Gail. "Ethnicity and State-Building: Accommodating Ethnic Differences in Post-Soviet Eurasia." In Beissinger and Young, *Beyond State Crisis?* 323–58.

Lapychak, Chrystyna. "Crackdown on Crimean Separatism." *Transition*, 26 May 1995, 2–5.

Lepingwell, J. "The Black Sea Fleet Agreement." *RFE/RL Research Report 2*, no. 28 (9 July 1993): 48–55.

Lewytzkyj, Borys. *Politics and Society in Soviet Ukraine, 1953–1980.* Edmonton: CIUS, 1984.

Lialikov, N. I. *Sovetskaia Ukraina: Ocherk ekonomicheskoi geografii.* Moscow, 1954.

Liber, George. "Imagining Ukraine: Regional Differences and the Emergence of an Integrated State Identity." *Nations and Nationalism* 4, no. 2 (1998): 187–206.

Lieven, Dominic. *Empire: The Russian Empire and Its Rivals.* London: John Murray, 2000.

Light, Margot. "Russian Foreign Policy Thinking." In *International Factors in Russian Foreign Policy,* edited by Neil Malcolm et al., 33–100. Oxford: Oxford University Press, 1998.

Lijphart, Arend. *Democracy in Plural Societies: A Comparative Exploration.* New Haven: Yale University Press, 1977.

Linz, Juan J., and Alfred Stepan. "Political Identities and Electoral Sequences: Spain, the Soviet Union, and Yugoslavia." *Daedalus* 121, no. 2 (1992): 123–39.

———, eds. *Problems of Democratic Transition and Consolidation: Southern Europe, South America, and Post-Communist Europe.* Baltimore: John Hopkins University Press, 1996.

Lipset, Seymour M., and Stein Rokkan. "Cleavage Structures, Party Systems, and Voter Alignments: An Introduction." In *Party Systems and Voter Alignments: Cross-National Perspectives,* edited by Seymour M. Lipset and Stein Rokkan, 1–64. New York: The Free Press, 1967.

Livingston, William S. "A Note on the Nature of Federalism." *Political Science Quarterly* 67, no. 1 (1952): 81–95.

Losev, Dmitrii, ed. *Obraz poeta: Maksimilian Voloshin v stikhakh i portretakh sovremennikov.* Feodosiia: Izdatel'skii dom Koktebel', 1997.

———, ed. *Krymskii al'bom.* Feodosiia and Moscow: Izdatel'skii dom Koktebel', 1997–2001.

Luther, Michel. *Die Krim unter deutscher Besatzung im Zweiten Weltkrieg.* Forschungen zur osteuropäischen Geschichte 3, 28–98. Berlin: Osteuropa-Institut an der Freien Universität, 1956.

Luzhkov, Iurii. "Russkaia Palestina." Preface to Losev, *Krymskii al'bom 1999,* 5.

Magocsi, Paul Robert. *A History of Ukraine.* Toronto: University of Toronto Press, 1996.

Maksimenko, M. M. "Pereselennia v Krym sil's'koho naselennia z inshykh raioniv SSR (1944–1960 rr.)." *Ukraïns'kyi istorychnyi zhurnal,* no. 11 (1990): 52–58.

Malcolm, Neil, et al. *International Factors in Russian Foreign Policy.* Oxford: Oxford University Press, 1998.

Malek, Martin. "Die Krim im russisch-ukrainischen Spannungsfeld." *Osteuropa* 43, no. 6 (1993): 551–62.

Mal´gin, A. V. "Pridnestrov´e, Krym, Zakarpat´e: Tri Sluchaia Postsovetskogo Regionalisma." *Krymskii kontekst*, no. 5, 1996, 72–81.

———. *Krymskii uzel*. Simferopol, 2000.

Markevich, Arsenii. *Tavricheskaia guberniia vo vremia Krymskoi Voiny.* Izvestiia Tavricheskoi Arkhivnoi Komissii 37. Simferopol´: Tipografiia Tavricheskoi Gubernii, 1905; reprinted Simferopol: Biznes-Inform, 1994.

Markov, Evgenii. *Ocherki Kryma: Kartiny Krymskoi Zhizni, Istorii i Prirody.* 3rd ed. St. Petersburg, 1902; reprinted Simferopol: Tavriia, 1995.

Markus, Ustina. "Crimea Restores 1992 Constitution." *Transition*, 10 June 1994, 9–12.

———. "The Ukrainian Navy and the Black Sea Fleet." *RFE/RL Research Report* 3, no. 18 (6 May 1994): 32–40.

———. "Black Sea Dispute Apparently Over." *Transition*, 28 July 1995, 30–34.

Marples, David R., and David F. Duke. "Ukraine, Russia, and the Question of Crimea." *Nationalities Papers* 23, no. 2 (1995): 261–89.

Martin, Terry. *The Affirmative Action Empire: Nations and Nationalism in the Soviet Union, 1923–1939.* Ithaca: Cornell University Press, 2001.

McCormick, Anne O'Hare. "Russia's Indifference to Popular Reactions in Berlin." *New York Times*, 1 March 1954, 24.

McFaul, Martin. "The Fourth Wave of Democracy and Dictatorship: Noncooperative Transitions in the Postcommunist World." *World Politics* 54, no. 2 (2002): 212–44.

McGarry, John, and Brendan O'Leary. "Introduction: The Macro-Political Regulation of Ethnic Conflict." In *The Politics of Ethnic Conflict Regulation*, edited by John McGarry and Brendan O'Leary, 1–40. London: Routledge, 1993.

Medvedev, Roy A. *All Stalin's Men*. Oxford: Basil Blackwell, 1983.

Medvedev, Roy, and Zhores Medvedev. *Khrushchev and the Years in Power.* New York: Columbia University Press, 1976.

Melvin, Neil. *Russians beyond Russia: The Politics of National Identity.* London: Royal Institute of International Affairs, 1995.

Michel, T. *Handbook for Travellers in Russia, Poland and Finland, including the Crimea, Caucasus, Siberia and Central Asia.* 5th rev. ed. London: John Murray, 1893.

Mill, John Stuart. *Considerations on Representative Government.* Reprint of 1861 edition. Oxford: Oxford University Press, 1974.

Ministerstvo Statystyky Ukrainy. *Natsional´nyi sklad naselennia Ukraïny.* Kyiv, 1992.

Miroshnik, O. S., et al., eds. *Regional'noe razvitie Ukrainy: problemy i perspektivy. Materialy Mezhdunarodnogo nauchno-prakticheskogo seminara g. Kharkova, 25–28 May 1995.* Kharkiv: Ukraïns'ka perspektyva, 1995.

Mizhrehional'nyi Blok Reform: Prohramni partiini dokumenty. Kyiv, 1995.

Motyl, Alexander J., ed. *Dilemmas of Independence: Ukraine after Totalitarianism.* New York: Council of Foreign Relations Press, 1993.

———. "After Empire: Competing Discourses and Inter-state Conflict in Post-imperial Eastern Europe." In Rubin and Snyder, *Post-Soviet Political Order*, 14–33.

Mychaijlyszyn, Natalie. "The OSCE and Regional Conflicts in the FSU." In Hughes and Sasse, *Ethnicity and Territory in the Former Soviet Union*, 194–219.

Nadinskii, P. N. *Krym v periode Velykoi Oktiabr'skoi Sotsialisticheskoi Revoliutsii, inostrannoi interventsii i grazhdanskoi voiny (1917–1920).* Vol. 1 of *Ocherki po istorii Kryma.* Simferopol, 1957.

Nahaylo, Bohdan. "The Massandra Summit and Ukraine." *RFE/RL Research Report* 2, no. 37 (17 September 1993): 1–6.

Natsional'ni vidnosyny v Ukraïni u XX st.: Zbirnyk dokumentiv i materialiv. Kyiv: Naukova dumka, 1994.

Naumenko, A. V., ed. *M. Tsvetaeva i Krym.* Simferopol: Tavriia, 1994.

Neilson, Andrew, Mrs. *The Crimea: Its Towns, Inhabitants, and Social Customs; By a Lady, Resident Near the Alma.* London: Partridge, Oakey and Co., 1855.

Nekrich, Alexander. *The Punished Peoples: The Deportation and Fate of Soviet Minorities at the End of the Second World War.* New York: W. W. Norton & Co., 1978.

Nemyria, Hryhorii. "Regional Identity and Interests: The Case of Eastern Ukraine." In *Between Russia and the West: Foreign and Security Policy of Independent Ukraine*, edited by Kurt R. Spillmann et al., 303–23. Bern: Peter Lang, 1999.

———. "Regionalism as a Dimension of State Building in Ukraine." In *The Experience of Democratization in Eastern Europe: Selected Papers from the Fifth World Congress of Central and East European Studies, Warsaw 1995*, edited by Richard Sakwa, 72–90. London: Macmillan Press, 1999.

Nesterenko, A. A., et al., eds. *Ocherki razvitiia narodnogo khoziaistva Ukrainskoi SSR.* Moscow: Izdatel'stvo Akademii nauk SSR, 1954.

Nikolaenko, Nikolai, ed. *Skvoz' veka: Narody Kryma.* 2 vols. Simferopol: Krymskii kontekst, 1995–96.

Nordlinger, Eric A. *Conflict Regulation in Divided Societies.* Cambridge, Mass.: Center for International Affairs, Harvard University, 1972.

North, Douglass. *Institutions, Institutional Change and Economic Performance.* Cambridge: Cambridge University Press, 1990.

Obolenskii, V. A. "Krym pri nemtsakh. Voina Kryma i Ukrainy." Part one of "Krym v 1917–1920-ie gody." *Krymskii arkhiv*, no. 2 (1996): 14–18.

Obrashchenie 1-i sessii III Kurultaia Krymskotatarskogo Naroda k Verkhovnomu Sovetu Ukrainy v Sviazi s Priniatiem Ukrainskoi Konstitutsii, 29 June 1996. Spektr 5. 1996.

O'Donnell, Guillermo. "Delegative Democracy." In *The Global Resurgence of Democracy*, edited by Larry Diamond and Marc F. Plattner, 94–110. Baltimore: John Hopkins University Press, 1996.

Offe, Claus. *Varieties of Transition: The East European and East German Experience.* Cambridge: Polity Press, 1996.

Ohloblyn, Oleksander. *Dumky pro Khmel'nychchynu.* New York: Orhanizatsiia oborony chotyr'okh svobid Ukraïny, 1957.

O'Leary, Brendan. "On the Nature of Nationalism: An Appraisal of Ernest Gellner's Writings on Nationalism." *British Journal of Political Studies* 27, no. 2 (1997): 191–222.

Osipov, K. *Velikaia druzhba.* Moscow, 1954.

Otdel po robote s mestnymi sovetami i territoriiami Sekretariata Verkhovnogo Soveta Kryma. *Informatsiia o khode podgotovki vyborov deputatov i predsedatelei sel'skikh poselkovykh, raionykh, gorodskikh sovetakh.* Simferopol, 1996.

Overing, Joanna. "The Role of Myth: An Anthropological Perspective." In Hosking and Schöpflin, *Myths and Nationhood*, 1–18.

Ozhiganov, Edward. "The Crimean Republic: Rivalries for Control." In Arbatov et al., *Managing Conflict in the Former Soviet Union*, 83–136.

Packer, John. "Autonomy within the OSCE: The Case of Crimea." In *Autonomy: Applications and Implications*, edited by Markku Suksi, Dordrecht: Kluwer Law International, 1998, 295–316.

Pallas, P. S. *Bemerkungen auf einer Reise in die Südlichen Statthalterschaften des Russischen Reiches in den Jahren 1793 und 1794.* 2 vols. Leipzig: Gottfried Martini, 1799.

Parliamentary Assembly of the Council of Europe. *On the Application by Ukraine for Membership of the Council of Europe.* Opinion no. 190 (1995). http://assembly.coe.int/Documents/AdoptedText/TA95/eopi190. HTM. Accessed 2 March 2007.

Parliamentary Assembly of the Council of Europe, Committee on Migration, Refugees and Demography, Rapporteur Lord Ponsonby, UK, Socialist Group. *Repatriation and Integration of the Tatars of Crimea.* Document no. 8655, 18 February 2000.

Pioro, I. S. *Krymskaia Gotiia.* Kyiv: Lybid', 1990.

Pirie, Paul S. "History, Politics and National Identity in Southern and Eastern Ukraine." PhD dissertation, University of London, 1998.

Pistrak, Lazar. *The Great Tactician: Khrushchev's Rise to Power.* New York: Frederick A. Praeger, 1961.

Plokhy, Serhii. "The City of Glory: Sevastopol in Russian Historical Mythology." *Journal of Contemporary History* 35, no. 3 (2000): 369–84.

Polkanov, A. I. *Krymskie karaimy.* Paris, 1995.

Popadiuk, Roman. "Crimea and Ukraine's Future." *Mediterranean Quarterly* 5, no. 4 (1994): 30–39.

Potichnyj, Peter J. "The Struggle of the Crimean Tatars." *Canadian Slavonic Papers* 17, no. 2–3, (1975): 302–18.

Predstavnytstvo Presydenta Ukraïny v Respublitsi Krym: Ukrepliaia vlast' i zakonnost'. Simferopol, January 1996.

Prizel, Ilya. *National Identity and Foreign Policy: Nationalism and Leadership in Poland, Russia and Ukraine.* Cambridge: Cambridge University Press, 1998.

Protokol Uchreditel'nogo sobraniia Krymskogo komiteta sodeistviia konstitutsionnomu protsessu v Ukraine. Simferopol, 12 April 1996.

Pushkin, A. S. *Sochineniia v trekh tomakh.* Vol. 1. Moscow: Khudozhestvennaia literatura, 1985.

Pyrih, R. Ia., and F. M. Prodaniuk. "Skoropads'kyi: shtrykhy do polytychnoho portreta." *Ukraïns'kyi istorychnyi zhurnal,* no. 9 (1992): 91–105.

Reclus, Eliseé. *L'Europe Scandinavie et Russe.* Vol. 5 of *Nouvelle Géographie Universelle: La Terre et les Hommes.* Paris: Librairie Hachette et Companie, 1880.

Reid, Anna. *Borderland: A Journey Through the History of Ukraine.* London: Phoenix, 1998.

Renan, Ernest. "Qu'est-ce qu'une nation?" Reprinted in *Nationalism,* edited by John Hutchinson and Anthony Smith, 17–18. Oxford: Oxford University Press, 1994.

Riasanovsky, Nicholas V. *A History of Russia.* 4th ed. Oxford: Oxford University Press, 1984.

Riazantsev, S. N., ed. *Sovetskoe Chernomor'e.* Moscow, 1954.

Roeder, Philip G. "Soviet Federalism and Ethnic Mobilization." In *The Soviet Nationality Reader: The Disintegration in Context,* edited by Rachel Denber, 147–78. Boulder: Westview Press, 1992.

———. "Peoples and States after 1989: The Political Costs of Incomplete National Revolutions." *Slavic Review* 58, no. 4 (1999): 854–84.

———. "The Rejection of Authoritarianism." In Anderson et al., *Postcommunism and the Theory of Democracy,* 11–53.

Rokkan, Stein, and Derek W. Urwin. *Economy, Territory, Identity: Politics of West European Peripheries.* London: Sage Publications, 1983.

Rothschild, Joseph. *Ethnopolitics: A Conceptual Framework.* New York: Columbia University Press, 1981.

Rubin, Barnett R. "Conclusion: Managing Normal Instability." In Rubin and Snyder, *Post-Soviet Political Order*, 162–79.

Rubin, Barnett R., and Jack Snyder, eds. *Post-Soviet Political Order: Conflict and State-Building*. London: Routledge, 1998.

Rudiakov, A. N., and V. P. Kazarin, eds. *Krym: Poeticheskii atlas*. Simferopol: Tavriia, 1989.

Rudnytsky, Ivan L. "Letter to the Editor." *New York Times*, 16 March 1954, 28.

———. Introduction to *Pereiaslav 1654: A Historiographical Study*, by John Basarab, xi–xxiii. Edmonton: The Canadian Institute of Ukrainian Studies Press, 1982.

———. "Pereiaslav: History and Myth." In *Essays in Modern Ukrainian History*, edited by Ivan L. Rudnytsky, 77–89. Edmonton: University of Alberta, 1987.

Rudnyts'kyi, Stepan. *Ukraine: The Land and its People: An Introduction to its Geography*. New York: Ukrainian Alliance of America, 1918.

———. *Chomu my khochemo samostiinoï Ukraïny?* Lviv: Svit, 1994. Reprint.

Rush, Myron. *The Rise of Khrushchev*. Washington: Public Affairs Press, 1958.

Rustow, Dankwart. "Transitions to Democracy: Toward a Dynamic Model." *Comparative Politics* 2, no. 3 (1970): 337–63.

Sagatovskii, V. N. "Tavrida internatsional'naia." In *Krymskaia ASSR (1921–1945)*, edited by Iu. T. Gorbunov, 33–37. Voprosy—otvety 3. Simferopol: Tavriia, 1990.

Salisbury, Harrison E. "Soviet Transfers Crimea to the Ukrainian Republic." *New York Times*, 27 February 1954, 24.

Sasse, Gwendolyn. "Die Krim—regionale Vielfalt im Spannungsfeld der Geschichte." *Österreichische Osthefte* 42, no. 3–4 (2000): 437–56.

———. "The 'New' Ukraine: A State of Regions." *Regional and Federal Studies* 11, no. 2 (2001): 69–100.

———. "Conflict-Prevention in a Transition State: The Crimean Issue in Post-Soviet Ukraine." *Nationalism and Ethnic Politics* 8, no. 2 (2002): 1–26.

Saunders, David. "Russia's Ukrainian Policy (1847–1905): A Demographic Approach." *East European Quarterly* 25, no. 2 (1995): 181–208.

Sbornik zakonov SSSR i ukazov Presidiuma Verkhovnogo Soveta SSSR, 1938–noiabr' 1958. Moscow: Gosizdat, 1959.

Schama, Simon. *Landscape and Memory*. London: Fontana Press, 1995.

Schapiro, Leonard. *The Communist Party of the Soviet Union*. 2nd revised ed. Fakenham: Cox & Wyman, 1970.

Schlögel, Karl. *Die Promenade von Jalta und andere Städtebilder*. Vienna: Carl Hauser Verlag, 2001.

Schmitter, Philippe. "The Influence of the International Context upon the Choice of National Institutions and Policies in Neo-Democracies." In Whitehead, *International Dimensions of Democratization*, 26–54.

Schöpflin, George. "The Functions of Myth and a Taxonomy of Myths." In Hosking and Schöpflin, *Myths and Nationhood*, 19–35.

Scott, Charles. *The Baltic, the Black Sea and the Crimea*. London: Richard Bentley, 1854.

Semin, G. I. *Sevastopol': Istoricheskii ocherk*. Moscow, 1955.

Sevdiiar, Memet, *Etiudy ob etnogeneze krymskikh Tatar*. New York: Fond Krym, 1997.

Seymour, H. D. *Russia on the Black Sea and Sea of Azof: A Narrative of Travels in Crimea and Bordering Provinces; With Notices on the Naval, Military and Commercial Resources of Those Countries*. London: John Murray, 1855.

Sezer, Duygu Bazoglu. "Balance of Power in the Black Sea in the Post–Cold War Era: Russia, Turkey, and Ukraine." In Drohobycky, *Crimea: Dynamics, Challenges, and Prospects*, 157–94.

Shapovalova, S. N., et al., eds. *Krym: Pamiatniki slavy i bessmertiia*. Simferopol: Tavriia, 1980.

Shevchuk, Andrii. "Krym: vnutrishnii protyrichchia ta rosiis'kyi vplyv." *Moloda Natsiia* 8 (1998): 46–88.

Shils, Edward. *Center and Periphery: Essays in Macrosociology*. Chicago: Chicago University Press, 1975.

Shulman, Stephen. "Competing versus Complementary Identities: Ukrainian-Russian Relations and the Loyalties of Russians in Ukraine." *Nationalities Papers* 26, no. 4 (1990): 615–32.

Shved, Vyacheslav. "Islamic Factor and National Interests of Ukraine." *Kryms'ki studiï* 3–4 (2002): 246–52.

Shvets, A. B., and D. A. Sinitsa, eds. *Kto est' Kto v Krymu?* Simferopol: Krymskii arkhiv, 1995.

Simonsen, Sven Gunnar. "'You Take Your Oath Only Once': Crimea, the Black Sea Fleet and National Identity among Russian Officers." *Nationalities Papers* 28, no. 2 (2000): 289–316.

Skocpol, Theda. "Bringing the State Back In: Strategies of Analysis in Current Research." In Evans, Rueschemeyer, and Skocpol, *Bringing the State Back In*, 3–43.

Skoropads'kyi, Pavlo. *Spohady: Kinets' 1917–Hruden' 1918*. Kyiv, 1995.

Smith, Anthony. *The Ethnic Origins of Nations*. Oxford: Blackwell Publishers, 1986.

———. *National Identity*. London: Penguin Books, 1991.

———. "Culture, Community and Territory: The Politics of Ethnicity and Nationalism." *International Affairs* 72, no. 3 (1996), 445–58.

Smith, Anthony, et al. *Nation-Building in the Post-Soviet Borderlands: The Politics of National Identities.* Cambridge: Cambridge University Press, 1998.

Smith, Graham, and Andrew Wilson. "Rethinking Russia's Post-Soviet Diaspora: The Potential for Political Mobilisation in Eastern Ukraine and North-East Estonia." *Europe-Asia Studies* 49, no. 5 (1997): 845–64.

Smolii, V. A., et al., eds. *Ukraïns'ko-rosiis'kyi dohovir 1654r.: Novy pidkhody do istorii mizhderzhavnykh stosunkiv.* Kyiv, 1995.

Snyder, Jack. "Reconstructing Politics amidst the Wreckage of Empire." In Rubin and Snyder, *Post-Soviet Political Order,* 1–13.

———. *From Voting to Violence: Democratization and Nationalist Conflict.* New York: W. W. Norton & Co., 2000.

Sochor, Zenovia A. "No Middle Ground? On the Difficulties of Crafting a Consensus in Ukraine." *The Harriman Review* 9, no. 1–2 (1996): 57–61.

Solchanyk, Roman. "The Crimean Imbroglio: Kiev and Moscow." *RFE/RL Research Report* 1, no. 40 (9 October 1992): 6–10.

———. "Russia, Ukraine, and the Imperial Legacy." *Post-Soviet Affairs* 9, no. 4 (1993): 337–65.

———. "Crimea's Presidential Election." *RFE/RL Research Report* 3, no. 11 (18 May 1994): 1–4.

———. *Ukraine and Russia: The Post-Soviet Transition.* Lanham, Md.: Rowman and Littlefield, 2001.

Solodovnikova, S. N., ed. *Legendy Kryma v pereskaze Eleny Krishtof.* Kerch: Kerchenskaia gorodskaia tipografiia, 2001.

Solov'ev, S. M. *Istoriia Rossii s drevneishikh vremen.* Reprint. Moscow: Mysl', 1988.

Solzhenitsyn, Aleksandr. *Russkii vopros k kontsu XX-ogo veka.* Moscow: Golos, 1995.

Sovet Federatsii, Postanovlenie Federal'nogo Sobraniia Rossiiskoi Federatsii. *Zaiavlenie "O statuse goroda Sevastopolia."* 5 December 1996.

SSSR: Administrativno-territorial'noe delenie soiuznykh respublik. Moscow, 1949.

Stalin, J. V. *Problems of Leninism.* Peking: Foreign Language Press, 1976.

Statisticheskoe upravlenie Krymskoi oblasti. *Narodnoe khoziaistvo Krymskoi oblasti.* Simferopol: TSU-SSR, 1957.

Stepan, Alfred. "Federalism and Democracy: Beyond the US Model." *Journal of Democracy* 10, no. 4 (1999): 19–34.

———. "Russian Federalism in Comparative Perspective." *Post-Soviet Affairs* 16, no. 2 (2000): 133–76.

Stetsenko, Vasilii. "Chernomorskii flot i Sevastopol'." In Losev, *Krymskii al'bom 1999,* 142–53.

Stewart, Susan. "Autonomy as a Mechanism for Conflict-Regulation? The Case of Crimea." *Nationalism and Ethnic Politics* 7, no. 4 (2001): 113–41.

Subtelny, Orest. *Ukraine: A History*. 2nd ed. University of Toronto Press, 1994.

Swearer, Howard R. *The Politics of Succession in the USSR*. Boston: Little, Brown and Company, 1964.

Sychyns′kyi, V. *Istorychnyi narys*. New York: Ukraïns′kyi Narodnyi Universytet, 1954.

Szporluk, Roman, ed. *National Identity and Ethnicity in Russia and the New States of Eurasia*. Armonk: M. E. Sharpe, 1994.

———. "The Fall of the Tsarist Empire and the USSR: The Russian Question and Imperial Overextension." In *The End of Empire? The Transformation of the USSR in Comparative Perspective*, edited by Karen Dawisha and Bruce Parrott, 65–93. Armonk, N.Y.: M. E. Sharpe, 1997.

———. "Ukraine: From an Imperial Periphery to a Sovereign State." *Daedalus* 126, no. 3 (1997): 85–119.

Tabachnyk, D. *Polozhennia pro Predstavnytstvo Prezydenta Ukraïny v Avtonomnii Respublitsi Krym*. N.p., 31 January 1996.

Tarle, Evgenii. *Gorod russkoi slavy: Sevastopol′ v 1854–1855 gg.* Moscow: Voen. izd-vo, 1954.

Tarlton, Charles. "Symmetry and Asymmetry as Elements of Federalism: A Theoretical Speculation." *Journal of Politics* 27, no. 4 (1965): 861–76.

Taubman, William. *Khrushchev: A Man and His Era*. New York: W. W. Norton, 2003.

Tefler, J. Buchan. *The Crimea and Transcaucasus, Being the Narrative of a Journey in the Kouban, in Gouria, Georgia, Armenia, Ossety, Imeritia, Swannety and Mingrelia, and in the Tauris Range*. 2 vols. London: Henry S. King & Co., 1876.

Tillet, Lowell. *The Great Friendship: Soviet Historians on the Non-Russian Nationalities*. Chapel Hill: University of North Carolina Press, 1969.

Tilly, Charles. "War Making and State Making as Organized Crime." In Evans, Rueschemeyer, and Skocpol, *Bringing the State Back In*, 169–91.

Tolstoi, Lev N. *Sevastopol′skie rasskazy*. Moscow: Khudozhestvennaia literatura, 1986.

Tolz, Vera. "Conflicting 'Homeland Myths' and Nation-State Building in Postcommunist Russia." *Slavic Review* 57, no. 2 (1998): 267–94.

Tomenko, Mykola, ed. *Abetka ukraïns′koï polityky*. Kyiv: Smoloskyp, 1998.

Tompson, William J. *Khrushchev: A Political Life*. Basingstoke: Macmillan, 1994.

Torbakov, Igor B. "Russian-Ukrainian Relations 1917–1918: A Conflict over

Crimea and the Black Sea Fleet." *Nationalities Papers* 24, no. 4 (1996): 679–89.

Tsentral´noe statisticheskoe upravlenie pri Sovet Ministrov SSSR. *Itogi vsesoiuznogo perepisi naseleniia 1959 goda: Ukrainskaia SSR*. Moscow: Gos. statizdat, 1963.

Tsybul´s´kyi, V. T. "Pereiaslavs´ka Rada 1654 roku v zarubezhnii istoriohrafii (1945–1990)." In Smolii et al., *Ukraïns´ko-rosiis´kyi dohovir 1654 r.*, 60–68.

Tulko, Alexander. "Conflicting Reports Fuel Crimean Tension." *Transition*, 28 April 1995, 16–18.

Tuna, Mustafa Özgür. "Gaspirali v. Il´minskii: Two Identity Projects for the Muslims of the Russian Empire." *Nationalities Papers* 30, no. 2 (2002): 265–89.

Tunmann [Thunmann], Hans Erich. *Krymskoe khanstvo*, translated from the 1784 German edition by N. L. Ernst and S. L. Beliavskaia. Simferopol: Tavriia, 1991.

Uehling, Greta. "Squatting, Self-Immolation, and the Repatriation of Crimean Tatars." *Nationalities Papers* 28 no. 2 (2000): 317–41.

Ukraïns´kyi nezalezhnyi tsentr politychnykh doslidzhen´. *Chy rozhoryt´sia kryms´ka kryza?* Kyiv: Zapysky Ukraïns´koho nezalezhnoho tsentru politychnykh doslidzhen´, 1995.

———. *A Russia That We… Views of Russia's Political Forces on the Future of Ukraine and the CIS and Views of Ukraine's Political Forces about Russia.* Kyiv: UCIPR, 1995.

———. *The Crimea: Chronicle of Separatism (1992–1995).* Kyiv: Ukrainian Center for Independent Political Research, 1996.

———. *Informatsiino-analitychne vydannia*, no. 3, 2002.

United Nations, *Crimea Integration and Development Programme: Overview of the Programme.* Simferopol: United Nations, 1996.

United Nations Development Programme. *Crimea: A Programme for the Future.* Geneva: United Nations, 1996.

Usov, Sergei A. "K voprosu o statuse Respubliki Krym: istoriia i sovremen-nye problemy." In Goble and Bordiugov, *Mezhnatsional´nye otnosheniia v Rossii i SNG*, 71–87.

———. "The Status of the Republic of Crimea: History and Present-Day Problems." *Russian Politics and Law* 34, no. 1 (1996): 59–72.

Velychenko, Stephen. "The Origins of the Official Soviet Interpretation of Eastern Slavic History: A Case Study of Policy Formulation." *Forschungen zur Osteuropäischen Geschichte* 46 (1992): 221–35.

———. *Shaping Identity in Eastern Europe and Russia: Soviet-Russian and Polish Accounts of Ukrainian History 1914–1991.* New York: St. Martin's Press, 1993.

Verkhovna Rada Kryma. *Statystychnyi zvit pro sklad deputativ mestnykh vyboriv (do kintsia 1995 r.)*. Simferopol, 1996.

Viatkin, A. R., and E. S. Kul'pin, eds. *Krymskie tatary: problemy repatriatsii*. Moscow: Institut Vostokovedeniia RAN, 1997.

Vidomosti Verkhovnoi Rady Ukraïny. 12 May 1992.

Virnyk, D. F. *Ukrainskaia SSR: Kratkii istoriko-ekonomicheskii ocherk*. Moscow: Gosudarstvennoe izdatel'stvo politicheskoi literatury, 1954.

Volobueva, O. V., and G. N. Iofis. "'Iskliuchitel'no zamechatel'nyi akt bratskoi pomoshchi.' Dokumenty i materialy o peredache Krymskoi oblasti iz sostava RSFSR v sostav USSR (ianvar'–fevral' 1954 g.)." *Istoricheskii arkhiv*, no.1 (1992): 39–54.

Voloshin, Maksimilian. *Koktebel'skie berega*. Simferopol: Tavriia, 1990.

von Hagen, Mark. "Does Ukraine Have a History?" *Slavic Review* 54, no. 3 (1995): 658–73.

Voprosy razvitiia Kryma: Nauchno-prakticheskii diskussionno-analiticheskii sbornik. Vol. 4. Simferopol: Tavriia, 1997.

Vozgrin, V. E. *Istoricheskie sud'by krymskikh tatar*. Moscow: Mysl', 1992.

Vsesoiuznaia perepis' naseleniia 1939 goda: Osnovnie itogi. Moscow: Nauka, 1992.

Vseukraïns'kyi perepys naselennia 2001. "Movnyi sklad naselennia Avtonomnoï Respubliky Krym." http://www.ukrcensus.gov.ua/results/general/language/crimea/. Accessed 10 January 2007.

———. "Natsional'nyi sklad naselennia.": http://www.ukrcensus.gov.ua/results/general/nationality/. Accessed 10 January 2007.

Whitehead, Laurence. "Three International Dimensions of Democratization." In Whitehead, *International Dimensions of Democratization*, 3–25.

———, ed. *The International Dimensions of Democratization: Europe and the Americas*. Oxford: Oxford University Press, 1996.

Wildavsky, Aaron. *Federalism and Political Culture*. New Brunswick: Transaction Publishers, 1998.

Williams, Brian Glyn. *The Crimean Tatars: The Diaspora Experience and the Forging of a Nation*. Leiden: Brill, 2001.

Wilson, Andrew. "Crimea's Political Cauldron." *RFE/RL Research Report*, 2, no. 45 (12 November 1993): 1–8.

———. "The Elections in the Crimea." *RFE/RL Research Report* 3, no. 25 (24 June 1994): 7–19.

———. "Presidential and Parliamentary Elections in Ukraine: The Issue of Crimea." In Drohobycky, *Crimea: Dynamics, Challenges, and Prospects*, 107–31.

———. *Ukrainian Nationalism in the 1990s: A Minority Faith*. Cambridge: Cambridge University Press, 1996.

Wilson, Andrew. *The Ukrainians: Unexpected Nation*. New Haven: Yale University Press, 2000.

Wittkowsky, Andreas. "Politische Eliten der Ukraine im Umbruch: Reformen und die Strukturierung von Interessensgruppen."*Osteuropa* 46, no. 4 (1996): 364–80.

———. *Fünf Jahre ohne Plan: Die Ukraine 1991–1996. Nationalstaatsbildung, Wirtschaft und Eliten*. Hamburg: LIT Verlag, 1998.

Wolczuk, Kataryna, *The Moulding of Ukraine: The Constitutional Politics of State Formation*. Budapest: Central European University Press, 2001.

Yevtoukh, Volodymyr. "The Dynamics of Interethnic Relations in Crimea." In Drohobycky, *Crimea: Dynamics, Challenges, and Prospects*, 69–85.

Zarechnyi, V. R. "Kontury tsentrizma." *Krymskii kontekst* 4 (1996): 5–14.

Zarubin, A. G., and V. G. Zarubin. "Krymskoe pravitel'stvo M. A. Sul'kevicha i ego politika." *Otechestvennaia istoriia* 3 (1995): 135–49.

Zimmerman, William, "Is Ukraine a Political Community?" *Communist and Post-Communist Studies* 31, no. 1 (1998), 43–55.

Zolotarev, Vladimir. "Federativnoe ustroistvo Ukrainy kak sposob preodoleniia krizisa." *Krymskii kontekst*, no.3 (1995): 70–77.

Zürcher, Christoph, and Jan Koehler. "Introduction: Potentials of Disorder in the Caucasus and Yugoslavia." In Zürcher and Koehler, *Potentials of Disorder*, 1–22.

———, eds. *Potentials of Disorder: Explaining Conflict and Stability in the Caucasus and in the Former Yugoslavia*. Manchester: Manchester University Press, 2003.

Index